IMPERIAL INFRASTRUCTURE

RACE AND RESISTANCE ACROSS BORDERS IN THE LONG TWENTIETH CENTURY

Volume 2

Series Editors:
Tessa Roynon, University of Oxford (Executive Editor)
Elleke Boehmer, University of Oxford
Victoria Collis-Buthelezi, University of the Witwatersrand
Patricia Daley, University of Oxford
Aaron Kamugisha, University of the West Indies, Cave Hill
Minkah Makalani, University of Texas, Austin
Hélène Neveu Kringelbach, University College London
Stephen Tuck, University of Oxford

PETER LANG
Oxford • Bern • Berlin • Bruxelles • Frankfurt am Main • New York • Wien

IMPERIAL INFRASTRUCTURE

AND SPATIAL RESISTANCE IN COLONIAL LITERATURE, 1880–1930

Dominic Davies

PETER LANG

Oxford • Bern • Berlin • Bruxelles • Frankfurt am Main • New York • Wien

Bibliographic information published by Die Deutsche Nationalbibliothek.
Die Deutsche Nationalbibliothek lists this publication in the Deutsche National-
bibliografie; detailed bibliographic data is available on the Internet at
http://dnb.d-nb.de.

A catalogue record for this book is available from the British Library.

Library of Congress Cataloging-in-Publication Data

Names: Davies, Dominic, 1988- author. | University of Oxford, degree granting
     institution.
Title: Imperial infrastructure and spatial resistance in colonial literature,
     1880-1930 / Dominic Davies.
Description: Oxford ; New York : Peter Lang, [2017] | Series: Race and
     resistance across borders in the long twentieth century ; 2 | Includes
     bibliographical references. | D.Phil. University of Oxford 2015 Humanities
     Division Faculty of English Language and Literature St. Anne's College.
Identifiers: LCCN 2017007737 | ISBN 9781906165888 (alk. paper)
Subjects: LCSH: English fiction--19th century--History and criticism. |
     English fiction--20th century--History and criticism. | Imperialism in
     literature. | Infrastructure (Economics) in literature. | Capitalism. |
     Great Britain--Colonies--In literature.
Classification: LCC PR878.I49 D38 2017 | DDC 823/.80936--dc23 LC record available
at https://lccn.loc.gov/2017007737

Cover image by Erica Lombard. Cover design by Peter Lang Ltd.

ISSN 2297-2552
ISBN 978-1-906165-88-8 (print) • ISBN 978-1-78707-451-4 (ePDF)
ISBN 978-1-78707-452-1 (ePub) • ISBN 978-1-78707-453-8 (mobi)

© Peter Lang AG 2017

Published by Peter Lang Ltd, International Academic Publishers,
52 St Giles, Oxford, OX1 3LU, United Kingdom
oxford@peterlang.com, www.peterlang.com

Contents

Figures

Acknowledgements

As a thesis-turned-book, this project has been long in the making, and I am indebted to the many friends, colleagues, mentors and institutions who have contributed in myriad ways throughout the years. The Arts and Humanities Research Council generously funded much of my DPhil as well as research trips to India and South Africa, without which the book would have been impossible. St Anne's College, University of Oxford, generously provided me with two Domus Scholarships in the project's early years, and just as importantly, Oxford's Vice-Chancellor's Fund removed financial strain from the crucial final year of the thesis. Particular thanks must go to The Leverhulme Trust, who funded the Network, 'Planned Violence: Post/Colonial Urban Infrastructures and Literature', giving me the opportunity to return once more to India and South Africa and to hone ideas about the relationship between infrastructure and literature in no less than four intellectually vibrant international workshops. Finally, the British Academy's Postdoctoral Fellowship Scheme privileged me with the time not only to explore new research areas, but to make those crucial edits and revisions that transform a PhD thesis into a critical monograph.

Oxford's intellectual and academic communities have been fundamental to my growth as a scholar, without which this book could not exist. In particular, Jan-Georg Deutsch, who generously invited me to join his African Research Seminar, is warmly remembered as a tutor and a friend. Similarly, the Postcolonial Writing and Theory seminar provided a fundamental platform where I cut my teeth as an active participant in critical discussion, and through which I made many long-lasting friendships, both academic and personal. I am indebted to the seminar's organisers, Elleke Boehmer and Ankhi Mukherjee, and particularly to Asha Rogers, Ed Dodson and Louisa Layne, who productively blurred the lines between the seminar room and the pub.

Elleke deserves an extra special mention for being such a diligent, tireless and supportive supervisor and mentor, for giving me the opportunity to run the 'Planned Violence' Network with her, and in more recent years for becoming such a wonderful friend, colleague and co-author. Alex Tickell and Pablo Mukherjee have also been terrific mentors, variously sharing ideas and opportunities, showing interest in my research, and welcoming me into an academic community outside of Oxford. The editors at Peter Lang have been similarly helpful with their time, and I'm grateful, too, for the valuable insights of the external reviewers who read the early drafts of this manuscript.

My parents' unwavering love and support has been invaluable. Mum, who has listened to me ramble endlessly over the years, still had the stomach to proofread so much of what is included in this book. Meanwhile, Dad affirmed the validity of my project by accepting my critical re-evaluations of some of his childhood bedtime stories and seeking out introductory books to postcolonialism. Thank you both for so much, but especially your faith in me.

Lastly, but just as importantly, I am indebted to Maja Založnik, Edward Still and Caroline Corke, for many evenings at Sunningwell and in the pub; to Ruth Davies, my incredible sister and friend; to Dave Lawrence and Chris Williams, for welcoming me to Brighton when I needed to let off steam; and to Joseph Macmillan, for organising things when I couldn't. My final love and thanks go to Emma Parker, who has been all of the above – critic, mentor, friend – and so much more, the best partner in crime.

Infrastructure, Resistance, Literature

Infrastructure and the Networked World-System

> Month by month the Earth shrinks actually, and, what is more important, in imagi-nation. We know it by the slide and crash of unstable material all around us. For the moment, but only for the moment, the new machines are outstripping mankind. We have cut down enormously – we shall cut down inconceivably – the world-conception of time and space, which is the big flywheel of the world's progress. What wonder that the great world-engine, which we call Civilisation, should race and heat a little; or that the onlookers who see it take charge should be a little excited, and, therefore, inclined to scold. [...] For the moment the machines are developing more power than has been required for their duties. But just as soon as humanity can get its breath, the machines' load will be increased and they will settle smoothly to their load and most marvellous output.
>
> — KIPLING (2010: 241)

Speaking at the Royal Geographical Society in 1914, Rudyard Kipling described the British Empire as a networked world-system facilitated by the expansion of physical infrastructural technologies, 'great world-engine[s]' that were, for him, both literal and symbolic manifestations of 'Civilisation'. Kipling understands this 'world-engine', and according to the terminology of world-systems analysis that I will draw on throughout this book, Britain's 'world-empire' and the capitalist 'world-system', as a networked web of uneven and unstable core–periphery relations. For Immanuel Wallerstein, as Kipling already intuited, it is crucial to 'note the hyphen in world-system and its two subcategories, world-economies and world-empires', because what is under analysis is not a 'social whole', but rather 'a spatial/temporal zone which cuts across many political and cultural units' (2004: 16–17). If Wallerstein's 'state-centric' map of the world-system is reductive, Neil Brenner's qualificatory focus on the 'historically specific socio-geographical infrastructures' that facilitated 'the annihilation of space through time' offers a more nuanced understanding of the 'historically specific patterns of uneven development' (2011: 103–106; Harvey, 1995: 205). Core–periphery relations are constituted not only between homogenous nation-states, but along and between infrastructural routes such as railway, shipping and telegraph lines, the development of which intensified, albeit unevenly, between 1880 and 1930. Facilitating resource extraction and trade, enmeshing peripheral landscapes and populations into exploitative economic and cultural relations, and offering imperial administrators, financial speculators and colonial writers alike with a symbolic reference point of supposed 'civilisation' and 'modernity', imperial infrastructures played a fundamental role in shrinking the 'Earth' both 'actually' and 'in imagination' during the half-century that is the focus of this book.

Kipling's conceptual and physical map of the economic, social and cultural relations that gave shape to the British imperial project is, this book will show, embedded within and reproduced by a much wider literary production of colonial space during this time. As has been well documented, the 'bard of empire', who travelled imperialism's extensive networks of 'railways and sea-lanes' (Bubb, 2013: 391–394), stressed both the economic and cultural capital invested in them, as important 'in imagination' as they were in their physical and economic actuality. For Kipling, the 'fifty thousand miles of railways laid down and ten thousand under survey' in India in the late nineteenth century made the subcontinent not only 'fit for permanent habitation' by its British rulers; these infrastructural circuitries facilitated the 'dream' of a networked world functioning on the principle of 'free trade' (Kipling, 1913: 233–235). His resulting fantasy – 'one great iron band girdling the earth' (235) – is indicative of the way in which physical infrastructure gave imaginative shape to this world-system by providing a metaphoric language with which to describe it. Though infrastructural metaphors were common to British colonial administrative writings (see

Mitchell, 1988: 157–158), it also bleeds into much anglophone colonial *literary* writing of the British Empire.

In this body of writing, which I loosely bracket beneath the term 'colonial literature', infrastructures as embodiments of empire proliferate, repeatedly using them to make sense of the various geographies in which they are set: railways and trains, telegraph wires and telegrams, roads and bridges, steamships and shipping lines, canals and other forms of irrigation, cantonments, the colonial bungalow, and other kinds of colonial urban infrastructure – all these physical edifices and lines demarcate and break up the landscape to facilitate literature's depiction and production of colonial space. For example, Edward Thompson's India is divided into urban and rural zones linked only by 'a single railway' (1931: 17); Edmund Candler's characters meander through the segregated urban environment of New Delhi; and in *Prester John* (1910), John Buchan's protagonist Davie Crawfurd locates himself in the Southern African terrain by drawing on the spatial referent of 'the railroad' as demarcated on his map (2008: 16–17).

As Colonial and Foreign Office archives make evident and as numerous critics have noted, cartography was a practice fundamental to the imperial enterprise (Mitchell, 2002: 9; Boehmer, 2005: 15).[1] It allowed governmental

---

1   In his essay, 'Geography and Some Explorers', published in *National Geographic* in March 1924, Joseph Conrad reflected on this enthusiasm for map-making. But whilst Conrad considered 'the honest maps of the nineteenth century' to be 'the most blameless of sciences' (1926: 10–14), it is clear that their spatial representations were in fact 'linked overtly and covertly with imperial power' (Butlin, 2009: 277). Jane Carruthers explains how 'cartography configured the "imagined community" of a nation and placed it before an international audience in a scientifically acceptable way', whilst 'some groups, particularly African communities, were wiped off the map' (Carruthers, 2003: 956). Harvey, amongst others, has argued that 'India, as a coherent geographical entity, was [...] very much a British imperial rather than indigenous conception' and that 'the fundamental moment in this definition was the mapping of the subcontinent by British surveyors' (Harvey, 2009: 47–49; see also Tickell, 2004). Paul Carter identifies the implicit ideological systems inherent in maps of Australia, South Africa, the United States and Canada (Carter, 2002: 150–152), demonstrating how they informed infrastructural development across different colonial environments: 'we live in the maps that the colonial surveyors bequeathed us. Inside their cadestral enclosures we have settled down. The roads

administrators, surveyors and engineers, settler colonials and freelance capitalists, financial speculators, investors and travelling labourers all to 'conceptualise, codify and regulate' a 'vision of the land' (Huggan, 1994: xv). Unsurprisingly, this is a trend registered in a number of colonial literary texts. Conrad's Marlow famously has 'a passion for maps' as he gazes upon 'the many blank spaces on the earth' (2006: 7–8), whilst Kipling's Kim has 'a great aptitude' for 'map-making' (2002: 139) and the novel is littered with '*kilta*[s] full of maps' (200). Franco Moretti, whom I follow in my application of world-systems analysis to a literary field (2000: 55–57), has argued that 'literary geography [...] can refer to two very different things': 'the study *of space in literature*; or else, the study *of literature in space*' (1998: 3). If they are 'essentially different', he continues, the 'two spaces may occasionally (and interestingly) overlap' (3). In this book, I develop a critical methodology that I call *infrastructural reading* which connects the representations of infrastructure *in* colonial literary writing to the infrastructures *of* that writing. Outlined in detail in this introduction, the methodology is then applied to selected colonial literature in each of the book's four chapters. By emphasising these spatial 'overlaps', *infrastructural reading*'s basic aim is to lever open a critical space within what is, predominantly, *pro*-imperial literature. In so doing, it mobilises an *anti*-imperial resistance to the various discriminatory ideologies that this colonial literature propagates. But this is not only a resistance to ideology – *infrastructural reading* as a critical practice heeds Fredrick Cooper's warning that a focus on '"textual colonisation" or a "metaphoric colonisation"', which he argues has become something of 'a cliché in literary studies', 'risk making colonialism appear everywhere – and nowhere' (2005: 47). Rather, connecting the infrastructures *in* and *of* these texts emphasises that literary writing set in specific *colonial* spaces was deeply complicit with *imperialism* as a cross-national project of exploitation, one underpinned by the globally uneven development of capitalism and its resulting social, political, cultural and economic inequalities (see Lazarus, 2011: 36–38).

---

we drive, the prospects they open up, and the alignment of the walls inside which coming home we agree to reside and sleep are all the linear offspring of those rulers' (2009: 17–19).

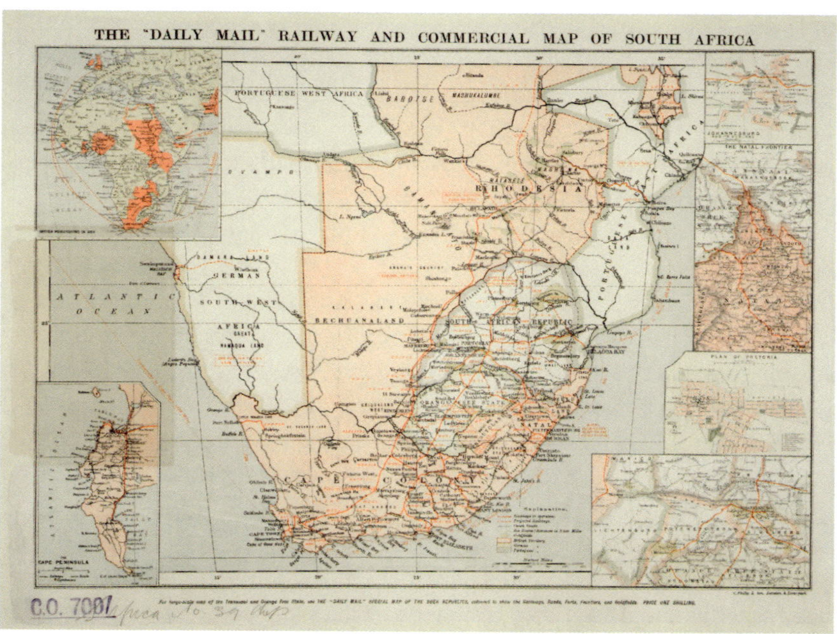

Figure 0.1: Sketch map of Southern Africa's railway system, commissioned and produced by the War Office and reproduced as an inset for the *Daily Mail* in 1899. Colonial Office Archives, 700/SouthAfrica39, National Archives at Kew.

As the commercial map of Southern Africa reproduced here demonstrates, cartographies of colonial space depended on arterial infrastructural routes to make sense of the landscape. Governmental and commercially funded maps of Southern Africa and India, surveyed and produced by colonial administrators and private companies alike, were repeatedly constructed around not only the lines of political borders, but also of infrastructures such as the railway, telegraph and shipping lines that cut across them. These infrastructures served not only as physical, but also ideological, political and economic reference points, and the cartographic depiction of them betrays the underlying motors of imperialism. Railway networks collect and condense around resource rich areas (Kimberley and the Witwatersrand in South Africa) or politically contested spaces (the North-West Frontier in India), before linking them to cross-national trading and communication networks. Indeed, whilst members of the Royal Geographical Society provided 'cartographic information and other knowledge for the organisation' (and by proxy, imperial governance), these individuals also often contributed 'capital through investment' in 'roads, railways, telegraphs, and administration systems' (Butlin, 2009: 277–278).

A focus on infrastructure, which has increasingly gained traction in recent social science research (see Larkin, 2013), thus reveals imperialism's underlying dynamics. As Brett Fischman summarises in his overview of some '[s]tandard definitions of infrastructure', these physical networks constitute 'the underlying framework of a system', ranging from '*transportation systems*' and '*communication systems*' to '*basic public services and governance systems*' (2012: 3–4); they are 'a system of substrates' that form 'part of the background for other kinds of work', even if they remain 'by definition invisible' (Star, 1999: 380; Easterling, 2014: 11). As Kipling intimated in 1914, the British Empire should be understood as constituted not by the ideologically expansionist blocked out chunks of pink on the imperial map, but rather as the thin, though very physical, networked world-system of infrastructures that it built and that tied it together, and along and around which its exploitative trades and imperial armies were circulated.

Michael Rubenstein, one of the few critics to discuss specifically *literary* representations of infrastructure, observes that the word itself only 'really comes into the English language after Roosevelt's New Deal during the era of the Great Depression' (2010: 6). For his study as for mine, the use of the term 'infrastructure' is therefore 'an anachronism in the historical and literary contexts in which I employ it' (6). According to the *OED*, the term first appeared in *Chambers's Journal of Popular Literature* on 14 May 1927 to describe 'tunnels, bridges, culverts and "infrastructure" work' (infrastructure, n. *OED*, 1989). But it was not until 13 April 1963, in an edition of *The Economist*, that the first use of the adjectival derivative, 'infrastructural', occurred in a discussion of 'various forms of infrastructural *development*' (infrastructure, n. *OED*, 1989; my emphasis). Similarly, recent editions of the *Dictionary of Environment and Conservation*, the *Dictionary of Geography*, and the *Dictionary of Economics*, all foreground the terms 'growth' and 'development' under their definition of infrastructure (2007;

2009a; 2009b). Infrastructure became, in the second half of the twentieth century, a conveniently visible (and physical) way to create and stimulate, as well as to measure and monitor, development and economic growth, particularly in post-imperial nation-states. Furthermore, the *language* of infrastructural development has been contaminated by associations variously rooted in the often racist and certainly unequal ideological frameworks of imperialism, from the paternalist humanitarianism of international NGOs (Barnett, 2014: 105–106) to the implementation of Structural Adjustment Plans (SAPs) that 'became the favoured means of disciplining postcolonial states, domesticating them and rendering them subservient to the needs of the global market' (Lazarus, 2011: 9).

This is unsurprising. Across the British Empire between 1880 and 1930, as I will explore, infrastructure functioned as a measure of 'modernity' – 'a marker of Europe's right to rule' (Cooper, 2005: 115) – for colonial administrators, travel writers, financial speculators and capitalist investors alike, even if the term 'public works', coined by Adam Smith in his *Wealth of Nations* to describe 'one of the most basic enabling institutions of capitalism', was more commonly used at the time (Rubenstein, 2010: 4). I contend that a retrospective application of the term 'infrastructure' accurately isolates and identifies the importance of these projects, the uneven development of which both sustained and challenged the world-system during this period of high imperialism. In addition, it draws to the fore the ways in which imperial infrastructures, through both their physical layouts and their associated ideologies (which are, as I shall also demonstrate, intimately connected), continue to shape the twenty-first-century world.

Infrastructural systems are 'at the heart' of 'wealth creation and capital accumulation' because they extend 'control and appropriation of labour power and all sorts of resources over distant territories, people, and ecosystems' (Graham, 2010: 4). A focus on the occurrence of infrastructure in imperial and colonial maps and, in turn, literary writing about these spaces, reveals the exploitative economic motor driving imperial expansion, even as fictional writing attempts to conceal these dynamics through the propagation of different pro-imperial ideologies. 'The combination of being oppressed, being exploited, and being disregarded is best illustrated', argued Walter Rodney in 1972, 'by the pattern of economic infrastructure of African colonies: notably, their roads and railways' (2012: 209). If, as Arjun Appadurai has commented, 'to study infrastructure is, in truth, to study the technologies and techniques through which the visible and invisible are separated' (2015: xiii), the study of literary representations of infrastructure allows for the excavation of a set of hidden ideological techniques and strategies that functioned as apologies for imperial exploitation. The damaging ramifications of the infrastructural circuitries laid during this period for the post-imperial world are matched only by the similarly dangerous ideologies that propagated their development, and with which they are still often associated. Of course, unequal infrastructural developments and ideological justifications for them have taken on new guises as planetary dynamics shift in the twenty-first century. However, a failure to acknowledge that the 'enduring consequences of empire can be implicated in creating and amplifying current problems' simply contributes, as Paul Gilroy has convincingly demonstrated, to 'an anxious, melancholic mood' that has 'become part of the cultural infrastructure' of post-imperial countries such as Britain (2004a: 2–15).

Functioning as fictional maps of a sort, it is important to emphasise that the literary depictions of colonial space with which I am concerned are, like colonial maps, repeatedly reliant on imperial infrastructures as a set of spatial and cultural reference points. Infrastructures are fundamental coordinates for the production of *space in literature*, whilst they simultaneously and historically facilitated the circulation of *literature in space* (Moretti, 1998: 3). In the interests of scope, this book confines its analysis to colonial fiction set in parts of Southern Africa and the Indian subcontinent, but its overarching argument relies on the recurrence of representations of infrastructure across a much larger body of colonial literature. Returning once more to Moretti's groundbreaking work, I am in part reliant on his notion of 'distant reading', where a quantitative analysis 'allows you to focus on units that are much smaller or much larger than the text: devices, themes, tropes – or genres and systems' (2000: 57). I therefore began this project by word searching a large body of anglophone colonial literature written by authors associated with the British Empire for different kinds of infrastructures (railways, telegraphs, cantonments, and so on). I included Kipling's vast *oeuvre*, of course, and Conrad's, but the work of many other writers as well: G. A. Henty, W. C. Scully, J. Percy Fitzgerald, R. L. Stevenson, Maud Diver, Alice Perrin, Henry Lawson, Hugh Clifford, Henry Newbolt, and so on. In addition, I word searched the complete literary writings of the eight authors discussed in detail in this book's four chapters: Flora Annie Steel, H. Rider Haggard, Olive Schreiner, William Plomer, John Buchan, Edmund Candler, Edward Thompson and E. M. Forster. From this, I was able to build a broad picture, or map, of the infrastructural networks that run, unevenly, through the literary geography of this colonial writing, tracing the patterns that emerged around infrastructure's repeated recurrence in this literature's spatial productions, but also noting its limitations.

I undertook this opening survey not simply to show that infrastructure is an important device for colonial literature. It is worth clarifying that this is not a book historical project, nor do I wish to argue that this colonial writing is somehow a kind of 'world literature', agendas that inform Moretti's methodological approach. Rather, my intention is to show how a focus on infrastructure allows for the excavation of anti-imperial resistance from what are mostly pro-imperial writings. This practice, as the book's four chapters demonstrate, needs to be conducted at a very close textual level. Though I explain my selection of texts and authors in greater detail in the final section of this introduction, I have followed Moretti once more by choosing authors who are *not quite* canonised – in the sense that Kipling and Conrad are – and instead look at their '*rivals*: contemporaries who write more or less like canonical authors [...] but not quite', and who are perhaps 'the largest contingent of the "great unread"' (2008: 66–67). Whilst the practice of *infrastructural reading* needs to be undertaken at the level of close textual analysis, then, the general conclusions that these micro-analyses reveal are, I am convinced, applicable to a much larger body of 'colonial literature', and I therefore use that much broader label throughout.

In this colonial writing, infrastructures are repeatedly invested with a symbolic capital that make them cultural equivalents of what might be understood as the economic 'core' in world-systems analysis, in relation to the (semi-)peripheral zones that they traverse. As Cara Murray argues, imperial 'traffic' – the numerous trade flows and infrastructural routes that cut across borders and constitute the circuitry of the world-economy – is enabled by the technologies of empire: 'roads, trains, telegraphs', but also 'novels', all of which 'give shape and form to landscapes' (2008: 12–13). Moretti implicitly connects the '[u]neven rhythm of literary evolution' to uneven infrastructural development, describing the European novel 'as a sort of literary railway' that weaves 'the network capable of covering a country in all its extension' (2008: 21–23). If this has, by the end of the nineteenth century, 'been basically accomplished' in Europe (23), it begins with a new ferocity in Europe's colonial spaces in the 1880s, where it describes, whilst *also functioning as*, a 'sort of literary railway'. Colonial literature is engaged in processes of export and import, both describing and itself enacting the investment of economic and cultural capital abroad. This can be seen to occur with greater clarity, as I will repeatedly argue, when we focus on its depiction of physical infrastructures. Infrastructural routes take on a cultural 'core*ness*' in this literary writing, linked as they are to a set of 'core-like production processes' through the socioeconomic motions of the unevenly developing world-system that they historically enabled (Wallerstein, 2004: 17).

Wallerstein himself acknowledges that, whilst 'we talk of core areas or core zones, peripheral areas and peripheral zones', without too much difficulty, an 'important confusion' arises when 'we talk of core states and peripheral states' because there is a 'lack of total coincidence between the economic processes and the state boundaries' (1982: 91–92). The world-system's 'units are not "national societies"', but rather 'lower-level historical loci of the system's operation and development' (87). In my reading of colonial literature, the cores of the world-system, and more specifically, the British world-empire, are conceived as 'vast, uneven chains of integrated production structures brought together through a complex division of labour and extensive commercial exchange' (Robinson, 2011: 727). Core zones are not national blocks, but rather webs, networks or lines, what the social historian of technology and infrastructure, Daniel Headrick, describes titularly as *Tentacles of Progress* (1988).

Colonial literature thus presents a conceptual (and physical) map of a networked core comprised of imperial infrastructures, marked by unevenly developed groupings, clusterings and lingering strands, variously patrolling and cutting through political borders and linking continental and oceanic spaces. In this sense, they are emblematic of what Herman Wittenberg identifies as the 'paradoxical notion' of 'imperial spatiality'; a spatiality somehow 'unitary and global', but also, and simultaneously, 'divided and fragmented' (1997: 130). As the Warwick Research Collective have recently argued by building on Fredric Jameson's notion of 'singular modernity' (which always associated 'technology' with 'progress' (Jameson, 2012: 7)), 'capitalist development does not smooth away but rather *produces* unevenness, systematically and as a matter of course' (WReC, 2015: 12). 'Capitalist modernisation entails development', they continue, 'but this "development" takes on forms also of the development of underdevelopment, of maldevelopment and dependent development' (13).

This emphasis on infrastructural development's unevenness allows us to see that whilst colonial authors 'claimed that they were "opening" the African continent', the 'domination and exploitation' that resulted was 'lumpy to an extreme' (Cooper, 2005: 104–105). Indeed, whilst Cooper critiques what is the deeply contested and even confused notion of 'modernity' (113–149), and though he finds the offerings of world-systems analysis to be dissatisfyingly 'rigid' (44–45), I wish to retain his emphasis on the 'network concept'. This allows for a more nuanced exploration of the way in which colonial literary writing used infrastructure as a physical demarcator of the unevenly developing world-system. An emphasis on *networks* not only more accurately describes imperial infrastructural developments as they were planned, constructed, mapped and reproduced in literary texts, but also works as a conceptual tool that is 'less sweeping, more precise', emphasising 'both the nature of spatial linkages and their limits' (93). Furthermore, it 'puts as much emphasis on nodes and blockages as on movement', drawing attention to 'the wide variety of units of affinity and mobilisation, the kinds of subjective attachments people form and the collectives that are capable of action' (108). It levers open the complex spatiality not only of pro-imperial literature, but of anti-imperial *resistance*:

> The spatial imagination of intellectuals, missionaries, and political activists, from the early nineteenth to the mid-twentieth century was [...] neither global nor local, but was built out of specific lines of connection and posited regional, continental, and transcontinental affinities. These spatial affinities could narrow, expand, and narrow again. (109)

Whilst Wittenberg is correct to observe the paradox of an imperial spatiality that integrates cultures and economies on a global scale in 'a fundamentally unequal way' (1997: 130), his spatial conception remains structured around a dual geographic binary 'between the colonial periphery and the metropolitan centre' (130). Such an approach is unable to move beyond the blocked out political borders of nation-states and colonial possessions. By contrast, I see the relationship between core and (semi-)peripheral zones to be occurring at the level of arterial and capillary infrastructural lines. From this perspective, the core of the world-system is comprised of networks with edges, but also with huge underdeveloped gaps in between and beyond it: the (semi-)periphery is realised not at the level of the exploited continent, subcontinent, region, city, or even town, but at the level of the coalfield and the diamond mine, the slum and the village, the developed road and the underdeveloped sidewalk. It is the manifestation of the unevenness of the world-system at this micro-geographical scale, in which core infrastructural routes cut through peripheral spaces (usually in order to underdevelop them all the more), that shows up again and again in colonial literature. Just as the colonial map-maker makes sense of colonial space through the core-peripheral dynamics signified by infrastructural lines, the writers of colonial literature and their fictional protagonists look to the physical embodiments of imperial infrastructure to give shape to the peripheral, underdeveloped conditions of their surroundings.

Throughout I will emphasise the resistant flip side to colonial literature's reliance upon the infrastructural core of the world-system. In its repeated return to infrastructure, this literature is forced to acknowledge the unequal and uneven development produced by the imperial project, undermining the civilising, modernising and humanitarian rhetoric that it so frequently draws on to justify that development in the first place. It is here that the second concept that structures this book – 'spatial resistance' – comes into play. This term is motivated by my efforts as a critic to re-politicise the body of fiction that I call 'colonial literature' through the excavation of moments in which it undoes imperial hegemony. If the imperial ideologies that colonial literature propagates have (in many cases ongoing) material consequences, it is my hope that as a methodology, *infrastructural reading* is able to counter these with a material resistance of its own. *Infrastructural reading* is specifically designed to excavate the ideological anxieties, limitations and silences concealed within the textual creases of colonial literature, as well as to unearth the more direct objections to and violent defiances of imperial control and capitalist accumulation that on occasion emerge in it. It then gathers these varying cracks and crevices within imperial ideology together and mobilises them under the broad category of 'spatial resistance'.

'The Colonial Present': Criticism as Resistance

This book has two central objectives. The first begins with the premise that, while colonial literature is undoubtedly structured by (often ugly) racial, cultural and political hierarchies – an argument widely accepted since Edward Said's foundational works, *Orientalism* (1978) and *Culture and Imperialism* (1993) – the subsequent avoidance of such texts can be defeatist. Indeed, this dismissal comes with the warning that critics who do engage with them might actually be in danger of perpetuating their ideological frameworks of inequality, discrimination and oppression. But to relinquish this body of fiction to the unread archive is, I believe, more dangerous: it ignores this literature's rich stock of insight into and, on occasion, subversion of those very frameworks, many of which have unfortunate contemporary resonances. Indeed, there is a political imperative for the present here. As Gail Low argues, 'the easy negation of such writing does not address the power of their myth-making': 'simply to point out the falsity' of these imaginative fictions is to leave 'untouched the psychic investments which determine the formation of the fictions that sustain the world we [continue to] live and act within' (1996: 2). This book's recovery of a series of critically under-read literary texts in order to excavate – rather than perpetuate – their complex ideological dynamics is, I argue, a project that might benefit the study of numerous, and in some cases ongoing, colonialisms.

The second central objective of the book is to develop a self-consciously political critical reading practice that might, tentatively, be considered a form of anti-imperial resistance in and of itself, or at least politically aligned with other resistant practices. Historians from Walter Rodney to Mike Davis have convincingly demonstrated that 'what we today call the "third world"' is a direct 'outgrowth' of the inequalities that were shaped 'most decisively in the last quarter of the nineteenth century' (Davis, 2010: 15–16; Rodney, 2012, 27). This book's political work is similarly and self-confessedly motivated by the often violent and material implications of the world-system's uneven and unequal development, particularly as they were shaped under the remit of the British Empire. The politics inform-ing its methodology are therefore affiliated with 'the writings of liberation movements that had inaugurated the interrogation of colonialism and imperialism' (Parry, 2004: 6). The book responds to Benita Parry's call to historicise British imperialism and its literary accompaniments 'within the determining instance of capitalism's global trajectory' (2004: 9). This task is, as I have already suggested, best achieved by focusing on colonial literature's representation of imperial infrastructure. Whether looking to H. Rider Haggard's 'King Solomon's road' or Flora Annie Steel's intermittent depic-tion of the telegraph, these texts can be made to confess that imperialism is about 'the construction of minimal and strategic infrastructure' designed to facilitate 'capitalism's urge to inset the non- or incipiently capitalist zones into its world-system', despite their propagation of pro-imperial ideologies suggesting the contrary (Parry, 2004: 9). It is through the 'cartography of colonial ideology' emerging from this book's constitutive chapters that I hope to practice a 'process of cultural resistance and cultural disruption'; that is, 'writing a text that can answer colonialism back' (27–28).

For this book, mapping physical imperial infrastructure as it appears in colonial literature allows for the dismantling of colonial ideology. It is worth returning here to Frantz Fanon, for whom, as historian of colonial urbanism Anthony King observes, the infrastructural layout of 'the segre-gated city' epitomises 'the entire colonial relationship' (1976: 282–283). A project concerned with the politics of infrastructure in the fraught dynam-ics of the colonial environment must recall Fanon's words at its outset:

> The colonial world is a world divided into compartments. [...] if we examine closely
> this system of compartments, we will at least be able to reveal the lines of force
> it implies. This approach to the colonial world, its ordering and its geographical

> layout will allow us to mark out the lines on which a decolonised society will be reorganised.
>
> The colonial world is cut in two. The dividing line, the frontiers are shown by barracks and police stations. [...] The settler's town is a strongly-built town, all made of stone and steel [whilst the town of the colonised] is a world without spaciousness; men live there on top of each other, and their huts are built one on top of the other. (2001: 29)

Fanon here understands the core and peripheral zones of the world-system occurring not at the macro-level of nation-states, but rather between specific infrastructural routes, boundaries and borders. Explaining Fanon's thought within the terms of world-systems analysis, arterial infrastructures such as a railways or roads are invested with and facilitate the economic and cultural flows of the core. In turn, the surrounding area is relationally produced by the world-system as a peripheral zone (Wallerstein, 2004: 17). The resulting 'periphery is not a state but a process', for which 'we have the noun peripheralisation': 'the inclusion of a unit, or an area, which was not previously involved at all, into the functioning of the world-economy', or the intensification of this process 'in a more unequal direction' (Hopkins and Wallerstein, 1982: 98–99). Whilst I analyse colonial literature's problematic representation of 'underdeveloped societies', it is equally important to acknowledge the presence of what Walter Mignolo, another cultural theorist to self-confessedly 'piggyback' on world-systems analysis, calls 'silenced societies': geohistorical locations where 'talking and writing take place but which are not heard in the planetary production of knowledge' (2002: 18, 71). In so doing, this book repeatedly refuses to subscribe to colonial literature's often explicit claim to represent colonial landscapes and peoples in their entirety, whilst nevertheless arguing that it gives voice to more than it realises. The resistance recovered by this book frequently revolves around moments in which colonial literature gestures towards those peripheral spaces of the world-system that exist beyond, beneath and between the infrastructural tentacles upon which it relies.

For Benedict Anderson, the novel as genre, form and material object is central to the way in which 'imagined communities' such as nations come into being (2006: 24–26), operating 'as a technology that functions like a railway or canal' by giving 'shape or form to landscapes' (Murray,

2008: 12–13). The infrastructural and governmental 'circuitry' of a colonising power can be damaging to the postcolonial society that inherits it, as it prescribes certain modes of governance and social interaction initially designed to facilitate the totalitarian rule and racially segregated living of the coloniser (Anderson, 2006: 160–161; Soja, 2010: 4). Fanon himself saw that colonialism's infrastructural organisation of physical space provided the coordinates on which the 'decolonised society' was 'reorganised' (2001: 29), and King further documents the way in which infrastructures of segregation and uneven development, both distinctive features of the colonial city, intensified spatial, social and economic inequalities in postcolonial nations (1976: 283–287).

Reliant on infrastructure to give shape to the landscapes it depicts, colonial literature contributes to the production of imagined geographies inflected with imperial ideologies (cities constructed around hierarchical zoning, regions demarcated along sectarian divisions), but that nevertheless find currency in early nationalist writings (a legacy explored at length in Chapter 4's discussion of nationalism in colonial fiction). It is therefore complicit in initiating and intensifying damaging cultural imaginings of these postcolonial spaces, from geographies of communalism, tribalism and sectarianism to infrastructures of inequality, hierarchy and corruption – physical and imaginative infrastructures that would, in many instances, have catastrophic consequences for the world's postcolonial citizens. Though a post-imperial analysis is beyond the scope of this book, it is these outgrowths and ongoing ramifications that inform the project's political urgency, remaining aware throughout of what Derek Gregory identifies as 'the continuities between the colonial past and the colonial present' (2004: 7). Fanon's words resonate throughout the following chapters, emphasising the inscription of inequality, oppression and exploitation into the infrastructures that gave shape to colonialism's physical spaces, whilst maintaining a combative and self-consciously resistant stance towards them.

It is thus for historical as well as methodological reasons that I respond to Fredric Jameson's call to engage with 'the political interpretation of literary texts', not as 'some supplementary method' but 'rather as the absolute horizon of all reading and interpretation' (2002: 1). Tony Bennett, too, argues that 'the activity of criticism is itself a preeminently *political* exercise' (2003: 111). This book proceeds *not* from the question of 'what literature's political effects *are*', but rather 'what they might be *made to be*' (111). As another materialist critic, Pierre Macherey, comments, 'criticism immediately dissents from the empiricist fallacy', instead aspiring 'to indicate a possible alternative to the given' (1986: 15). Reading this colonial literature for that which 'lurks, deceptively, *behind* its real meaning' (22) – its 'political unconscious', as Jameson would call it (2002) – the book attempts to build an alternative, broad map of the colonial literary field through a series of highly focused and specific micro-analyses. Indeed, the textual readings of which the chapters are comprised are certainly very 'close'. Though Moretti has since advocated the practice of 'distant reading', he elsewhere emphasises that 'the *minutiae* of language reveals secrets that great ideas often mask [...] the false starts, the hesitations, the compromises' (2013: 19). It is my hope that when these attentive close readings are read cumulatively and across several colonial authors and texts, the larger map that I am attempting to sketch will emerge. But as I shall repeatedly demonstrate, the idea is not simply 'to tell the truth that colonial discourses did not tell' – not simply 'to tell the truth over lies', as Mignolo frames it – but rather 'to think otherwise' about colonial literature and the task of the literary critic reading it today; 'to change the terms, not just the content of the conversation' (2012: 69–70).

The tension between the book's broader mapping efforts and the close textual analysis of its constituent parts is contained by its methodological strategy. Throughout, I draw on a range of different, though related, materialist critics – from Macherey, Terry Eagleton and Barbara Harlow to Harvey, Parry and James C. Scott, amongst others. These critics and the reading techniques they have developed are selected tactically at each stage in order to 'make' the particular text under analysis '"reveal" or "distance" the dominant ideological forms to which they are *made* to "allude"', thereby mobilising 'them politically in stated directions' (Bennett, 2003: 114–115). This strategic use of different critical techniques across the four chapters is woven together through the framework of the networked world-system, which is retained as an analytical lens throughout. The resulting dual movement (close and distant) allows for *infrastructural reading*'s simultaneous close-textual nuance and wider generalisation, as well as for its future applicability. Each chapter is organised around a specific theme, refracting the methodology through four of the period's most dominant ideological paradigms: 'humanitarianism', 'segregation', 'frontiers' and 'nationalism'. The chapters negotiate colonial literary texts that are mostly (though not strictly) arranged chronologically so that the book's broader methodological contribution builds cumulatively over the historical period as well as across these four themes. Whilst Chapters 1 and 3 are shorter, author-specific studies (Flora Annie Steel and John Buchan respectively), Chapters 2 and 4 each offer more sustained, comparative readings of multiple authors and are designed to bring colonial literature's *recurrent* and *intersecting* trends, tropes and traumas to the surface. *Infrastructural reading* builds cumulatively as a coherent methodology throughout the book, but it is necessary to take the time to outline it in more detail now.

Infrastructural Reading: The Infrastructures in and of Colonial Literature

The methodological reading practice that I call *infrastructural reading* is rooted in a dualistic, yet connected use of the word 'infrastructure' as a critical tool for opening up and comprehending a mutually sustaining relationship embedded within colonial literary narratives. The first is the use of infrastructure *in* the text, both physically and symbolically – what Sarah Nuttall would call the 'literary infrastructures', or 'imaginary infrastructures that surface in fiction' (2008: 198–200): roads, railways, cantonments, the colonial bungalow, and so on. This is, in many ways, the more conventional side of the infrastructural coin, in that it simply means the occurrence of a certain type of infrastructure in the literary text. In South Africa, for example, Olive Schreiner's novel *Undine*, written during the 1870s, depicts mining headgear, a fundamental infrastructure for Kimberley's diamond industry, whilst William Plomer's short story, 'Ula Masondo' (1927), represents the urban infrastructural layout of walls, roads and compounds that were built in Johannesburg in the early twentieth century.

The second usage is the more complex notion of the infrastructure *of* the text. By this I mean the historical raw material, be it social, economic or geographic, out of which the literature, as a specific crystallisation of cultural patterns and trends, is carved. Given that world-systems analysis informs my approach, I perhaps unsurprisingly read these most often as the infrastructures *of* the unevenly developing cross-national capitalist economy during this period. As the close textual readings throughout this book demonstrate, the infrastructures *in* the text and the infrastructures *of* the text are intimately related. In the process of mapping colonial literature's narrative depiction of imperial infrastructures, I have consistently found that when they surface *in* the text, the economic and political infrastructures *of* imperialism (and the capitalist world-system) are *at least* acknowledged, if not explicitly engaged. This simultaneity of signification means that the imperial rhetoric of 'civilisation' and 'modernity', which was often sustained by those lines of physical infrastructure, collide with the socioeconomic and political realities of imperialism – that is, the processes of economic exploitation and uneven and underdevelopment that those infrastructures historically enabled. The result is a productive clash, or generative friction, that results in the production of gaps from within which various forms of anti-imperial resistance can be excavated and (re)mobilised.

Whilst infrastructure is fundamental to the way in which colonial literature *represents* colonial space, it also allows us to see how this literature might *produce* it. My use of the word *production* is taken here from the work of Henri Lefebvre in his landmark text, *La Production de L'Espace* (*The Production of Space*, 1974). Wallerstein has been rightly critiqued for conceiving of the world-system within a 'morphologically static territorial matrix', but combining his insights with Lefebvre's allows for a more '*historical* and *dynamic*' conceptualisation 'of social space' (Brenner, 2011: 102). Within this framework, colonial literature produces what Lefebvre would call 'representational spaces', 'space as directly *lived* through its associated images and symbols and hence the space of its "inhabitants" and "users", but also of some artists and [of those] who describe and aspire to do no more than describe': these literary writings can therefore be conceived as cartographic productions that 'overlay physical space, making symbolic use of its objects' (1998: 39). For literary descriptions and surveys of the colonial landscape, the 'objects' most obviously available are these physical embodiments of empire: imperialism's infrastructural routes that carve up the geographical terrain, though as we shall see, distinctive topographical features also at times perform a similar function. These literary productions therefore perpetuate the use of infrastructures as spatial sense-making technologies, feeding back into the broader infrastructural strategies of the colonial project and, in the cross-national physical and economic circuitries of those infrastructures, an imperial one. Colonial literature can be understood as an intervention into 'the dialectical relationship that exists within the triad of the perceived, the conceived, and the lived' that necessarily always 'grasp[s]', but also produces, 'the concrete' (38–40). To view this dialectical relationship as nothing more than an 'abstract "model"' is, Lefebvre argues, to reduce the process 'to no more than that of one ideological mediation amongst others' (40).

Read through this lens, colonial literature can be seen to have contributed materially to imperialism's infrastructural development. As Neil Smith observes of Jameson's use of spatial terminology, space must not be reduced 'to metaphor' with its 'materiality still unrealised'; rather, it is imperative to understand 'the mutuality of material and metaphorical space' (Smith, 2008: 223). Anthropologist Brian Larkin, in his summary discussion of the recent critical reevaluation of infrastructure, argues that it is by 'being alive to the formal dimensions of infrastructures' that an understanding of the 'sort of semiotic objects they are' and an analysis of 'how they address and constitute subjects' can be developed (2013: 329). At close textual levels, colonial literature offers a crystallised moment in which the 'formal dimensions of infrastructures' are expressed. With a little 'reverse-engineering', as Moretti aptly calls it, it might therefore be made to reveal 'the problem it was designed to solve' (2013: 14). Studying occurrences of infrastructure in literature as momentary pauses in the Lefebvrian dialectic, it is possible 'to elucidate', to use Nirvana Tanoukhi's words, 'the diverse forms of entanglement between literary history and the history of the production of space' (2011: 94–95).

In this literature, fictional narrators repeatedly profess cartographic accuracy, whilst other characters constantly make use of maps and other spatially enabling technologies (such as compasses, field-glasses and so on). Practicing imperialism as a 'metaphoric and cartographic – as well as legalistic – undertaking', observes Elleke Boehmer, 'colonisers relied on and scattered about them the stock descriptions and authoritative symbols that lay to hand' (2005: 15–17). 'The imaginations of readers across the British Empire were led along parallel grooves', she continues (52), but I want to emphasise that these 'parallel grooves' were as fundamentally the *actual* iron girders of the colonial railway as they were the metaphoric lines of the realist novel. Understood in this way, we can see how colonial literature, through its representation of infrastructures, participates in what Edward Soja, since Lefebvre, has called the 'socio-spatial dialectic' (2010: 4). As a spatial sense-making technology itself, colonial literature draws on infrastructures to give shape to its own representations, and in turn (re)produces a colonial landscape shaped by imperial ideologies and their subsequent socialities (racial and class hierarchies, for example). It is complicit in the production of what Jason Moore calls *'abstract social nature'*, the 'family of processes through which states and capitalists map, identify, quantify, measure, and code human and extra-human natures in service to capital accumulation' (2015: 194). In this sense, colonial literature is one of imperialism's 'productive forces', 'tools and technological systems' that, like infrastructure itself, work 'toward definite ways of producing and reproducing life' (195). Running through the textual surface of colonial literature, these infrastructural networks give it social and economic shape; it follows that the exploitative dynamics of core–periphery relations are embedded in, if also thinly concealed by, its various narrative formations. Colonial literary texts can on occasion be made to confess their complicity with the uneven accumulation of capitalist imperialism: Buchan's Davie Crawfurd may use the railroad as a spatial referent and symbolic object that allows him to navigate the South African landscape, but the reason he travels that railroad in the first place is, after all, to 'open up new trade among the natives' (2008: 15).

It should be apparent by now that, by developing the methodology of *infrastructural reading*, I want to consider the way in which the literary and cultural terrain is interacting with the fraught territorial contest between methods of imperial expansion, exploitation and control, and resistance to these processes. If Said reminds us that '[t]he actual geographical possession of land is what empire in the final analysis is all about', and that 'the culture associated with it affirms both the primacy of geography and an ideology about control of territory', for him, the 'territories, lands, geographical domains, the actual geographic underpinnings' of imperialism underly 'social space' and the 'the cultural contest' (1993: 93). The two terrains remain detached or separate, the former somehow located 'beneath' or 'below' the latter. Infrastructure, as the physical, economic and symbolic scaffolding of empire, connects these multiple spheres, becoming, as my discussion will go on to show, the most fruitful point at which they can be seen to interconnect and collide. Political and ideological nuances coagulate around these infrastructural routes, creating textual moments in which they can most productively be captured, isolated and analysed.

As noted in this book's opening comments, processes of 'mapping' and 'map-making' are crucial here. Certainly, colonial literature 'functions as a form of mapping' by 'offering its readers descriptions of places, situating them in a kind of imaginary space, and providing points of reference by which they can orient themselves and understand the world' (Tally, 2013: 2). But it also maps something else: the literature charts the contours not only of imperial geographies, but also ideologies, revealing, to use Jameson's words, 'the limits of a specific ideological consciousness' and surveying 'the points beyond which that consciousness cannot go' (2002: 32). The literature's varying genres, forms and plot-sequences register, to varying degrees in different cases, these ideologies and their limits. An infrastructural analysis of colonial literature refutes the ostensible 'objectivity' of its geographical 'mapping' project. Rather, the texts produce a politically charged landscape that binds different ideologies unevenly, and often tactically, to different segments of the colonial landscape. Space becomes, as Soja explains, 'predominantly related to the reproduction of the dominant system of social relations' (1989: 91). It is for this reason that I preface the four titular themes of each chapter with the word 'mapping', as each analyses both their infrastructural and ideological formations. For Edmund Candler, for example, nationalist resistance is restricted to the topographical feature of 'the cave', where it is spatially isolated and contained, no longer a threat to the Raj's hegemony. Haggard, too, positions Southern Africa's Black population in a geographical zone separated from white settler society. By contrast, William Plomer intertextually rewrites the imperial romance in order to subvert this segregationist ideology, thereby undermining 'the production of space, the territorial structure of exploitation and domination [and] the spatially controlled reproduction of the system as a whole' (Soja, 1989: 92).

By demonstrating colonial literature's participation in the production of space, the book's mapping of a cultural onto a geographic and socioeconomic terrain avoids what John Tagg, in his discussion of the 'reductive and economistic Immanuel Wallerstein', calls 'the primitive architecture of the base and superstructure model of the social whole' (2000: 156). Though heeding this warning, the application of world-systems analysis to the dual, though deeply interconnected types of infrastructural networks – *in* and *of* – that run through this body of literature allows an assessment of the impact of physical embodiments of empire on its cultural corollary and vice versa. It becomes possible to assess the impact that cultural terrains, that I will show to be littered with fissures, tears and fragments of resistance, might have upon the physical geographies and socioeconomies of imperialism. As Gramsci argued, though 'material forces are the content and ideologies are the form', this 'distinction has purely indicative value, since the material forces would be inconceivable historically without form and the ideologies would be individual fancies without the material forces' (1988: 200). I arrive here at Raymond William's replacement of 'the formula of base and superstructure with the more active idea of a field of mutually if also unevenly determining forces' (2005: 20). Though this study is clearly influenced by a number of 'postcolonial' critics, then, its focus on the infrastructure of the world-*system* thus rejects the 'antecedent lexicon of "post"-theory' and its preoccupation with the 'untotalisable fragment', instead following WReC's recent work that emphasises 'vertical and horizontal integration, connection and interconnection, structurality and organisation, internal differentiation [and] a hierarchy of constitutive elements governed by specific "logics" of determination and relationality' (2015: 6–8).

By emphasising imperialism's uneven infrastructural development, the uneven representational and production practices of colonial literature can be foregrounded and the reproduction of its ideological frameworks – or, just as bad, the assimilation of anti-imperial resistance into its hegemonic apparatus – can be avoided. In order to resist rather than perpetuate imperial ideology, it is necessary both introduce the conceptual and political spaces that lie beyond its ideological and representational contours, whilst finding ways to prevent the assimilation of those spaces into its cartographic endeavours. If, according to Wallerstein and others, '[o]pposition to oppression is coterminous with the existence of hierachical social systems', even when it remains 'latent' (Arrighi et al., 2011: 29), literary representations of infrastructural networks should contain clues, at their sub-textual or marginal levels, of ongoing 'anti-systemic' resistance. Though 'the work cannot speak of the more or less complex opposition which structures it', the literary text, when read strategically, '*manifests*, uncovers, what it cannot say' (Macherey, 1986: 84). The presence of resistance, if not the fully fledged articulation of it, becomes configured within colonial literature's mapping project: the frontispiece map in the opening pages of *King Solomon's Mines* may depict an apparently consolidated, infrastructural route, but in order to do so it must also include the swathes of peripheral, unmapped landscape that surround it (Haggard, 2008: 21). Resistant spaces – or a kind of *spatial* resistance – are written into colonialism's literary landscapes as they are dialectically produced by physical infrastructures and cultural representations of them.

Hobson, Luxemburg, Lenin: Why 1880 to 1930?

The capitalist underpinnings of the British Empire, and the processes of 'accumulation' that I take to be the drivers of its uneven infrastructural development during this period, are grounded in theories of economic imperialism elaborated by a number of contemporaneous anti-imperialist and anti-capitalist thinkers. Though world-systems analysis provides the over-arching framework for *infrastructural reading*, using its diagnostic tools is by no means an entirely retrospective – nor anachronistic – act. In this section I wish to stress the connections between anti-imperial critiques produced coterminously with British imperial hegemony and my own reassessment of colonial literature. For Soja, at the end of the nineteenth century 'every scale of life was being restructured to meet the urgent demands of capitalism in crisis', resulting in a new spatiality that manifested in 'poetry and painting, in the writing of novels and literary criticism, in architecture and what then represented urban and regional planning' (1989: 34). If in 'social science and scientific socialism, a persistent historicism tended to obscure this insidious spatialisation', there were exceptions: between them, these exceptions – 'Lenin, Luxemburg, Bukharin, Trotsky, and Bauer, the key figures leading the early twentieth-century modernisation of Marxism' – laid a 'rich foundation for a Marxist theory of geographically (as well as historically) uneven development' (32), and it is to two of these theorists in particular that this section will turn.

First, however, we must begin with J. A. Hobson. Though not a Marxist as such, his influence on later Marxist writers and other anti-imperialist thinkers 'cannot be ignored' (Brewer, 2001: 73). Not coincidentally, Hobson's critique of imperialism grew out of his experience as a journalist in South Africa, where he witnessed the swift but uneven infrastructural growth of Johannesburg in 1899 firsthand: 'the golden city of Africa, with its eighty miles of streets', reached 'out its tentacles on every side' and connected the urban centre to 'its mining villages' (Hobson, 1900: 10). Vocal in his criticisms of the 'encroachments of Great Britain to the north' and 'the annexation of the Kimberley diamond fields' (130), Hobson highlighted the appetite for resource accumulation that drove the development of infrastructural networks such as the telegraph and railway northward into the African continent. He shed light on the way in which Cecil Rhodes and a cartel of other transnational capitalists had in the 1890s 'designed to use the money of the British taxpayer to obtain for himself and fellow-capitalists that political control of the Transvaal which was essential to his economical and political ambitions' (206–207). The Anglo-Boer War was, Hobson argued, 'being waged in order to secure for the mines a cheap adequate supply of labour' (231), in turn giving rise to contradictions addressed in greater detail in Chapters 2 and 3 of this book.

The use of imperial rule to facilitate capital accumulation – in Wallerstein's terms, the world-system developing under the 'temporary hegemony' of the British 'imperium' (Hopkins and Wallerstein, 1982: 52) – underpinned Hobson's slightly later and more theoretical work, *Imperialism, A Study* (1902). There he defined imperialism as 'the use of the machinery of government by private interests, mainly capitalists, to secure for them economic gains outside their country' (1988: 94). The metabolisms of profitable capitalist industries fuelled imperial expansion, inverting the popular political 'dogma' of the time 'that "Trade follows the Flag"' (33). There was, Hobson writes, a 'great expenditure of public money upon ships, guns, military and naval equipment and stores', one that fed 'business and professional interests [...] in opposition to the common good' (48), producing underdeveloped zones and impoverished peoples not only in colonial spaces, but also in metropolitan Britain. For Hobson, the economic 'core' of the world-system is again more helpfully configured at the level of networked infrastructural development than at that of the nation-state. Capitalism survived, Hobson argued, by generating vast 'public debts' in the imperial centre and loaning these to 'colonies' and 'foreign countries that come under [Britain's] protectorate' through investments in 'rails, engines, guns' and the 'making of railways, canals, and other public works': that is, the fixed capital of imperialism's unevenly developing infrastructural projects (49).

Karl Marx first theorised the notion of 'the accumulation of capital' in Part IV, Volume 1 of *Capital* in 1867 (1999: 315–362), and more specifically the idea of 'primitive accumulation' in Part V (363–380). Though, as David McLellan points out, 'the phenomena of imperialism are largely absent from *Capital* because 'the main colonial push came after its publication' (xxvi), Marx wrote numerous articles and letters that addressed imperialism's infiltration of the Indian subcontinent in the years leading up to the 1880s, building a 'critique of capital' that 'was far broader than is usually supposed' (Anderson, 2010: 237). Infrastructural development crucially informed his analysis of these processes of capital accumulation. Writing in an article published in August 1853, Marx foresaw that:

> the English millocracy intend to endow India with railways with the exclusive view of extracting at diminished expenses, the cotton and other raw materials for their manufactures. But when you have once introduced machinery into the locomotion of a country, which possesses iron and coals, you are unable to withhold it from its fabrication. You cannot maintain a net of railways over an immense country without introducing all those industrial processes necessary to meet the immediate and current wants of railway locomotion, and out of which there must grow the application of machinery to those branches of industry not immediately connected with the railways. The railway system will therefore become, in India, truly the forerunner of modern industry. (2006: 48–49)

Marx theorised these insights a few years later in the *Grundrisse*, where he emphasised the importance of 'the physical conditions of exchange – of the means of communication and transport' to 'the annihilation of space by time', a process that facilitated capital's need to 'drive beyond every spatial barrier' (1993: 524). However, whilst Marx anticipated the expansion of the world-system through the construction of a variety of infrastructural and industrial technologies, it is Rosa Luxemburg who, in *The Accumulation of Capital* (published in 1913, midway through the half-century analysed here), applied it to a specifically imperial context. Luxemburg criticises Marx for failing to see that, as Iqbal Husain describes, 'surplus value in capitalist production could be "realised" by the capitalists only through the enforced system of commodity exchange with precapitalist (colonial and peasant) economies' (Marx, 2006: xlvi–xlvii). For Luxemburg, it was a geographically expansive process of 'accumulation' that was integral to 'feeding' capital's metabolism, a relationship that, she argued, took place not *within* the capitalist system, but between that system and the pre- or non-capitalist societies that lay beyond it. The accumulation of capital, she wrote, 'corrodes and assimilates'; it depends upon the 'continuous and progressive disintegration of non-capitalist organisations' (2003: 397–398). Of course, this binary configuration of accumulation taking place 'between the ever-expanding domain of capital and the surrounding "medium and soil" of static, closed natural economies' is, as Anthony Brewer argues, 'surely too simple' (2001: 68), and is productively complemented by the emphasis placed on *uneven* development as undertaken by more recent commentators, to which I shall turn in a moment. However, Luxemburg still saw that these processes occurred 'at the margin where capitalist and pre-capitalist economic systems meet', a margin that 'exists within countries rather than between them' (72) and again emphasises the networked composition of the world-system's core–periphery relations.

Luxemburg drew on the specific historical contexts of both South Africa and South Asia in order to develop her critique. Her analysis cut through ideologies of humanitarianism – what Pablo Mukherjee has called 'palliative imperialism' (2013: 18), discussed in greater detail in Chapters 1 and 4 of this book – to conclude that 'British capital had no object in giving the Indian communities economic support or helping them to survive. Quite the reverse, it aimed to destroy them and deprive them of their productive forces' (Luxemburg, 2013: 356). Likewise, in South Africa after the discovery of the diamond and gold fields in 1867 and 1876 respectively, Luxemburg analysed the rise of 'mining capital' in the region: the Union of South Africa was a moment in which, with the formation of 'a great modern state, as envisaged by Cecil Rhodes' imperialist programme', 'capital officially took over the reins' (396). For Luxemburg infrastructure is again fundamental here, the 'forward thrusts of capital [...] approximately reflected in the development of the railway network' (400). Infrastructures such as railways exported resources from and imported manufactures to the colonies, whilst also proving a 'well-tried measure for civilising and pacifying the natives' (395). However, whilst intimating a networked picture of the world-system, her spatial paradigm remains constituted of blocked out segments of landscapes rather than unevenly developing infrastructures. This led Luxemburg to conclude that once 'external' geographical spaces were assimilated into the world-system, capitalism would no longer survive. 'Since', she argued, 'the earth is finite and the acquisition of new markets must some time come to an end, the time will come when the question can no longer simply be adjourned' (223). Luxemburg failed to predict that capital was as much responsible for *underdevelopment* as it was development – that it's development was uneven – and that it actively produced peripheral spaces to which it might return through a series of spatial expansions and contractions, manifesting often at the level of infrastructural development.

For Luxemburg, it was in the 1880s that capital ran out of the 'absolute' space into which it could expand (Smith, 2008: 134). According to Neil Smith, by the final decades of the nineteenth century capital's expansionist movement was restricted by solidifying political boundaries as they were drawn by competing imperial powers and, in turn, often adopted by emerging anticolonial nationalisms:

> The absolute expansion of nation states and of their colonies came to an end with the final partitioning of Africa in the 1880s. Certainly there were some internal islands of non-development, and indeed at the urban scale the process was not yet complete, but mopping these up would not on its own sustain the necessary economic expansion of capitalism. (2008: 119–120)

Smith refers here to the Berlin Conference of November 1884, when competing imperial powers partitioned Africa between themselves and planned the imposition of around 50,000 miles of colonial frontiers across the continent between 1885 and 1914 (Griffiths, 1995: 34; Packenham, 2009). Meanwhile, in South Asia, we find the almost coterminous formation of the Indian National Congress in Bombay in 1885, an organisation that would become 'the focus of the longest-lived nationalist movement in the modern colonial world' and the 'model for nationalist movements everywhere, above all, South Africa' (Metcalf and Metcalf, 2002: 136). On a global scale, in 1884 the world was demarcated into a system of time zones with the Greenwich Meridian at its centre, a process that cartographically positioned Britain at the heart of its world-empire – by 1913 this system spanned almost the entire face of the globe (Osterhammel and Petersson, 2003: 82–83). Despite these tectonic global shifts, however, for Headrick as for this book, the 'most noticeable transformation of the late nineteenth century was the triumph of the technologies introduced in the previous 100 years', of which '[r]ailroads and steamships were the most conspicuous' (2009: 111).[2]

---

2   Headrick points out elsewhere that this era of the 'new imperialism' coincided 'with the creation of modern underdeveloped economies in Asia and Africa', arguing that it is a 'consideration of the technologies involved', primarily manifested in imperial infrastructural developments, that 'can shed some light on this question' (1988: 4).

It is not my intention to argue whether or not capital did, indeed, run out of 'absolute' space in the 1880s. This timeline has been the explicit argument of geographers such as Smith, who maintains that at the end of the nineteenth century there was a 'geographical transition from the absolute expansion of global capitalism to its internal expansion and differentiation, and the emergence of the classical pattern of uneven development' (2005: 108–109). Clearly, however, Smith's is a general rather than exact commentary: internal differentiation occurred prior to this moment and at the same time as global expansion, with that expansion itself developing unevenly in different regions and at different times and speeds. More recently, critical contributions have argued for readjustments of the timescale of the instantiation and development of the capitalist world-system, de-emphasising 'the immediate practices and structures of European imperialism' and stressing that it was 'the "new" imperialism of early modernity', beginning with the Iberians in the late sixteenth century, that created 'a new way of seeing and ordering reality' (Moore, 2015: 190). For Wallerstein, 'the pushing of outer boundaries of the world-economy to the limits of the earth' were only just 'being approached' in the 1880s (1979: 278), but this fails to account for the 'internal islands', to use Smith's phrase (2008: 120), not necessarily of 'non-development', but of underdevelopment. And clearly, 'capitalist forms and relations exist alongside "archaic forms of economic life" and pre-existing social and class relations' even today, speaking to the 'combined' aspect of what WReC, following Trotsky and others, have emphasised as capital's 'combined and uneven development' (2015: 11). If, at 'first glance, the new empires had more effective technological and organisational means of exerting and maintaining power', Cooper maintains that what resulted was 'a patchwork of economic exploitation rather than a systematic transformation' (2005: 157). As he continues, all sorts of 'varied networks shape the nature of capitalism and its highly uneven effects', and there have been numerous '[c]ommunications revolutions, capital movements, and regulatory apparatuses' that 'all need to be studied' (111–112). For this book, it is the infrastructural networks of British imperialism that are placed centre-stage, and an emphasis on their *unevenly networked* composition, rather than any hegemonic totality, leaves room for the complexities of alternate infrastructural activity and socioeconomic organisation in its methodological approach to colonial literature.[3]

From this perspective, the motions of global capital were clearly foregrounded in the 1880s by the boom in communication and transport technologies, resulting in an acute unevenness that was most clearly demarcated by infrastructural development. This was in turn accompanied by an increase in the global imaginary of metropolitan and colonial subjects alike, or what Moore would call their 'way of seeing and ordering reality' (2015: 190), as Kipling observed so perceptively in 1914. In 1883, the historian John Seeley observed the 'simple and obvious fact of the extension of the English name into other countries of the globe' (1914: 9), an ideology of national expansion that could, albeit somewhat simplistically, be mapped onto an economic terrain (see Sassen, 2006: 132). As Hannah Arendt argues: 'imperialism, which grew out of colonialism and was caused by the incongruity of the nation-state system with the economic and industrial developments in the last third of the nineteenth century, started its politics of expansion for expansion's sake no sooner than around 1884' (2004: 159). This 'new version of politics' – imperialism – is 'born', for Arendt as for Hobson, 'when the ruling class in capitalist production came up against national limitations to its economic expansion' (170). Significantly, like Hobson and Luxemburg, Arendt developed these ideas out of her analysis of the historical example of South Africa at the turn of the twentieth century, a 'sensitivity to the significance of the violence perpetrated at the colonial limit' that is 'part of Arendt's debt to the work of Rosa Luxemburg' (Caygill, 2013: 153).

Raymond Williams, too, argues that '[f]rom about 1880 there was [a] dramatic extension of landscape and social relations [and] a marked

---

3   In this sense, the methodology follows WReC member Sharae Deckard's call for 'a critical practice that unites a theory of combined and uneven development across the striated cores and peripheries of the world-system with a conceptualisation of capitalism as a world-ecology constituted by ecological regimes' (2016: 244). These ecological dynamics are implicit throughout the book before being addressed specifically in Chapter 4's discussion of the urban-rural tensions embedded in late colonial literature.

development of the idea of England as "home"' (1973: 281). In this configuration, the developed and industrialised 'consuming capital' of London
begins to be imagined in direct contrast to the 'rural' areas of colonial
landscapes, transformed 'by economic and political force [into] planta-
tion economies, mining areas [and] single-crop markets' (284), with an
increased depth and virility, even if these relational dynamics had been
in play since the fifteenth century (Rodney, 2012: 95–100). For the first
time, Williams continues, 'a model of city and country' moves beyond 'the
boundaries of the nation-state, and is seen but also challenged as a model of
the world' (1973: 279). Williams's analysis, like Arendt's, builds on Hobson's
earlier contribution, highlighting the material underpinnings of 'political
imperialism' and translating this into a view of the British Empire as an
unevenly developed network of core-peripheral relations. Impoverished
populations – '[t]he unemployed man from the slums of the cities, the
superfluous landless worker, the dispossessed peasant' – are produced within
both the colonised countries *and* the imperial nation (283).[4] As Wallerstein
concedes, core and periphery 'are simply phrases to locate one crucial part
of the system of surplus appropriation by the bourgeoisie': if the 'proletarian is located in a different country from this bourgeoisie' this results
'in patterns of "uneven development"' (1991: 293). Cores and peripheries
are distributed, colonial literature reveals, unevenly across the face of the
globe, regardless of political and national borders, and was best measured
through the symbolic objects of imperial infrastructure.

It is for these reasons that Smith, in his book-length discussion of
uneven development, turns from Luxemburg's important theoretical contributions to focus instead on Lenin's later work, especially his *Imperialism,
the Highest Stage of Capitalism* (1916). Lenin was attuned to the more
spatially complex methods by which capital sustained its accumulative
metabolism. As Lenin hypothesised, though 'the colonial policy of the

---

4   Williams also emphasises the post-imperial outgrowths of the '[m]assive investments'
    in 'economic and political infrastructure' made during this period, often couched as
    'aid', but that continues to develop peripheral 'economies towards metropolitan needs'
    through 'the preservation of markets and spheres of influence' or 'the continuation
    of indirect political control' (1973: 284).

capitalist countries has *completed* the seizure of the unoccupied territories on our planet' this does not mean that '*a new partition* is impossible – on the contrary, new partitions are possible and inevitable':

> For the first time the world is completely shared out, so that in the future only *redivision is possible*; territories can only pass from one 'owner' to another, instead of passing as unowned territory to an 'owner'. (1987: 227)

This occurred, Lenin continues, during 'the period of the enormous expansion of colonial conquests [...] between 1860 and 1880, and it was also very considerable in the last twenty years of the nineteenth century' (228). As Smith reads Lenin, capitalist development therefore sustains itself 'not through absolute expansion in a given space but through the internal differentiation of global space, that is through the production of differentiated spaces' (2008: 120). Lenin begins to theorise the notion of uneven development across and between nations, but also at the lower geographical scales of the networked world-system: 'The uneven and spasmodic character of the development of individual enterprises, of individual branches of industry and individual countries, is inevitable under the capitalist system' (1987: 215). For Lenin, like Marx and Luxemburg before him, the physical infrastructures of imperialism were both the economic *and* symbolic expression of cross-national capitalism. He writes in the preface to the French and German editions of *Imperialism*, published slightly later in 1920:

> Railways are the summation of the most important branches of capitalist industry, coal and iron; the summation and most striking indices of the development of the world trade and bourgeois-democratic civilisation. [...] The uneven distribution of the railways, their uneven development, are the summation of modern monopolist capitalism on a world scale. (1934: 10)

Both Smith and Harvey have since emphasised the centrality of infrastructure as enabling, expressing and reproducing the processes of uneven development. The 'frantic geographical expansion' of capital accumulation 'requires a continuous investment of capital in the creation of a built environment for production': 'Roads, railways, factories, fields, workshops, warehouses, wharves, sewers, canals, power stations'; infrastructures that function as 'geographically immobilised forms of fixed capital, so central to the progress of accumulation' (Smith, 2008: 159–160). As Harvey explains, 'capitalism seeks to overcome spatial barriers through the creation of physical infrastructures that are immobile in space'; infrastructures function as a 'spatial fix' that resolves – if only temporarily – 'the internal contradictions of capitalism' (1999: 379–380, 393). The 'concentrations of capital and labour' that congregate in metropolitan areas seesaws with 'sprawling far-flung development' into peripheral zones, as these infrastructures open up new pools of labour-power and material resources and offer financial capitalists the opportunity for speculative investment – 'roads and railways litter a landscape that has been indelibly and irreversibly carved out according to the dictates of capitalism' (373). Seeking a spatial fix in the form of 'an immobile environment for production' (fixed infrastructure), 'external space' is unevenly produced *within and as part of the global geography of capitalism*, manifesting as 'social inequality blazoned into the geographical landscape' (Smith, 2008: 187, 198, 206). At this spatial-historical crisis-point in the development of the world-system, as both contemporaneous and retrospective analysts here conceive it, the production of space – physically and economically, but also ideologically – becomes fundamental to the resolution of capitalism's deep-set contradictions.

It is my argument, then, that the depiction of infrastructure in colonial literature from the 1880s onwards functions, correspondingly, as what Stephen Shapiro calls a 'cultural fix': 'Just as the spatial fix involves opening new geographies, the cultural fix, likewise, looks to establish new identities for control' (2014: 1262). Cultural fixes 'serve to normalise otherwise unacceptable appropriations of global natures, human and extra-human' (Moore, 2015: 199). Operating on a cultural terrain, colonial literature tries to 'fix' contradictions in imperial ideology by looking repeatedly to infrastructures as spatial reference points and (re)producing their uneven geographical developments. Colonial literature becomes obsessed with the production of spaces that might satiate the accumulative appetite of the capitalist world-system and resolve the ideological tensions it throws up, creating cultural maps of uneven infrastructural development in order to do so. *Infrastructural reading* focuses on the occurrence of infrastructure in colonial literature in order to unpick this 'cultural fix' as it manifests in textual form. Focusing on these representations of infrastructures allows us to see how they contribute to uneven geographical development within the imperial imagination and, through its (re)production of space, to the very material inequalities that shape the colonial environment. It is in these moments, and often despite its best efforts, that colonial literature confesses to imperialism's complicity in the 'development of underdevelopment' (WReC, 2015: 13).

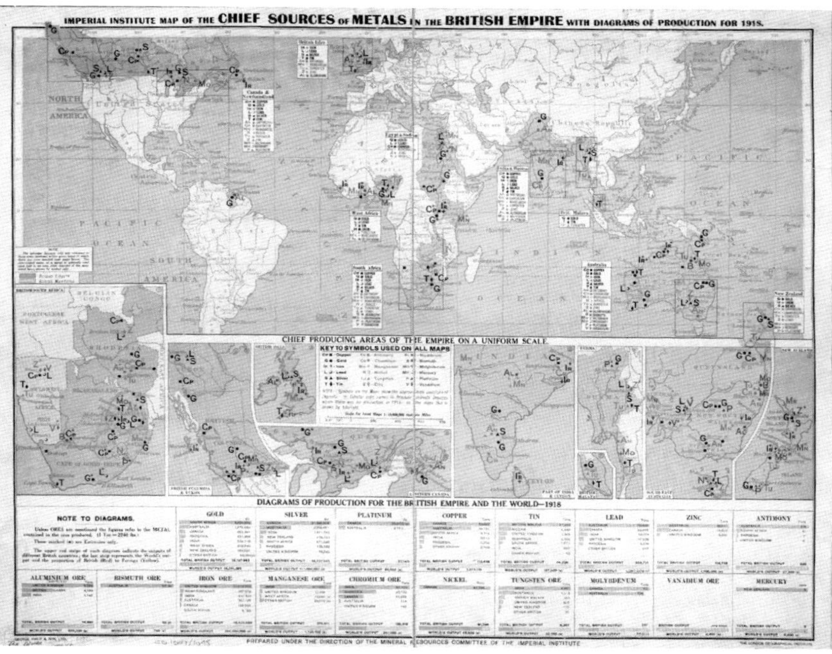

Figure 0.2: Map produced by the Imperial Institute in 1918 charting the 'Chief Sources of Metals in the British Empire' and accompanied by 'Diagrams of Production for 1918'. Colonial Office Archives, 1047/1045, National Archives at Kew. It is demonstrative of the way in which colonial cartographic practice (in literature as well as maps) transforms the '*basic* fact' of geology into 'a *historical* fact' by revealing 'the historically co-produced character of resource production' (Moore, 2015: 179).

If Lenin concludes that imperialism, spatially conceived, 'means the partition of the world', his discussion of effective, revolutionary resistance is similarly spatial and rooted in material geographic space – something that 'the social-liberal Hobson is unable to perceive' because, Lenin indicts, of his tendency 'to substitute petty-bourgeois reformism for Marxism' (1987: 249–250, 258). For Lenin, it is through both the formation of cohesive nationalist identities and anti-imperial solidarities unified by class-consciousness that resistance to imperialist world-economies can be conceived and effectively initiated.[5] Though I am primarily concerned with the excavation of elusive moments of resistance from colonial literature, I also want to emphasise that, especially in fiction written towards the end of the half-century of 1880 to 1930, the geographic and territorial shape of the post-imperial nation begins to haunt these cultural productions of space. What results is a fundamental contradiction that produces deep rift within the ideological fabric of colonial literature; as Hopkins and Wallerstein point out, 'integrating production on a world-scale' and the formation of 'strong national-states' are the world-system's 'two broad', though 'deeply contradictory', 'organising tendencies' (1982: 43).

The conception of both South Africa and India as independent national units no longer under the political domain of the British world-empire occurs *not only* in nationalist and other anticolonial writings, *but also* within colonial literary productions of space. As Anderson has demonstrated, the nation is 'an imagined political community' that comes into being as an 'inherently limited and sovereign' entity bound to a static geographical territory (2006: 5–6). The contours of the imagined post-imperial nation are debated and shaped by contemporaneous anticolonial and nationalist movements throughout the final decades of the British Empire's global hegemonic supremacy, but this contest is also played out in the subtexts and infrastructural frameworks of much of this colonial literature. Colonial texts written and published in the 1910s and '20s are already preoccupied with the disintegration of formal British rule, the emergence of newly independent nations and the infrastructural foundations and geographical perimeters that will shape them. It is for this

5 See specifically Lenin's *State and Revolution* (1917), where he positions 'the organisation of national unity' as a core ingredient for a movement that 'totally rejects not only capitalism, but also all Western political forms and institutions' (Lenin, 1987: 271, 308–310).

reason – as well, of course, simply for issues of scope and focus – that the book ends in 1930, rather than extending its analysis right up until, say, Indian independence in 1947.

The title of the latest novel discussed at length in this book, Thompson's *A Farewell to India* (1931), is indicative of the concerns circulating at this time. Historically speaking, this is perhaps unsurprising. On 2 March 1930, then Viceroy of India, Lord Irwin, 'received an ultimatum in the form of a polite letter from Gandhi' (Newsinger, 2010: 141). Ten days later, Gandhi began his famous march to the sea with the intention of breaking the 'British enforced monopoly on the sale and production of salt', 'a masterpiece of political mobilisation' that targeted exploitative economic policies of imperial administration (141). As Dietmar Rothermund has argued, this event, which led to the Civil Disobedience campaign of 1930–1932, 'recruited the younger generation of many groups who had not so far participated in nationalist politics' (1970: 23), and in January 1930 that the Indian National Congress 'celebrated "Independence Day" for the first time' (Heehs, 2010: 172). This anti-imperial activism had been accelerated by the first Non-Cooperation campaign of 1920–1922, the first time that, according to Jim Masselos, 'grievances against the British had brought the country together in one movement under one leader' (2010: 168–169). Though these resistant activities would ebb away through the mid-1920s, their return towards the end of the decade makes 1930 a poignant year with which to conclude this study.

Though less obviously a landmark date in South African history, 1930 can still be situated within the context of political unrest and anti-imperial resistance, though 1910 is of more central concern to authors such as Buchan. When 'Boer Generals and the British capitalists swore blood-brotherhood in the Union of 1910', the flames of both Afrikaner nationalism and Black activism were fed, leading in turn to the formation of the South African Natives National Congress (later the African National Congress) in 1912 and the gradual decline of British imperial influence in the region (McClintock, 1995: 368–369). However, Shula Marks and Richard Rathbone argue that the years between 1870 and 1930 were 'formative', 'dominated by the imperatives of mining capital'; for them, 'the thirties' constitute a suitable 'cut-off date' (1982: 11–12). Thomas Karis and Gwendolen Carter have noted the intensification of 'African protest' between 1920 and 1935, as efforts were made by Black Africans to challenge 'their growing disadvantages within the system' (1972: 148–149). These culminated in events such as 'the National European-Bantu Conferences', 'called yearly from 1929', and the Non-European Conferences, convened first in 1927 and then in 1930, 1931 and 1934, all with the aim of raising 'nonwhite grievances' and passing 'numerous resolutions recording opposition to government policy' (151–152).

Taking account of the increased vocalness of these anti-imperial movements specific to various local and (sub)continental contexts, 1930 was also a significant year for the waning of Britain's global hegemony. At the Imperial Conference of 1926, the dominions were pronounced 'autonomous communities within the British Empire, equal in status', and five years later, in 1931, 'the report was given legal status by the Statute of Westminster' (Johnson: 2003: 158). Economically speaking, the Great Depression 'forced Britain to abandon the gold standard in 1931 and free trade through the Import Duties Act in 1932' (166–168). It is for these reasons that, in his discussion of the 'cultural and spatial foundations of the world urban system', King cites 1931 as a landmark date for the height of British imperial economic hegemony, after which its supremacy began to dwindle (1991: 5–6).

Given the centrality of nationalism to this history, a final note is necessary on how it is factored into the methodology of *infrastructural reading*. For Partha Chatterjee, the 'perception of uneven development creates the possibility for nationalism; it is born when the more and the less advanced populations can be easily distinguished in cultural terms' (2011: 4). Mitchell similarly argues that in 'the later nineteenth and early twentieth centuries, practices such as the demarcation and policing of frontiers' (a recurring concern for colonial literature and studied in detail in Chapter 3), as well as 'the overcoming of distances through the construction of railways, roads, shipping canals, and telegraphs', created the nation as a 'postimperial political topography' (2002: 78–83). Indeed, as Wallerstein and others point out, 'antisystemic movements have more and more taken on the clothing of "national-liberation movements"' (2011: 27). I want to emphasise that nationalist resistance needs to be understood as more than simply a product of, or response to, uneven infrastructural development. Rather, nationalism plays an active role in the shaping of that uneven*ness*. This reconfiguration embeds the presence of resistance, albeit implicitly, within, between and beyond the infrastructural networks that run through colonial literature, as a counteracting force rather than a passive byproduct or 'derivative discourse', in any simplistic sense (Anderson, 1988: 29).

Colonial literature registers on formal, thematic and symbolic levels, uneven and differentiated internal infrastructural development in the same moment that it negotiates the formation of the post-independent nations as distinct geographic and political entities. For example, in both *Siri Ram – Revolutionist* (1912) and *Abdication* (1922), Edmund Candler attempts to delegitimise the arguments of emerging nationalist movements whilst simultaneously producing the unevenly and unequally developed landscapes that justified many of their arguments in the first place. These are coterminous ideological projects that are inextricably woven together within colonial fiction's uneven literary geographies. Reading nationalisms through colonial literature in this way should not be seen as a 'backward projection of the post-1960s world of nation-states into a two-century-long path of inevitability', which limits 'the diversity of opposition' to imperialism (Cooper, 2005: 24). Of course, numerous anti-systemic movements have operated across and between the political borders of nation-states. Rather, an assessment of colonial literature's engagement with early nationalisms reveals that, as Stephen Clingman has argued, the national community (and, I would argue, territory) is 'gapped, divided, and incoherent in ways Anderson's model could not fully conceive' (2009: 4). A focus on colonial literature's depiction of infrastructures allows us to disaggregate the traditional cartography of geopolitical borders and global hierarchies as constructed by nineteenth-century imperialisms into a more complex, uneven geography. This understanding of the nation's terrain reframes what is, for Clingman, a 'fundamental question': we should not ask 'whether boundaries exist – because they do, they always do – but what kind of boundaries they are' (4–5). Analysing colonial literature's production of geographies of division, segregation and partition might, then, also contain clues for how nationalisms' imaginative and physical ordering of the world, rooted in and building on the infrastructures that shape the way those national spaces are still imagined and inhabited today, can be transgressed, complicated and at times, undone.

Spatial 'Resistance': The Politics of a Term

Throughout the book I wish to argue that the fissures, crevices and cracks in the ideological field of colonial literature can be quantified as a mode of resistance, or even *mobilised* as an *actively resistant* force. However, whilst I do not wish 'to romanticise anticolonial movements in their triumph', I am troubled also by arguments that claim that 'colonialism was *as much* threatened by fissures within its modes of action and representation as by the threat' and actual acts of anticolonial resistance (Cooper, 2005: 32; my emphasis). Though I continue to use the term 'resistance' throughout, I remain concerned by the extent to which such a term overstates the gravity of the critical work that this book undertakes. In this section I will therefore expand upon my use of that hanging, qualificatory adjective included in this book's title – '*spatial* resistance' – to show how this addresses some of these concerns, whilst further reflecting on the concept of 'resistance' more broadly. To begin, however, it is necessary to outline the four different kinds of resistance that I have found to occur with any significant regularity across the broad field of colonial literature:

1. Violent resistance, be it a coherent anti-imperial campaign (such as Zulu resistance to the British in South Africa in the 1870s and '80s) or a spontaneous outburst against imperial agents or infrastructures (for example, isolated acts of peasant resistance).
2. Non-violent resistance, from the passive blockage of imperial movement and infrastructural development to active interventions into those circuitries and the economic dynamics they facilitated (such as the *swadeshi* campaigns in India).
3. Emerging nationalist campaigns self-consciously mobilised against imperial rule with the ultimate aim of achieving independence from it (for example, Gandhi's nationalist movement).
4. The representation of (semi-)peripheral zones signified by underdeveloped geographical space, indifferent colonised populations, and a range of alternative social, cultural and economic activities practiced regardless of the imperial presence ('what Gramsci refers to as the "practical

activities" of "the man in the mass"' and 'Lefebvre refers to as "everyday life"' (Harvey, 2009: 238)).

Given the self-consciously pro-imperial agendas and historically racial, cultural and often economic privilege of so many of these colonial authors, the most frequently occurring kind of resistance is the fourth in this list. Often, anti-imperial resistance is situated *beyond*, or *on the cusp of*, the landscapes, plots and characters of these literary texts; it resides, latent, or implicit, in the subtextual constructions of the cultural and geographical terrain that colonial literature produces – it is *inscribed into colonial literature's infrastructure*. This literature is reliant upon, but also restricted to, the world-system's unevenly developed physical and symbolic infrastructural networks, and must therefore necessarily acknowledge the limits of its representations and productions of colonial landscapes. Highlighting these *spatial* limits and listening for the silences and stirrings that lie beyond them allows us to map numerous moments of implicit subversion within colonial literature, even when these remain residual, abeyant, waiting to be reignited and re-mobilised. When read cumulatively out of several texts from a range of different geo-historical locations, these momentary subversions coalesce into a cartography of resistance that is embedded within the colonial literary terrain. This resistance is always spatial, in that it is in and through its dispersed, networked spatiality that imperialism – as a stage in the development of the world-system – is resisted.

Critical discussions of resistance repeatedly emphasise its 'hiddenness', or 'evasiveness', before developing specific techniques in order to make these hidden moments 'speak'. Whether it is 'Antonio Gramsci's concept of counterhegemony, Karl Polanyi's notion of countermovements, [or] James C. Scott's idea of infrapolitics', it is always necessary to 'dig deep to excavate the everyday individual and collective activities that fall short of open opposition' (Mittelman, 2000: 166). As Scott comments, '[i]f the decoding of power relations depended on full access to the more or less clandestine discourse of subordinate groups, students of power – both historical and contemporary – would face an impasse' (1990: xii). Analysts must look for what Scott calls 'the hidden transcript' that, though located 'beyond direct observation by powerholders', remains present, 'albeit in disguised form' (xiii, 4–5). Theorists of resistance therefore frequently take gaps and ruptures in the archive of the dominant power to be symptomatic of more coherent systems of resistance existing beyond its purview. As Louise Amoore argues, '[w]here we do see the instances of open collective protest or the loud headline-grabbing demonstrations, these are but ripples on the surface of a deeper and more diffuse pattern of struggles' (2005: 8). These 'less visible practices of resistance' are not 'meaningfully separable from the overt expressions' – in fact, the opposite is often the case: it may be these day-to-day, invisible strategies that actually 'make the grand gestures possible' (8). Discussing the colonial archive in particular, Ann Laura Stoler looks to the 'storied edges' where 'the faultlines of colonial ethnography may more fully reside, in the interstices of sanctioned formulae, in the descriptions of what it meant to say' (2002: 143–144); those 'ragged edges of proto-col' that were produced by 'the administrative apparatus as it opened to a space that extended beyond it' (2009: 1–2). Likewise, the *Subaltern Studies* collective has sought to subject colonialism's 'hegemonic presumption to thoroughgoing critique', reading between the archival lines to show that, in the Indian context, 'there is nothing in the record of the Raj [...] to justify any pretension to a rule by consent' (Guha, 1998: xviii). Our task, then, is to continually develop new ways of decoding latent forms of resistance, an ambition that motivates the practice of *infrastructural reading*.

Hopkins and Wallerstein argue that tracing the 'phasings of formal colonisation and informal empire [...] for the system as a whole' allows 'the interrelations between these phasings and the presence or absence of various modes or forms of opposition – "primitive rebellion" (Hobsbawm), "wars of independence", "wars of liberation", "nationalist movements", and the like – to be sketched' (1982: 29). For Hobsbawm, the conditions to which this resistance reacts 'comes to [oppressed groups] from outside, insidiously by the operation of economic forces which they do not under-stand and over which they have no control, or brazenly by conquest' (1959: 30). However, this suggests that it is only with the arrival of imperial rule that resistance begins. It is framed only as a backlash to the imposition of imperial infrastructures, occurring temporally *after* or *in response* to their arrival. Conceived in this way, resistance is put on the back foot and its active agency reductively limited. Instead, as Steve Pile and Michael Keith have argued, 'resistance needs to be considered on its own terms, and not as simply the underside of domination' (1997: xi). Though of course anti-colonial struggles could not take place until the various territories to which they were home had been colonised, the construction and imposition of different kinds of imperial infrastructure took place historically *in response* to different kinds of resistance.

Howard Caygill, in a discussion of the criticisms levied against Michel Foucault for his apparent nullification of resistant agencies, quotes an interview with the French historian that shows how the biopolitical tactics of governmental rule are actually developed in response to the resistance they encounter:

> if there was no resistance there would be no relations of power. Because everything would simply be a question of obedience. From the moment an individual is in the situation of not doing what they want, they must use relations of power. Resistance thus comes first, it remains above all the forces of the process, under its effect obliges relations of power to change. I thus consider the term 'resistance' to be the most important word, the key word of this dynamic. (Foucault, 2001a: 1559–1560; translated in Caygill, 2013: 8)

By reframing resistance in this way, traces of anti-imperial defiance can actually be found inscribed into and actively shaping the literary depictions of infrastructural networks analysed here. Colonial fiction's ideological strategies (its 'cultural fixes'), which congregate around its depiction of imperial infrastructure, do not occur temporally prior to anti-imperial resistance. Rather, they are already a response to resistance that has taken place and that is, in many cases, ongoing. As the individual chapter studies will show, resistance actually shapes the colonial narratives propagated by these texts. If resistance dictates the infrastructural shaping of an unevenly developing capitalist world-system as it is read through this literary fiction, it is therefore most productively configured in its *spatial* manifestations.

A 'spatial understanding of resistance necessitates a radical reinterpretation and reevaluation of the concept' (Pile and Keith, 1997: xi): by conceiving of resistance as spatial, *infrastructural reading* shows how resistance inflects and gives shape to the infrastructures of the world-system whilst refusing to assimilate, and thus neutralise, its resistant potential.

This highlights what Caygill calls '[t]he resistance of resistance to analysis' (2013: 7). For Caygill, resistance 'is rooted in practice and articulated in tactical statements and justifications addressing specific historical contexts', with the consequence that 'defining a concept of resistance' becomes a tricky, if not impossible task (6). However, this is 'not necessarily a disadvantage': defining resistance actually 'risks making it predictable, open to control and thus lowering its resistance' (6). In order to trace the contours of resistance it must be continually 'situated within a complex and dynamic spatio-temporal field' (2). This allows us to build a 'consistency' across occurrences of resistance (thereby revealing and emphasising the weight of their impact as a coherent sociopolitical force), without 'imposing unity' on those resistant occurrences (and thus defining, quantifying and limiting that same sociopolitical impact) (7). As Jopi Nyman and John Stotedbury argue, 'resistance emerges as a context-bound phenomenon solved differently in different spaces; there is no single centre to be resisted but many' (1999: 1). Similarly, Joanne Sharp and others 'talk about "entanglements" to indicate that the domination/resistance couplet is always played out in, across and through the many spaces of the world' (2005: 1). Predicated on a networked conception of an unevenly developing world-system, *infrastructural reading* can therefore trace, and subsequently analyse, multiple sites and forms of resistance as they shape colonial literature. It realises a level of cumulative 'consistency' across different geo-historical occurrences of resistance, whilst avoiding the imposition of a limiting, or oppressive unity upon them.

The spatiality of resistance ensures it remains active and alive within the colonial literary archive. If Lenin and Luxemburg were important theorists of imperial exploitation, their work is similarly attentive to methods of resistance. All of Lenin's critical writings are oriented toward a radical, anti-systemic politics. As Alex Callinicos argues, 'what Lenin showed more effectively than any other Marxist was the importance of theoretical analysis of capitalism in strategically situating political actors' (2007: 36). However, because of his formally political preoccupations, for Lenin resistance always manifests 'in terms of the clash of solids' necessarily constituted, as Caygill explains, amongst a community of 'integrated and conscious class subjects' (2013: 46–47). Lenin warns against *spontaneous* development of the labour movement', its 'lack of consciousness' risking its eventual subordination 'to bourgeois ideology' (1987: 82–84). Conversely, for Luxemburg resistance does not need to 'fit into the kind of continuous logical and temporal narrative contrived by Lenin', instead operating 'as the movements of fluid forces made up of diverse currents moving at different velocities' (Caygill, 2013: 47). This is conveyed in her account of the 1905 Revolution, when social unrest spread across the Russian Empire. There she emphasises the 'spontaneous' revolutionaries 'shaking and tugging' on the 'chains of capitalism' (1970: 171). These movements flow, Luxemburg writes,

> like a broad billow over the whole kingdom, and now divides into a gigantic network of narrow streams; now it bubbles forth from under the ground like a fresh spring and now is completely lost under the earth [...] all these run through one another, run side by side, cross one another, flow in and over one another – it is a ceaselessly moving, changing sea of phenomena [...]. (182)

For Luxemburg, resistance is dispersed and spatial rather than linear and chronological, a conception more useful for this book's mapping of moments of resistance that remain uneven in their trajectories, manifestations and tactics across the colonial literary field. This recalls Gramsci's notion of the 'war of manoeuvre', in which 'different strategic options' are mobilised to increase their effectiveness in different contexts (Gramsci, 1988: 230; Caygill, 2013: 141). As David Lloyd argues in his reading of Gramsci, by defining the subaltern as 'that which resists or cannot be represented [...] its "episodic and fragmentary" history can be read as the sign of another *mode* of narrative, rather than an incomplete one' (1993: 127). Whilst a paradigm of uneven development informs infrastructures of colonial literature during this period, a scattering of uneven but ever-present modes of resistance likewise, and just as importantly, shape the world-system and, in turn, the literary field's mapping of it.

Of course, it is important to stress the limitations of such a project. I would not want to go so far as to reframe these often pro-imperial writings as what Barbara Harlow calls 'resistance literature'; regardless of the resistance practices latent within them, the texts studied here mostly fail to 'challenge both the monolithic historiographical practices of domination and the unidimensional responses of dogma to them' (1987: 30). Often, and especially at the levels of character and plot, colonial fiction struggles to maintain and perpetuate a violent set of racial, social and economic hierarchies that enabled imperial domination and capital accumulation. However, the critical methodology of *infrastructural reading* allows us *to read colonial literature resistantly*, to show how this literary archive can provide, to cite Harlow once more:

> developed historical analyses of the circumstances of economic, political, and cultural domination and repression and through that analysis raises a systematic and concerted challenge to the imposed chronology of what Fredric Jameson has called 'master narratives', ideological paradigms which contain within their plots a predetermined ending. (1987: 78; see also Jameson, 1991: xi)

In its undertaking, then, this book joins other efforts to correct 'the revisionist accounts of imperial and colonial life that have proliferated in recent years', arguments that, as Paul Gilroy observed in the first years of the twenty-first century, 'compound the marginality of colonial history' and make 'the formative experience of empire less profound', whitewashing its violent realities 'in order to promote imperialist nostalgia' (Gilroy, 2004a: 2–3). Unfortunately, his commentary seems even more relevant as I write a decade on. What Renato Rosaldo once called 'imperial nostalgia' – an emotional fantasy that transforms 'the responsible colonial agent into an innocent bystander' (1989: 108) – appears to have returned with renewed aggression in recent years; a 2014 poll revealed that 59 per cent of respondents believed the British Empire was 'something to be proud of' (Andrews, 2016). If a critique of these contemporary repercussions of empire and colonialism are beyond the scope of this book, I wish to emphasise throughout that the four overarching ideologies addressed in the book's four chapters are *directly* related to current manifestations of post-imperial violence, from recent surges in racially motivated hate crimes to broader institutional and structural forms of discrimination (see Hall, 2016).

It is in this sense, then, that I *align* the book with, though *do not* necessarily consider it a direct act of, contemporary praxis and practices of 'decolonial resistance'. For Mignolo, decolonisation is not a one-off, historical event now passed, but rather an ongoing process that must be continually (re)mobilised: 'While liberation framed the struggle of the oppressed in the "Third World" and the history of modern coloniality, decoloniality is an even larger project' (2012: 457). If imperial nostalgia has intensified in recent years, so too have these decolonising efforts, especially on university campuses indelibly and infrastructurally marked by their imperial pasts – most notably the Universities of Cape Town (UCT) and Oxford. The 'Rhodes Must Fall' (RMF) campaign, which mobilised effectively around the removal of the statue of arch-imperialist Cecil Rhodes from the UCT campus, asserts a 'decolonial gaze' that 'deliberately remembers the violence of colonialism, the exploitation of extractive settler economies [and] the disfigurement of African communities and culture – all of which are concealed by grand narratives of development and modernisation' (Luckett, 2015: 416). As I will discuss throughout the book, by emphasising infrastructural development, imperialists like Rhodes were able to promote a narrative that concealed colonial exploitation beneath a benevolent, '"pastoral power" (that is not overtly authoritarian), which characterised an aspect of British imperialism' (Kros, 2015: 156), and that is still repeated by critics of RMF today (see Lowry, 2016: 329–330).

Figure 0.3: Photograph of the statue of Cecil Rhodes being removed by crane from the University of Cape Town's campus on 9 April 2015, a symbolic culmination of ongoing decolonial protests by the Rhodes Must Fall campaign.

Nevertheless, if infrastructure fixed, spatially and culturally, some of the key contradictions of imperial capitalism and its corresponding ideologies, critically focusing on them allows for the (re)disturbance of the smoothing over they facilitated and, in turn, creates space for resistance to them. *Infrastructural reading* creates crevices and fissures that make room for alternative histories and resistant practices previously silenced by the colonial archive – it allows us to read these archives '"against the grain"; to challenge and expand them' (Luckett, 2016: 425). Decolonial movements such as RMF are 'about more than simply removing colonial and apartheid era symbols, increasing the number of black academics and including African texts in the curriculum'; they address 'a violent phenomenon' in order to look forward to 'the creation of a new humanity' (Prinsloo, 2016: 165). Because this book's methodological effort embraces RMF's 'strong emphasis on the democratic potential around notions of voice, representation, and speaking up or talking back' (Bosch, 2016: 9), it places a self-conscious emphasis on *listening* for and to the silences in colonial literature, silences that, when ignored, can 'become forms of violence against decolonisation' (Pillay, 2016: 157): 'it is not only important to speak', notes Tanja Bosch, 'but also to be heard' (2016: 9–10). Pedagogically, this book is intended as an attempt to develop 'the analytical and methodological tools for debating, challenging and deconstructing inherited canons' (Luckett, 2016: 425), a process that can in turn be translated into 'real action' (Prinsloo, 2015: 166). To use Stuart Hall's words, my development of *infrastructural reading* is accompanied by an 'intellectual modesty', conceived 'as a practice which always thinks about its intervention in a world in which it would make some difference, in which it would have some effect' (1992: 286). For this reason, *infrastructural reading* should not itself be quantified as resistance, but rather seen as an effort to *create space for* resistance; to initiate, that is, a *spatial resistance*.

Colonial Literature: Why These Texts?

Further to my opening remarks on the archive referred to here as 'colonial literature', I wish to conclude this introduction by clarifying more exactly the parameters of this cultural field. Of course, Kipling's writing is arguably the most representative example of colonial literature, and it is indicatively obsessed with technological developments, imperial forms of infrastructure and literary depictions of them. However, 'postcolonial' commentaries on his fiction have gained significant traction since Edward Said's reading of *Kim* (1901) in *Culture and Imperialism* (1993: 159–196), as critics have thoroughly dismantled the pro-imperial ideologies propagated by his jingoistic poetry and reevaluated his prose for its more 'modernist', subversive content (Low, 1996; Randall, 2000; Nagai and Rooney, eds, 2010). Indeed, in his 'Note on Modernism', Said distinguishes between the 'narrative progression and triumphalism' of texts such as Haggard's *She* (1887) and the 'extreme, unsettling anxiety' in the work of authors as wide-ranging as Conrad, Forster, Malraux, T. E. Lawrence, T. S. Eliot, Proust, Mann and Yeats. Undoubtedly, writings by these authors do exhibit the kinds of resistant strategies excavated by *infrastructural reading*, as numerous materialist and postcolonial critics have convincingly shown. Some of these studies have been concerned in particular with the 'spatiality' of these texts, emphasising the genre's preoccupation with 'absences and gaps to grids and maps' and their 'numerous abstract tropes and topographical stereotypes', many of which, this book will show, are characteristics of colonial literature more widely (Childs, 2007: 84). One collection has even linked the two spheres of 'modernism' and 'colonialism' via the contemporaneous development of imperial infrastructures (Begam and Moses, 2007: 2).

Perhaps most famously, however, is Fredric Jameson's emphasis on the connection between the spatiality of modernist form and the coterminous period of Britain's accelerated expansionism in his essay, 'Modernism and Imperialism' (1990). Here, Jameson argues that when a 'significant structural segment of the economic system' is exported to an 'unknown and unimaginable' space 'over the water', the 'new spatial language' of 'modernist style' is produced (1990: 51–58). Unsurprisingly, this has has been critiqued for relating modernism to imperialism through 'a single linear narrative of cause and effect' (Booth and Rigby, 2000: 6). However, Patrick Williams is sympathetic to the political import of Jameson's work. He acknowledges that Jameson's 'spatialising effect' is a product of 'the attempted mapping of the restructuring of the imperial world system' before turning to Said's more resistant work (2000: 21–23), which emphasises the 'disturbing effect' that modernism's spatiality might bring to 'imperial ideology' (Said, 1993: 226). Clearly, this effort to assess the historical impact that moments of what might be described as a kind of 'spatial resistance' in modernist literature to imperial ideology is in line with this book's own critical task. Indeed, Williams concludes by complicating Jameson's paradigm through the application of a '"combined and uneven development" perspective' to 'modernism and imperialism', a theoretical shift that, as for this project, allows a more nuanced analysis of 'imperialism on a world scale' (2000: 32).

Though I arrive at the critical application of uneven development to a literary-cultural field through a different methodological route, there are many fruitful overlaps here and these should be seen as mutually constructive and, I would stress, political projects. The book does, however, make a crucial departure from this work: it is my contention that the world-system historically underpinning the British Empire is registered formally and generically *not only* by modernist literature. Instead, I follow Elleke Boehmer who, in the introduction to her *Anthology of Colonial Literature, 1870–1918*, defines some of the key traits of this alternate literary archive:

> assumptions of supremacy and hierarchy captured in images of work, 'improvement', and 'progress'; visual bafflement at 'impenetrable' and apparently featureless foreign landscapes; stories and poems of encounter, conflict, and connection; and also preoccupations with cultural difference, dislocation, and 'taint' [...]. (1998b: xix)

It is my contention that, when read *infrastructurally*, this colonial literature, which certainly does *not* exhibit typically 'modernist' formal and generic conventions, can also be made to reveal conflicts, tensions and fissures at the level of ideology. 'If nothing else', Boehmer writes elsewhere, this literature offers us some 'insight into the imperial imagination' and, even more importantly, 'some purchase on the occlusions of human loss that operated in colonial representation' (2005: 21).[6] Colonial literature responds to a number of

---

6   Boehmer makes a further distinction between 'colonial' and 'colonialist' literature, the former including 'literature written in Britain as well as in the rest of the Empire during the colonial period', the latter being 'specifically concerned with colonial expansion' (2005: 3). Whilst all the literature analysed here is *colonialist*, in this sense, it is sometimes authored by figures who, returned from the colonies, write *from* Britain, and it is for this reason that I use the more encompassing term, 'colonial literature', throughout.

issues, from the hypocritical arguments of benevolent imperialisms, to the violent ramifications of uneven capital accumulation and infrastructural development, to the presence of anti-imperial and nationalist resistance campaigns. It is for this reason, and despite the fact that they are similarly built around the representation of infrastructure, that I move away from much-studied 'colonial' novels such as *Kim* and *Heart of Darkness* (1899) – though because of Kipling's undeniable importance, his writing shadows much of my discussion, and on occasion makes an explicit appearance.

Primarily, I turn my critical gaze to a much broader cross-section of what mostly remains *under*-analysed colonial literature. The work of writers such as Flora Annie Steel, William Plomer, John Buchan, Edward Thompson and Edmund Candler, studied here at length, has yet to receive sustained critical engagement from postcolonial and materialist critics. As discussed earlier, it is important to emphasise that these author-specific readings are undertaken against a back-drop of a much wider, 'distantly read' archive of colonial literary writings, many of which remain mostly forgotten, yet to be critically interrogated. There are exceptions; for example, I apply *infrastruc-tural reading* to Rider Haggard's much-discussed *King Solomon's Mines*, the archetype of the imperial romance genre. The formal characteristics of the imperial romance recur throughout much under-read colonial literature and so using Haggard's text as a reference point bolsters my arguments at various stages. Furthermore, despite my pronounced departure from convention-ally modernist writers, I have also included two (proto-)modernist-colonial authors: Olive Schreiner and E. M. Forster, in the second and fourth chap-ters respectively. As with Haggard, I use these writers as contemporaneous intertexts that, when juxtaposed with their more explicitly pro-imperial counterparts, serve to enhance the *infrastructural readings* that I undertake and to illuminate the resistance that remains latent within colonial literature.

It remains to be said that the colonial literature analysed throughout this book is almost always set in, or written from (or both), the socioeco-nomic and cultural context of the colonial environment.[7] This literature

---

7   There is a notable exception to this: as Chapter 3's discussion of John Buchan shows, the tropes of the South African frontier continue to pervade the political uncon-scious of his *The Thirty-Nine Steps* (1915), set in Britain, a geographical fusion that

might broadly be described as a form of 'popular culture' – alongside other forms such as 'the music hall' and 'the melodrama theatre' (Bennett, 1982: 18) – and undoubtedly had a wide readership in Britain at the time. But it also circulated through the colonial spaces it depicts, 'from company offices to the guest-rooms of government houses to the libraries of hill-stations' (Boehmer, 2005: 52), feeding into, shaping and reproducing the imperial imagination of colonial space. It was also woven into more interdisciplinary colonial cartographic productions, as the literary text's 'verisimilitude was checked against other fabrications – the books, reports, surveys, army officers, missionaries, journalists, explorers and travellers' (Parry, 2004: 18); as Boehmer observes, there was an 'overproduction under colonial administration of reams of documentation, ethnographic and scientific studies, journals, accounts, censuses, dispatches, laws, etc. To colonise something was to pile writing, a grammar, a structure, upon it' (2005: 92). This body of literature forms a disciplinary 'territory' that Parry identifies as 'The Literature of Empire or The Colonial Fiction' (2004: 17). Though I irreverently de-capitalise both the adjective and noun of this label throughout the book, Parry's definitional criteria – that it is affiliated 'to the hegemonic explanatory order and written within the same ideological code as the discourse of colonialism' (17) – usefully groups the texts analysed here together.

As already mentioned, the book's four chapters are organised around four ideological paradigms that occur with especial potency in the texts analysed therein, offering a set of categorisations that lends focus to their respective *infrastructural readings*. Chapter 1, 'Mapping Humanitarianism', focuses on the work of Flora Annie Steel. It begins with her most widely read 'Mutiny' novel, *On the Face of the Waters* (1896), which takes as its subject matter an event of concerted anti-imperial resistance – the Great Rebellion of 1857 – in India. Historically, this event sparked a significant increase in infrastructural development across the subcontinent and, as Steel's novel shows, this act of violent, anti-imperial resistance came to dominate imperial consciousness throughout the half-century covered by this book. The chapter then turns to a selection of Steel's short stories, written throughout

emphasises the 'prominent, if under-recognised, role' that Southern Africa has played 'in British self-imagining, or "worlding"' (Chrisman, 2003: 10).

the 1880s and 1890s, to explore how notions of humanitarian development and famine relief, ideologies that justified infrastructural development, are actually subverted by Steel's anxieties about the socioeconomic conditions that those infrastructures actually facilitated. Drawing on Macherey and others, this chapter focuses on the 'silences' in colonial literature to show the ideological limits of Steel's texts and to suggest that the resulting spaces look forward to different kinds of anticolonial resistance.

Chapter 2, 'Mapping Segregation', turns to Southern Africa to explore how different narrative forms and genres are deployed to map a landscape that throws up the polarities of core and periphery in particularly stark infrastructural manifestations and racial segregations. Here, I track the ways in which these narrative forms might themselves be resistant when their intertextual relations with one another are highlighted. Beginning with a study of the genre of the imperial romance through a reading of H. Rider Haggard's *King Solomon's Mines* (1885), the chapter first deconstructs that text by reading it topographically, excavating what James C. Scott would call its 'hidden transcript' and arguing that it is deeply preoccupied with the vast infrastructural projects taking place in South Africa during the period of its publication. It will then turn to the work of Olive Schreiner to show how her writings interrogate ideologies of segregation that had been generated by the specific context of the emerging mining industries. The chapter's reading of *The Story of an African Farm* (1883) alongside her other, critically neglected literary writings, demonstrates how Schreiner's mapping of a peripheral landscape enables the production of a meta-narrative that deconstructs the linear confidence of imperial romances such as Haggard's, as well as the arch-imperial infrastructure project of Cecil Rhodes' 'Cape-to-Cairo' railway route. Schreiner's resistant strategies are supplemented and emphasised by a turn to William Plomer's depiction of South Africa's specifically urban spaces in 'Ula Masondo' (1927). His short story directly resists the imperial imagining of South Africa's literary geographies through its explicit re-writing of the romance genre, whilst initiating through its resistant writing a range of what Harvey would call 'revolutionary trajectories' (2012: xvii).

Developing this focus on South Africa and the imperial romance, Chapter 3, 'Mapping Frontiers', embarks upon a study of the early fiction of

John Buchan in order to isolate and dissect a very specific strand of imperial ideology. The chapter calls this 'frontier consciousness' and proceeds by isolating its key features, as well as excavating some of its central contradictions, through a reading of Buchan's first novel, *Prester John* (1910). A survey of the geographical and topographical space within and across which the novel's action takes place reveals that it is inflected with – indeed, has inscribed into its multi-dimensional infrastructure – the hallmarks of settler colonial ideology. Written slightly after the boom in imperial romance writing of the late nineteenth century of which *King Solomon's Mines* is representative, Buchan's efforts to reproduce the frontier narrative can be read as a 'cultural fix' that tries – and fails – to smooth over a contradictory crisis in imperialism's uneven development. The chapter then moves away from South Africa to study Buchan's first 'Hannay' novel, *The Thirty-Nine Steps* (1915), arguing that the frontier consciousness epitomised in *Prester John* is present also in Britain where the contradictions of capitalist accumulation were similarly being felt. By mapping the production of peripheral zones *within* the metropolitan country, which are always linked in some way – most often through their topographical features and frontier-like attributes – to the South African spaces of *Prester John*, this chapter reveals how uneven infrastructural development in cities such as London warp Buchan's literary form.

The book's fourth and final chapter, 'Mapping Nationalism', returns to the Indian subcontinent, bringing the insights of the previous three chapters together to explore the way in which colonial literature interacts with emerging nationalist movements through the work of E. M. Forster, Edmund Candler and Edward Thompson. By using Forster's novel, *A Passage to India* (1924), as a subversive intertext, the chapter follows on from its study of Buchan to highlight the way in which the geographical spaces of core and periphery produced by Candler and Thompson are inflected with the hierarchies of colonial ideology. Whereas the colonial literature studied in the previous three chapters has yet to come to terms with the disintegration of Britain's Empire, Candler and Thompson explicitly acknowledge the imminence of Indian independence. The shift of this political anxiety from subtext to surface shows how these later writings are concerned both to delegitimise nationalist movements, whilst simultaneously imagining the infrastructural coordinates of the world-system – primarily configured through a geographic split between rural and urban zones – that would linger after the formal dissolution of British rule. Despite these ideological efforts, the chapter argues, expressions of anti-imperial resistance can still be located in the contradictions and literary motifs that emerge in these late colonial writings.

Throughout these different studies the axis of infrastructure and resistance, which come together beneath the methodology of *infrastructural reading*, are deployed to activate a materialist critique of colonial literature. By highlighting the literature's complicity with the world-system and the physical infrastructures that facilitated its accumulative processes, a pattern of resistance emerges across the different chapter studies that build cumulatively to produce an alternative map of this literary field. Though the focus of the book is the way in which colonial literature helped to build the infrastructure of the contemporary world-system, as Kipling observed, both 'actually, and, what is more important, in imagination' (2010: 241), it shows how this system has always been riddled with locales, acts and expressions of anti-imperial resistance. The resulting survey thus charts not 'the high-glass print of history writ-large', but rather 'the space of its production, the darkroom negative'; following Stoler, it maps a set of 'historical negatives whose reverse-light traces disturbances in the colonial order of things, whose shadows trace the lineaments of potential dissent and current distress' (2009: 108–109). In conclusion, I will suggest that if the world-system remains entrenched in increasingly uneven and unequal ways in the twenty-first century, despite the dissolution of the British Empire's formal hegemony, *infrastructural reading* still has much work left to do.

Mapping Humanitarianism: Flora Annie Steel and the Contradictions of Colonial Capitalism

Introduction: From Contradiction to Resistance

> I accepted everything as a strange part of the Great Mystery of humanity and the world, though no child could have been more ignorant of natural happenings than I was. [...] my distaste to realities was overborne by a desire to understand. I think that even in those early years my mind was working along definite lines, which in later years were to crystallise into intense belief.
>
> — STEEL (1930: 29)

Written more than sixty years after the occasion, these lines from Flora Annie Steel's autobiographical account of her first arrival in India in 1868 suggest a sensitivity to the realities of her new surroundings, albeit underpinned by an overriding ideological commitment to British imperialism in the subcontinent. Several critics have commented on the apparent duality of Steel's political consciousness in relation to the subcontinent and its peoples. Throughout her life, Steel was proud of her 'desire to understand' colonised Indians and their problems. However, she could never fully relinquish the 'definite lines' of Anglo-India's racial hierarchies and condescending paternalisms. Steel learned this compromised humanitarian ideology from the Government of India (G. O. I.), who used it to justify their infrastructural developments and public works policies in the latter half of the nineteenth century.[1] Though Steel attempted

---

1   David Archard defines the concept of paternalism as 'an interference with another's freedom for the purpose of promoting that other's good; and for some the interference

to meet and befriend many Indians, 'she was unable to enter anything but a paternalistic relationship' with them (Parry, 1972: 128). Nevertheless, and as Parry acknowledges, despite the 'prejudice and social conformity' that 'shackled her imagination', the tensions embedded in Steel's thought produces, within her literary fiction at least, 'provocative contradictions which place her apart' from many of her contemporary Anglo-Indian authors (129). For Jenny Sharpe, 'Steel, perhaps more than anyone else, embodies the memsahib in all of her contradictions' (1989: 93). Similarly, Nancy Paxton monitors the levels of 'complicity' and 'resistance' in Steel's writing, mapping this tension onto Steel's fictional and non-fictional writings, where the former shows 'more than usual insight into and sympathy with the lives of her Indian characters', the latter 'a self-importance inflated by the authority she claimed as a memsahib' (1992: 163). This chapter demonstrates that Steel's ideological 'muddle', to borrow Parry's term (1972: 129), produces what Alan Johnson, in his discussion of Anglo-Indian writing, has described as 'a discursive "fuzzy" space' (2011: 70).

Though retaining Johnson's spatial conceptualisation, I trace Steel's ideological ambivalence along more clearly delineated textual fractures and fragmentations, reading these as manifestations of the contradictions of colonial capitalism in India in the final decades of the nineteenth century. Careful historicisation of a number of Steel's literary works reveals the discrepancies between the humanitarian ideologies underpinning the Raj's imperial project and the material geographies to which those ideologies gave shape. In Steel's writing, the friction created by these inconsistencies is foregrounded when attention is paid to her depiction of imperial infrastructures. Tracing the symbolic, metaphorical and literal emergences of infrastructure in Steel's fiction allows us to map moments of resistance that reside within, and emerge through, its textual crevices. These moments are

---

must be coercive' (1990: 36). As Michael Barnett points out, '[h]umanitarianism and paternalism overlap in various ways', and 'nineteenth-century missionaries and liberal humanitarians were paternalistic, quite often unapologetically so, on the assumption that these childlike populations needed adults to civilise them' (2013: 33, 41). Similarly, Daniel Bivona identifies 'Mid-Victorian "humanitarianism"' as 'implicitly (and sometimes explicitly) expansionist', an '"imperialism" [that] would become much more evident after 1850' (1998: 14–15).

excavated from a selection of Steel's texts by combining readings of the ideological limitations and borders that are written sub-textually into her narratives with her more outright criticisms of a profit-oriented imperial enterprise.

Steel's early biographer, Daya Patwardhan, rightly observes that if writers such as Kipling use the 'weapons' of 'satire and even cynicism [...] to lash Anglo-Indian society', Steel's critique of empire is more outspoken, manifesting in 'direct comments, especially in her stories of rural life' (1963: 70). Though Patwardhan feels this 'spoil[s] their artistry', that there 'are no stories written for mere amusement of the reader' highlights the polemic underpinnings of Steel's fiction (71). This chapter concludes with a discussion of these more 'direct' critiques that, as Patwardhan rightly claims, are to be found in Steel's short stories rather than her novels. In these stories, Steel's narratives lay the '*ideolegeme*' of what Pablo Mukherjee calls 'palliative imperialism' – 'the idea of imperialism as an act of care' that obscures and legitimises 'those structural inequities that produced the disaster events in the first place' – open to dissection (2013: 18). As Shampa Roy argues, Steel brought into focus the 'contradictions and inadequacies in the Imperial reform projects and the assumptions of benevolent impact that underwrote them' (2010: 72). Steel wrote at a time when the notion of humanitarianism was becoming increasingly 'associated with compassion across boundaries': the creation of the International Committee of the Red Cross (ICRC), 'the world's first official international humanitarian organisation', in 1863, shortly before Steel arrived in India, marks a 'tipping point' for the increasing virility of this ideology (Barnett, 2013: 19).

Steel's humanitarianism is dogged throughout by her problematic paternalism – 'an unsavoury legacy of the nineteenth century', argues Michael Barnett, 'that best captures the nature of power in the ethics of care' (2013: 12, 223). This chapter understands humanitarianism as complicit with 'capitalism's unquenchable drive to expand', legitimising the 'need to govern and integrate' those peripheral societies that inhabit the world-system's 'borderlands' (24; see also Duffield, 2001: 309). However, the ideological nuances played out in Steel's fiction reveal its contradictions and hypocrisies, especially as and when they are oriented around the development of imperial infrastructure. Whilst these 'contradictions' have been highlighted the critics cited here, by drawing a thread through a selection of textual moments this chapter recovers a consistent, if not coherent, counter-narrative of anti-imperial resistance. This counter-narrative registers the sorts of ongoing peasant uprisings documented by the *Subaltern Studies* group whilst also, on occasion, looking forward to early formations of more cohesive Indian nationalisms. Steel's *oeuvre*, when read *infrastructurally*, demonstrates that 'there is nothing in the record of the Raj, considered on empirical grounds alone, to justify any pretension to a rule by consent' (Guha, 1998: xvii).

This chapter begins, however, with an analysis of Steel's best known novel, *On the Face of the Waters* (1896), which 'cemented her reputation as a popular and critically-acclaimed author' (Goodwin, 2013: 441). Depicting the Great Rebellion in India, the novel fictionalised an event since described by historian Richard Gott as 'the climactic moment of the first century of empire, an anti-British explosion that threatened the entire enterprise' (2012: 448). The huge socioeconomic, infrastructural, political and cultural impact of the Great Rebellion on and across the networks of Britain's world-empire, especially during the half-century this book takes as its focus, make this an apt event with which to begin its close textual studies. Steel's literary account of this landmark moment of direct anti-imperial resistance and her self-conscious engagement with its 'social and historical raw material' gestures immediately towards the ideological politics of her narratives (Jameson, 2002: 135). Nevertheless, in his reading of Steel's novel, David Thomas repeats a warning already acknowledged in this book's introduction: that, as critics, 'we cannot account for the psychological and social dynamics by which the problem of empire could come to appear to the Victorians and their heirs as a problem of morality or justice at all' (1995: 157). As I have already emphasised, it is at no point my intention to give authorial credit where it is not due, nor to reproduce the cultural and political hierarchies that are embedded within Steel's texts. However, I do believe that complete adherence to this caution risks relinquishing a body of colonial literature to the unread archive and thereby ignoring its stock of insight into and nuancing of imperial ideologies. Indeed, notions of 'humanitarianism' continue not only to justify and shape different kinds of foreign interventionism in the twenty-first century, but to mobilise a complex set of 'spatial organisations and physical instruments' that have become 'the crucial means by which the economy of violence is calculated and managed' on a global scale (Weizman, 2011: 4).

Proceeding cautiously then, I seek to expose the 'social dynamics' – or infrastructure – of Steel's humanitarian justification of empire through a sustained reading of her 'Mutiny novel' and a selection of her short stories. Whilst Thomas argues that 'the empire in India would be near its actual end before mainstream British authors – for instance George Orwell in *Burmese Days* (1934) – would directly represent the status quo in India as illegitimate', he does concede that 'public discourse already in the late Victorian period prepared the way for such views' (168). This anticipation of later, more sustained and direct critiques of British imperialism, can be retrospectively understood as a central preoccupation of Steel's *literary* narratives. Indeed, a focus on colonial *literature*, as opposed to the 'reams of documentation' of the 'colonial administration', from governmental reports to imperial speeches (Boehmer, 2005: 92), enables a shift of the historical time frame outlined by Thomas to an earlier moment. As we will see, many of the occurrences of spatial resistance excavated in this and following chapters rely on a close analysis of textual *form*, where it is warped or broken, fractured and fragmented by the unevenly developed colonial landscape that it depicts. Focusing on these literary qualities, flashes of anti-imperial resistance and contradictory crises in imperial ideology can be seen to emerge not only in the final years of the British world-empire, as Thomas argues, but also at the height of its global hegemony and at the historical moment in which some of its most outspoken – and still lingering – ideologies were forged. Despite her efforts to smooth over the conflict between her 'progressive attitudes and traditional values' (Goodwin, 2011: 519), this chapter argues that Steel, in her literary fiction, unwittingly preempts the surge in post-1900 non-fictional critiques of imperialism by commentators such as Hobson, Luxemburg and Lenin. Furthermore, I will show that this occurs most distinctly through her representation and reproduction of imperial infrastructures as symbolic and material indicators of the frequently violent motions of the capitalist world-system.

The 'Gaps' of Colonial Capitalism in *On the Face of the Waters* (1896)

In her opening 'Author's Note' to *On the Face of the Waters*, Steel claims that her fictional account of 'the Indian Mutiny [...] is scrupulously exact, even to the date, the hour, the scene, the very weather', claiming that she has 'not allowed fiction to interfere with fact in the slightest degree' (2005: 9). In her autobiography, *The Garden of Fidelity* (posthumously published in 1930), Steel recounts her efforts to ground her 'Mutiny novel' in historical 'fact' by drawing on the imperial archive:

> I had asked the Panjab [*sic*] Government for leave, in view of the book I was writing about the Mutiny, to inspect certain confidential boxes of papers which I knew existed in the Delhi offices. The answer was long in coming, and when it did come I laughed, though it contained full licence to see everything and anything. For it was so exceedingly crafty. It began by expressing full reliance on my discretion, my judgement, my loyalty, my everything in short. So, having thus tied my hands, it proceeded to allow me everything! (1930: 213)

Steel simultaneously distances herself from the imperial regime whilst reaffirming her 'loyalty' to it – though finding the G. O. I.'s 'crafty' censorship laughable, she concedes and submits to its demands. The novel's prefatory claims to factual documentation are, she reveals in this later account, not only predicated on an imperial archive that is itself selective and partial, but is further refracted through a pro-imperial ideology that is a condition of her access to it. As Paxton argues, 'constrained by her role as the wife of a British civil servant under the Raj', Steel was forced 'into a position of complicity', the Government demanding that she 'define' herself as either 'loyal or disloyal to British civilisation' (1992: 161).[2] However, Steel's

---

2   If Steel falls into ideological step with the imperial government then it is, Gráinne Goodwin argues, 'little wonder': she 'fell into the category of women whose positions as helpmeets, facilitating their husbands imperial careers, rendered them incorporated as wives and working partners in empire' (2011: 511). Her co-authored non-fictional work, *The Complete Indian Housekeeper and Cook*, testifies to her alignment of 'wifely and domestic management with the wider project of colonial governance' (511; Steel, 2010). She was, in effect, a colonial governor and administrator herself.

conscious self-censorship is further embedded within the dominant narrative of the 'Indian Mutiny of 1857' which, as a memorialised event, had accumulated a virile currency by the 1890s in India, Britain and across the Empire. She not only neglects the fact that her historical documents were all written by British soldiers, government officials, and civil servants, and thus that resistant accounts are occluded from the outset. She further claims that within the 'confidential boxes of papers' she 'found [a] corroboration of my fiction by facts' that meant she 'had not to alter one single thing in my projected story of the Mutiny' (1930: 214). Informed by a hegemonic memory of the 'Mutiny', Steel's narrative framework is already in place. Historical documents are then assimilated into this framework, bolstering rather than challenging the version of events accepted and propagated by imperial ideology.

In 1925, Edward Thompson, whose literary writings are discussed in Chapter 4 of this book, wrote a non-fictional polemic entitled *The Other Side of the Medal*. There, he was one of the first Britons to identify and condemn 'the uncritical and incurious character of [the British] people's minds' in their general acceptance of 'the version of the Mutiny that was imposed upon us when it finished' (1930a: 48). He continues: 'The raking up of the mud of atrocities committed by Indians has never ceased, as any English account of the Mutiny will show, while the Indian case is not known to our people' (84). The reframing of a sustained moment of anti-imperial resistance as evidence of Indian savagery and the propagation of British victimhood that took place in the years following 1857 has been discussed by Patrick Brantlinger: 'the racist pattern of blaming the victim' was contemporaneously expressed 'in terms of an absolute polarization of good and evil, innocence and guilt, justice and injustice' (1988: 199–200; see also Sharpe, 1989: 61–80). Taking George Otto Trevelyan's *Cawnpore* (1865) as emblematic of this 'Mutiny' literature, Brantlinger notes that novel's graphic accounts of 'the massacres at Cawnpore' that subsequently became 'the primary focus of all popular accounts' (1988: 202; see also Tickell, 2012: 95–134). Writing in the mid-1920s, Thompson understood that this focus on the violence committed by Indian Sepoys against Britons at Cawnpore 'makes it possible for readers, who are ordinarily critical and wide-awake enough, to miss the way in which gaps are slurred over and inconvenient questions begged or burked', concluding that 'there is nothing in our history books more emphatically calling for revision than their accounts of the Mutiny' (1930a: 97).

Brantlinger acknowledges that by 'the end of the century a deeper critical perspective does almost emerge', citing Steel's *On the Face of the Waters* as an example. Her shift of perspective from the massacres at Cawnpore to the ongoing struggles that took place across the subcontinent, particularly in Delhi, suggests an effort to construct a more historically accurate account of the British suppression of Indian resistance than her predecessors. However, Brantlinger further notes that Steel's 'apparently balanced view leaves untouched the pervasive impression of the Mutineer's barbarism, cruelty and irrationality' (1988: 220–221). Indeed, Steel's self-professed effort to present a 'historically factual' account actually functions more covertly to disavow its own historical oversights and selective inclusion of eyewitness accounts. The ideological virility of the term 'Indian Mutiny' – its evocation of injustice, its reduction of anti-imperial resistance to a mutineering military class, its rejection of the participation of peasant activity and refusal to acknowledge any coherent national or political Indian consciousness – would not be fully corrected until Utpal Dutt's re-staging of the event in his *Mahavidroh*, or *The Great Rebellion* (1989). This literary renaming, as Nandi Bhatia has described, 'invokes a conscious political effort and resistance on the part of those who participated' in what was 'a powerful moment of anticolonial resistance in Indian history' (Bhatia, 1999: 171–172). Throughout this analysis of *On the Face of the Waters*, I will therefore use the term 'Rebellion' to refer to the actual historical event, whilst the term 'Mutiny' will be reserved to signify the ideological framework that shaped colonial accounts of it.

In *Mahavidrah*, Dutt foregrounds 'the exploitative context that provided the grounds for rebellion' (Bhatia, 1999: 171–172), issues that, as Thompson describes, formed 'gaps' within early representations of the Mutiny (1930: 97). These gaps operate as what Pierre Macherey has described as textual 'silences', absences in which 'the presence of ideology can be most positively felt' (1986: 155; see also Eagleton, 2002: 32), and which, as Patrick Williams reminds us, are 'built into the material processes and social and historical circumstances' that 'relate to the text' (2016: 87). This reading of Steel's novel is designed not to 'fill in' these gaps; this work has already been done effectively by literary authors such as Dutt and the historians of the *Subaltern Studies* group, amongst others. Rather, following Terry Eagleton's reading of Macherey, this chapter seeks to draw out the text's 'conflict of meanings', thereby demonstrating how 'this conflict is produced by the work's relation to ideology' (2002: 33). Such a reading re-inscribes resistance back into Steel's text by uncovering the peripheral zones both located within its purview, but which remain beyond its direct narrativising processes. These peripheral spaces are located alongside, and emerge in response to, both the infrastructures *in* and *of* the text, as the novel narrates the violent processes whereby the Indian subcontinent was enmeshed into the infrastructure of Britain's world-empire throughout the nineteenth century.

There are brief criticisms of Britain's imperial policy in India in Steel's novel that, despite its ideological limitations, justify the Rebellion as an historical event. Articulated in *On the Face of the Waters*' opening pages, they sit in sharp contrast to the violent retribution and ideological resolution with which it closes, as the novel attempts to overshadow the issues it has unwittingly raised. Here, Steel gives voice, through an Anglo-Indian auctioneer, to the exploitation of the colonised by the coloniser: "'it's slave-drivin' to screw bids for beasts as eats hunderweights out of poor devils as 'aven't enough for themselves, or a notion of business as business'" (2005: 13). This articulation is swiftly contextualised by an omniscient authorial voice which directly addresses the reader, a frequent trait of Steel's fiction (Patwardhan, 1963: 70). The auctioneer's comment, Steel writes,

> gave expression to a very common feeling which in the early [eighteen] fifties, when the commercial instincts of the West met the uncommercial ones of the East in open market for the first time, sharpened the antagonism of the [Indian] race immensely. (2005: 13–14)

Steel directly acknowledges the provocation of the intensification of exploitative capitalist relations, under the aegis of the British world-empire, into what she repeatedly *portrays* and *produces* as a pre-capitalist socioeconomic space. This intervention immediately undermines ideological justifications for the British humanitarian presence in the subcontinent. The conflict raised by the novel is aggravated if we consider that by the time of the novel's publication in 1896 the British had expanded and consolidated their economic and governmental security via investments in a vast range of transportation, communication, legal and administrative infrastructures, entangling large sections of the subcontinent into an increasingly uneven world-system.

Britain's construction of the railway network in India increased political unity and government security by allowing the swifter mobilisation of troops, as well as sparing them the long, tiring marches across vast stretches of the subcontinent's terrain. In the twenty-two years that Steel lived in India, from 1867 until 1889, there were huge infrastructural developments across these spaces, so that by 1890 'India had one of the world's top rail networks' (Headrick, 1988: 56). In 1850, there were no railways operating in India; by 1875 'an extensive network of trunk lines' had been established; and by 1900, 'trunk and branch lines extended over 25,000 miles of track' (Kerr, 1995: 1). The telegraph was equally important in consolidating imperial security. In 1851 there were just a few miles of telegraph line; by 1856 there were over 4,250 miles; by 1865, 17,500 miles; and an astonishing 52,900 miles by the end of the nineteenth century (Arnold, 2000: 113). This infrastructural development was, however, fuelled by the unequal trade relations of the world-system. India became 'Britain's best customer for iron and steel productions', a 'decision made in Britain at India's expense, for it diverted demand away from a potential Indian industry' (Headrick, 1988: 84, 282). The result, Headrick notes, was that India 'emerged from colonial rule with a "developed" rail network and an "underdeveloped" economy' (50).

The British Government also laid telegraph lines between Britain and India to allow for instantaneous communication with the Raj. A 4.5 per cent return was guaranteed to encourage speculators to invest in the project, almost matching the 5 per cent guarantee on Indian railway investment first offered in the early 1850s, and exemplifying what Harvey would describe as partially '[s]tate-funded infrastructural projects' designed 'to re-kindle economic growth' and provide capital with a 'spatio-temporal fix' (2014: 151). When the intercontinental telegraph was successfully completed in 1866, the cable was laid using Isambard Kingdom Brunel's steamship, the SS Great Eastern, 'symbolically linking the pioneer of both railway and steamship with this new element of communications innovation' (Latham, 1978: 32). This cross-national telegraph network sped up global trade by carrying 'information about prices, quality and delivery dates' and allowing 'goods to be bought and sold long before they arrived in Europe or America [...] without having to be stockpiled in London first' (37). Though satiating British anxieties about the prospect of future political unrest in India by increasing governmental security, these infrastructures equally, if not primarily, served to facilitate and intensify the world-system's accumulative processes.

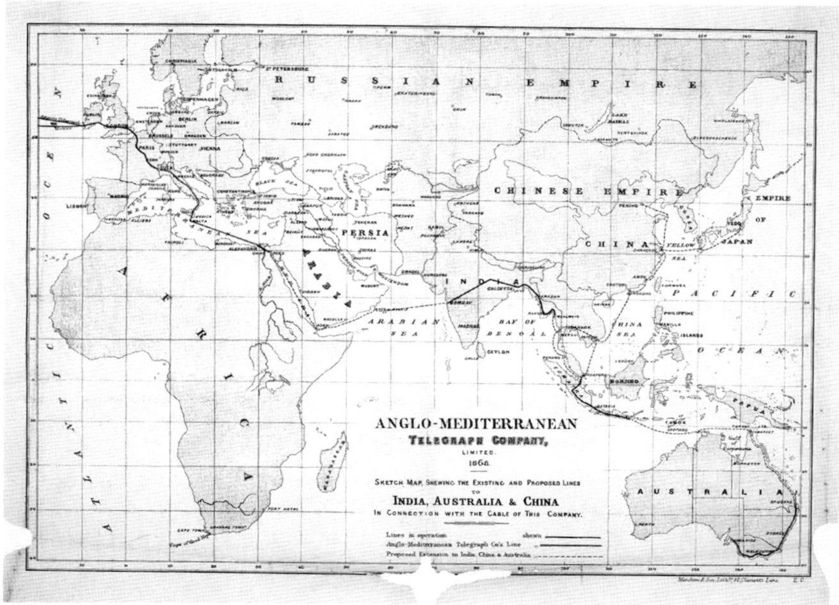

Figure 1.1: Map produced for the Anglo-Mediterranean Telegraph Company showing the existing and proposed telegraph lines connecting Britain to India, Australia and China. Lithographed by Metchim and Son, 32 Clement's Lane, in 1868. MPD 1/207, National Archives at Kew.

Steel's novel raises concerns about the imposition of colonial legal systems that facilitated these infrastructural dynamics. The text perpetuates problematic ideological hierarchies whilst implicitly criticising the G. O. I.'s complicity with an exploitative capitalism: '[O]ne stroke of an English pen', Steel writes, deprives Lucknow, 'the most profligate town in India', of the '*raison-d'être* of its profligacy', as it is 'bidden to live as best it could in cleanly, court-less poverty' (2005: 15). The repetition of 'profligate', alongside the word 'cleanly', allude to Steel's racialised conception of a 'degenerate' Indian society, a set of 'moral, biological and sexual referents' that Stoler identifies as typical of the '"colonial branch" of eugenics' discourse (2002: 62–63). Stoler continues: 'European women were vital to the colonial enterprise and the solidification of racial boundaries' (62), a theme identified in Steel's fiction by both Johnson (1998: 507–513) and Mukherjee (2013: 193–195). But this imperial infiltration of the peripheral zone of Lucknow, which is reflected here in the city's sparse, or underdeveloped physical infrastructure – 'the dome of a mosque or the minaret of a mausoleum told that the town of Lucknow, scattered yet coherent, lay among the groves' (2005: 15) – is also framed in terms of the ramifications of the world-system's cross-national economies.

> So, already, there were thousands of workmen in it, innocent enough panderers in the past to luxurious vice, who were feeling the pinch of hunger from lack of employment; and there were those past employers also, deprived now of pensions and offices, with a bankrupt future before them. (15)

Beginning this paragraph with '[s]o, already', Steel emphasises the effects of global capitalism upon this peripheral space. The text narrates two of the key 'trends of capitalism' identified by Wallerstein: the infiltration of the 'outer boundaries of the world-economy' into the city of Lucknow that produces it as an underdeveloped zone, whilst also transforming a population of '"quasi-federal" semiprolaterians' into fully fledged 'proletarian wage labour' (1991: 278–279). That this results in a 'lack of employment' highlights the fact that their surplus labour has been assimilated into a cross-national system, whilst the legal structures serve the economic interests of the coloniser. This manifests in a pattern of 'uneven development' at the levels not only of social and cultural relations, but also of physical infrastructural developments and the industrialisation and urbanisation they facilitated.

These textual allusions to systems of exploitation surface briefly some forty pages later before being silenced by the circumstances of the Mutiny with which the novel then becomes preoccupied. Steel's omniscient narrator presents Mr Gissing, who is 'not a Government servant' but rather a colonial capitalist, 'a vulgar creature, but an excellent businessman, with a knack of piling up the rupees which made minor native contractors, whose trade he was gradually absorbing, gnash their teeth in sheer envy' (2005: 53). Gissing claims that 'the Western system of risking all to gain all was too much opposed to the Eastern one of risking all to gain little, for the hereditary merchants to adopt it at once'; the complaints of the 'native contractors' against his exploitative trading become nothing more than stories to be told at 'luncheon parties' (53). Though acknowledging and directly critiquing the exploitative tendencies of colonial capitalism, Steel uses her characterisation of Gissing to distinguish these forces from her conception of imperialism as a benevolent, or humanitarian force. This is symptomatic of Steel's thought on imperialism where, as Patwardhan observes, she gener-ally 'blames the money-lender rather than the British Government whose policy of exploiting the poor people is really responsible for the poverty of the peasants' (1963: 143–144). Separated from the paternalistic structure of the imperial government, traders such as Gissing enable a convenient 'fictive resolution' – or 'cultural fix' – that allow Steel to maintain her faith in a humanitarian, or 'palliative' imperialism, whilst also criticising the exploitative effects of an international economy upon colonised peoples.

However, as Patwadhan continues, the Indian's 'enemy was not so much the money-lender as the foreign ruler' (144), a critique that emerges within Steel's text in relation to the imperial government's investment in infrastructure. Gissing uses the 'facility of transport given by roads' con-structed by the G. O. I. to legitimise his colonial presence. For Gissing, these investments in infrastructure justify

> the right of Government to benefit – er – slightly – by these outlays. Commerce isn't a selfish thing, sir, by gad! If you don't consider your market a bit, you won't find one at all. So I stepped in, and made thousands; for the Commissariat, seeing the saving here, of course asked me to contract for other places. It serves the idiot uncommon well right; but it will benefit them in the end. If [the Indians are] to face Western nations they must learn – er – the – the morality of speculation. (2005: 54)

As Mukherjee argues, the novel acknowledges that the '[i]mperial extrac-tion of wealth' is 'criminal (an Englishman is bound to rob a native)' whilst framing it as 'historically inevitable (the Indians misread as robbery what is actually the cutting-edge development in the world economic system)' (2013: 197). Nevertheless, Gissing's uneasy hesitations become conspicuous 'silences', undermining the ideological conviction that imperial infrastruc-tural development is driven primarily by its humanitarian ethos. These silences write the economic exploitation that such development had in fact facilitated, and from which Gissing has 'made thousands', unevenly into the ideological fabric of the text. He alludes to the ongoing accumu-lation of capital 'for other places', a cross-national commerce that is once again 'contracted' by the Raj. The text reveals the ideological complicity of humanitarian notions of imperialism with an exploitative colonial capi-talism, despite Steel's efforts to separate them from one another. Written at the end of the nineteenth century, the subtextual motions of the novel confess the ideological hypocrisies later identified by Mike Davis, who has shown how 'newly constructed railroads, lauded as institutional safeguards against famine, were instead used by merchants to ship grain inventories from outlying drought-stricken districts to central depots' (2010: 26). But at this point the novel swiftly leaves the 'morality of speculation or gambling' behind, turning to its account of the 'Indian Mutiny' in an attempt to repair these conspicuous tears in its ideological fabric.

Consolidating Ideology: Flags, Telegraphs and Governmental Reports

A symbol that recurs sporadically throughout Steel's novel, and around which, like the victorious colonial soldiers who retake Delhi in its closing scenes, her most ideologically consolidated narrative moments collect, is 'the English flag' (2005: 367).[3] This symbol of imperial power echoes Alfred Tennyson's patriotic tribute to the British troops who fought in the Mutiny, 'The Siege of Lucknow' (1880). Documented in obsessive infrastructural and spatial detail by Colonel G. B. Malleson in his book-length account, *The Indian Mutiny of 1857* (1857, but which ran to eight editions, the last of which appeared in 1901), narrative text was accompanied by visual plans such as the image reproduced here, demonstrating the importance of cartography for the Raj's regulation and production of colonial space. As for these retrospective cartographic plans, the opening lines of Tennyson's imperial poem emphasise the enduring nature of Britain's imperial presence: 'Banner of England, not for a season, O banner of Britain, hast thou/ Floated in conquering battle or flapt to the battle-cry!' This refrain is echoed at the

---

3   That Steel, who was herself Scottish, emphasises that this is the *English* rather than *British* flag, might at first appear to be suggestive of an ambivalence towards, or detachment from, a pro-imperial dogma. However, as the symbolic work of Tennyson and Kipling mentioned here indicates, the interchangeable use of 'English' flag and 'British' Empire is in fact a semantic slippage common to the period, and in this sense Steel is actually reproducing rather than challenging the ideology associated with what was undoubtedly an important patriotic symbol for rallying pro-imperial sentiment.

climax of each of the poem's seven sections as 'ever upon the topmost roof our banner of England blew' (1998: 59–63). It was a similarly important symbol for Kipling who infamously asked, in his 1891 poem 'The English Flag', 'what should they know of England who only England know?' (2006: 178–179). Specifically in British India, the flag formed the centrepiece of the Imperial Assemblages and durbars, displays of power that plotted, spatially, a range of social and political hierarchies through their temporary infrastructures of wooden stands and camps (see Cohn, 2009: 636–679).

Steel strategically employs this culturally significant symbol throughout the novel, enabling a systematic regulation and reassertion of imperial ideology that counteracts the repeated moments of resistance it documents. At first, the 'English flag drooped *lazily* in *calm* floods of yellow light' (2005: 15); five months after the outbreak of violence at Lucknow, 'the English flag [...] floated there now, *serenely, securely*, with an air of finality in its folds' (79); 'in front of the big mess-tent the English flag drooped from its mast in the *still* night air' (119); 'any risk was needless when, to a *certainty*, the English flag would be flying over the city' (255; emphases all mine). The systematic recourse to this symbol enacts, to use Macherey's terminology, 'an imagined order, projected onto disorder, the fictive resolution of ideological conflicts' – a 'resolution' that remains, however, 'so precarious that it is obvious in the very letter of the text where incoherence and incompleteness burst forth' (1986: 155). The 'fictive resolution', or cultural fix, performed by Steel's use of the flag can, when juxtaposed with the novel's more peripheral moments, be unpicked, enabling the excavation of the ideological conflict that the text seeks to conceal. This is best identified in the most ideologically saturated moment of the flag's final mention, when the British soldiers have successfully recaptured Delhi and the Rebellion has been suppressed:

> It was the English flag.
> The men, forgetting everything else, cheered themselves hoarse – cheered again when an orderly rode past waving a slip of paper sent back to the General with the laconic report:
> *'Blown open the gates! Got the palace!'* (2005: 367)

Evoking patriotic hype, Steel's narrative asks the reader to forget 'everything else', including the injustices of colonial rule to which the text itself drew attention in its opening pages. But the detail of colonial capitalism's economic exploitation remains present, situated within 'the very letter of

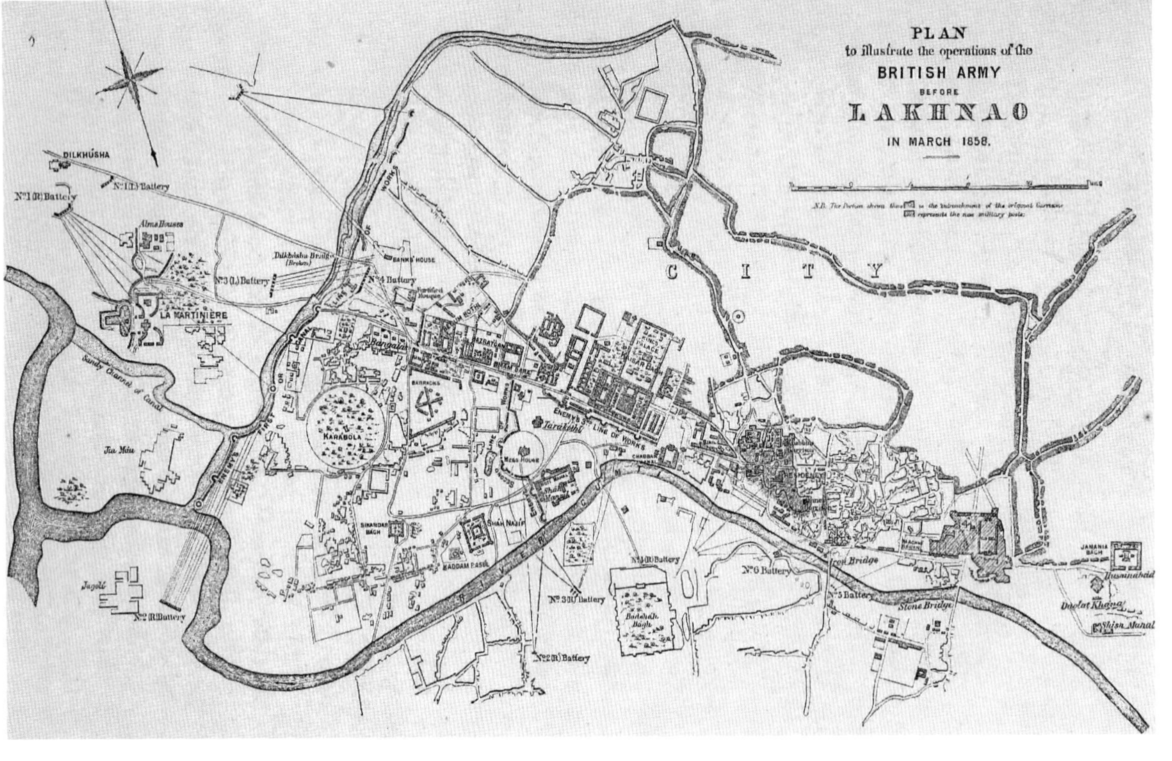

Figure 1.2:   Plan included in the 1901 edition of Colonel G. B. Malleson's *The Indian Mutiny of 1857, with Portraits and Plans*, illustrating the spatial movements of the British Army during the siege of Lucknow in March 1858.

the text' that now attempts to erase it: if anything, the 'fictive' nature of the novel's 'resolution' is intensified by the 'absence' of these earlier concerns in this climactic scene and that, as Macherey would argue, 'enables us to identify the active presence of a conflict at its borders' (1986: 155).

This climactic scene points not only to the British victory over the Indian rebels, but to another crucial thematic and infrastructural vein that runs through *On the Face of the Waters*: the *communication* of that victory. As Thomas has demonstrated, 'the opening of Steel's novel situates the crisis of the Sepoy rebellion within a framework of what we might call communicative inaction' (2009: 177). This 'theme of imperial communication and its impediments', Thomas argues, is developed throughout the novel 'at several textual levels, including word choices, formal patterns in plotting and structure, and narrative incidents' (177). As already noted, telegraphic development had exploded like a web across the subcontinent from the early 1850s (Arnold, 2000: 113). Indicatively, in his landmark historical study of the 'Mutiny' Saul David cites the words of a Financial Commissioner to the Punjab in the subtitle of his prologue: 'The Electric Telegraph has saved us' (2002: xix–xxiii). By tracing the network of textual references to the telegraph that occur spatially within Steel's novel, it becomes evident that the context in which this specific infrastructure appears serves the broader ideological motions of Steel's plot.

The novel's early references to the telegraph stress its importance in communicating 'news' to the broader 'Empire'. It is designed not so much to enable communication within India, but rather to alert the broader imperial world, and the imperial centre in London, to the outbreak of Rebellion. Don Randall points out that even the telegraph's 'electric speed' was, at this historical juncture, 'retarded by intercontinental relays', taking 'at least six weeks' to reach Britain (2003: 4). It was this 'lag' in communication time, he continues, that allowed the 'disparities between discourse and event' to blossom into 'those events known as the "Mutiny"' (6, 15). Interestingly, Steel's narrative points to this production of 'tales', as capitalism's 'time-space compression' alters 'how we represent the world to ourselves' (Harvey, 1995: 240), in the novel's first reference to the telegraph:

> there were so many tales nowadays. Of news flashed faster by wires than any, even the Gods themselves, could flash it; of carriages, fire-fed, bringing God knows what grain from God knows where! Could a body eat of it and not be polluted? Could

> the children read the school books and not be apostate? Burning questions these,
> not to be answered lightly. (2005: 21)

One infrastructure references another, moving from telegraph to steam train to emphasise the 'God-like' speed they facilitate. But Steel's narrative is also tinged with sarcasm, as it suggests the mis- or overuse of these new communications technologies in a subtle critique of Anglo-Indian society. There is also an implicit register of the historical function played by these new communications and transport infrastructures in the facilitation of what Dadabhai Naoroji, in 1876, had called 'drain theory'. Naoroji argued that the Indian economy was 'being steadily drained by exports', a process of impoverishment that could only be solved 'once the British presence was removed' (Masselos, 2010: 72–73; Naoroji, 1901). This analysis was reaffirmed a few years after the publication of Steel's novel by Romesh Chunder Dutt in his *Open Letters to Lord Curzon on Famines and Land Assessment in India* (1900) and his slightly later *Economic History of India in the Victorian Age* (1904). There, Dutt argued:

> that the manufacturers lost their industries; that the cultivators were ground down
> by a heavy and variable taxation which precluded any saving; that the revenues of the
> country were to a large extent diverted to England; and that recurring and desolating
> famines swept away millions of the population. (1950: xviii–xix)

Steel's narrative acknowledges that this 'grain' comes from a peripheral zone ('God knows where!'), thereby demonstrating the way in which infrastructures such as the railway contributed to the uneven development of the world-system. As M. L. Dantwala explains, infrastructures such as '[r]ailways and even irrigation development were oriented towards facilitating the drain', exporting 'raw materials needed by British manufactures' and importing 'British goods' (1973: 14). Though it took the more direct polemic work of Naoroji and Dutt to more fully outline the devastating ramifications of this process, the manifestation of infrastructure *in* Steel's text registers the infrastructures *of* the text, as her pro-imperial ideology fractures, warping the novel's narrative form.

However, as for the novel's other criticisms of colonialism's exploitative practices, this is overshadowed by the events of the Mutiny to which the next textual reference to the telegraph points: 'the strangest telegram that ever came as sole warning to an Empire that its very foundation was attacked' (2005: 160). Only pages later, as the Mutiny takes hold, 'the telegraph wires had been cut' (172), resulting in 'a new world without posts or telegraphs, laws or order; time itself turned back hundreds of years and all power of progress vested absolutely in [...] the Great Moghul!' (243). This temporal disjunction, a 'new' world simultaneously located 'hundreds of years' in the past, disrupts the progress of Western development, reinforcing an ideology that Dipesh Chakrabarty identifies as the 'homogenising narrative of transition from a medieval period to modernity', repeatedly characterising the Indian as 'a figure of lack' (2008: 32). It is this linear conception of development that WReC, as discussed in this book's introduction, seek to correct through their emphasis on the Jamesonian singularity of modernity (2015: 12–13). Nevertheless, and as Anthony King documents, the ideological formulation that '"modernisation" was necessarily "Westernisation"' became a synonymity that has drastically intensified inequalities and created problematic and ongoing rifts into the post-colonial era (1976: 34–40). More recently, humanitarian notions of 'developing' and 'developed' worlds continue to split the globe into neat geographical categories positioned on a singular, progressive line with the 'modern' West at the forefront of 'civilisation' (McEwan, 2009: 120–121).

Despite the novel's early ideological investment in telegraphic infrastructure, the failure of these communication technologies at the novel's midway point results in a crucial concession:

> to all intents and purposes, the English were annihilated, during that short month of peace between the 11th of May and the 8th of June 1857; for Delhi knew nothing of the vain striving, the ceaseless efforts of the master to find tents and carriages, horses, ammunition, medicine, everything save, thank Heaven once more! courage, and the determination to be master still. (2005: 244)

In this passage, Steel's narrative admits the fragility of the imperial project before beginning once again to restore, like the military reassembly it describes, confidence in the superiority of the English 'master'. This self-conscious restoration of order, embedded in the minutiae of the novel's text, allegorises the governmental authority that, by 1896, the Raj had mostly reinstated through the web of infrastructures with which it had criss-crossed the subcontinent in the intervening decades, even as it reveals the extent to which this resolution is merely a 'fictive' one. Indeed, its syntactical *struggle* to move from the annihilation of the English to the reassertion of imperial dominance is signified by the premature position of the exclamation mark before the end of the sentence, an oddity suggestive of momentary insecurity. Following Jameson, this 'wrenching use' of punctuation suggests anxieties 'buried' within the infrastructure *of* the text (Roberts, 2000: 81). The shifting socioeconomic realities and political tensions of post-Rebellion India warp the narrative at this close textual level, just as these ideological fault lines in turn feed back into, and disrupt, the Raj's political and socioeconomic foundations. As Johnson comments of the novel more broadly, *On the Face of the Waters* 'shows how memory of the Mutiny is double-edged: it provides both the traumatic origin for the consolidation of Imperial power, but also the origin of national identity that will lead to the overthrow of that power' (1998: 512).

Pursuing Steel's textual references to the telegraph, the move from the communication network's trivial misuse to its sabotage and subsequent ineffectiveness begins now, from this central moment onwards, increasingly to enable the reclamation and consolidation of British hegemony. This reflects, in condensed narrative and historical time, the telegraphic developments constructed by the G. O. I. in post-Rebellion India: some 17,500 miles by 1865, a huge 52,900 miles by the end of the century, and an intercontinental telegraph directly linking India to Britain completed in 1866 (Arnold, 2000: 113; Latham, 1978: 32). As the 'unchecked conflagration of mutiny' spreads 'swiftly' through Steel's novel, 'men elsewhere telegraphed the same question': a call for a siege of Delhi, the final military move towards which the narrative leans (2005: 263). The multiplicity and speed of the communication of this demand causes 'the General, finally' to give 'a grudging assent': in a final electric surge before this last extended military engagement, 'the telegrams, the letters [...] the orders' come 'pouring in to take Delhi – to take it at once!' (276). Returning again, then, to the novel's climactic scene, the General's 'laconic report' (367), though not specifically a telegraph, a message that will most likely become one (it is short enough), functions to isolate and condense the imperial victory. It produces a 'fictive resolution' that, echoing the succinct symbolic and ideological power of the 'English Flag', writes an 'imagined order' across the acts of disorderly rebellion documented by the novel, apparently consolidating British authority and imperial domination. The telegraph networks that run through Steel's narrative undercut and control the spreading sites of resistance, enabling the production of a novel that, despite its 'gaps' and 'silences', was not deemed in need of further censorship by the G. O. I. when it appeared in 1896.

Steel's novel finishes with an appendix consisting of copies of a Governmental Report on the Mutiny written by 'A. Dashe, *Coll. and Magte*', who appears briefly as a fictional character earlier in the plot, and which operates as a metafictional addendum to the novel's closing scene. The date, recipient and signature's allusion to Dashe's high governmental position suggests an official document that draws attention to the fictionality of the preceding novel. Though consistent with Steel's self-professed attempt to root her novel in 'historical facts', the inclusion of this appendix counteracts her claim in the opening author's note that she 'has not allowed fiction to interfere with fact in the slightest degree' (2005: 9). This final document highlights the construct*ness* of the novel's main narrative, drawing attention to the 'imagined' nature of its sequential (as well as selective) ordering. However, her use of an 'original' document to draw her account of the 'Mutiny' to an 'official' close decisively consolidates the text's overarching ideological goals: the establishment of what Francis Hutchins calls 'the illusion of permanence', required at a time when, 'at the turn of the [twentieth] century [...] the Empire itself was becoming no longer viable' (1967: 196). Dashe's narrative follows on directly from, and decisively ends, Steel's own, as he claims that after the 'fall of Delhi', the 'mutinous fugitives [...] literally melted away, and the public mind seemed to become aware that the contest was over, and that the struggle to subvert British rule had ignominiously failed' (2005: 385–386).

This recourse to the direct quotation of Governmental Reports grows out of Steel's own experience of British rule in post-Rebellion India, where she lived from 1867 to 1889 as the wife of a Civil Servant, Henry William Steel, and during which she herself wrote a number of Governmental Reports. 'Steel's reputation was built largely on her experiences as one of the the first female officials of the British Government' in India, writes Rebecca Sutcliffe, as she contributed to the massive increase in written documentation that, collected and reprinted in Foreign Office or Colonial Office Blue Books, worked to 'tighten the centre's control over what happened in the periphery by constructing systematic, regularised ways of communicating activity' (1998: 157–159). This surge in the production of bureaucratic documentation was combined, post-1857, with massive infrastructural developments: the telegraph, already noted above; the railway, which, as shall become evident in a discussion of Steel's short stories, is an important symbolic and physical structure; and a vast web of legal, administrative and economic systems, the contradictions of which, though touched upon in *On the Face of the Waters*, come under greater scrutiny in Steel's shorter fiction.

In *The Rise and Expansion of the British Dominion in India* (1907), imperial historian Alfred Lyall encapsulated the way in which the 'Indian Mutiny of 1857' justified the continuation and formalisation of British rule in India, as well as the infrastructural development that sustained it. 'In suppressing the wild fanatic outbreak of 1857', he writes, the 'supremacy' of the Raj 'now stands uncontested' (1907: 323–324):

> The sepoy-mutiny of 1857 was reactionary in its causes and revolutionary in its effects; it shook for a moment the empire's foundations, but it cleared the area for reconstruction and improvement. [...] With the complete pacification of the country came leisure for organisation, for placing the executive authority of the various local governments on a definite footing, and substituting laws properly framed for unmethodical procedure and discretionary ordinances. (368–369)

Fuelled by this ideological conviction, as Ira Klein has since documented, 'Western dominion in late nineteenth-century India was perhaps never more actively [nor more] optimistically involved in India's improvement than in the decade following the Mutiny' (2000: 566). The government 'constructed and commissioned' railways, roads and canals, and distributed 'small loans to agriculturalists' and 'funds for the upkeep of irrigation' (566), as part of a conscious effort 'to implement the Free Trade idea of development through increased agricultural production and international commerce' (566; see also Davis, 2010: 31; and Singh, 1996: 22–23). Karl Marx himself, writing in the late 1850s, remarked upon the way in which the 'Mutiny' narrative was mobilised to consolidate imperial power and intensify economic exploitation, specifically through infrastructural development. 'Political "unity", imposed by the British sword', Marx wrote, would 'now be strengthened and perpetuated by the electric telegraph': the 'day is not far distant when, by a combination of railways and steam vessels', the travel and communication time between England and India would be drastically reduced and 'that once fabulous country [would] be annexed to the Western World' (2006: 47). As Brantlinger writes, if Marx 'emphasised economic exploitation and interpreted the Mutiny as at least foreshadowing a full-scale nationalist revolution', he also 'predicted that the British would crush the rebellion and assume a more repressive dominion afterward' (1988: 202). Though Marx 'never rejected the idea that colonialism was essential for bringing capitalism to Asia', after 1857 he began, argues Pranav Jani, 'to see colonised Indians as agents in their own history, who, as in the classic model of the bourgeois-proletarian relation, needed to struggle *against* the colonisers to win their liberation' (2004: 83). If Marx shared Lyall's view about the 'progressive role of colonialism', he did so only because he saw capitalism itself as a necessary though progressive evil; efforts 'to portray Marx as an enthusiast of colonialism would logically have to portray him as an admirer of capitalism as well' (Ahmad, 2008: 225–226).

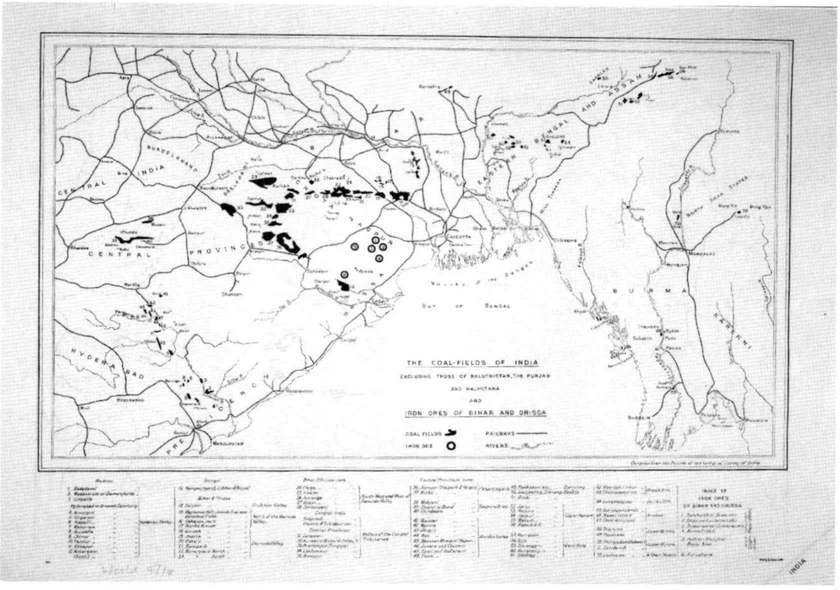

Figure 1.3: A late nineteenth-century map of north-eastern India, showing the strategic development of railways to connect the coal fields and iron ore reserves to the port city of Calcutta and to other parts of the British Empire. Colonial Office Archives, 1047/1054, National Archives at Kew.

Marx was not wrong. Despite Lyall's rhetoric of 'reconstruction and improvement', the prospect of a profitable international economy underlay the sudden intensification of infrastructure construction in the decades following the Rebellion. The Peninsular & Oriental Steam Navigation Company (P&O), it was observed, would make 'enormous savings' if, instead of 'stripping bunker coal from British coalfields', the infrastructure could be developed that would allow it to 'tap into Indian coalfields' (West, 2009: 2). The first railway lines laid in India facilitated these processes, reflecting the Raj's 'need to provide transport for her exports': the very first line of 21 miles opened in India in 1853, linking the cotton fields of the Deccan to the port of Bombay, whilst the second linked Calcutta to the coalfields in the northwest (Latham, 1978: 17). As the map compiled by the Geological Survey of India reproduced here indicates, infrastructural routes were repeatedly constructed to connect resource deposits to coastal ports, their development shaped by the logic of capital. Similarly, as already mentioned, the telegraph was equally conducive to the development of global economic transactions, allowing the easy transmission of prices, orders and market information. Historical circumstances further intensified these processes: the failure of the American cotton crop in 1846 forced British cotton mill owners to look elsewhere for a 'new source of raw material', and the American Civil War ensured that these lobbies intensified throughout the 1860s (Harnetty, 1972: 46–47). A memorandum drawn up in 1862 by the Manchester Chamber of Commerce argued that government subsidisation of transport links within India, such as roads, canals and railways would not only 'ensure new supplies from India', but would be of advantage to the subcontinent as a beneficial system of public works, 'whether or not they were remunerative of separate enterprises' (49) – an argument strikingly reminiscent of those made by Steel's character Gissing, and of which her literary writing is deeply critical. As noted in the introduction, Hobson had argued that though a belief that 'trade follows the flag' underpinned late nineteenth-century imperial ideologies (an observation that resonates with Steel's symbolic use of 'the English flag'), more often the occupation of colonial territories actually followed the 'expanding importance of trade' (1988: 47–48).

Of course, we should not reduce the spatial arrangements of imperial and other infrastructures purely to 'the requirements of accumulation' or 'the demands of capital'; as Doreen Massey argues, '[s]patial structures are established, reinforced, combated and changed' through a range of social, political and economic strategies, including the 'determined resistance' of the workforce (1995: 82, 87). Indeed, Sutcliffe points to the multiple agendas of infrastructural developments in late nineteenth-century India, detailed in the Governmental Reports that accompanied them: 'someone writing a report on the building of a canal through hostile territory could be said to be practising military, technical, diplomatic, or business writing' (1998: 158). However, Steel's own reports, first published as an appendix to the report of the Director of Public Instruction as part of the June 1884 volume of *Proceedings of the Government of the Punjab*, move between a 'rigid systematisation of record-keeping' and what Sutcliffe describes as 'figurative, inflammatory language, creating an emotional tone of outrage' (1998: 163, 167). If her outraged language reduced the effectiveness of Steel's call for accuracy and objectivity' (Sutcliffe, 1998: 167), the transposition of her knowledge and experience into her short fiction, the first of which was also published in 1884, enabled her to put together momentary, and on occasion sustained, literary critiques of an exploitative international economy and violent imperialism. Through this combination of prose form and her more polemic, 'direct comments', there is embedded within her narratives an implicit register of anti-imperialist resistance and, on occasion, an anticipation of more coherent nationalist movements.

In the reading of Steel's stories that follows, I seek to recognise and reemphasise these moments of resistance as they occur in response to imperialism's uneven infrastructural development. However, these moments are complicated by her adamant refusal to relinquish an overarching ideological affiliation to the supremacy of the imperial government. By unearthing the resulting conflict between notions of humanitarian infrastructural work and the socioeconomic realities of an unevenly developing world-system within Steel's literary writings, it becomes possible to lever open this ideological fissure as it manifests at the level of textual form to uncover moments of spatial resistance.

The Silences of Steel's Short Fiction

The title of Steel's story, 'In the Permanent Way' (1897), puns on a dual meaning. It enunciates an infrastructural security or 'permanence', whilst also evoking the 'permanent' presence of Indian resistance to imperialism. The phrase is reiterated throughout the story, with increasingly severe consequences, by the 'overseer' of the construction party building the railway: 'Craddock, a big yellow-headed Saxon' (Steel, 1971: 146). Ian Kerr has documented in detail the processes involved in 'the formation of the [railway] line', beginning with the mapping and planning of the route, the 'ballasting and laying of the permanent way' and the subsequent development of signalling devices, telegraphs, water towers and roads that were constructed around the arterial route (1995: 130). These networks were accompanied by an 'emerging web of capitalist relations', as construction processes were intwined with 'the more intensive intrusion of the practices of capitalism, with tight contracts, specifications, expectations of performance and notions of legally enforceable responsibilities' (67–68). The physical demarcations of infrastructural routes, invested with both an economic and symbolic 'core*ness*', sutured these spaces into an increasingly uneven world-system. Infrastructural development, celebrated as a symbolic hallmark of 'modernity' and 'civilisation' by pro-imperial commentators, simultaneously aggravated (and aggravates) the processes of peripheralisation through the 'development of underdevelopment' (WReC, 2015: 13); as Wallerstain reminds us, the terms 'coreness-peripherality' are fundamentally relational, reflecting 'the geographical structure of the economic flows' (2011: 31–32). The threads of the networked world-system manifested historically in these physical infrastructural routes forces Steel's short stories to map a similar geography of core–periphery relations on a cultural terrain.

Kerr estimates that somewhere 'between 126 and 155 [Indian] workers were employed per construction mile' between 1850 and 1900, the colonised providing a replenishing pool for cheap and unskilled manual labour. Meanwhile, the overwhelming majority of skilled roles were occupied by British administrators and engineers (1995: 42) – indeed, as Kerr notes elsewhere, the 'Indianisation of employment on the railways' would become 'a major goal of Indian nationalists' in the 1920s (2003: 308). Acknowledging the work of the *Subaltern Studies* group, Kerr reluctantly concedes that the '[n]ineteenth-century construction workers will always be mute: people spoken of, who left no first-hand accounts of their own' (1995: 14). Perhaps unsurprisingly, the silence of these workers is reproduced by Steel's short story. There are recorded moments of resistance to railway construction: strikes and violence were often catalysed by the 'subtle and pervasive' exploitation that was a 'feature of the wage relationship', irresponsible employers, and unreliable hiring based on short-term contracts and a disposable workforce (168). For example, the Santhal uprising of 1856 was in part a retaliation against the 'bullying' of Santhal labourers and the 'disgracing' of Santhal women by 'European railway builders in the Rajmahal hills' – the uprising was 'brutally suppressed' by the British military 'as the death toll of some 20,000 Santhals attested' (35). However, the Indian character in Steel's 'In the Permanent Way', whilst inhabiting the peripheral space into which the railroad infiltrates, exhibits a form of resistance markedly different from the violent outbursts of labouring classes assimilated into the lowest rungs of the capitalist economy. Rather, he passively, though adamantly, refuses to be assimilated into an infrastructural and socioeconomic network that is in turn explicitly portrayed as a cross-national project, one emblematic of the global relations of the world-system.

Steel's fictional narrator 'heard this story in a rail-trolly on the Pind-Dadur line, so I always think of it with a running accompaniment, a rhythmic whir of wheels' (1971: 142). Travelling along the 'permanent way', 'you could almost fancy yourself sitting on a stationary engine, engaged in winding up an endless ribbon' (142), as the construction of the infrastructural route appears literally to feed what Luxemburg would call capitalism's 'metabolism' – the processes of accumulation that 'corrodes and assimilates' (2003: 397). The narrative marks the rhythm of capital accumulation with the 'wheels that spin like bobbins', introducing an extended metaphor also employed by Kipling in his poems 'The Exile's Line' (1890) and 'The Song of the English' (1893). In these verses, Kipling conceptualises the British Empire's networks of shipping lines as a vast 'web' spanning the face of the globe, the ships that transport goods between colony and metropole flying back and forth like 'shuttles' on a 'loom' (Kipling, 2006: 129–131).

As Boehmer interprets Kipling's later poem, 'Britain had built for itself an industrial loom spanning the globe, in which the shuttles flying to and fro were the ships of the British merchant marine' (2005: 36). This metaphor alludes to the cotton trade between Britain and India, a process of extracting raw materials from India for Manchester and Lancashire cotton mills whose manufactures were then resold at a profit back to the subcontinent (Harnetty, 1972: 58, 124; Latham, 1978: 77). As Davis points out, somewhat rhetorically, 'in the age of Kipling, that "glorious imperial half century" from 1872 to 1921, the life expectancy of ordinary Indians fell by a staggering 20 percent'; 'Where were the fruits of modernisation, of the thousands of miles of railroad track and canal?' (2010: 312).

The central Indian character of Steel's 'In the Permanent Way' anticipates the methods of non-violent resistance, or *satyagraha*, outlined and employed by Gandhi, in a direct obstruction of the railway under construction (see Gandhi, 2007: 291–292).[4] Gandhi combined these methods of *satyagraha* with other non-violent forms of resistance, specifically that of 'Khadi', which promoted the Indian production of its own cotton manufactures so as to undermine the economic profitability of British imperial policy (Gandhi, 2008: 168). Steel's Indian character exhibits a religious simplicity that prefigures Gandhi's own self-constructed nationalist identity:

> It was a man. For further description I should say it was a thin man. There is nothing more to be said. [...] The only thing I know for *certain* is that he was thin. The *khalassies* said he was some kind of a Hindu saint, and they fell at his feet promptly. (1971: 144)

This 'bronze image', who retains a suggestive anonymity throughout the story, meditates peacefully on a patch of land that lies directly in the path of the permanent way. He does not respond to the imperial attempt to 'annex the only atom of things earthly to which he still clung', nor does he

---

4   Though I have described Steel's character as 'passively' resistant, it is not my intention to suggest that this passivity is some kind of weakness, nor that it resembles pacifism, especially when I point to the similarities between Steel's character and Gandhi's later campaigns. Though Gandhi himself used the term 'passive resistance' in South Africa, he quickly 'disowned this term in favour of his neolocution, "*satyagraha*"', to indicate instead an active but non-violent resistance method that certainly did not advocate 'turning the other cheek in every situation' (Fox, 1997: 70).

retaliate when Craddock 'just lifted him right up, gently, as if he had been a child, and set him down about four feet to the left' (146–147). However, despite portraying him as a passive 'child', Craddock finds that the 'next day he was in the old place', and though never retaliating violently, the Indian figure repeatedly returns to his inconveniencing position. 'It was no use arguing with him', so the construction team simply resort to moving 'him out of the way when we wanted' (147).

Within this narrative context Steel's title, 'In the Permanent Way', becomes invested with dual meaning, signifying both infrastructural development and the obstruction of it. Taken at face value, this is a reiteration of a structural line that 'permanently' marks the colonial landscape and, in that adverb, contributes to the Raj's 'illusion of permanence' (Hutchins, 1967). However, this 'Hindu saint' is himself 'permanently' in the 'way' of this construction process: 'the narrowing red ribbon' of the infrastructural route is 'barred by that bronze image' (149). As Craddock repeatedly puns, reiterating the title throughout the text: 'Look here, sonny, [...] you're in the way – in the permanent way' (147). Reading this textual conflict and its associative imagery as an anticipation of Gandhian *satyagraha* does not put us in danger, as Cooper warns, of 'doing history backward' (2005: 18). Methods of non-violent resistance were already commonplace in post-1857 India: in Bengal, peasants had deployed these methods during the great indigo struggle of 1859–1860 and the Pabna rent strike of 1873, and Bholantha Chandra's call for '"non-consumption" of foreign goods' was 'followed by a boycott pledge taken by some Dacca youths in 1876' (Sarkar, 1985: 50). These historical examples of anti-imperial resistance fuel the 'buried', 'unconscious anxiety' that can be excavated out of the contours of Steel's plot structure, levered from 'the very letter of the work' (Macherey, 1986: 155). Like the construction of the railway her story documents, the narrative's propagation of imperial ideology is 'unmade even in its making' (155).

Nevertheless, Steel's story takes on a grim physical reality at its climax, a violence that builds through layers of imagery that accumulate as the narrative progresses:

> The whistle rang shrill over the desert of sand, which lay empty of all save that streak of red with the dark stain upon it; but the stain never moved, never stirred, though the snorting demon from the west came racing up to it at full speed. (1971: 151)

The 'streak of red' and 'dark stain' conjure up images of blood, in sharp contrast to the previously clean, 'tinsel edge' of the 'steel railway', thereby drawing attention to what Anupama Rao and Steven Pierce would call the 'corporeality' of the colonised subject. As they write, it was this 'temporal coexistence of corporeal and disciplinary modes' that 'fuelled humanitarian criticism of colonial corporeal technologies' (2006: 17). In this passage, 'the west' and its infrastructural invasion of the Indian landscape is literally demonised. The dangers of the permanent way are compounded in the final moments of the story when the train kills not only the 'bronze image', but also Craddock, as the construction worker attempts to save the life of Steel's persistently resistant Indian character. Returning to Roy's more general observation of Steel's short stories, 'the contradictions and inadequacies in the Imperial reform projects and the assumptions of benevolent impact that underwrote them' are here brought sharply 'into focus' (Roy, 2010: 55).

However, 'In the Permanent Way' offers one further insight into the nuances of imperial ideology and its response to infrastructural development. Steel's fictional narrator concludes:

> When a whole train goes over two men who are locked in each other's [*sic*] arms it is hard – hard to tell – well, which is *Shivers-Martha Davy*, and which is *Wishnyou Lucksmi*. It was right out in the desert in the hot weather, no parsons or people to object; so I buried them there in the permanent way. (1971: 158)

The story gives literal shape to the way in which infrastructural development, itself justified by the 'humanitarian' ethos of a supposedly 'palliative' imperialism, in fact results in a vivid and corporeal violence, producing for the coloniser a 'troubled dialectic between violation and protection, between governance and atrocity' (Pierce and Rao, 2006: 3). In an effort to craft a 'fictive resolution' to this conflict, both coloniser and colonised are 'locked' together and destroyed, quite literally 'buried' within, and by, the text. But the monument constructed to mark the place of their death, like the story that commemorates them, remains, pointing to the 'absence' where the inconsistencies of the 'ideology can be most positively felt' (Eagleton, 2002: 32). Gesturing to the monument in the story's final paragraphs, the narrator's companion claims: 'You see it does for both of them' (1971: 159). Documenting, meta-textually, its own efforts to culturally fix this conflict, the story still suggests the failure of such an effort. As the narrator concludes in the final sentence that brings Steel's narrative to an abrupt close: 'The jar of the points prevented me from replying' (159).

Craddock, the colonial hero of 'In the Permanent Way', is resuscitated and appears in another story that revolves around a railway, whilst Steel's passively resistant figure is left 'buried' within the text. 'A Danger Signal' (1897) is, however, told directly from the perspective of two Indians (Steel, 1971: 160). This perspectival shift reduces the 'funny white people' – Anglo-Indians – to 'stuffed dolls', and Steel's Indian characters, 'old Dhunnu and his granddaughter', Dhunni, are empowered by the imperial government through the redeployment of what has already been identified as a significant symbol in Steel's writing: the 'flag', 'green' for 'line clear', 'red' for the 'danger signal' of the story's title (164). Located at 'level crossing number 57', an infrastructural intersection where the road is 'not visible to the passing eye' (160), Dhunnu and Dhunni have the power to halt 'the great caterpillar with red and green eyes' (162). The locomotive becomes a metonym for 'the passing of civilisation' (165), as the story takes up the symbolic currency of Steel's other writings to identify the infrastructural line as a manifestation of 'modernity' and 'civilisation'. In contrast to the train that speeds past them, Dhunni and Dhunnu are described as 'two motionless figures' (160), signifying a peripheral zone that is conspicuously static in relation to the dynamics of global capitalism but that is invested with the capacity to interrupt its accumulative processes.

However, Dhunnu refuses to allow his granddaughter to act on this implicitly political power with a metaphor that further indicates the narrative's allegorical work: 'that will never be', he tells her, 'since east and west is there no cause sufficient to check progress; and as *that* is by order the green flag, so the green flag it will be' (162). As the metonymic weight of the train as a signifier of Western infrastructural and economic development accumulates, the conflict between Dhunnu's refusal and Dhunni's desire to intervene – to resist giving '"line clear", as it were, to a whole world, of which she knew nothing' (164) – is located within their generation gap. Across the three generations that cover the story's time frame (c.1860 to 1890), Steel's narrative gestures, albeit implicitly, towards the evolution of an anti-imperial agency, one that would crystallise historically, as shall be shown in greater detail in Chapter 4, in emerging nationalist movements. It is when Dhunnu is on one occasion absent that Dhunni begins to question the infrastructural line and, finally, decides quite literally to stop the steam engine's progress in its tracks.

> She was on her feet in an instant, listening, waiting. Ah! this was new, certainly. This she had never seen before. An engine with a single carriage coming full speed out of the golden West. Was she to give 'line clear' to this? or – (168–169)

Operating at the metonymic level that the story itself has foregrounded, Dhunni's 'listening, waiting', gives shape to an anti-imperial agency, silent but present within the infrastructure *of* the narrative. In the textual moment that Dhunni actually intervenes in the train's progress, once again framed as synonymous with the 'golden West', Steel's narrative breaks down into a hyphenated silence. The borders of the ideological material out of which Steel carves her narrative can be mapped at this close formal level, as the text 'resorts to an eloquent silence' (Macherey, 1986: 79). By intervening in Steel's story with the critical practice of *infrastructural reading*, it becomes possible, as outlined in the introduction, to 'deliver the text from its own silences by coaxing it into giving up its true, latent or hidden meaning' (Bennett, 2003: 86) – that is, to understand this textual silence as an acknowledgement of the historically ongoing anti-imperial resistance to the Raj's exploitative economic enterprise.

There is, however, a further dimension to Steel's story that emerges in its plot structure, one that complicates a simple dualistic opposition between coloniser and colonised, or socioeconomic separation between core and periphery, instead highlighting the extent to which they are related to one another. Ironically, Dhunni's spontaneous decision to raise the 'scarlet veil' actually prevents the destruction of the train by the 'narrowest escape' (173).

> no one had thought it could possibly be done – that the warning could possibly be given in time. It was the veriest piece of luck. Briefly, just after the mail had passed, a big culvert had given not two miles farther down the line. They had telegraphed both ways of course, though, as no train was due for hours, there was plenty of time for repairs. Then had come the return wire, telling of the boy's start to overtake the mail on urgent business. Everyone had said it was too late; and, after all, it had

been a matter of five minutes or less. The veriest luck indeed! If they had been five minutes earlier ...! (174)

After the failure of two forms of infrastructure, both railway and telegraph, Dhunni's action actually prevents a train crash by undercutting these infrastructural networks, intervening in the temporal and physical space they have left unregulated. But her intervention goes largely unrecognised, the avoidance of catastrophe ascribed instead to the 'veriest luck'. The more hesitant disintegration of this paragraph – an ellipses rather than a hyphen – again suggests an ideological fragmentation, or fault line, beyond which resides an assertion of Indian agency. In the story's final sentences, the narrative once again stumbles at a close syntactical level, as it fails to resolve anxieties around infrastructural failure and imminent anti-imperialist resistance. Dhunni stands 'gazing after the red and green lights with a dazed look on her face. The danger signal had come into her life – the train had stopped, and then – and –?' (176). Unable to contemplate an alternative to imperial rule and a narrow conception of 'modernity' as allegorised by the train – the infrastructures *of* the text manifesting as the infrastructure *in* the text – the narrative falters, stutters, and falls, once again, into silence.

In his book-length analysis of what he describes as the indirect 'murder' of millions of Indians by the 'sacred' *laissez-faire* 'principles of Smith, Bentham and Mill' in British India, Davis gives rich historical texture to these underlying inconsistencies, anxieties and hypocrisies (2010: 9). In so doing, he sheds light on the damaging effects and violent ramifications of 'palliative imperialism' (Mukherjee, 2013: 18). Reflecting on his own retrospective condemnation of these policies and their consequences, Davis asks: 'how do we weigh smug claims about the life-saving benefits of steam transportation and modern grain markets when so many millions, especially in British India, died alongside railroad tracks or on the steps of grain depots?' (2010: 9). Davis's impassioned language reflects his explicit acknowledgement of his political responsibilities as a critic and historian of empire that, as explained in the introduction, this book shares. An *infrastructural reading* of Steel's short fiction allows a clearer delineation of the ideological complexities born out of the fraught historical circumstances described by Davis, and of which he is rightly so vocal in his condemnation.

The combination of Steel's fragmented narrative form and the more direct criticisms that her stories articulate gesture towards the socioeconomic realities of a violent colonial system, functioning, I argue, as a political critique of the imperial government's complicity with the uneven and unequal developments of the capitalist world-system.

Another of Steel's stories, 'Surâbhi, A Famine Tale' (1903), identifies the incompatibilities of pre-existing Indian cultural and economic systems with imposed imperial ones, whilst simultaneously condemning 'the official neglect' that limited the potentially beneficial impact of infrastructures such as the 'British railroad and canal construction', 'local irrigation' and famine relief (Davis, 2010: 290). Once again, this acknowledgment of acts of 'atrocity' by a government priding itself on its 'protection' of its subject peoples requires a cultural fix, one that can only manifest within the narrative as a final, conspicuous 'silence'. The dilemma at the heart of 'Surâbhi' is the G. O. I.'s assumption that 'when cattle starve it is not a famine' (1971: 27). This means that the story's Indian protagonist, Gopâl Das, not only falls outside of imperialism's networks of humanitarian relief, but that his suffering is actually exacerbated by them. Das's only 'cow' was 'all things, wife and child, earth and heaven' to him (23), and he therefore feeds the animal his ration of 'famine bread' rather than eating it himself. The system in place then requires him to contribute the cow's milk back to the Raj's centralised relief effort, rather than allowing him to drink it himself. He therefore becomes 'appreciably more lank, more skeleton-like' (28) until, 'like any child', he falls 'forward insensible with outstretched, petitioning hands' (35).

> [The] last calf had long since become an ox, and drifted away from the village to fill a gap in the great company of ploughers and martyrs who give the coffer of the Empire all its gold and die in thousands – long before famine touches humanity – without a penny piece from that coffer being spent to save them from starvation. (26)

This surprisingly severe critique of a capitalised 'Empire' – signifying not just money-lenders such as Gissing, but Britain's cross-border cultural and economic world-empire as a whole – informs the story's overtly political, if not anti-imperial, context. As Roy argues, Steel here draws 'attention to the confused aspirations and frustrated desires, despair and even death that the poorly visualised, inefficiently administered reform projects cause'

(2010: 40–41). However, the description of Gopâl as 'only a baby himself' indicates that the story's ideological scaffolding is not entirely subverted, but is rather stretched to accommodate its critique. Whilst, as Mukherjee notes, the story 'alert[s] us to the unease [...] about the oppressive nature of imperial benevolence' (2013: 193), Steel is unable to acknowledge that it is the presence of the 'foreign ruler' that is, in the end, the 'enemy' of the peasant (Patwardhan, 1963: 144). This failure to see the broader, structural violence of empire is generally representative of her autobiographical thought. As late as 1929, when ideas of Indian nationalism and independence were circulating widely (and to which I will return in Chapter 4), Steel still believed that:

> there is no Eastern language which contains the equivalent of 'national'. *Swaraj*, of which we have so much nowadays, is simply 'self-government' and would apply equally well to a caste or race; but not to a nation. In fact, the national idea is foreign to the Indian. He has learnt it, doubtless, but it is alien. (Steel, 1930: 190)

By contrasting the two extended quotations above, the first from the short story, the second from the autobiography, the contradictions of Steel's ideological framework can be thrown into relief. Despite her often astute criticisms of the imperial enterprise, the concept of an independent, post-imperial India remains unintelligible. Nevertheless, on a textual level, the story reveals the presence of this historical activity, as the story's culminating sentence seeks to resolve these anxieties whilst confessing its own inability to do so: 'Then there was silence' (Steel, 1971: 36). The text points to its own 'eloquent silence' (Macherey, 1986: 79), marking a failed attempt to fix, culturally, this crisis in imperial ideology.

Perspectival Shifts: Resisting Infra-Structural Violence

Crucial to the critical purchase of Steel's short fiction is its tendency to shift the narrative perspective from the coloniser to the colonised. Though they continue to adhere, if implicitly, to Steel's hierarchical paternalism, this shift still allows Steel's stories to analyse the Raj's infrastructural machine from the peripheral zones that lie beyond imperialism's core networks, both physical and symbolic. These narratives frequently begin in, and emerge from, what Lefebvre would call the 'blank or marginal spaces', the '"holes in the net"' that lie beyond and between the 'pathways' and 'networks' of the structured landscape (1998: 132). By writing from these geographical and socioeconomic spaces, Steel's stories highlight the contradiction between imperialism's rhetoric of infrastructural development as a symbol of humanitarian progress and the development of underdevelopment that those infrastructures so often facilitated. Whilst the massive infrastructural developments furnished the British with 'proof of their material superiority' by drawing 'almost every part of India' into the railway's 'spider web of steel' (Arnold, 2000: 109–110), these infrastructural routes simultaneously facilitated capitalism's accumulative metabolism by linking, according to Bipan Chandra, both the landscape and its peoples 'with the growing world market', setting them 'on the path of capitalist development' and integrating the subcontinent's 'non-European peasantries' into the 'world economy' (2006: 77). By repeatedly adopting and approaching these infrastructures from the perspective of the colonised, Steel produces literary geographies that both directly and sub-textually criticise the G. O. I.'s failings – the resistance that emerges from the resulting ideological fractures, as they are registered in textual form, are thus most effectively configured *spatially*. These spaces implicitly acknowledge an ongoing and increasingly disruptive Indian resistance, and this chapter concludes with a final comparative reading of two more of Steel's short stories to demonstrate that her writing's 'silences' and 'absences' contains, on occasion, explicit and even violent anti-imperial intrusions.

The protagonists of Steel's 'The Great Durbar' (1897) and 'Harvest' (1894) are Indian peasants – Nânuk and Jaimul respectively – and at the beginning of each story, both are situated geographically 'beyond' or 'outside of' the networks of imperial infrastructure and the cross-national circuitries of the world-system. Nevertheless, both protagonists are subject to the impoverished socioeconomic conditions – the development of underdevelopment, or the process of peripheralisation – that those same imperial infrastructures have created. For Nânuk, 'fate' has 'decreed that in his old age the peasant farmer should have neither furrows nor water-wheel of his own. How this had come about needs a whole statute-book of Western laws to understand' (Steel, 1971: 352). Steel's satirical reference to 'fate' here serves as an implicit metaphor for the inadequate famine relief and misplaced reforms that have dealt Nânuk out of the tools he requires to produce enough food simply to sustain himself and his family. Meanwhile for Jaimul, the 'empire' lies 'far from his simple imaginings; and yet he, the old peasant with his steady hand of patient control, held the reins of government over how many million square miles? That is the province of the Blue Book, and Jaimul's blue book was the sky' (374–375). As the satirical tone of these sentences implies, Steel's short fiction works to disrupt the 'assumptions' of the 'benevolent impact' that 'underwrote' the imperial reform projects (Roy, 2010: 55). But what sets these stories apart from the short fiction already discussed is the active intent, or agency, of both Nânuk and Jaimul, as they attempt to seek out 'justice' from, if not directly to resist, the infrastructural and bureaucratic web of the imperial government. The stories not only expose the hypocritical contours of humanitarian ideology, but describe an active intervention into the exploitative dynamics of the capitalist world-system.

In his extended historical documentation of peasant resistance, David Hardiman has argued that though the continuing outbreaks did not 'pose a direct threat to British rule between 1858 and 1914', they did provide 'a continual rebuttal to the claims made by colonial officials that India had become a more prosperous and stable society under the British' (1992: 1–2). But despite these continuing movements, little 'understanding or sympathy was shown for the peasants' motives, nor analysis undertaken' (2). Within the historic and economic context in which these stories are set – from the 1870s onwards – there was, Hardiman documents, 'a slump in agricultural prices due to the opening up of huge areas of virgin farmland' across the British Empire in Australia and Canada and beyond it, in North and South America and Russia (5). Because of Britain's refusal 'to impose tariffs' and thereby 'protect small agriculturalists from the influx of cheap grain', the expansion of 'communication and market networks' – facilitated by the development of infrastructures such as the railway and telegraph – actually 'prevented rather than encouraged the emergence of

a class of peasants able to benefit from commercial agriculture' (5). It is
the ramification of these global forces upon the day-to-day lives of Indian
peasants that informs the critical thrust of Steel's stories, which explore the
wider structural conditions of the world-system and its uneven development as they are refracted through the experiences of poorer populations
situated on its periphery. A focus on the occurrence of infrastructure in
these stories foregrounds the structural critique that Steel undertakes in
these literary writings, as she reveals the conflict between the G. O. I.'s
claims to humanitarian benevolence and its strict adherence to exploitative
free trade policies. Furthermore, by contextualising Nânuk's and Jaimul's
actions within these broader structural conditions, Steel accounts for, if
not going so far as to justify, constant resistance to the Raj's rule, which
culminates here in an account of a violent, anti-imperial act.

Figure 1.4: Photograph showing the architectural layout of the
Delhi durbar of King George V in 1911.

Both Nânuk and Jaimul know 'nothing of Statutes of Limitation or
judgments of the Chief Court' (Steel, 1971: 378), but they nevertheless
address their assertions of agency to symbolic manifestations of British
imperialism. Nânuk travels, by foot, to the material and symbolic heart of
the Indian empire and a grand architectural and infrastructural feat, 'The
Great Durbar' (352–353). Here, Steel fictionally recreates Lord Lytton's

Imperial Assemblage held in Delhi between December 1876 and January 1877 which was designed 'to announce, enhance and glorify British authority' (Cohn, 2009: 662), an event that was repeated with similar architectural grandeur and spatially demarcated hierarchies in 1911, as the image reproduced here demonstrates. Anthony King has documented the extensive infrastructural development of the 'cantonment road system and the road network' that linked the geographical area cleared for the Imperial Assemblage in 1876 with the 'Civil Lines' and the main city: '40 miles of new roads were constructed within a 25-square mile area' along with '26.5 miles of broad gauge and 9 miles of narrow gauge railways' (King, 1976: 224–228). Stumbling upon these massive infrastructural projects, Nânuk walks past a 'mountain of wheat cumbering the railway platforms all along the line', a sight that provokes

> wonder in his slow brain how it could be that the increased demand for wheat and its enhanced price should have gone hand-in-hand with the financial ruin of the grower.
>   To say sooth, however, such problems as these flitted through the old man's thought. (361)

Though there is only a momentary insight into the economic inequalities produced by cross-national infrastructural development, the narrative still implies that these infrastructures facilitate the world-system's intensification of unequal disparities between core and peripheral zones. The focus on the slowness of Nânuk's brain and the fact that his observation is 'half forgotten' a few sentences later might be indicative of an ideological belittlement of the Indian's sustained political consciousness. But there still remains a direct recognition of the Raj's exploitative economic policies, and Nânuk's 'slow brain' is as much due to his state of starvation as it is his de-politicised mind. Historically, the year of the Imperial Assemblage, 1876, was also the first year of the Madras famine. By drawing on a number of contemporaneous and retrospective sources, Davis has estimated that 'the great drought of 1876–1879' resulted in the deaths of between 6.1 and 10.3 million people (2010: 6–7). He also cites an English journalist who 'later estimated that 100,000 of the Queen-Empress's subjects starved to death in Madras and Mysore in the course of Lytton's spectacular *durbar*' alone (28). Cohn has also drawn attention to the durbar as an 'example of the callousness on the part of imperial rulers who spent large sums of public money at a time of famine' (2009: 676), and Steel's story is shaped, in both content and form, by the violent ramifications of imperial rule.

Nânuk works his way towards the Viceroy's dais, the central symbolic manifestation of an event designed 'to express and make manifest and compelling the British construction of their authority over India' (Cohn, 2009: 677). He finds himself

> beneath what had been the goal of all his hopes [...] the flagstaff whereon the Standard of England hung dank and heavy [...] So far so good. This was the '*Standard of Sovereignty*' no doubt [...] the guide by day and night to faithful subjects seeking justice. (1971: 367)

In a re-writing of the ideological symbol that runs through *On the Face of the Waters*, the satirical dryness of Steel's narrative voice finds literary embodiment in the 'English Flag' which, no longer floating 'serenely, securely', has become 'dank and heavy'. The text's discordant parody of the flag is reinforced by the soldier who encounters Nânuk: Private Smith 'was drunk enough to be intensely patriotic', his 'little lilt' keeping time 'to the stave of "God Save our Gracious Queen" which he was whistling horribly out of tune' (368). The Private's aggression towards Nânuk – 'you won't drink 'er 'elth, you mutineering nigger?' – warps the adamant patriotism that pervades Steel's Mutiny novel into an explicit racism that the narrative works to condemn (370). This scene ends with 'the first gun of the hundred and one which are fired at daybreak on the anniversary of her Most Gracious Majesty's assumption of the title [Empress of India] boomed out across the fog' (371) – the capitalisation of 'Most Gracious Majesty' and the word 'assumption' again highlight the sharp, satirical undertones of Steel's prose. Importantly, however, Nânuk does 'not hear' this symbolic expression of imperial dominance. Weary with fatigue and lack of food, he 'had stumbled to his feet and fallen sideways to the ground', in a textual juxtaposition that allegorically writes the peripheral, famine-stricken areas of rural India into the very centre of the Imperial Assemblage, suggestively and *spatially* undermining its benevolent, protectorate and authoritative claims with the violent realities of its economic policies (371). If, as Barnett observes, 'a new ideology of humanitarianism' meant that the 'British colonial state was partly built on the skeletal remains of the Indians' (2013: 64), Steel's story condemns the violent hypocrisies of this paternalistic humanitarianism with a similarly visceral and politicised imagery.

In 'Harvest', Jaimul, another impoverished peasant, takes his case to the 'District Court', where 'the long, carefully-woven tissue of fraud and cunning blinded even the eyes of a justice biassed in his favour' (1971: 385). The description of this textual fabric – the 'records of Indian law-courts' that 'teem with such cases', the 'long array of seals' and 'the strands which formed the net' (386) – critiques the dense bureaucratic machinery and Governmental Reports that Steel would later condemn in her autobiography for being 'too legal, too systematised, for the ignorance with which it had to deal' (Steel, 1930: 249). Though the autobiographical comment is again symptomatic of Steel's racialised paternalism, the literary representation of the Indian's negotiation of the Raj's bureaucratic system throws the broader contours of imperialism's structural violence into sharp relief. It contextualises what Slavoj Žižek identifies as an obvious signal of violence – 'crime and terror, civil unrest' – by detailing 'the contours of the background which generates such outbursts' (2008: 1). By adopting Jaimul's perspective, the text steps back, allowing readers 'to disentangle' themselves 'from the fascinating lure of this directly visible' violence, 'performed by a clearly identifiable agent', to foreground instead imperialism's '"systemic" violence' – that is, 'the often catastrophic consequences of the smooth functioning' of imperialism as a political and socioeconomic system (1–4). In so doing, Steel's story not only acknowledges anti-imperial resistance, but begins to justify and legitimise its right to political, even violent intervention.

In the final pages of the story, Jaimul turns to violence in his search for justice. But because the subject of Steel's critique is the systemic inequalities perpetuated by the Raj's economic policies, the narrative never actually condemns the peasant's violent outburst. Rather, it shows how Jaimul's act of 'behavioural violence' is, in fact, a product of those structural inequities.[5]

---

5   The plot of this story is strikingly similar to Leonard Woolf's slightly later novel, *The Village in the Jungle* (1913). There, the structural violence instigated by the imperial government's dense and unevenly developed legal systems drive a Sri Lankan peasant, Silindu, like Jaimaul, to commit an act of violence against his headman.

The scene is scattered with references to '[t]he land! [...] hardened by many a dry year of famine', and the 'good ground', the 'Good soil!' (388–389). By emphasising the physical terrain upon which Jaimul's act of violent resistance – the murder of the headman, symbolically a 'white figure on a white horse' (388) – takes place, the narrative places the politics of colonial rule, understood as a set of 'activities of domination and exploitation' that are 'acting in and on the material world' (Young, 2008: 408), centre stage. Though the 'face' of the British headman is 'beaten to jelly', described a few sentences later as 'formless' and 'the horror' (1971: 389), Steel's perspectival shift to that of the peasant reveals the structural conditions that have induced Jaimul's violent act:

> he was not sorry, or ashamed, or frightened – only dazed at the hurry of his own act. Such things had to be done sometimes when folk were unjust. They would hang him for it, of course, but he had at least made his protest, and done his deed as good men and true should when the time came. (389–390)

Steel's story intertextually foreshadows Joseph Conrad's 'horror', which is, by some critical accounts, at least in part a response to the violence of Belgium's imperial exploitation of central Africa (Conrad, 2006: 70; Hawkins, 1982; Brantlinger, 1988). It also looks forward to George Orwell's non-fictional account of a hanging of a colonial prisoner in Burma, an essay equally critical of imperial hypocrisy and violence (2000: 14–18). So though Thomas argues that 'the empire in India would be near its actual end before mainstream British authors – for instance George Orwell in *Burmese Days* (1934) – would directly represent the status quo in India as illegitimate' (1995: 168), Steel's story highlights a fundamental contradiction in imperial ideology at this earlier historical moment. Furthermore, despite the constant ideological citation of the violence committed against Britons during the 'Indian Mutiny' as a justification for violent governmental retaliation – a move to which Steel herself resorts in *On the Face of the Waters* – the final paragraph of 'Harvest' draws on that ideology

Furthermore, and as I have written elsewhere, Woolf's novel is narrated, like Steel's short story, from the perspective of the colonised, thereby throwing the contours of imperialism's structural violence into relief (see Woolf, 2008; and Davies, 2015).

to intensify, rather than nullify, its critique of the exploitative nature of British imperialism in India:

> The usurer's boys, it is true, forced the utmost from the land, and sent all save bare sustenance across the seas [...] Perhaps the yellow English gold which came into the country in return for the red Indian wheat more than paid for these trivial losses. Perhaps it did not. That is a question which the next Mutiny must settle. (392)

In this final sentence Steel at last shifts the 'significant silences' with which this chapter has been concerned to an open acknowledgement of the inevitability of anti-imperialist resistance. Retaining the use of the term 'Mutiny', its textual location suggests that by invoking the 'wild tales of horror' that proved 'remarkably durable' within the British and Anglo-Indian imagination (Randall, 2003: 5), Steel warns her readers of forthcoming anti-imperial violence. By ending, like 'The Great Durbar', with a provocative textual juxtaposition, for its time the narrative is radical in its comparison of the violence of the Mutiny with the violence of the Raj's exploitative economic and infrastructural policies. The global dynamics of these policies, emphasised here in Steel's concluding paragraph, reflect imperialism's subservience to the dynamics of the capitalist world-system and its complicity with the development of underdevelopment in the subcontinent. This is a socio-economic violence enabled, as has been shown, by the infrastructural and technological developments that were themselves justified by ideologies of humanitarianism. Steel's fiction demonstrates an acute awareness of this fundamental contradiction, an ideological inconsistency that makes space for, and even on occasion justifies, anti-imperial resistance at these close syntactical and infrastructural levels.

In this first chapter I have made preliminary efforts to show how an infrastructural approach to colonial literature allows us to see how its narratological configurations of anti-imperial resistance are not simply anticolonial or anti-governmental, but in fact constitute what Arrighi, Hopkins and Wallerstein have called 'anti-systemic movements' (2011: 1). Because Steel is aligned, both biographically and ideologically, with the Raj's imperial governance, the 'peripheralisation processes' of the world-system – the extraction of resources, the international division of labour (Hopkins and Wallerstein, 1982: 98–99) – remain implicit, concealed within the frameworks of her humanitarian ideology. In the case of South Africa, British governance was historically not so concerned with humanitarian intervention. There, as the next chapter will show, infrastructures were not justified by palliative ideologies but took on a more obviously systemic role, rendering the region's mineral resources accessible and building complex systems of segregation in order to maintain a compliant and regular workforce. Whilst the anti-imperial resistance of Steel's fiction is rooted in her criticisms of the G. O. I. for its colonial capitalist tendencies, the fiction of Haggard, Schreiner and Plomer, all of which are set in industrialising South Africa, more explicitly reveal infrastructure to be a symbolic demarcator of the intensification of capitalist relations. Nevertheless, because of the historical and political context to which Steel's literature responds, and the cross-national core–periphery networks that can be traced through its production of India's colonial spaces, the contradictions manifested in her fiction should still, I argue, be configured as interventions into and disruptions of the mechanics of the capitalist world-system as a whole.

Mapping Segregation: Literary Geographies of South Africa

Introduction: Industrialisation, Urbanisation, Segregation

> Industrial revolution is one thing when it is the natural movement of internal forces, making along the lines of the self-interests of a nation and proceeding *pari passu* with advancing popular self-government; another thing when it is imposed by foreign conquerors looking primarily to present gains for themselves, and neglectful of the deeper interests of the people of the country.
>
> — HOBSON (1988: 292)

By 1921, a glance at a railway map of Southern Africa such as the one reproduced below would reveal with astonishing starkness the extent to which imperial infrastructure had been constructed to serve the interests of foreign capital, as Hobson observed. The region's industrial revolution, sparked by the discoveries of diamonds in Kimberley in 1867 and gold on the Witwatersrand in 1886, occurred at a furious pace, tearing apart 'the fabric of African life' so that where prior to 1870 'the majority of Africans in southern Africa lived in independent chiefdoms', by the 1920s South Africa was home to huge urban centres with large black populations (Marks and Rathbone, 1982: 1; Karis and Carter, 1972: 4). Whilst in India infra-structural development was certainly shaped by the prospect of resource extraction (primarily from the subcontinent's coalfields), as discussed in the previous chapter, railway, road and telegraph construction in Southern Africa and the resulting processes of industrialisation and urbanisation were more obviously dictated by 'the imperatives of mining capital' (1982: 12). Infrastructural development was infrequently justified by claims to

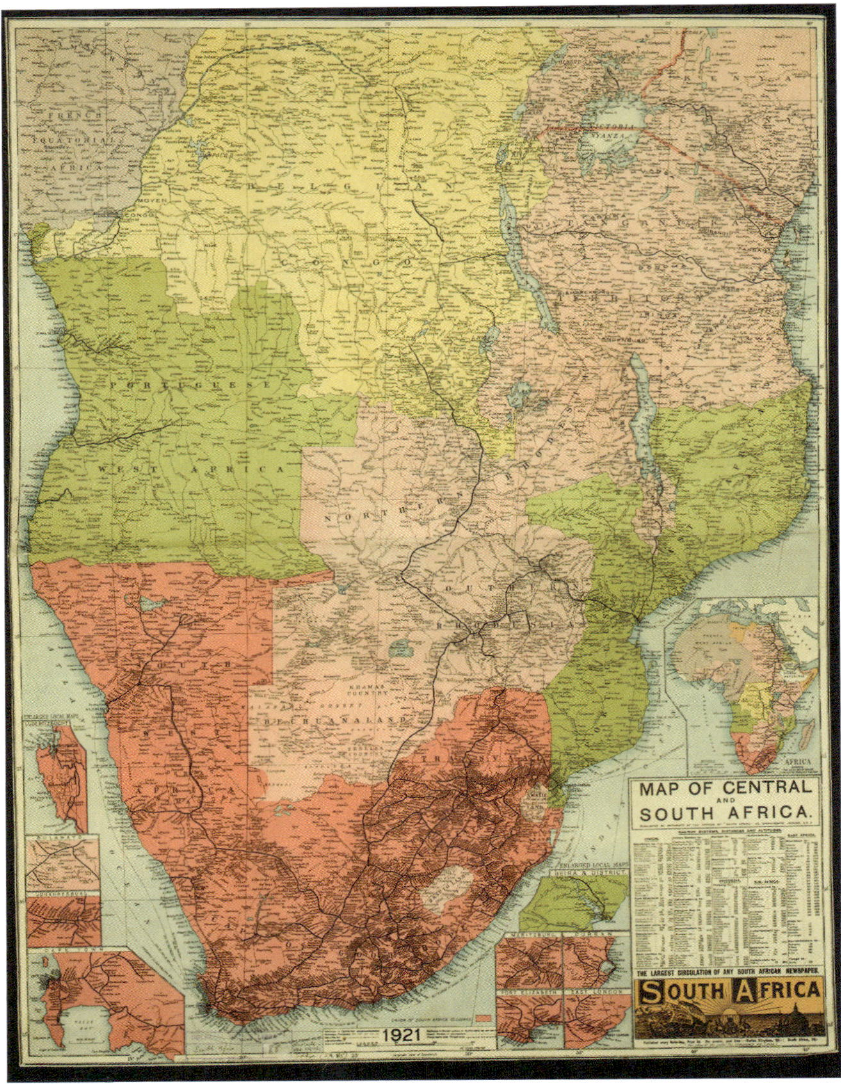

Figure 2.1: Map of Central and South Africa, including insets of the African continent as a whole and of the major colonial port cities and their environs. Printed at 125 miles to an inch for the newspaper, *South Africa*, in 1921. Colonial Office, 1047/203, National Archives at Kew.

humanitarian intervention. Rather, it was explicitly designed to export resources, import manufactures and move labour forces to the new industrialising centres. Looking to the accompanying map once more, the unevenly developed arterial routes cluster around identified areas of rich mineral deposits and link them to coastal ports, whilst on occasion unravelling to cast exploratory threads into the continent's interior spaces.

South Africa's industrial revolution was not, as Hobson observed, simply 'neglectful of the deeper interests of the people of the country' (1988: 292). Rather, black Africans were its fuel; this is why, as Achille Mbembe writes, 'from the start, a dense nexus of overlapping and interweaving threads connected migrancy and modernity in South Africa' (2008: 42). The assimilation 'of the colonised peoples primarily as an urban working class' resulted in a 'bewildering array of discriminatory laws and practices' in the emerging industrial heartlands, specifically designed to keep 'workers cheap and pliable' (Clark and Worger, 2011: 8, 14–15). These uneven geographies and racialised demographies manifest in colonial literature primarily, as this chapter will show, in increasingly complex infrastructural and ideological systems of segregation. For Wallerstein, 'racism' is 'a cultural pillar of historical capitalism' (2011: 80). It enables 'the stratification of the work-force inside the historical system' so as 'to keep the oppressed groups inside the system' rather than 'expel them' (103). As the infiltration of capitalist relations into Southern Africa intensified, a complex geography of segregation was required to encrust the racial 'boundaries' that facilitated 'the hierarchisation of the work-force and its highly unequal distributions of reward' (78). Whilst facilitating capital flows in and out of the region, physical infrastructures also played a central role in maintaining these boundaries in both actual and imagined space, laying the foundations for the phenomenon that would overshadow South Africa for much of the remainder of the twentieth century: apartheid (Ferro, 1997: 144–145). Johannesburg, a city constructed from the settlements that originally congregated around the gold mines of the Witwatersrand, lies at the centre of these historical processes. As with New Delhi in India, as I will show in Chapter 4, the historical sedimentations of Johannesburg's physical and infrastructural arrangements tell the story of 'the rise, fall and reconstruction of the segregated city' (Nuttall and Mbembe, 2008: 10). Literary representations of South African geographies, like those of India, have been both complicit with, and resistant to, the production of this deeply racialised and segregated space.

By the time of the Berlin Conference on African Affairs and the 'Scramble for Africa' in the 1880s, South Africa had been 'transformed from a service station en route to India to a global centre of industrial production' (Chrisman, 2000: 23–24). Literary texts such as H. Rider Haggard's *King Solomon's Mines* (1885) brought 'the "Dark Continent" into vibrant colour' for the imperial imagination (Pocock, 1993: 62–63). However, it was not until 1910 that, as Luxemburg wrote, a 'million white exploiters of both nations sealed their touching fraternal alliance within the Union with the civil and political disenfranchisement of five million coloured workers' (2003: 396). The unification of four former British colonies, rich in natural resources and exhibiting 'enormous potential for economic development', was, Luxemburg argued, a seminal moment in the consolidation of white power and the disenfranchisement of blacks in South Africa (Griffiths, 1995: 71). Reflecting on the political situation in 1896, Olive Schreiner and her husband Samuel Cronwright-Schreiner argued that 'the Native Question' was in fact 'only the Labour Question complicated by a difference of race and colour' (1896: 109). For Schreiner, the creation of an impoverished black proletariat in South Africa's new urban environments by 'the foreign Speculator, Capitalist, and Shareholding class' was 'the very core within the core, and the kernel within the kernel, of the South African problem' (1923: 315–316). This is a preoccupation that, as this chapter will show, is made manifest by the infrastructures not only of, but also *in* her literary texts.

The systematic infrastructural regulation of a constant supply of black labour was reinforced via a number of legal measures during the years that led up to the publication of Plomer's 'Ula Masondo', which appeared in his first collection of short stories, *I Speak of Africa*, in 1927, and to which this chapter will turn in its conclusion. The Natives Land Act, passed in 1913, legalised 'the principle of territorial segregation' and prohibited Africans from lawfully acquiring land outside of 'native reserves' (Meredith, 2008: 522–523). As Sol Plaatje would write in his polemic condemnation of the Act, 'the South African found himself, not actually a slave, but a pariah in the land of his birth': 'the locations form but one-eighteenth of the total area of the Union. Theoretically, then, the 4,500,000 natives may "buy" land in only one-eighteenth part of the Union, leaving the remaining seventeen parts for the one million whites' (2011: 186–188). The Act forced black populations into the cities to work in the mines on short term contracts as they failed to feed themselves – never mind pay taxes imposed by the new government – on the small portions of land available to them. In the years immediately prior to the publication of Plomer's short story, a string of further acts were passed that increasingly restricted the spatial movements of the black population, this time specifically within the urban environment into which so many had been forced: the Native Urban Areas Act (1923), the Industrial Conciliation Act (1924), the Wages Act (1925) and the Mines and Works Amendments Act (1926). Finally, in 1927, the Native Administration Act was passed, 'giving the Department of Native Affairs control over all matters pertaining to Africans' and restricting them to large reserves, whilst retaining them as a labour supply for the mining districts of the cities (Clark and Worger, 2011: 23).

In his book-length study of the architecture of occupation and segregation in Israel/Palestine, Eyal Weizman has emphasised the role of infrastructure in embodying and instituting legal apparatuses, noting the 'almost palindromic linguistic structure of law/wall' that, as Steel's literary interrogations of the Raj's railway and legal infrastructure also showed, is indicative of 'an interdependency that equates built and legal fabric' (Weizman, 2012: 210). Like Steel, the three authors addressed here are preoccupied with the complex infrastructural and legal arrangements required not only to contain anti-imperial resistance, but also to assimilate that population into the industrialising centres as its fundamental economic powerhouse. In her reading of Luxemburg and her reflections on the long-term effects of the invasion of capital into South Africa, Arendt argues that 'the permanent attraction of South Africa, the permanent resource that tempted permanent settlement, was not the gold but this human raw material' (2005, 258). Peripheral zones and disenfranchised populations had to be infrastructurally incorporated *into* South Africa's core industrial spaces. But whilst the increasing complexity of these geographies of segregation become evermore central to the literature's concerns, there also emerges an increased capacity to resist these 'law/walls', one that plays out spatially within their textual forms and themes. As Weizman writes: 'The un-walling of the wall invariably becomes the undoing of the law' (2012: 210).

Mapping the region's rich mineral resources became a central preoccupation of one literary genre in particular: the imperial romance. Its ideological agendas are inscribed into the contours of its narrative structures and the industrialising landscapes of settlements and cities such as Kimberley and Johannesburg are conspicuous in their absence. As many critics have observed, 'champions of [the] romance' offered 'imperial adventure as an antidote to the effete world of high capitalism' (Reid, 2011: 152–178), producing narratives that 'justify seizing the spoils of conquest' (Macdonald, 1994: 213) and that accommodate 'the politics of imperialism' (Katz, 1987: 50). Furthermore, as Bill Schwarz argues, they were central in transmitting 'stories of empire' to the population in imperial Britain, producing a 'strange compound of knowledge and ignorance' that enables the colonised – and specifically Southern African – landscape to serve as a 'pure counterpoint to the decay, degradation, and dirt of domestic England' (2011: 22, 79). Taking up this observation, Chapter 3's exploration of 'frontier consciousness' will show through its discussion of John Buchan's novels that these processes can be mapped, in turn, onto the uneven motions of capital accumulation. Whilst it might seem counterintuitive to map 'segregation' chronologically before 'frontiers' in this book, the literary frontier writing in fact proliferated during the first decades of South Africa's industrialisation. The intensification of capitalist relations, manifested physically in uneven infrastructural developments, creates proximal demographies troubling to imperial and racial ideologies. The production of frontiers thus becomes an increasingly urgent and complex task for colonial literature, as my reading of Buchan will show. If *King Solomon's Mines* is, at least ostensibly, a frontier novel, I argue that it can and should be understood as laying ideologically informed spatialities and segregationist infrastructural imaginaries that would go on to underpin apartheid, the ramifications of which linger on, albeit with notable alterations, into the post-apartheid era (see Bremner, 2010: 97–100).

It is for this reason that I begin this chapter with an infrastructural reading of Haggard's imperial romance, a text that, as Laura Chrisman argues, 'established the prototype' for this extraordinarily popular genre (2012: 226). Norman Etherington similarly emphasises the genre-defining nature of Haggard's text: '*King Solomon's Mines* [is] the first and still more widely read of the romances' (1978: 74), whilst Wendy Katz argues that the 'most striking by-product' of Haggard's time in South Africa was 'the development of romance literature' (1987: 4). My analysis of this much-read novel traces the romance's simplistic production of segregated space, arguing that it reflects and reproduces a wider currency of reductively linear infrastructural imaginings that were circulating in contemporaneous ideas about a Cape to Cairo railway. As Moretti has argued, similarly writing with one eye on early colonial maps of Africa and another on the imperial romance, 'the single, one-dimensional line [...] has been the standard sign of African explorations in map after map'; it is 'an isolated line, with no deviations, no lateral branches', one that is replicated in 'the linear plot' (1998: 59–60). For Moretti, '[i]deology and narrative matrix, here, are truly one and the same', and the plot of *King Solomon's Mines* undoubtedly follows what he calls 'the spatial logic of colonialism': 'Penetrate; seize; leave' (60–62). However, by looking more closely at the infrastructure *in* the text, I will show that this linearity is in fact deeply troubled by a central 'contradiction' in imperial ideology that arises in response to the processes of industrialisation and subsequent urbanisation in South Africa – the infrastructures *of* the text. This contradiction is rooted in 'the intrinsically paradoxical nature of segregationist politics':

> The very concept of urban segregation, after all, is self-contradictory. Cities are places where many different people come together, congregate, and create great agglomerations – where geographical distances between people are diminished, not increased. For whites who dominate multiracial cities, this contradiction often translates into a real political dilemma. (Nightingale, 2012: 10)

As Alan Lester observes, this 'contradiction' was 'central to South Africa's subsequent social, economic and political development', hinging on a tension 'between large-scale African labour requirements, inclining social structures towards racial integration, and ideologies and administrative systems of spatial separation' (1998: 55). This contradiction produces a series of more complex geographical strategies that are complicit with the foundation of an infrastructure of discrimination, separation and segregation, and 'the practical application' of these 'spatial forms' would go on to provide 'the structures which the apartheid ideologues would seek to consolidate' (Lester, 1998: 83).

These contradictions, already at play in *King Solomon's Mines*, also surface in some critically under-read segments of Schreiner's fictional and non-fictional writings as they turn to South Africa's industrialising and urbanising centres. Turning to the only novel that Schreiner published during her lifetime, *The Story of an African Farm* (1883), the chapter then explores the way in which it shifts the perspectival and geographical focus of the imperial romance so as to originate in, and emerge from, a peripheral zone within the capitalist world-system. This spatial reorientation allows Schreiner's novel to produce a subversive meta-narrative that deconstructs, if not actually resists, the linear narrative of the imperial romance. The chapter concludes with William Plomer's short story, 'Ula Masondo', which not only continues Schreiner's ideological work by laying the thematic and formal groundwork for a radical turn to the production of South Africa's urban space, but does so through its engagement with, and illumination of, the implicit politics of the romance genre. It is for this reason that, at this stage, I draw on James C. Scott's terminologies of 'hidden' and 'public transcripts' – the former used 'to characterise a discourse that takes place "offstage", beyond direct observation by powerholders', the latter as 'a short-hand way of describing the open interaction between subordinates and those who dominate' (1990: 2–5). The accumulation of mineral resources and the assimilation of colonised populations into a cross-national labour force are inscribed into what Scott would call the 'infrapolitics' of the imperial romance, an 'unobtrusive realm of political struggle' that, though 'beyond the visible end of the spectrum', are detectable when these texts are read infrastructurally (183). Of course, the resistance embedded within Schreiner's and Plomer's writing is by no means direct, complete or unproblematic, but they do gain much of their political gravity through their intertextual – if not inter-geographical and inter-infrastructural – relationship with the romance. They throw the 'discrepancy *between* the hidden transcript and the public transcript' into relief, a spatial dislocation that makes visible the romance's ideological limits (5). Indeed, Plomer's radical re-writing of the romance might be considered a 'public declaration of the hidden transcript', the 'mobilising capacity' of which, argues Scott, 'as a symbolic act is potentially awesome' (227).

The Infrastructure of the Imperial Romance:
King Solomon's Mines

Recalling his role in Britain's first attempt to annex the Transvaal on 12 April 1877, a peaceful and anti-climactic affair that took place in the empty Market Square of Pretoria, Rider Haggard felt that 'for the moment I was the representative of England' (Haggard, 1926: 105; Packenham, 2009: 40–41). Through his extensive journalistic and fictional writings, Haggard would go on to contribute to the structural formation of a 'recognisable' imperialist ideology (Katz, 1987: 29). The importance of Haggard's romance writing in the production of South African geography for the metropolitan imagination is evident from contemporaneous reviews of *King Solomon's Mines*, many of which praised the supposed verisimilitude of its descriptions: 'Haggard is so correct in his descriptive touches and pictures of African life', wrote one, while another commended 'the writer's acquaintance with African scenery and manners' that gave 'reality and vigour to his pages' (Haggard, 2002: 246, 251). Haggard's 'social and historical raw material' – Southern Africa – was inextricably linked to the 'generic model' that he pioneered: as another reviewer commented, Haggard had 'shown the old distinction between the novel and the romance' (249). This inter-relationship between the infrastructure *of* the text and the formal and generic structures of its narrative follow Jameson's conception of genre, one that is not directly 'causal', but is rather 'a limiting situation: the historical moment is here understood to block off or shut down a certain number of formal possibilities available' (2002: 134–135). It is not my intention to reveal 'the "causes" of a given text or form' – in this case, the historical reasons *why King Solomon's Mines* is an imperial romance – but rather to map its 'a priori conditions of possibility' (2002: 134–135). Read in this way, it becomes possible to get closer to what the romance performs ideologically as a cultural fix. Again, I argue that his is most effectively achieved by focusing on the occurrence of infrastructure *in* the text, as it enables Haggard to produce a Southern African geography that bears the imprint of imperial ideology in its contours.

Haggard returned to Britain on 1 September 1881 after just a few years in the colony, never to return. Haggard's geographical distance from the

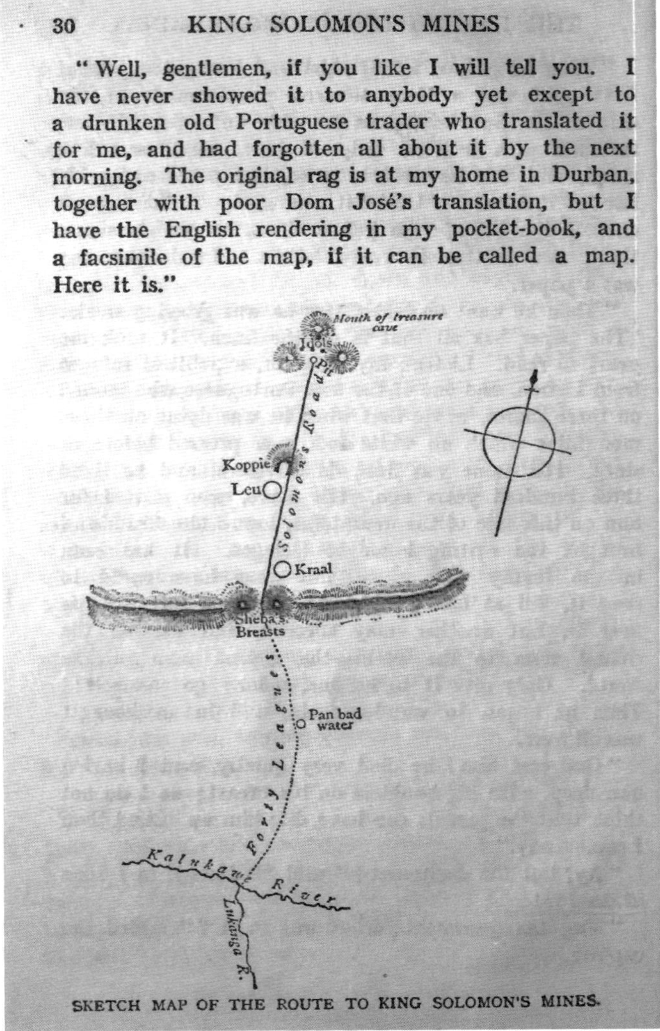

Figure 2.2: The map included in the opening pages of H. Rider Haggard's
King Solomon's Mines.

landscape that *King Solomon's Mines* describes is surely significant. As Thomas Pocock observes, Southern Africa could continue to exist 'in his imagination' as he looked out on 'the oaks and elms of the Norfolk countryside' (1993: 53). On returning to England, Haggard was considered, and considered himself, an authority on Southern African affairs. He wrote articles for *The South African* magazine, sent letters to *The Standard* and *St James Gazette* newspapers and regularly purchased the Government's 'Blue Book' reports to supplement his knowledge of the region (56–57). Removed from what Mary Louise Pratt would call the 'contact zone' (2003: 8), in his literary writing Haggard was able to occlude the physical realities and indigenous populations that did not accord with the metropolitan imagination of Southern Africa. However, mapping these occlusions can in turn reveal some of the deepest contradictions of imperial ideology, a process best achieved by reading the infrastructural traces *in* the text as clues to the infrastructures *of* it.

The map that appears in the first few pages of *King Solomon's Mines* details a plot trajectory that will structure the novel's entire narrative arc (Haggard, 2008: 21). This map has received much critical attention, predominantly for its 'explicitly sexualised' representation of the South African landscape (Stott, 1989: 77–79; McClintock, 1995: 1–4). Despite its apparent simplicity ('the single, one-dimensional line that has been the standard sign of African explorations in map after map' (Moretti, 1998: 58)), this is in fact a deeply layered document. When set within its historical context, the map does more than 'open up' the landscape to the 'landscanning European eye' (Pratt, 2003: 60), though this it certainly does. The 'linear plot' of *King Solomon's Mines*, as with other imperial romances, narrates the extraction of resources (in this case 'diamonds') located in the 'treasure cave' and their release onto 'the world market' (Moretti, 1998: 61–62). However, it also concludes with a segregationist geography that divides the novel's white and black populations, inscribed into the map via the mountain range that cuts it horizontally in half. The novel's ideological predicates are, quite literally then, written into, and can be read out of, the map's contours. However, if the Southern African landscape is divided here into core and peripheral zones, it is not between the segments of landscape located either side of Sheba's Breasts. Rather, a networked conception of the world-system means that, as for Flora Annie Steel's 'Permanent Way', Solomon's Road *itself* functions as the 'core', with the large vacant expanses to its east and west functioning as relationally peripheral zones. The infrastructural route along which Haggard's protagonists move enables the assimilation of the landscape's mineral resources – its 'treasures' – into the world-system at the end of the novel: Haggard's characters return with such wealth that they have to 'sell by degrees for fear we should flood the market' (2008: 198).

The infrastructural line of Solomon's Road functions as a Lefebvrian 'symbolic object' (1998: 39), allowing the novel's protagonists both to make sense of the African landscape and to reap its material rewards. By invoking this 'skeletal landscape', the map offers a framework that keeps the novel 'on track', a literary infrastructure that the narrative can then flesh out (Chang, 1998: 43–44). As Robert Tally observes, just as the 'plot' of a narrative 'is also a plan, which is to say, a map', this map is simultaneously the plot, 'establishing [its] setting, setting [its] course' (2013: 49). Similarly, to 'colonise', argues Mitchell, it is 'necessary "to determine a plan"', to make the landscape 'readable, like a book' (1988: 33). Quartermain, Haggard's narrator-protagonist, decides that 'the best plan would be to tell the story in a plain, straightforward manner, and leave [other] matters to be dealt with subsequently in whatever way may ultimately appear to be desirable' (2008: 7–8). The 'plan' is indeed 'straightforward'; straight and forward along the line so clearly demarcated on the map, cutting through the landscape it will go on to depict. Quartermain's reference to the subsequent dealings of other matters, such as contrasts between 'Zulu and Kukuana dialects' and the 'magnificent system of military organisation in force in that country' (7), alludes to the potential that this text might itself become a map upon which future representations of Southern Africa may draw: the text predicts its own entry into the creation of 'a field of textual genres' that creates 'ways of seeing' the colonised landscape (Chang, 1998: 57).

However, implicit in the invasive confidence of its linearity – or as Quartermain describes it, his 'blunt way of writing' (Haggard, 2008: 47) – is an acknowledgement of the limitations of the narrative's geographical scope, one that reveals its 'mapping project' to be 'incomplete, provisional, and tentative' (Tally, 2013: 53). Returning to Macherey, the imperial romance's 'linear simplicity' should in fact be understood as the text's 'most superficial aspect' (1986: 39). By providing the 'answers' to his novel so early on in the narrative – the inevitable culminations of the plot (resource extraction, racial segregation) as inscribed on the map – the 'question which gave rise' to this goal is 'ignored': as Macherey continues, 'concealed under the answers, the question is rapidly forgotten' (8–9). Indeed, not only is the quest to seek out Sir Henry's brother quickly forgotten, a plot device that is, of course, absent from the map. The historical tensions that shaped Haggard's experience of South Africa also remain largely omitted from the geographical space that the novel produces. These absences are primarily orientated around, first, infrastructural development, introduced in order to facilitate mineral resource extraction and the industrialisation of new mining centres; and second, the prevalence of violent resistance from African tribes that posed a dangerous threat to British rule throughout Haggard's time in South Africa.

It is no coincidence that the line that runs through the centre of Haggard's map – 'Solomon's Road' – is a physical infrastructure embedded within the landscape, leading directly to a mine in which diamonds and gold are buried. After its appearance on the map, Solomon's 'great white road' recurs with systematic regularity throughout the text as Haggard's protagonists progress along it (Haggard, 2008: 47). It reorientates and reveals the economic focus of imperialism by providing the invading characters with a set of material coordinates. As Paul Carter observes, the 'straight line' presupposes the possession of a 'goal' (2002: 39). This goal allows Haggard's imperialists always to locate or relocate themselves in relation to the *somewhere* – in this case, Solomon's mine – at which they are bound to 'arrive'. After all, the 'white ribbon of Solomon's great road', like the novel's plot, finds its 'terminus' in a chapter entitled 'The Place of Death'; death being the final culmination of the narrative's progression, the 'goal' to which, from the introduction of the map at its very start, it has been ceaselessly moving towards (2008: 158).

Though the mythological road has not actually been built by British imperialists, it is described by Quartermain within the terms of imperial infrastructural development. 'As for the road itself, I never saw such an engineering work', he comments, concluding that '[n]o difficulty had been too great for the Old World engineer who designed it' (69). There is no topographical feature that this infrastructural route cannot traverse: in places it is 'cut in zigzags out of the side of a precipice five hundred feet deep', whilst in others it 'tunnelled right through the base of an intervening ridge a space of thirty yards or more' (69). Sir Henry compares it to 'the great road over the St. Gothard [*sic*] in Switzerland', an engineering project that built a 'carriage road' between Switzerland and Italy in the 1820s and tunnelled through the mountains in the 1870s (69, 207). This comparison with what was, at the time, one of Europe's most impressive infrastructural feats, the fact that it is eventually attributed to an ancient white civilisation, and even the very colour of the road itself – 'white' (47, 161) – alludes to contemporaneous imperial infrastructural development whilst also, as Etherington notes, discounting 'African ability' (1978: 75). If the text functions 'as an outlet for fears of African resistance', however, Chrisman observes that there is also inscribed within the infrastructure of the now abandoned, racially white empire of King Solomon, 'a reversal of imperial practice' (2000: 38). Besides its infrastructural legacy, the Phoenician civilisation to which the construction of the road is credited has disappeared and only black Africans remain. Focusing on infrastructure here reveals the novel's subtextual postulation that 'Africans have erased imperialist history' (38). The anti-imperial resistance that the text rediscovers through its encounter with ancient infrastructure is refracted specifically through the labour relations introduced by the mining industry in the 1860s and 1870s. As Chrisman continues, the 'threat to the Zimbabwean mines of the past was from African slave labour and/or marauding "Bantu" peoples' (2000: 46), as the novel uneasily establishes 'ideological connections' between the ancient 'practice of mining and that of present South Africa' (34).

These 'ideological connections' are historically unsurprising. In 1881, during Haggard's final months in the region, the formation of a host of joint-stock companies brought the era of independent diggers to an end. As Martin Meredith observes, the 'rush to invest in joint-stock companies was as hectic as the original diamond rush of the 1870s' (2008: 107). By 1885, the year of *King Solomon's Mines'* publication, the first railways extended some 1,000 kilometres inland from the Cape to Kimberley, opening up the South African interior for the first time and operating as the 'vehicle for imperial expansionism' (Griffiths, 1995: 35). These new infrastructures, combined with the reinvigorated interest in the extraction of diamonds from the Kimberley mines, permeate Haggard's text despite its attempts to produce a Southern African geography devoid of the historical realities of industrialisation. His questing trio are, after all, 'independent' diggers, detached from any governmental or corporate cross-national organisation. Haggard conspicuously attempts to write 'the activity of trade', its 'association with urbanism' and 'profiteering' and its implications of 'industrial and financial capitalism' *out* of the novel's literary geography (Chrisman, 2000: 49). Furthermore, the infrastructure in and around the mines was itself, in Kimberley and then later Johannesburg, constructed according to the 'growth and slump' of 'cycles of speculation', resulting in 'unevenly developed districts' and 'unevenly joined parcels of real estate' that 'eluded' the rational ordering of other colonial cities: 'speculation rather than orderly planning ruled the day' (Kruger, 2013: 3–4; Turrell, 1982: 57–58). Infrastructures were left to decay as investors speculated on more lucrative plots and geographical zones, juggling the tension between 'pressing transportation needs and the impossible economics of railroads' (Headrick, 1981: 193). In this sense, the abandoned infrastructural vein that runs through the literary landscape of *King Solomon's Mines*, when set within its historical context, alludes to the uneven infrastructural development of the world-system, as the text attempts to fix culturally one of its fundamental economic contradictions.

Haggard's infrastructural line thus becomes an ideological border upon which the genre's project of geographical romanticisation hinges, gesturing towards the 'political unconscious' of the text (Jameson, 2002: 32). Contemporaneous maps demonstrate that infrastructural lines – and railways in particular – were central to the configuration of both Southern African and Indian space, promoting a culture of profitable resource extraction that *King Solomon's Mines* both drew on and perpetuated. These lines of transport and communication run between colonial ports and the mining centres of Kimberley and the Witwatersrand through what is depicted as an otherwise empty landscape, 'redirecting the local economy *outwards*: towards the sea, the metropolis, the world market' (Moretti, 1998: 61). However, the resulting industrialisation of areas such as Kimberley – the first cycle of production took place between 1877 and 1885 – had resulted in 'the extensive acquisition of fixed capital in the form of steam machinery' and 'the intensification of labour exploitation' in the region (Turrell, 1982: 57). Previously 'empty' spaces on the map were increasingly enmeshed into complex infrastructural webs, processes that betray the uneven contradictions and crises of the world-system.

In response, Haggard's romance writes these industrialising centres out of its literary geographies not only to smooth over the challenges that infrastructural development posed to the metropole's conception of Southern Africa as an redemptive, romanticised geography. It also registers the cyclical processes of capital investment: 'the collapse of the European diamond market in late 1882 [and] the impact of the economic depression began to be felt seriously in Kimberley' in the years leading up to the publication of *King Solomon's Mines* (Turrell, 1982: 58). The novel's depiction of abandoned imperial mining infrastructure extrapolates into ancient history the local effects of global capital's uneven investment cycles. In addition, the significant increase in cheaper African (rather than European or Coloured) labour 'between 1881 and 1884' resulted in spatial proximities that threatened ideologies of racial segregation (58), anxieties reflected in Haggard's literary geography. The novel's imperial protagonists leave black Kukuanaland behind, segregated from Kimberley and the Cape Colony; as Quartermain writes, 'I need hardly state that we never again penetrated into Solomon's treasure chamber' (2008: 187). But despite the ideological resolution – or cultural fix – of the text's conclusion, the historical realities and ramifications of infrastructural development remain embedded, albeit mythologically, within the novel's underlying cartographic project.

It is, then, a focus on the ancient imperial infrastructure *in* the text that foregrounds the infrastructures *of* it. The mine to which the road leads is repeatedly compared to those found in Kimberley: 'the formation is the same', observes Quartermain, as he superimposes his prior experience as a trader in Kimberley's 'Diamond Fields' onto 'Solomon's Diamond Mine'

(Haggard, 2008: 11, 156, 160). However, it is not only 'diamonds' that, at least initially, Solomon's mines yield:

> On the opposite side of the chamber were about a score of wooden boxes, something like Martini-Henry ammunition boxes, only rather larger, and painted red. [...] Pushing my hand through the hole in the lid I drew it out full, not of diamonds, but of gold pieces. (171–172)

The earliest discoveries of gold on the Witwatersrand dated back to the 1850s, whilst the 'first significant gold deposits in a reef formation' were 'uncovered in the Barberton district in 1884' (Beavon, 2004: 20). Rumours of these discoveries fed 'speculation about the likelihood that even richer gold deposits would be found' (Meredith, 2008: 207). As these were extensively covered throughout the 1870s by the colonial press and 'Blue Books', Haggard was undoubtedly aware of these developments in the Transvaal – indeed, Quartermain himself mentions the settlers 'in what is now the Lydenburg district of the Transvaal' who have 'again lately been prospecting for gold' (Haggard, 2008: 17). *King Solomon's Mines* itself then popularised, and was itself made more popular by, the culture of speculation that flourished when formal discoveries were made in 1886, just a year after the novel's publication. This is evidenced by its prolific publication history: at least one new edition, in some cases more, appeared almost every year between 1885 and 1926. Indeed, Haggard made some revealing amendments to the Revised New Illustrated Edition, first published in 1905. Whereas in the 1885 edition Quartermain grabs only 'a couple of handfuls' of diamonds (2008: 181), in the 1905 reissue he also picks up an empty basket and fills that 'with great quantities of the stones' as well (212), despite the threat to his life that such a decision poses. He lays 'down the basket, wishing to be rid of its weight, but on second thoughts took it up again. One might as well die rich as poor, I reflected' (212). Haggard increases his protagonist's imperial appetite for Southern Africa's material wealth to accord historically with speculative interest in the region. Capitalist relations infiltrate more intensely into Haggard's fictional text, reflecting the culture of finance capitalism and speculation as they manifested materially in infrastructural developments around the Witwatersrand gold mines in the two decades intervening the publication of the first and revised editions.

Racial Segregation and the Cape to Cairo Railway

Embedded within *King Solomon's Mines* is a trace of the mineral wealth that transformed the physical and social geography of Southern Africa in such explosive and violent ways. The significance of the gold buried in King Solomon's mine, when extracted from the bare geology of the text and situated in a richer historical topography, comes to the fore. Gold became the economic foundation for twentieth-century South Africa's most spatially constrictive and politically contested urban space: the 'edgy city' of Johannesburg (Kruger, 2013). Nevertheless, a cartography of segregation lurks within the infrastructure, both *in* and *of, King Solomon's Mines*, one that proliferates especially when the novel is analysed through the lens of African resistance to imperialism. Dennis Butts charts the geography of *King Solomon's Mines* against the map that accompanied the first publication of Fred Selous's *A Hunter's Wanderings in South Africa* (1881), a British explorer on whom, it has been suggested, Quartermain's character may be based (Haggard, 2008: 200–202). As discussed in the introduction, the prevalence of British cartography 'burgeoned' from the 1850s onwards, operating, like Haggard's fictional map, to legitimise 'European penetration of Africa' and rendering its material wealth both accessible and retrievable (Carruthers, 2003: 990). By the 1870s, however, the Transvaal government, in an attempt to seek out 'precious minerals and mining leases', began 'encouraging its own cartographical reconnaissance' (968). Friedrich Jeppe, a young German cartographer whose political allegiances were ambiguous, but who was certainly not opposed to the British annexation of the Transvaal, led this cartographic exercise. His 1877 map of the Transvaal, which first appeared in the *Journal of the Royal Geographical Society* and that is reproduced here, was a comprehensive depiction of the region and included insets of street plans of Pretoria and Delagoa Bay, as well as illustrations of Great Zimbabwe that, it has been argued, inspired Haggard's own fictionalised ancient infrastructures (Etherington, 1978: 74). Its success was such that it was subsequently used in the 1877 Blue Book, entitled *Correspondence Respecting the War between the Transvaal Republic and Neighbouring Native Tribes* (Carruthers, 2003: 970–971).

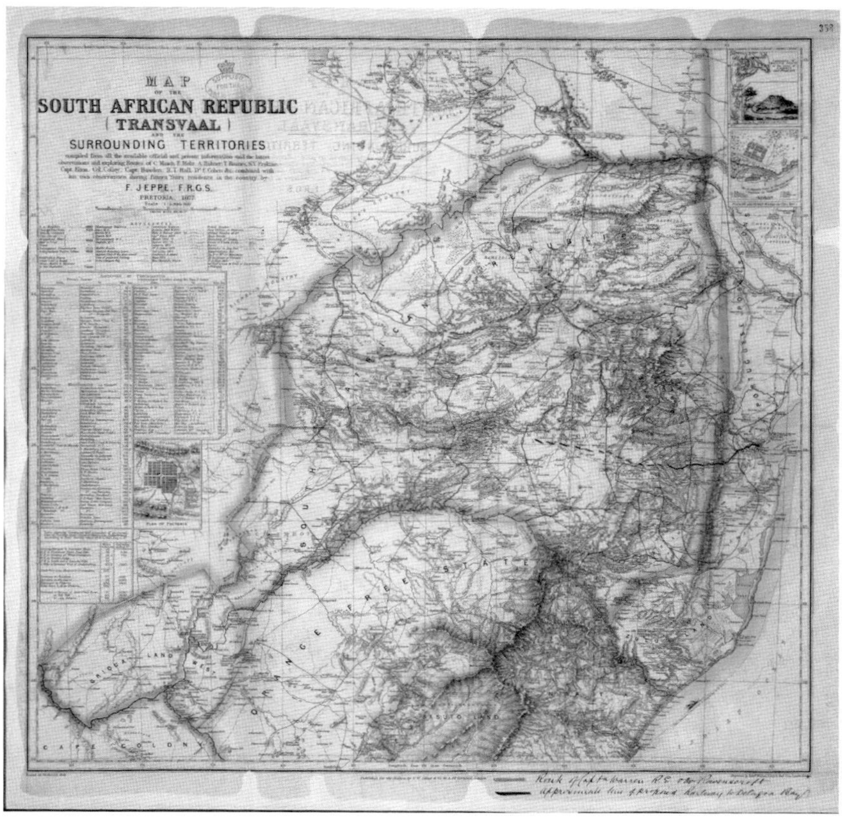

Figure 2.3: The map of the South African Republic, particularly Pretoria and the Transvaal as well as surrounding territories, by Friedrich Jeppe, produced for the Royal Geographical Society in 1877. MPG 1/1119/3, National Archives at Kew.

Haggard's voracious consumption of Blue Books makes it likely that he was acquainted with this document, the title of which registers ongoing anti-imperial resistance. In his autobiography, written in 1926, whilst recalling his 'leisurely progress over the plains, the mountains, and the vast rolling high veld of the Transvaal territory', Haggard also noted the 'great danger with which the Transvaal was threatened in 1877': a 'Zulu attack' (Haggard, 1926: 76, 80). The memories of his time in Africa, recorded in *The Days of My Life*, are littered with acts of deadly Zulu resistance, culminating in the 'disaster at Isandhlwana' (1926: 145), when the Zulus responded to British troops marching into Zululand by attacking Lord Chelmsford's column, killing 858 white men and 471 blacks (see Afigbo et al., 1986a: 278–279; and Packenham, 2009: 70). These acts of anti-imperial violence left a strong impression upon Haggard:

> One of the last things that happened before I left South Africa was the slaying of the Prince Imperial by a Zulu outpost. Well can I remember the thrill of horror, and, I may add, of shame, that this news sent through all the land. [...] Nothing is more terrible than a sudden rush of savages on a little party that does not suspect their presence, especially when the attacking force may perhaps be numbered by the hundreds. (1926: 145)

Against this historical backdrop, the presence of black Africans in *King Solomon's Mines* is significant. Blank spaces dominate Haggard's map, 'holes in the net' that exist between those places that are 'marked, noted, named' (Lefebvre, 1998: 118), or 'marginal spaces' that allude to the 'indeterminate social struggles' – the *spatial resistance* – with which 'the production of space and place is shot through' (Harvey, 2009: 194). Haggard's text removes Africans from the landscape of the Transvaal of all native presence, conspicuously ignoring the violent uprisings that were so pervasive during his time there. If Quartermain does recall that he 'had been one of Lord Chelmsford's guides in the unlucky Zulu War, and had had the good fortune to leave the camp in charge of some waggons the day before the battle' (Haggard, 2008: 33), by the time of the fictional quest, the landscape is deserted. In the second paragraph of an early chapter, entitled 'Our March into the Desert', Quartermain observes:

> [There was] a scattered native settlement with a few stone cattle kraals and some cultivated lands down by the water, where these savages grew their scanty supply of grain, and beyond it great tracts of waving 'veldt' covered with tall grass, over which herds of the smaller game were wandering. To the left was the vast desert. This spot appeared to be the outpost of the fertile country. (2008: 44)

At this 'outpost of the fertile country', the border of the Transvaal, there is an extended description of a black African presence, their crops and herds peacefully inhabiting the landscape. However, 'the Kaffir kraals are merely part of the beautiful wilderness' (Low, 1996: 76), and the physical existence of an African population is carefully written out of the landscape. Haggard's novel is conspicuously silent 'about the place of the black man in the pastoral idyll'; as J. M. Coetzee observes of white South African writing more generally, 'its truth lies in what it dare not say for the sake of its own safety' (1980: 81).

When a black population is eventually encountered, the party have successfully traversed an almost impassable geographical boundary. As Chrisman observes in her comparison of the Zulus and Haggard's fictional Kukuana tribes – a comparison invited by Quartermain himself (Haggard, 2008: 7) – the 'key to their difference is geography. [...] where the Zulu are connected to white South Africa, the Kukuana are isolated from it' (2000: 68–69). Inscribed into the novel's production of space, Chrisman argues, is 'an ideology of separatism: segregation of African and white society' (70).[1] But despite this, a closer look at *King Solomon's Mines* reveals that the text itself confesses the limitations of its segregationist ideology, embedded in the partiality of its geographical knowledge. As early as Chapter V, Quartermain concedes that their party's 'future' is 'completely unknown' (2008: 50). A page later, Captain Good whistles a popular British marching song that originated during the Napoleonic Wars (with symbolically imperial connotations), but that, in this landscape, fails to reignite his imperial zeal: his patriotic 'notes' begin to sound 'lugubrious in that vast place, and he gave it up' (51). It becomes 'evident that no great faith could be put in the map' and, as Quartermain surveys the landscape, he admits that 'language seems to fail me. I am impotent even before its memory' (56–57). In a revealing use of spatial terminology, the

---

1   Gail Low similarly reads the demands made of Ignosi, who at the text's conclusion becomes the African ruler of Kukuanaland, 'to rule justly, to respect the law, and to put none to death without cause' (Haggard, 2008: 189), as 'comparable with the changes brought about by the formations of Locations in contemporary Southern Africa' (1996: 83).

geographical space becomes increasingly 'beyond' Quartermain's 'power to explain' (61).

Haggard's ideologically consolidated cartography in fact a 'fictive resolution of ideological conflicts', one 'so precarious that it is obvious in the very letter of the text' (Macherey, 1986: 155). Graham Huggan has shown how maps often appear as a 'frontispiece', 'directing the reader's attention towards the importance of geographical location in the text that follows, but also supplying the reader with a referential guide to the text' (1994: 21). However, as Huggan continues, the juxtaposition of two mediums – the visual and the verbal – actually invites the reader to consider, if not interrogate, 'the duplicating procedures of mimetic representation' (21–22), throwing the ideologies embedded within each medium into relief. It is through the discrepancies between map and narrative – one professing clarity of vision, the other confessing its limitations – that it becomes possible to draw forth the 'infrapolitics' of Haggard's literary geography (Scott, 1990: 183). Haggard's implicit ideological strategies crystallise when, constrained by its linear infrastructure, the narrative admits to the spatial limitations of its cartographic practice, or what Said would call its 'consolidated vision' (1993: 204). Indeed, the Zulu threat was nowhere more explicit than in, or rather on, the novel's first edition, published by Cassell & Company in 1885: the cover of this original publication bore not only the title and author's name, but also a design of a Zulu shield, weapons and elephant tusk (Monsman, 2002: 11–12). The text that sought to write the threat of violent Zulu resistance out of the Southern African landscape was itself shrouded in the symbolic presence of that polity.

Chrisman is correct to assert that the novel's concluding racial geography is invested with 'an ideology of separatism' (70). However, this simplistic geographical division fails to negotiate the realities of an unevenly developing world-system which, as Wallerstein argues, needed 'to keep the oppressed groups inside the system' as its stratified labour force, 'not expel them' (2011: 103). Friedrich Jeppe's cartographic career, whilst reflecting Haggard's concerns in the late 1870s and early 1880s, exemplifies an increasingly complex spatial politics of segregation taking plce in

South Africa at this time. Between 1871 and 1875 there were already some 50,000 'natives from the interior' arriving in Kimberley each year. The gold mines on the Witwatersrand employed only 15,000 Africans in 1890, but this would increase to 105,027 in 1907 and to 189,253 by 1912 (Turrell, 1982: 47, 83). Where Jeppe had, like Haggard, written the African presence out of his early depictions of South African space, his last map of the region, produced in 1899, demarcated distinct African reserves to which, as noted earlier, repeated legislations would confine the black population throughout the early years of the twentieth century (Carruthers, 2003: 974). The geography of segregation mapped out in *King Solomon's Mines* – white settlers colonising the southern peninsula and coastlines, black Africans exiled and isolated in the northern interior – was replaced with a much more complex patchwork of contested political boundaries and unevenly developed economic zones. It was not only that the industrialising centres of Kimberley and the Witwatersrand were now home to thousands of black migrant labourers from the North. In the 1890s, under the guidance of Cecil Rhodes and his Charter Company, white settlers moved towards the interior from the South, following Haggard's fictional 'roadway, which headed steadily in a north-westerly direction' (Haggard, 2008: 78) and establishing Southern Rhodesia after a bloody war won with the Maxim gun in 1893 (Packenham, 2009: 384). Lobengula, who Quartermain dismisses rhetorically as 'a great scoundrel' (Haggard, 2008: 36), 'fled to die in exile', leaving the new country to consolidate itself as 'a northwards extension of the South African system of white domination' (Afigbo et al., 1986b: 233–234).

It was at this historical moment that perhaps the most powerfully symbolic infrastructural line of the period was conceived by Rhodes: a railroad that spanned the entire African continent to connect its southern tip in Cape Town to Cairo in Egypt. For Rhodes, railways were the 'girders of empire, weapons used to revitalise imperial hegemony' (Wilburn, 1991: 28). This intended infrastructural line would span some 9,600 kilometres, cutting through and linking up all 'territories coloured red on the map', and became a crucial cartographic coordinate in the British imperial imagination (Griffiths, 1995: 38). Rhodes sought speculative investment for 'my railway to Egypt, my telegraph to Egypt' (Rhodes, 2000: 143–144), giving speeches that compared the infrastructural developments taking place in Africa's northern and southern segments:

> I look upon this Bechuanaland territory as the Suez Canal of the trade of this country, the key of its road to the interior. [...] The question before us really is this, whether this Colony is to be confined to its present borders, or whether it is to become the dominant state in South Africa – whether, in fact, it is to spread its civilisation over the interior. [...] What did we build railways for? To secure the trade of the interior. Suppose we lie down oppressed with present difficulties, and say, 'We will not extend our railways any further; our liabilities are too great, and we will do no more.' [...] I claim the development of the interior as the birthright of this Colony. (Rhodes, 1900: 62–67)

Rhodes references that other avenue of trade, the Suez Canal, located at the northernmost tip of the Cape to Cairo project, to justify economically imperial infrastructural development northward from the South. With its 'severe straight lines and high banks', the Canal was depicted as cut off from the 'more fluidly rendered desert', propagating 'the idea that technology itself was Western, even before technology became a fully-fledged concept' (Murray, 2008: 1). Drawing on this ideology of infrastructural supremacy and the rhetoric of 'civilisation', Rhodes himself alludes to the material infrastructures *of* his imperial ambitions in the same speech: 'We know that all sorts of "fuel" are said to be in the country, and Imperial interference in Bechuanaland would be one source of fuel' (66). This fuel, recorded in suggestive inverted commas, references the black labour that Rhodes intended to secure for the thriving mining industries, their workforce providing an economic motor upon which the new South African nation would be founded. For Rhodes, mining capital would drive the nation's prosperity and geographical expansion as it (re)enmeshed the continent – through infrastructural and communication routes such as the Cape to Cairo railway and its accompanying telegraph – unevenly into the world-system.[2]

2   This was not a new 'enmeshing', since Africa had been on the periphery of the world-system and subject to the development of underdevelopment 'ever since slavery', which itself required 'development funds [...] necessary for more efficient exploitation in the

The British South Africa Company's extension of the railway system from Cape Town into the 'interior', depicted in the period's proliferation of maps of the region, strategically bypassed the political borders of the then Dutch-ruled Orange Free State and Transvaal. This infrastructure became not 'merely a reflection of [a] political vision', to use Weizman's words; rather, 'the folds, deformations, stretches, wrinkles and bends in the route' plotted out 'the influences' of different political and economic interests (2012: 162). The arterial route fed into numerous other lines of demarcation, including projected railways and telegraphs, as well as a patchwork of political borders ruled by different sovereignties, all of which broke up and shaped the landscape: 'through a complex web of mines, railways, and land developments, the Company maintained its economic hegemony over both Northern and Southern Rhodesia' (Hanes, 1991: 52).

Exemplifying the symbolic impact of these processes is a colossal five-volume tribute to Rhodes entitled *The Story of the Cape to Cairo Railway and River Route, 1886–1922*, edited and compiled by Leo Weinthal (also then Chief Editor of the journal, *The African World*) in 1922. More than forty-five literary and journalistic writers contributed to the first volume alone, resulting in a mammoth documentary work that compiled maps, poems, extracts from prose literature, newspapers, journal articles and photographs to chart the linear narrative-geographical progression of the Cape to Cairo railway – even though, as Peter Merrington observes, by the early 1920s Britain's imperial and political purchase in South Africa was beginning to wane (2001: 353). The volumes moves northwards through the African landscape, with photographs of and literary tributes to key infrastructures when and where they were under construction, building a narrative of historical and geographical continuity around landmark infra-structural projects such as the 'Iron Link', the great bridge over the Zambezi river. The narrative's clustering around these infrastructural achievements root the text physically in an explicitly 'conquered' terrain, whilst the reali-ties of pre-existing African territories are conspicuous by in their absence.

---

long run', though these investments did remain mostly restricted to the continent's coastline (Rodney, 2012: 212–214).

Figure 2.4: The bronze statue of Cecil Rhodes at the centre of the University of Cape Town's campus with Kipling's words inscribed in the stone beneath, removed in 2015 in response to protests led by the Rhodes Must Fall movement. Photo by the author.

Though, as Merrington argues, Weinthal's project is 'a postwar nostalgic fantasy' that 'constantly if unintentionally' pronounces the 'artificiality' of the Cape to Cairo idea (2001: 353), Rhodes's imperial infrastructural ambitions remained, until very recently, fossilised in the centrepiece of the University of Cape Town's campus. From 1934 until 2015, a pondering bronze statue of Cecil Rhodes gazed out across the Cape Flats, the colonial gaze of the 1880s and '90s surverying its 'Empire to the northward' – words that, belonging to Kipling, were quite literally inscribed into the foundation stones of the university.[3]

> Hail! snatched and bartered oft from hand to hand.
>   I dream my dream, by rock and heath and pine,
> Of Empire to the northward. Aye, one land
>   From Lion's Head to Line! (2006: 139–140)

The words come from Kipling's 'The Song of the Cities', a poem that celebrates the emerging international network of imperial urban hubs by offering four-line impressions of each one, encapsulating an emerging, infrastructurally interconnected world-empire in a few succinct lines of rhyme. In this verse, Kipling's lines look north from 'Lion's Head', the distinctive cone-shaped peak that stands beside Table Mountain, up into the African continent to the equatorial 'Line', envisioning Rhodes's dream of 'one land' stretched out in between – the architectural layout of statue and verse suggested that the 'I' was indeed Rhodes himself. As contemporaneous South African newspapers demonstrate, in the final years of the nineteenth century the colonial geographical imagination wove itself around the symbolic and alliterative infrastructural route. Plomer, to whom I will return later in this chapter, commented on the railway's imaginative

---

3   It is important to recall that, as discussed at greater length in the introduction to this book, the 'manufactured historical narrative' of which this statue was arguably the 'most conspicuous feature' has not only been recognised in recent years, but actively contested by decolonial movements such as the Rhodes Must Fall campaign (Kros, 2015: 152).

attraction in his satirical biography of Rhodes. Quoting the journalist
W. T. Stead, he wrote in 1933:

> If the Cape and Cairo had possessed different initials, the suggestion of a through
> continental line might never have suggested itself to Mr Rhodes. But the notion
> of linking the two places, each of which commenced with the same capital letter,
> 'caught on', and the gigantic enterprise is already making progress from the realm of
> the imagination into the domain of accomplished fact. (Plomer, 1984b: 142)

The Cape to Cairo railway, sections of which were realised as 'accomplished
fact' whilst others existed only in the imperial 'imagination', was arguably
one of imperialism's most potent 'symbolic objects' during this period, and
certainly an indicative one. Maps of an African continent carved in two by
one linear, uninterrupted infrastructural route, 'erases and hides the contested, political, representational nature of the world it portrays' (Mitchell,
2002: 117). Meanwhile, as Weinthal's volume demonstrates, accompanying
narratives about and photographs of the occasional infrastructural success
or completed project embedded an ideology of progress and 'civilisation'
physically in the landscape. The alliterative slogan thus concisely smoothed
over the contradictions of imperialism's deeply uneven and exploitative
infrastructural development that disregarded pre-existing social formations and indigenous populations, and bracketed the entire continent as a
British possession during a time of intense imperial rivalry.

An *infrastructural reading* of Haggard's ancient 'white road', when
linked to Rhodes's Cape to Cairo project, reveals the latter's ideological contours as they were lent further virility through the verbal circuitries of Kipling's verse. Haggard's geography of racial segregation, with
its entrenched topographical boundaries and simplistic binary divisions, attempted to smooth over the contradiction created by the mining
industry's violent appetite for black labour and the prospect of profitable
resources in the 'interior'. Rhodes himself was well aware of these spatial
contradictions and the segregationist technologies necessary to contain
them. He talked of the need to unify the various British protectorates and
Boer States before he could embark upon his arch-imperial infrastructural
project: 'if you were to go up in a balloon', he commented in 1899, on the
eve of the Anglo-Boer War, 'how ridiculous it would appear to you to

see all these divided States, divided tariffs, divided peoples [...] you can draw imaginary lines but we are all one' (2000: 143–144). Yet the region's infrastructural development undermines this rhetorical wish for a unified South African state. The physical layout alone of his infrastructural projects reveal that they served the economic interests of only a few cross-national capitalists, rather than the peaceful unification of the region under British imperial rule. As Hobson commented in 1900, Rhodes used 'the money of the British taxpayer to obtain for himself and his fellow-capitalists that political control of the Transvaal which was essential to his economical and political ambitions', waging the Anglo-Boer (or South African) War 'in order to secure for the mines a cheap adequate supply of labour' (1900: 206–207, 231).

Though calling for the eradication of political 'borders', Rhodes was not interested in deconstructing 'barriers'. As Weizman reflects, '[b]arriers are indeed different to borders: they do not separate the "inside" of a sovereign, political or legal system from a foreign "outside", but act as contingent structures to prevent movement across territory' (2012: 172). The infrastructural practices of Rhodes's diamond cartel, De Beers – a monopoly formation that, for Lenin, had 'at the end of the nineteenth century [...] become one of the foundations of the whole of economic life' under cross-national capitalism (1987: 183) – developed systems of spatial control. In a supposed effort to limit the theft of diamonds by African labourers, De Beers transferred the infrastructural techniques it had used 'to supervise convicts' to the labour population more generally, constructing a series of 'compounds' in which to house their workers (Lester et al., 2000: 105). These compounds were economically profitable, allowing De Beers to accommodate migrant labourers more cheaply, whilst the 'closed space of the compound' also made it easier to suppress strikes and other forms of resistance, distancing the black migrant labourers from the whites 'who lived permanently in the town' (105–106). The creation of a black labour force demanded these more complex spatial and infrastructural frameworks as part of a racialised policy of 'influx control' (Nightingale, 2012: 252–254). It required fluid political borders (for the influx of migrant labour) whilst solidifying barriers at a local level (to maintain racial and class divisions). Read infrastructurally, the Cape to Cairo imaginary becomes emblematic of the reductive portrayal of uneven development to a symbolic and physical manifestation of 'a linear march of progress', one that presumes 'to deterministically reorganise economies, societies, cultures, and geographies in increasingly urban ways', whilst disguising the 'social biases' inscribed into these 'systems' (Graham 2010: 4, 13). Leaving Haggard's simplistically linear 'cultural fix' to one side, it is at this point that a turn to Schreiner's fictional interrogation of imperial infrastructure allows for a more sustained analysis of the ways in which colonial literature unpicks, and on occasion spatially resists, Rhodes's imperial-capitalist ideology.

Grounding Meta-Narrative: Olive Schreiner's Geographies of Resistance

Olive Schreiner, born in 1855 and living in South Africa until her death in 1920 (apart from some years in London and Europe in the 1880s), witnessed firsthand the tumultuous processes of its hurried industrialisation.[4] Politically engaged and formally experimental, her writing often reveals the contradictions that linear infrastructural imaginaries sought to conceal, exposing the racial ideologies informing them and the dangers and discriminations of the increasingly segregationist policies that were introduced during her lifetime. In 1901, she revealingly reflected on the region's demography by attempting to draw 'a racial map of South Africa':

> no possible line which can be drawn across it will separate the colours one from another, or even combine their darker shades. [...] should we wish to make our map

4   I have up until this point in the chapter mostly referred to 'Southern Africa', in part because the Union of South Africa wouldn't exist as a formal political entity until 1910 (discussed further in Chapter 3), but also because both Haggard and Rhodes are writing of a geographical region that extends beyond South Africa northwards into Rhodesia. Schreiner, by contrast, was invested more specifically in a unified South Africa and her fiction is unambiguously set in that country's various parts, even if much of it was written before the Union in 1910.

> truly representative of the complexities of the South African problem, it will be necessary to go further, and across this intermingled mass of colours to draw at intervals, at all angles, and in all directions, lines of ink, which shall cut up the surfaces into squares and spaces of different sizes. If these lines be truly drawn they will be found to bear no relation to the proportions of the colours beneath them; they will run straight through masses of colour, cutting them into parts; and except in the case of some of the smallest divisions, where the dark predominates, it will be impossible to trace the slightest connection between the lines and the colouring. (1923: 52)

Schreiner could here be speaking of the African continent as a whole, commenting on the arbitrary partition in the 1880s that, as discussed in the introduction, stimulated a new urgency and divisive complexity in colonial literature's production of space. Focusing specifically on South Africa, however, she draws on her experience of its demographic and physical landscape to emphasise the disjunction between imperial ideology's shaping of colonial space and the political realities its infrastructural developments attempted to contain. By highlighting the interrelations between different kinds of spatial production – the written sentence, the drawn map and the spatial markings of political boundaries and infrastructural routes – Schreiner is able to isolate and deconstruct the ideological contours embedded within them. As I shall argue, it is because, unlike Haggard, she is situated in the peripheral economic zones of South Africa that she is able to produce a self-consciously spatial meta-narratological style in her literary writing, revealing the processes of the development of underdevelopment that shaped them. Grounded in the 'holes in the net' of imperialism's infrastructural developments (Lefebvre, 1998: 118), she exposes their limitations and mobilises a *spatial* resistance to the 'progressive' imperial ideologies that informed them.

From Man to Man, first published posthumously in 1926, was, Paul Foot observes, 'quite literally, her life's work' (Schreiner, 1982: xii). She worked on the manuscript sporadically from the age of eighteen, when she first visited Kimberley's diamond fields, until her death forty-seven years later. Though she attempted to publish an early version of it in 1881 under the title 'Saints and Sinners', it was rejected and she never tried again (van de Vlies, 2007: 23). The resulting text is therefore comprised of multiple layers of 'revising and rewriting', as Schreiner 'grafted on the thoughts and experiences of her later life' (Schreiner, 1982: xiii). If much of the text reads as political 'propaganda at the expense of the novel' (xiv), this representative of the larger trajectory of Schreiner's writing career. Beginning by writing literary texts in the 1880s and '90s, from the early 1900s until her death she wrote mostly polemic pamphlets in which, as McClintock observes, she 'was unusual in her anti-racism' and activism on behalf of the rights of black Africans (1995: 268). Given Schreiner's spatial and sociopolitical consciousness and the experimental formalism of some of her published literary writings, it is perhaps unsurprising that one of the novel's most striking segments speaks specifically to the concerns of infrastructure, segregation and resistance, and it is to this that I now turn.

Talking to her children, Schreiner's protagonist, Rebekah, infuses the imagined community of the South African nation with a multi-racial demography that, through its spatiality, highlights the limits, if not the impossibility, of segregationist ideology. Recalling her beliefs as 'a little girl', the now adult Rebekah remembers that she 'could not bear black or brown people. I thought they were ugly and dirty and stupid [...] I felt I was so clever and they were so stupid; I could not bear them' (Schreiner, 1982: 435). The simplicity of the narrative tone conflates this racism with a childlike naivety, a tactic that intensifies as Rebekah recalls her childhood imagining of a simplistically linear infrastructural demarcation, her racial ideology manifesting in geographical segregation:

> I always played that I was Queen Victoria and that all Africa belonged to me, and I could do whatever I liked. It always puzzled me when I walked up and down thinking what I should do with the black people; I did not like to kill them, because I could not hurt anything, and yet I could not have them near me. At last I made a plan. I made believe that I built a high wall right across Africa and put all the black people on the other side, and I said, 'Stay there, and, the day you put one foot over, your heads will be cut off.'
>
> I was very pleased when I made this plan. I used to walk up and down and make believe there were no black people in South Africa; I had it all to myself. (1982: 435)

Rebekah's childish imagining of a linear infrastructural barrier both recalls Haggard's geography of racial segregation whilst also satirising its naive simplicity. That Rebekah is 'playing' at being 'Queen Victoria' levels a belittling textual critique at British imperial policies of segregation in Africa

as they were justified by the hypocritical rhetoric of '"pastoral power"
(that is not overtly authoritarian)'; an ideology that, for Cynthia Kros,
is symbolised by 'the Rhodes Memorial' (2015: 156) and that, as we have
seen, similarly informed Steel's humanitarian justification of imperial
infrastructural development. For Rebekah, however, such segregationist
efforts can be no more than 'make believe'. By portraying ideologies of racial
segregation as childish fantasies, the text levers open the gap between the
spatial mappings and physical realities of South Africa – that is, 'the space
of separation between the land and the map' that allowed the nation to
emerge in the imperial imagination (Mitchell, 2002: 90), an issue that will
be taken up in greater detail in Chapters 3 and 4. As Rebekah continues,
a few pages later:

> [A]s I grew older and older I got to see that it wasn't the colour or the shape of the
> jaw or the cleverness that mattered; that if men and women could love very much
> and feel such great pain that their hearts broke, and if when they thought they were
> wronged they were glad to die, and that for others they could face death without a
> fear [...] then they were mine and I was theirs, and the wall I had built across Africa
> had slowly to fall down. (1982: 437–438)

For Burdett, '[m]othering here is expressly set against the violence of a
colonial imagination, exemplified in the wall which has to fall down as
Rebekah recognises human kinship through suffering' (2001: 107). But
there is also a historical temporality, marked by Rebekah's age – as she
grows 'older and older' – which, perhaps proleptically if not prophetically,
predicts both the implementation of a system of racial segregation as well
as, beyond that, its disintegration.[5]

---

5   Rebekah's 'wall', which Burdett describes as the 'fantasy of apartheid avant la lettre'
     (2001: 105), resonates with twenty-first-century geographies of segregation. As
     Weizman observes in his discussion of the 'separation barrier' that has cut through
     East Jerusalem and divided the West Bank from Israel since 2003, the notion of a
     dividing wall has 'become particularly associated with the word "apartheid", although
     even at the height of its barbarity the South African regime never erected such a
     barrier' (2012: 171).

However, whilst taking into account the critical forcefulness of these paragraphs, it is *The Story of An African Farm* that mobilises the most sustained spatially constructed resistance to imperial ideology. As Burdett points out, the novel 'rigorously' confines itself 'to a colonial reality' (2001: 30). It is located in a peripheral section of the African 'veld' that, when Schreiner was writing in the 1870s, was situated in the second development 'belt' around what was then the 'only major regional "core"' of Cape Town – though of course, by the time the novel was published in 1883, two new 'resource frontiers' and soon to be regional core zones were emerging in Kimberley and on the Rand (Lester, 1998: 47). Kimberley's conspicuous absence from the text is emphasised by another of Schreiner's novels, which she worked on coterminously but probably finished before *African Farm* appeared in its final form: *Undine*, published posthumously by her husband, S. C. Cronwright-Schreiner, in 1928. As he estimates in his preface to the novel, it is likely that *Undine* 'was completed in South Africa before she left for England in 1881' (Schreiner, 1928: ix), whilst *African Farm* was first published in 1883, two years after Schreiner had arrived in London.

Suggestively, the 'first mention of *Undine* appears in [Schreiner's] New Rush journal' – 'New Rush' being the name for the diamond fields when Schreiner travelled there in 1872, a year before the settlements were renamed 'Kimberley' in 1873 (ix-x, 246). The economic activity, infrastructure construction and labour exploitation that Schreiner experienced first-hand in Kimberley are placed centre-stage in *Undine*'s second half, as the narrative moves geographically from a peripheral African farm to the metropolitan centre – London – before then returning back to South Africa, only this time towards the mines at New Rush. If *African Farm* has a similar bipartite structure, it is not shaped, like *Undine*'s, by a geographical journey towards regional and global cores. Rather, it remains resolutely situated within the peripheral zone of the veld, barely straying even toward lines of networked infrastructure such as railways, or semi-peripheral towns and urban enclaves. Its dual structure comes instead from its formal experimentation: as this analysis will show, whilst the novel's first section confines itself to a linear narrative, the second firmly embeds itself within the peripheral landscape through a series of formally experimental chapters that deconstruct the imperial ideology propagated by texts such as Haggard's *King Solomon's Mines*.

A comparison of *African Farm*'s geography with *Undine*'s contrasting preoccupation with the diamond fields is therefore illuminating. The first halves of *Undine* and *African Farm* are strikingly similar: their narratives are constructed around their female protagonists – Undine and Lyndall respectively – who both live in an 'old Dutch farmhouse'. In the opening pages, the narrative's linear temporality is measured by the protagonists' obsession with the passing of time, manifested in the 'tick, tick, tick' of the 'inexorable old clock' (Schreiner, 1928: 5) ('Tick – tick – tick – tick! One, two, three, four! (2003: 49)). Both protagonists are even accompanied by a friendly dog, similarly described in each novel (1928, 23; 2003: 110). Nevertheless, the contrast between the geography and content of the two novels, as they at first align and then depart from one another, highlights the importance of the peripheral landscape for the development of *African Farm*'s anti-imperial meta-narrative. The geographical spaces situated *beyond* the webs and zones of infrastructural and economic development are, this comparison reveals, fundamental to the novel's anti-imperial project.

After returning to South Africa from Britain at more or less the novel's midway point, Undine is 'attracted, like all others who were near enough to feel its influence, by the great magnet that draws to itself all who are good-for-nothing vagabonds, wanderers, or homeless – the Diamond Fields' (Schreiner, 1928: 244). Significantly, the text indicates the historical moment in which it is set by highlighting that there is, as of yet, no railway to transport Undine from Port Elizabeth to Kimberley – a distance, a footnote informs the reader, of '485 miles' (244). Instead, she must travel on a 'great buck waggon, with its long span of red oxen and heavy freight of wires and buckets [...] along the sandy road' (249), a mode of transport that recalls Quartermain's extensive travels across South Africa with a 'wagon-load of goods [*sic*]' (Haggard, 2008: 14). This is not the only intertextual resonance between *Undine* and *King Solomon's Mines*. Of particular interest are the similarities between each text's description of its respective mining infrastructure – Kimberley for the former, King Solomon's mine for the latter. Through this intertextual reading, *Undine* vocalises the 'hidden transcript' of Haggard's romance narrative by detailing the close co-existence of different racial groups that was a product of South Africa's industrialising centres.

Figure 2.5: A drawing of the interior view of the Kimberley Diamond Mine between 1886 and 1887, first published in Volume 30 of the journal *Popular Science Monthly*.

Standing on the 'edge' of the 'vast hole' of King Solomon's mine, Quartermain looks out at 'the pit marked on the old Don's map, [where] the great road branched in two and circumvented it' (160). The physical geography of this landscape, in which Haggard's central infrastructural demarcation splits and circles the mouth of the mine, resonates with Schreiner's description of 'the Circus', 'the poorest and most wretched part of the camp' in Kimberley that is described as a 'wilderness of canvas': 'round tents, square tents, torn tents, and whole tents [...] canvas houses and wooden houses and iron houses, and non-descripts' (1928: 282–283). This 'Circular Road' encompasses the 'Kop', or central diamond mine. For *Undine*, 'the glare of the sun on the *white* road was almost blinding' (291, my emphasis), recalling the whiteness of Solomon's road. As Undine walks through this industrial settlement, she observes 'troops of niggers going to work at the Kop, and sharp little diamond-buyers going to look for the worm' (287), emphasising, racist language aside, the co-mingling of different racial groups along this central infrastructural route that Haggard's text worked so hard to deny.

Perhaps most revealing is Undine's response to the 'crater' of the diamond mine which, as Cronwright-Schreiner observes in his 1928 footnote, was an 'immense circular hole [that] is now claimed to be the largest hole ever sunk into the earth by man' (298). Looking 'down into the crater', Undine actually begins to mythologise, if not *romanticise*, this infrastructural feat:

> The thousand wires that crossed it, glistening in the moonlight, formed a weird, sheeny, mistlike veil over the black depths beneath. Very dark, very deep it lay all round the edge, but, high towering into the bright moonlight, rose the unworked centre. She crouched down at the foot of the staging and sat looking at it. In the magic of the moonlight it was a giant castle, a castle of the olden knightly days; you might swear, as you gazed on it, that you saw the shadows of its castellated battlements, and the endless turrets that overcrowned it: a giant castle, lulled to sleep and bound in silence for a thousand years by the word of some enchanter. (298)

Undine narrates the transformation of Kimberley's modern infrastructures that facilitate the exploitation of the landscape's minerals into a romanticised infrastructural edifice that is thousands of years old; a King Solomon's mine, of sorts. Schreiner's description of the physical apparatus of the mining industry, when read alongside Haggard's imperial romance, meta-narratalogically demonstrates the way in which a specific set of ideological agendas can warp colonial literature's production of space. Reading Haggard's romanticised landscapes through the lens of *Undine*'s spatial productions, the ideology inscribed into the contours of the former's literary mappings can be excavated, their limitations and obscurations identified, and their implicit politics drawn out. It's worth recalling that, though the inner cave of King Solomon's mines is called, in a chapter title, 'The Place of Death' (Haggard, 2008: 169), Haggard's protagonists escape from the mine unscathed and having retrieved its mineral wealth. For Undine, however, the Kimberley diamond mine quite literally becomes her 'place of death'. Alone and unable to find sufficient work to provide herself with food and accommodation,[6] Undine is exposed to the elements and, in the novel's final dreamlike paragraphs, collapses and dies on the edge of the mine.

> Presently the moon rose and looked over the ridge of the tent into the little yard among the gravel-heaps. The glowing stump [of the candle] had burnt out and gone to ashes between the great round stones.
>
> Before them, in her little purple print, with her feet crossed and her head resting on one arm, lay Undine. [...]
>
> There was nothing else to be seen in the little yard. (374)

The calm moonlight anticipates the stillness of *African Farm*'s opening description of the peripheral farm, to which I shall return in a moment, and shortly before her death Undine recalls with fondness 'the thatched roofs and stone walls of the old farm on the Karoo' (370). It is as though Undine *regrets* her geographic movement from the peripheral space of the farm to the region's emerging economic core. Read intertextually and inter-geographically alongside *African Farm*, Schreiner's second novel (and

---

6   Carolyn Burdett explores the 'symbolic resonance' of 'food and hunger' throughout Schreiner's *oeuvre*, one that conflates 'the land-hunger of imperial greed' with 'starving Africans' (2001: 126–128). As Chrisman has likewise argued, Schreiner's preoccupation with food emphasises how colonialism 'cannot replicate domestic pastoralism. The colonial setting necessarily reverses the dynamics: from producing food for others to producing others for food' (2000: 136).

indicatively, perhaps, the one that was published) functions as a fictional second chance for Schreiner. Where *Undine* succumbs to the speculative allure of the mining industry by moving towards and writing about it, *African Farm* adamantly resists geographical movement towards these core spaces. And when Lyndall does eventually leave the farm in the novel's closing pages, she too, like Undine, quickly becomes weak and dies. A comparison of the geographic trajectories of Schreiner's two female protagonists maps the movement from periphery to core onto the relational binaries of life and death, condemning the speculative culture surrounding the mining industry – whilst this remains implicit in *African Farm*, in *Undine*, Schreiner explicitly foregrounds the 'wild and reckless' speculation that bears 'the same irresistible fascination that the gaming table had for many' (1928: 110). However, and unlike Haggard's romance, *African Farm*'s attempts to distance itself from industrialising South Africa and its restriction to a peripheral geographical location actually allows it to mobilise a more sustained and formally nuanced critique of an exploitative imperialism.

For Jed Esty, *African Farm* performs a 'systematic assimilation of an uneven and markedly colonial temporality into its plot structure, characterisation, and figurative language', one that 'challenges the formal dictates of the Goethean *Bildungsroman* (with that genre's conventional sense of teleological and masculinist destiny)' (2007: 408). If, as Moretti argues, the *Bildungsroman* is 'the symbolic form that more than any other has portrayed and promoted modern socialisation' (2000: 10), that Undine's and Lyndall's deaths are consequent upon their varyingly brief encounters with the world-system suggests a failure – if not a refusal – to be assimilated into it. Esty compares *African Farm*'s 'underdeveloped zone' to the settings of Conrad's *Lord Jim* (1900), Woolf's *The Voyage Out* (1915) and Joyce's *A Portrait of the Artist as a Young Man* (1916), arguing that the 'geographical frame' of these texts produces an experimental narrative form that resists 'the "tyranny of the plot"' (2007: 411). This is akin to the connection between 'Modernism and Imperialism' established by Jameson, in which the economics of an expanding world-system shape the 'new spatial language' of 'modernist style' (1990: 51–58). Schreiner's modernist tendencies have been discussed by a number of critics (McClintock, 1995: 280–281; Burdett, 2001: 9), and Esty's study responds to Patrick Williams's call for the application of a '"combined and uneven development" perspective' to 'modernism and imperialism' (2000: 32). As Esty argues, the spatiality of Schreiner's text configures the 'structuring contradiction between the progressive imperial ethos of worldwide modernisation and the stubborn facts of uneven or under-development in the colonial periphery' (2007: 423).

Building on Esty's insights, I want here to use Williams's return to the work of Said to emphasise the 'disturbing effect' that the text's spatiality might bring to 'imperial ideology' (2000: 21–23; Said, 1993: 226), a reading best achieved by positioning *African Farm* in relation to *King Solomon's Mines*. The uneven spatiality of Schreiner's novel undoes the rigid ideological contours of texts such as Haggard's and, further, ideologies of linear progress embedded in infrastructure projects such as the Cape to Cairo railway. Its textual silences, the 'gaps and absences' that emerge from within the Southern African landscape of its geographical setting, are made explicit by Schreiner's meticulous meta-narratological construction, making 'the presence of ideology [...] most positively felt' (Macherey, 1986: 84; Eagleton, 2002: 32). Coetzee emphasises the 'silences' of the twentieth-century 'South African farm novel' more generally, arguing that the genre's 'truth' is found 'in what it does not know about itself: in its silences' (1980: 81). As the founding novel of this genre, *African Farm* employs a series of meta-narratological techniques to draw her reader's attention to these silences, transforming the implicit into the explicit. These meta-narratives are embedded within and enabled by its production of the landscape, as South Africa's mineral-based industrial revolution occurs out of sight of, but still impacts on, the novel's geography.[7] Finally, its intertextual evocations of the imperial romance highlight that genre's cartographic limitations: its productions of South African space, rather than opening up the region

---

7   Burdett notes that 'Lyndall's dream of wearing diamonds in her hair alerts us to Schreiner's own historical advantage in knowing that, by the 1870s, the Colony's economy had been transformed by the discovery of diamonds' (2001: 42) and the pseudonym under which Schreiner first published the novel, 'Ralph Iron', itself alludes to the iron that is embedded within the 'ironstones of the kopjes' (Monsman, 1991: 79).

to the 'landscanning European eye' (Pratt, 2003: 60), actually render the landscape 'alien, impenetrable', without a 'language [...] in which to win it, speak it [or] represent it' (Coetzee, 1980: 7).

In the 'Preface to the Second Edition' of the novel, Schreiner acknowledges 'a kind critic' who claims 'that he would better have liked [*African Farm*] if it had been a history of wild adventure; [...] "of encounters with ravening lions, and hairbreadth escapes"' (Schreiner, 2003: 41). Writing for the *Saturday Review*, this anonymous critic clearly refers here to the imperial romance. Schreiner's response to the criticism is revealing, rooted in her conception of how the local, peripheral geography of her African farm fits into the cross-national networks of the world-system: '[s]uch works are best written in Piccadilly or in the Strand', she argues; 'there the gifts of the creative imagination, untrammelled by contact with any fact, may spread their wings' (41). Conversely, Schreiner emphasises that it is her direct experience of South African geography and the spatial realities of its peripherality thats reveal the linear form of the imperial romance to be inadequate to 'paint the scenes', she tell us, 'in which' she 'has grown' (42). The text's spatiality levers open the gap between imperial 'imagination' and 'any fact' to throw the ideological contours of the romance's geography into relief.

This rejection of the romance's linearity is played out at the levels of both form and content. In the novel's climactic scene, Lyndall, on her deathbed, rejects a book with a linear narrative:

> 'Will you open the window', she said, almost querulously, 'and throw this book out? It is so utterly foolish. I thought it was a valuable book; but the words are merely strung together, they make no sense.' (262)

Lyndall exhibits a meta-narratological awareness, reflecting on the way in which linear narratives are constructed, before literally throwing the book out of the window. This meta-textual image builds from the novel's opening scenes, when Lyndall, sitting 'on the floor threading beads', is asked by her cousin, Em, why her beads never fall off her needle; she replies, 'I try [...] That is why' (50). Lyndall's metaphor alludes to the 'thread' of the novel's narrative which, if an eye is not kept on its 'sequential ordering', can be lost — as narratologist Mieke Bal explains, an emphasis on the effort required to 'thread' a text together becomes 'literary narrative's way of achieving a density that is akin to the simultaneity often claimed for visual images as distinct from literature' (1997: 82). The self-referential web of Schreiner's text, which cuts across the novel's multi-layered imagery and into its Preface, deconstructs the linearity of its own narrative. In so doing, it excavates the ideology of a 'progressive imperial ethos' embedded within linear – and often infrastructural – productions of space (Esty, 2007: 423).

Further meta-textual threads are inscribed into the broader motions of the plot. *African Farm*'s opening section adheres to a conventionally linear narrative form as it charts the early life of its child protagonists. Here, the farm is invaded by a comic villain called 'Bonaparte Blenkins', whose name references a broader imperial and historical context and whose Britishness makes his allegorical signification of imperial hegemony explicit. Lyndall's earlier discussion, and admiration, of Napoleon Bonaparte draws these imperial undertones to the fore (2003: 58). In the novel's second section, this narrative style fragments. After two philosophical chapters which focus on the landscape, the novel returns to a plot that becomes disjointed and anti-chronological. Though invoking the narrative style of the *Bildungsroman*, which details the process of 'world socialisation' through the '*interiorisation of contradiction*', the formal shifts of the second half of Schreiner's novel resist these ideological processes by highlighting those contradictions – her young protagonists refuse to 'learn to live with it' (Moretti, 2000: 10).

This resistance to socialisation is expanded to, and rooted in, the text's geo-historical allusion to the violent ramifications of the capitalist world-system and its oppression and dispossession of native Africans. Schreiner mobilises the peripheral landscape as a space of resistance from the novel's opening paragraph: 'The full African moon poured down its light from the blue sky into the wide, lonely plain' (2003: 47). The reader's attention is drawn by the light of the moon to the broad landscape: the 'solemn monotony of the plain', flat and two dimensional, is 'broken' by the three dimensional 'stunted "karoo" bushes, the low hills [...] the milk-bushes [and] the small solitary "kopje"' (47). The moonlight, like the narrative, lays bare the scene, framing these objects in an 'oppressive beauty' that meta-textually highlights the oppressive nature of its representational processes. The narrative's attempt to register the expansive space of the underdeveloped veld results in the production of a text that gestures towards socioeconomic spaces that resist assimilation into the world-system, working in turn to challenge it directly.

Schreiner understands that, for the coloniser, narrative functions as a way of 'mastering, looking from above, dividing up and controlling' geographical space, a process that 'ignores [...] the density of its lived-in quality'; in this case, the native Africans who 'lived in' the land prior to colonial occupation (Bal, 1997: 147; Mitchell, 1988: 32–33). As Bal argues, it is by 'providing a landscape with a history' that memory is spatialised, a process that 'undoes the killing of space as lived' (Bal, 1997: 147–148). Schreiner gives the landscape this history early in the novel in the form of 'some Bushmen-paintings', the 'red and black pigments' of which have 'been preserved through long years' (2003: 55). Deborah Shapple points out that these paintings allude to 'a suppressed precolonial history', whilst simultaneously denying 'their creators or ancestral interpreters [...] access to the present narrative moment' (2004: 113). However, though the native Bushmen are themselves silent, Schreiner's male protagonist, Waldo, gives voice to them in a speech-act that significantly interrupts Lyndall's reflections on Napoleon Bonaparte's imperial ambitions. Whereas for Lyndall, Napoleon, acting here as a metonym for British imperialism, is 'the greatest man who ever lived', Waldo is more interested in the 'Physical geography' of the kopje on which they sit, interrupting Lyndall's reflections: '"If *they* could talk, if *they* could tell us now!"' he says, moving his hand over the surrounding rocks (58, 60). Schreiner's narrative dislodges Lyndall's account of Napoleonic imperialism by introducing a segment of geographical space upon which the voiceless histories of the dispossessed are inscribed. As Bart Moore-Gilbert argues, Waldo's reading of the peripheral geographical zone is comparable to subaltern histories, as he searches for 'signs of the increasingly occluded "Bushman" histories' inscribed within its contours (2003: 96).

This spatiality is mobilised throughout the novel to resist the ideological frameworks of a specifically British imperial enterprise. The text's two central chapters, 'Times and Seasons' and 'Waldo's Stranger', fragment the plot's teleological development in a spatial rupture that is rooted in the physical geography of the peripheral South African landscape (Schreiner, 2003: 137–170). Waldo, as Carolyn Burdett has noted, is 'frequently represented as lying or squatting close to the ground' (2001: 41), and 'Times and Seasons' begins with him lying 'on his stomach on the sand' (Schreiner, 2003: 137). The linear narrative is broken up into short, chronologically numbered segments that begin with awkward temporal statements: 'And then a new time rises' (139), 'Then a new time comes' (140), 'Then a new time' (145), 'Then at last a new time' (148). This constant 'starting again' disrupts the novel's linearity, as what has gone before is erased with the arrival of each new narrative section. This chapter ends with the following sentence:

> And so, it comes to pass at last, that whereas the sky was at first a small blue rag stretched out over us, and so low that our hands might touch it, pressing down on us, it raises itself into an immeasurable blue arch over our heads, and we begin to live again. (154)

The narrative emphasises its own ability to convey, through the spatial dislocations of its form, a more accurate depiction of the South African landscape, implicitly infusing these with an expression of anti-imperial resistance. The imperial ideological frameworks that confine narratives such as the romance to their generic linearity – 'pressing down on us' – are first evoked and then resisted, as the landscape is now seen as 'immeasurable', beyond the romance's regulatory narrative structure. The text suggests a new ideological terrain through the colonial landscape that it produces, and from which an anti-imperial and distinctly spatial resistance emerges.

For Coetzee, Schreiner's portrayal of the 'idleness of life on her late nineteenth-century farm' actually 'underscores the centrality of the question of labour in the South African pastoral' (1980: 4), a genre that, as Nicole Devarenne has argued, 'would develop, by the 1930s, into an ideologically important genre justifying colonial subjugation and white supremacist claims to Afrikaner ownership of the land' (2009: 627). The 'chief labour' of the few native Africans represented in the novel 'is to perform boundary work. They stand at thresholds, windows and walls, opening and shutting doors' (McClintock, 1995: 268).[8] In Chapter VIII,

---

8   In her later novella, *Trooper Peter Halket of Mashonaland* (1897), though 'the land' is 'as bare of black men' as Haggard's depiction of the Transvaal, this absence is more explicitly ascribed to imperial violence: 'all native habitations had been destroyed

entitled 'The Kopje' – a naming that again reemphasises the text's geographical coordinates – Lyndall draws the attention of the 'new man, Gregory Rose', another invading Englishman, to 'a Kaffir' (Schreiner, 2003: 219). As Lyndall turns to converse with him she closes 'her book' and folds 'her hands on it' (219), once again conflating imperialism and linear narrative before rejecting it. By drawing Gregory's attention to the 'Kaffir' who is, she claims, 'the most interesting and intelligent thing I can see just now', despite the presence of a British male, she demonstrates her affinity with a subjected native African population (219). If the novel's critique is compromised by the reproduction of contemporaneous racist ideologies ('Doss', Lyndall's dog, is, she considers, more intelligent than both the 'Kaffir' and Gregory), these are complicated by Lyndall's anti-imperialism, which are in turn conflated with her critique of the native African's own male-dominated social structures: 'he is going to fetch his rations, and I suppose to kick his wife with his beautiful legs when he gets home. He has a right to; he bought her for two oxen' (219). Lyndall's sarcasm indicates her ideological rejection of a British imperialist narrative as she sides, if only by default, with the absent black African female. Lyndall confounds her white male interlocutor who, 'not quite sure how to take these remarks [...] half laughed and half not, to be on the safe side' (220; see also Barends, 2015: 102). Significantly, Gregory's 'one tiny room' is 'profusely covered with prints cut from the *Illustrated London News*' (Schreiner, 2003: 171), as he attempts, quite literally, to 'wall' out South Africa's geographical realities with imperial writings about it. Lyndall subverts his belief that romances written 'in Piccadilly or in the Strand' can represent accurately the South African landscape, rooting her resistance in a peripheral socioeconomic, geographic and cultural zone, situated beyond (though increasingly shaped by) the infrastructural and economic circuitries of the world-system.

---

within a radius of thirty miles' by the 'Colonial Englishmen'; 'forty miles off kraals had been destroyed and two hundred black carcasses were lying in the sun' (2009: 36).

Rewriting the Imperial Romance: The Revolutionary Trajectories of 'Ula Masondo' (1927)

Whilst Schreiner mobilises literary depictions of a *peripheral* landscape into a narrative form that dismantles imperial ideology, this chapter concludes by turning to the literary production of South Africa's *urban* space, and specifically Johannesburg, as it began increasingly to shape the region's physical and imagined geographies. Literary responses to Johannesburg proliferated throughout the twentieth century, often condemning and resisting its geographies of segregation. Texts such as Peter Abrahams' *Mine Boy* (1946, suggestively described by the *African Writers Series* as 'The First Modern Novel of Black South Africa' (Abrahams, 1963: front cover)) critiqued the exploitation of black labour in the gold mines, whilst Alan Paton's *Cry, the Beloved Country* (1948) interrogated the corrupting power of the metropolis. But it was in 1927 that Plomer published his short story, 'Ula Masondo', which began to construct the 'literary infrastructures' of Johannesburg's urban space (Nuttall, 2008: 195–218). Plomer's story looks in two directions, simultaneously offering an intertextual and subversive rewriting of the imperial romance whilst also, as Craig Mackenzie observes, setting the thematic and generic coordinates for 'the "Jim comes to Jo'burg" mould' (2012: 371). By building on Schreiner's literary resistance to imperial ideology, 'Ula Masondo' looks forward to the work of Abrahams, Paton and others, creating a literary template for future representations of, and resistance to, urban segregation, at the levels of both content and form. If the ways in which 'we write the city invents it, brings it into being, allows it to exist in very specific ways' (Bremner, 2010: 4), then 'Ula Masondo' can be said to enact what Loren Kruger calls 'performative archaeology': it 'includes not only the excavation of buried structures, but the reconstruction of performances that inhabited, shaped, and contested those structures', thereby imagining 'future alternatives' (2013: 11–12).

Like Schreiner, Plomer developed an outspoken anticolonial perspective, albeit articulated from a position of both economic and racial privilege. His self-alignment with Johannesburg's marginalised populations are perhaps due to his sexuality: if in 1924 'there was no law forbidding miscegenation in South Africa', there were 'laws (modelled on those of Britain)' that made 'homosexuality a crime', alienating Plomer, who was himself gay, from the legal system (Alexander, 1989: 81). In 1911, Plomer's father, Charles, had moved to Johannesburg to work in the central pass office at the Department of Native Affairs where, as the head of a complex system of clerks, interpreters and police, he administered increasingly restrictive policies to black Africans working in the gold mines (Alexander, 1989: 16). Reflecting on this period in his autobiography, Plomer recalls 'the unskilled black migrants of many tribes' who 'came as strangers, uneducated and bewildered, to the white man's new, urban, industrial world', as he witnessed the complex 'pass system' and other segregationist policies firsthand (1975: 94). In the years leading up to the publication of 'Ula Masondo' in 1927, a number of legal mechanisms ensured that only Africans who 'served white needs' were permitted access to the city (Meredith, 2008: 523). This segregationist 'legal fabric' was manifested in Johannesburg's 'built' environment, embodying Weizman's analysis of the mutually sustaining 'law/wall' formula (2012: 210) and maintaining 'the hierarchisation of the work-force and its highly unequal distributions of reward' (Wallerstein, 2011: 78).

The contradiction generated by the need to have black labour '"on site" from early dawn until after sunset' whilst maintaining clear spatial distinctions between racial groups led to the development of 'segregated and areally confined Locations well away from "white space"', underdeveloped 'inner-urban slumyards' and white residential areas within the city's municipal boundaries (Beavon, 2004: 80). In the early twentieth century, the British spent a colossal £3.5 million on the development of urban infrastructure – 'sanitation, sewerage, roads, stormwater drainage, water supply, electric tramways' – though 'almost exclusively in areas occupied by white people' (71–72). After the first formal establishment of the city's municipal boundary in 1901, the surrounding 'townships' became suburbs, a term that, during apartheid, would become colloquially used 'to refer exclusively to the "black areas" and particularly those initially called "Locations"' (75). The city's racial demography quite literally shaped, and was in turn shaped by, its internal uneven development (see Beall et al., 2002: 198), as it was constructed around proliferating boundary lines and borders that had been ideologically crystallised in the segregationist geographies of the imperial romance. Nevertheless, the city remained riddled with peripheral zones, spaces of economic impoverishment that existed outside of the infrastructural parameters of the city's governmental administration – as Mitchell writes more generally of the colonial city, even though its 'modernity is something contingent upon the exclusion of its opposite' and 'maintaining the barrier that keeps the other out', a close look reveals that 'the identity of the city could be understood to include its excluded exterior' (1988: 165, 174). As these boundaries and barriers were systematically enforced in Johannesburg's physical and conceptual space, they nevertheless remained 'fluctuating, porous and ill-defined' (Bremner, 2010: 160). In writing 'Ula Masondo', Plomer set out to demonstrate the ways in which the city's infrastructural ordering was repeatedly transgressed and resisted by marginalised populations from the outset.

'Ula Masondo' appeared as one of the longer stories in Plomer's first collection, *I Speak of Africa* (1927), a 'bold' title that implies both 'an outright declaration of content (Africa) and of intention (plain talk, straight from the shoulder)' (Gray, 1986: 53). Like Schreiner and unlike Haggard, Plomer wrote the stories of which this collection is comprised from within the immediacy of the 'contact zone' (Pratt, 2003: 8). He explicitly inverts the infrastructural linearity of the imperial romance to emphasise instead its fragility, exploring through an experimental literary form how this rewriting might initiate what Harvey calls 'revolutionary trajectories' (2012: xvii). The story is framed by the perspective of a 'white storekeeper', whose ambition is to open up trade with a rural native population by setting up 'a second Harrods here in Lembuland' (Plomer, 1984a: 51–52). Lembuland, a fictional location that is also the setting of Plomer's first novel, *Turbott Wolfe* (1925), is a railway journey of about 'two days and two nights' north of Johannesburg, a geographical location towards the African interior where Haggard's text is also set (until 1995 part of the Transvaal Province, since then Mpumalanga). Plomer thus de-mythologises the romance's geography, satirically introducing the socioeconomic realities – 'Harrods' – of colonial capitalism into King Solomon's realm. After these opening paragraphs have documented this white, profit-orientated perspective, the one-dimensional narrative breaks down and its progression falters. Though only thirty pages long, 'Ula Masondo' is fragmented into nineteen short chapters or sections, each of which exhibit sharp perspectival and geographical shifts, formally deconstructing the linear movement mapped by the imperial romance. At the beginning of section two, the narrative perspective moves from the white trader to a black African, the titular Ula Masondo; section three changes yet again to the perspective of Ula's father; and section four, one page later, throws the reader straight into a 'crowded' train as Ula makes his way from the rural northern territory down to the mining centre of Johannesburg (52–55).

'Ula Masondo' deliberately invokes several of the imperial romance's generic traits. It narrates Ula's journey into a dangerous landscape in search of the wealth buried within it, and contains detailed descriptions of this environment, presenting them as new and alien to an implied reader through Ula's perspective: 'the air was full of foreign newness' (1984a: 56). Ula becomes part of a small group unified in the face of socioeconomic difficulty ('financial adversity kept them together' (64)). Entering the gold mine, Ula becomes trapped in a 'cave' when there is a 'fall of rock' that leaves him 'cut off from the world' (69). Finally, after escaping the mine's 'entombing rock' (70), Ula realises his fortune and returns to his homeland wealthier than he left it, laden with symbols of his newfound materialism.

However, Plomer's adventuring protagonist is not a white imperialist but a black African who, rather than travelling inland from South to North, instead moves in the opposite direction, down from the rural North to the region's industrial centre. This landscape is not empty, penetrated by only one, linear infrastructural route. 'The thin brown grass of the veld' gives way to the 'mine dumps, sticking up beyond the horizon like the summits of snow-mountains' – recalling Quartermain's description of 'Sheba's snowy Breasts' (Haggard, 2008: 67) – and 'the great Reef Road' that runs 'parallel' to the train leads past 'bitter citadels of unreasoning industry' to the heart of Johannesburg (1984a: 55). This road is bustling with 'an incessant traffic of cars, bicycles and pedestrians' and the cityscape becomes increasingly saturated with 'streets', 'shacks of corrugated iron', 'trams, buildings, shops, many voices' (55–56). The train, in an inversion of the 'Place of Death', the final destination of Haggard's infrastructural line (2008: 158), here stops 'in the great terminus like a cavern, like a nightmare, like a dread' (1984a: 56). It is a landscape not of redemptive, romanticised space, where, as Schwarz argues, the 'prescriptive ideal of the figure of the white man' is at its most 'absolute' (2011: 118). Instead, it is littered with barracks, compounds and mines, and instils in Ula a taste for the materialism of the metropole: 'the wearing of clothes', 'methylated spirit at the price of French brandy' and 'cigarettes' (Plomer, 1984a: 57, 60, 62).

Working as a labourer in the gold mines, Ula becomes trapped after a 'fall of rock' blocks his exit: the 'entombing rock' is not a mythologised King Solomon's mine located in a romanticised African landscape, but an active gold mine in the region's economic centre. Whilst trapped in the mine, Ula has a peculiar dream-like hallucination, slipping out of consciousness because of the claustrophobic conditions: 'he found himself confined in a small space without light, or air, or any sound save that of his blood singing thickly in his ears' and 'his lungs seem to be full of earth' (69). It is at this point, as Ula's hallucination begins, that the prose form of Plomer's narrative transforms into a set of poetic verses of uneven and differing length:

> The cavern can keep
> Its secrets in stillness,
> In darkness, enfolded
> In the wild fig trees,
> Whose sinews are moulded
> To the curves of the stone,
> And whose roots are thrust
> In a crevice of dust,
> Clinging tightly within
> To the nerves of the quartz [...]
> Far down, far down,
> Where are the savage
> Cities of the future? [...]
> What are you doing,
> Ula Masondo?
> Do you follow the Bushmen?
> Do you travel to the valley
> This side of the city? (71–74)

This poetic intervention grapples with the *topographical*, or multi-dimensional geology of the landscape, tracing 'the curves of the stone' and 'the nerves of the quartz', as well as '[t]he cave-paintings of the Bushmen' that are daubed onto its surface, recalling *African Farm*'s depiction of the 'Bushmen paintings' (2003: 55). Plomer's form unpicks the romance's linear infrastructure, challenging its ideological project to map the South African landscape and its resources as open and accessible. Whereas Haggard flattens the 'landscape' out 'before us like a map' (Haggard, 2008: 68), Plomer's narrative, like Schreiner's, achieves 'a density that is akin to the simultaneity often claimed for visual images as distinct from literature' (Bal, 1997: 82). This density is infused with a politics that emphasises the historical effects of imperialism. As the poetic formal interlude ends and the regular prose returns, Ula has a prophetic premonition of 'valleys' that do not resemble the 'promised land', 'like Paradise', of *King Solomon's Mines* (Haggard, 2008: 70). Rather, they are 'threaded with the smoke of occasional trains, with telegraph wires', with 'the houses of men of property', and 'humming motor-cars, shining and powerful' (Plomer, 1984a: 75–76) – he envisions a landscape marked by the uneven infrastructural development of global capital.

After surviving the rock fall, Ula decides to leave the mines: he 'received his wages', 'paid his debts' and – just as Quartermain and his companions opt to leave Kukuanaland – decides to return to Lembuland (78). Even Ula's newfound material wealth parodies the huge financial wealth that the romance's imperialists are able to extract. He carries 'a suitcase of plum-coloured cardboard embossed to look like leather [...] in a hand resplendent with cheap rings' and wears swinging 'ear-rings' and 'streamers of pink wool' on his wrists (78–80). In a final parodic enactment of the romance's racist ideology, when he returns from the city Ula dismisses his mother as a 'bloody heathen', in reaction to which she commits suicide (80–81). This depiction of how the movement of migrant labourers between rural and city spaces channelled 'new, urban behaviour patterns back to the reserves', thereby challenging 'traditional African structures' (Lester, 1998: 87), might suggest a tone of nostalgia for, or romanticisation of, a pre-capitalist, pre-industrial African society. However, in the story's closing frame narrative, which returns to the perspective of the white trader in conversation with his wife, the narrative retargets its satirical focus back at this tendency toward romanticisation and questions 'capital's attempts to acquire labour power from colonised, yet "traditionally" oriented, or, as they were called by whites, "raw" Africans' (Lester et al., 2000: 108):

> '[…] By jove, there's an example for you, of a boy going away all right, and coming back with all this Christian dandy business that I can't stand at any price. Give me the raw nigger any day, is what I have always maintained.'
> 'Oh, go on, Fred, you're the one that's always talking about increasing their wants, and getting the trade built up for little Freddy –'
> 'Yes, that's all very well, but if that Ula Masondo ever comes here again, won't I give him a piece of my mind!' (81)

In this closing interchange, a contradiction in imperial ideology emerges as the white colonial traders *lament* the creation of a black urban proletariat, even as they themselves facilitate that process. The romanticisation of the rural landscape and the image of the 'noble savage' – a trope that, as Chrisman argues, was commonly used in imperial romance narratives to 'articulate and then resolve anxieties' created by black resistance to white rule (2012: 237) – cannot be reconciled with the simultaneous incorporation of a black labour force into the capitalist world-system. Plomer illuminates this fundamental contradiction which underpins capital accumulation, a recursive pattern to which I will return in the next chapter's discussion of John Buchan's 'frontier consciousness'. Even as Fred's wife begins to point out this tension, gesturing towards the economic function of the colonies as a new market for capitalist production, she is cut short by her husband, reducing this fundamental contradiction to a Machereyan 'silence' or 'absence', a faltering that marks the text's ideological contour (1986: 79). But the argument still remains, 'in the very letter of the text' (151), the white trader making it even more conspicuous by his explosive interruption.

By parodying the imperial romance's key features in this way, Plomer's narrative brings its 'hidden transcript' into 'public discourse' (Scott, 1990: 5). It draws attention to the 'discrepancies' between its own narrative and the conventions of the romance genre, exposing and interrogating, before finally rupturing through, that genre's ideological borders. The imperial romance attempted to construct, as Jameson might remark, 'imaginary or formal "solutions" to unresolvable social contradictions' by producing a South African space conspicuously evacuated of both industrialising cityscapes and black labour (2002: 64). In his rewriting of the imperial romance Plomer foregrounds the tensions concealed within its genre's infrastructure, producing a South African geography marked by vast infrastructural webs and increasingly urban environments. However, to conclude this chapter I want to read 'Ula Masondo' on its own terms to show how it also explores various forms of resistance that these spatial configurations and their segregationist underpinnings actually provoked and enabled.

Michael Wade, in his 'preliminary investigation' into the relationship between 'the historical processes of industrialisation and urbanisation in South Africa' and 'their literary inscriptions', identifies the railway as one of its most potent and 'multivalent symbols' (1994: 76). Wade argues that whilst configured as 'the symbol of penetration', the railway's power is in fact 'necessarily dualistic' (78). The train 'brings together' only to 'set apart': it becomes a 'mediating environment' that both 'symbolically and actually brings white and black groups together' (78–84). Indeed, within the duration of the short story's narrative, Ula actually appropriates, to use Wade's words, 'the representative symbol of the industrial-political power of the South African state' (90). As Ula approaches Johannesburg, the train 'window' reveals to him its 'bitter citadels of unreasoning industry', leaving among Ula and his 'compatriots in the train' the 'silence of apprehension' (Plomer, 1984a: 55). However, by the end of the narrative, after Ula's inauguration into the metropolis, the carriage is no longer a location of uneasy revelation. Instead, as 'the rushing train' returns Ula to Lembuland in the story's penultimate section, the infrastructural line is not the 'white' road of King Solomon, but is rather described, significantly, as 'black' (80). Ula is comfortable in the crowded station amongst the 'many moving forms of noisy and emerging humanity' and his refusal to recognise his mother reinforces the shift in his social and spatial affiliations from tribal to urban environments (80).

The appropriation of this arterial transport infrastructure is matched by Ula's familiarity with, and ability to move between, the city's segregated urban spaces. Arriving in Johannesburg, Ula is at first restricted to the regulatory structures, both spatial and temporal, that are in place: 'he suffered and never forgot the routine of work and rest at the Simeon and Steck Amalgamated', moving past only 'the engine-house on his way to the compound' (56). Historically, however, compound managers did offer 'the discretionary issue of "special passes"' to workers, allowing them 'to move about the Witwatersrand, particularly on weekends' (Moroney, 1982: 260). Sure enough, as Ula soon discovers, on 'Sunday afternoons life improved' (Plomer, 1984a: 57). In these moments of freedom, Ula begins to drink, gamble and befriend a small group of other black workers. After the group's gambling habits land them 'several pounds in debt', they begin to devise ways of increasing their acquisition of material wealth:

> Stefan suggested that they should join his friends, who knew a good way of making money, their custom being to station themselves on a lonely road behind the kopjes near the Simeon and Steck, and to lie in wait for cyclists and pedestrians, on whom they would rush out with a volley of sticks and stones. After the assault there was robbery, and after the robbery there was flight. The scene of these operations had lately been changed, so there was little danger of arrest. (61)

Ula, Stefan and their friends locate themselves in a geographical space that is within the infrastructural web of the urban landscape, yet simultaneously beyond its regulatory apparatuses: both police and compound managers, though nearby, are evaded. They situate themselves in what Harvey, in a discussion of Lefebvre, calls 'liminal social spaces', where '"something different" is not only possible, but foundational for the defining of revolutionary trajectories' (2012: xvii) – indeed, the 'progressive growth of urban crime' in early twentieth-century Johannesburg has been read as 'evidence of African resistance to the control imposed by the mining industry' (Richardson and Van-Helten, 1982: 92). It becomes 'the custom' of Ula's gang 'to meet in a thicket of [...] bushes on an unfrequented part of the kopje near the mine', where they are, significantly, 'unseen by the rest of the world', despite being located deep within the networks of global capital (Plomer, 1984a: 62). The 'something different' they enact begins to arise, as Harvey would argue, not necessarily as part 'of a conscious plan, but more simply out of what people do, feel, sense, and come to articulate as they seek meaning in their daily lives' (2012: xvii). Plomer's story narrates this process as Ula and his fellow workers, ground down by their heavy labour, seek hedonistic indulgence to make their life bearable and eventually resort to crime to fund this lifestyle. The spatially segregated areas within which the white population is situated are transfigured, in Plomer's text, into the source of wealth that improves Ula's material condition, as the urban environment enables a form of resistance that was unrealisable in the rural geographies of the romance. As one member of Ula's gang comments, 'There is no money in Lembuland [...] All the white people there are policemen or missionaries. How can you get money in such a place?' (68).

The revolutionary trajectory to which the gang's spontaneous actions give rise becomes increasingly coordinated as they seek increased financial reward by stealing from their 'masters' (65). Each individual plays a different, pre-designated role in the robbery, which is predicated on the gang's ability both to cross over the boundary wall that surrounds the white master's home and to penetrate the building's entrances and exits. Ula is able, quite easily, to 'peep' over the wall, and does so 'just in time to see Emma leaping out of the back door with a jingle of jewellery' in an act that empowers her – a black African woman – to remove embodiments of material wealth from the home of a white man (65). With this distraction in place, Stefan is able to 'dart' into the house, and after stealing the 'box' in which the money is kept, 'hurdles' over the wall (66). This transgression of physical boundary lines – infrastructures of segregation inserted to maintain racial and class divisions – results in a successful act of resistance. 'If the walls attempt to harness the natural entropy of the urban', argues Weizman, 'breaking it would liberate new social and political forms' (2012: 210). Plomer's protagonists render 'the wall' – symbolic of the barriers of the segregated city – to be 'no longer physically or conceptually solid or', within the 'law/wall' paradigm, 'legally impenetrable': 'the functional spatial syntax that [the wall creates] collapses' (Weizman, 2012: 210). Here, it is Plomer's textual syntax that deconstructs the order implemented by Johannesburg's rigid infrastructural segmentations. 'Ula Masondo' engages in the process of 'performative archaeology', an excavation of social and physical urban space that not only contests its structures but, as Kruger argues, 'imagine[s] future alternatives' to them (2013: 11–12).

This urban environment, which attempts to regulate a black African labour force, here becomes the location of a disruptive, if not revolutionary, black proletariat that threatens that environment's stability. This transformation results in the functioning of the city, to return to Harvey, 'as an important site of political action and revolt': the 'physical and social re-engineering and territorial organisation' that has been central to the industrialising process becomes 'a weapon in political struggles' (2012: 117–118). As Gray argues, during this period, Plomer was engaged in a project of 'demystifying and de-exoticizing what before him had been the vast romantic emptiness of the non-Eurocentric world' (1986: 60). Fundamental to this process was the representation of urban environments that, as sites of sociopolitical contestation, were repeatedly written out of the imperial romance's South African geographies. Plomer's 'Ula Masondo', in Scott's terminology, produces a 'public declaration' of its 'hidden transcripts' by re-orientating its perspective and producing a hitherto unmapped area of South African space (1990: 5). The effect of Plomer's literary intervention is to expose the limits of the romance's spatial productions, revealing the ideological and geographical borders of the genre's cartographic project. However, 'Ula Masondo' also looks forward to the conceptualisation of Johannesburg not only as a city of segregation and domination, but as an arena of narrative possibility that initiates resistance to, and transgressions of, its spatial structures. As Nuttall and Mbembe remark more generally, if 'the black migrant worker is constrained to experience the metropolis as a site of radical uncertainty, unpredictability, and insecurity', it is under these conditions that 'culture and aesthetics become an open-ended construction built in existing and often misused infrastructures' (2008: 23).

Even if the half-century following *King Solomon's Mines'* publication was marked by South Africa's industrialisation and proliferating uneven infrastructural development, imperial romances still continued to be published and circulated widely. The genre's literary geographies were modified and adapted in response to the region's infrastructural and urban shifts – aspects of the romance genre would even shape literary texts responding to India's deeply uneven infrastructural development in the 1920s and '30s, as this book's fourth chapter will show. In the next chapter, I therefore return to the imperial romance in its slightly later incarnation, documented here in the work of John Buchan. Though both Schreiner's and Plomer's literary writings throw the 'infrapolitics' of Haggard's romance into relief, Buchan's texts produce more nuanced literary geographies that cannot be so easily resisted through the intertextual connections that I have analysed so far.

By assessing what I will call Buchan's 'frontier consciousness', the next chapter will show how Buchan's literary texts continue to be complicit with the processes of capitalist accumulation and uneven infrastructural development, attempting to offer a cultural fix to the various spatial and ideological contradictions that they generated. However, I will also show how, despite producing a more complex, topographical production of the South African landscape than Haggard's romances, these contradictions continue to warp the formal smoothing over that colonial literature attempts. These contradictions can, I will continue to show, be most clearly delineated by focusing on the infrastructures *in* and *of* Buchan's writing.

CHAPTER 3

Mapping Frontiers: John Buchan and the Topographies of Imperial Ideology

Introduction: Frontiers and Borderlands

Despite the industrialisation and urbanisation of South Africa's core regions and a corresponding literary interest in them, imperial romances continued to flourish, albeit with various new formal traits, thematic concerns and increasingly complex geographical preoccupations. Of note was the writing of John Buchan, a Scot who spent much of his political career at the heart of the British imperial establishment – he had been president of the Oxford Union and would become, in later years, Governor General of Canada. Perhaps most importantly, however, he worked as a colonial administrator on the South African 'highveld' in the aftermath of the Second Anglo-Boer War, or the South African War (1899–1902). For Buchan, the distinctive topography of the highveld functioned as a spatial fix for the contradictions of not only South Africa's, but also Britain's industrialising and urbanising spaces, and this fix comes through in the cultural terrain of his literary writing. As he reflected in 1903:

> [the highveld's] vast spaces [...] are built on a scale other than ours; man's labour has in the last resort no power to change them. [...] It is England, richer, softer, kindlier, a vast demesne laid out as no landscape gardener could ever contrive, waiting for a human life worthy of such an environment. (1903: 126)

The topographical 'depth' of the 'highveld', its 'absence of points of purchase for the eye' and its 'lack of strategic frames of geographical reference, such as roads, towns and the accurate measures of distance', made it a 'landscape that lacked enclosure, orientation and articulation' (Foster, 1998: 333–334).

For Buchan, it was a 'frontier', 'the boundary between civilised settlement and untamed nature, and between the colonial settlers and the various non-white, mainly but not exclusively indigenous peoples' (Schwarz, 2011: 111–112). Pratt cautions against the use of the term 'frontier' because of its implicit Eurocentrism – 'the frontier is a frontier only with respect to Europe' – preferring instead her phrase 'contact zone', which readjusts this geographical 'point of view' (2003: 6–7). Though I follow Pratt's corrective agenda, it is necessary to foreground the term 'frontier' here because it illuminates a specific strand of imperial ideology. For Buchan, the veld is 'nature' itself, an '*external*' entity, 'the raw material from which society is built, the frontier which industrial capitalism continually pushes back' (Smith, 2008: 11). Nature's supposed externality spatially fixes crises in capital accumulation, and Buchan's preoccupation with the production of frontiers should be understood as a corresponding cultural fix. His writing 'abstracts' the landscape into 'social nature' – that is, the process 'through which states and capitalists map, identify, quantify, measure, and code human and extra-human natures in service to capital accumulation' (Moore, 2015: 194). Focusing on the infrastructures that litter Buchan's novels, it is possible to (re)disturb the resolution, or fix, that frontiers perform for imperial ideology, and from those disturbances, to open up a spatial resistance to it.

Delivering the annual 'Romanes Lecture' at the University of Oxford in 1907, Lord George Curzon, Viceroy of India from 1899 to 1905, spoke on 'the subject of frontiers' (1907: 3). Contrasting 'the boundaries of the British Empire in Asia' with recent political border negotiations in 'every part of Africa', he observed that '[o]utside of the English Universities no school of character exists to compare with the Frontier' (56). The frontier was an ideological pressure valve for the various class and racial conflicts foregrounded in urban environments, as Plomer's 'Ula Masondo' made clear, functioning as both a spatial and cultural fix for the contradictions of capital. 'Frontiers made it possible for capital to voraciously consume both the geological accumulations and biological configurations of unpaid work with ruinous increase in the costs of production', writes Moore; 'the natural fertility of the soil may "act as an increase in fixed capital"' (2015: 174–175). Ashis Nandy observes that 'by opening up alternative channels

of social mobility in the colonies and by underwriting nationalist senti-
ments through colonial wars of expansion', colonial frontiers 'blurred the
lines of social divisions' and 'shunted off to the colonies certain indirect
expressions of cultural criticism: social deviants unhappy with the social
order and buffeted by the stress within it' (1983: 33). Imperialism's proliferating infrastructural development created a contradictory crisis in capital
accumulation, one that demanded the production of new frontiers: 'As
the vacant spaces of the earth are filled up, the competition for the residue
is temporarily more keen', Curzon observed (1907: 7). By 1924, Joseph
Conrad would write nostalgically of 'the geography of open spaces and
wide horizons, built up on men's devoted work in the open air', lamenting
'its approaching end with the death of the last great explorer' (1926: 14), a
spatial fiction that Buchan's literary writing sought to recover.

Speaking a few months after Curzon, as he was working on drafts
of the manuscript that would become his first novel, *Prester John* (1910),
Buchan himself discussed this ideology of the frontier, or what I will call
his 'frontier consciousness'. He conflated the economic benefits of emigration to the colonies with the frontier rhetoric of the imperial romance, for
which Haggard had set the generic coordinates:

> These new countries give a man a horizon and an ideal which he may not be able to
> find at home. He has his chance, and the look-out ahead for him is not a lifetime
> spent in working at small wages, for others. [....] The emigrant has romance in his
> life, for he knows there is the chance of the unforeseen, and this chance puts enter-
> prise and ambition into men [...] It is as the residuary remedy for social disorders
> that we must advocate it, and it is a remedy which must be increasingly used if both
> the Mother Country and the outlying Empire are to remain in social and economic
> health. (1940b: 127–128)

For Buchan, the frontier fixed both economic *and* ideological crises in this
moment of capital accumulation. Through readings of his novels *Prester
John* (1910) and *The Thirty-Nine Steps* (1915), this chapter will demonstrate
how Buchan's fiction sets out more fully the paradox that was identified in
the concluding scene of Plomer's short story, in which his white characters
lament the industrialisation of South Africa whilst themselves facilitating capital's accumulative processes. Buchan's literary writings reveal this

fundamental contradiction: they must relentlessly move outwards to produce new frontiers, but the processes of mapping and narrating involved in this production of space paradoxically obliterates frontiers in the moment of their realisation. The frontier therefore has to be constantly *re*produced; as Schwarz describes, 'the frontier itself proliferates' (2011: 259). Buchan's fiction realises this contradiction in its production of space before immediately reengaging in it. These oscillating motions are best excavated out of the infrastructural coordinates of Buchan's novels by focusing, as I will show, on the occurrence of infrastructure *in* his texts. Buchan's physical infrastructures transport his protagonists into frontier spaces, whilst simultaneously facilitating what Hopkins and Wallerstein would call the processes of 'peripheralisation' (1982: 99). This peripheralisation process intensifies, rather than satiates, the need to produce more space 'beyond' in order that capital's accumulative processes might continue. In Buchan's 'imaginative geography', to use Gregory's term (2004: 17), the 'vast spaces' of the South African highveld are able momentarily to fix this contradiction, before the paradox embedded in his frontier project reemerges and once again disturbs this aspect of imperial ideology.

Like Haggard, Buchan spent a remarkably short time in South Africa. Arriving in 1901 and leaving in 1903, he returned only once to Cape Town in May 1905. But the experience gripped his imagination: 'Those were wonderful years for me, years of bodily and mental activity, of zeal and hope not yet dashed by failure', he recalled in his autobiography, written in the year of his death, noting that 'it is the land itself which holds my memory' (1940a: 110–111, 115). Buchan was a key player in an intense, though short-lived, British imperial project. Appointed to the Land Settlement Department in Pretoria, he was a member of the 'so-called "kindergarten"', a group of young men with 'nearly unfettered power' led by Alfred Milner, the new High Commissioner of South Africa (Kruse, 1989: 43–44). Milner, an 'imperial zealot', was determined in the aftermath of the Anglo-Boer War to transform the Transvaal into a 'thoroughly British' domain (Meredith, 2010: 365–367, 482). British infrastructural projects in Johannesburg, documented in the previous chapter, were accompanied by policies of cultural imperialism that encouraged British immigration and settlement, and introduced British education systems to promote anglicisation and 'denationalise'

Dutch-speakers. By the time Milner was recalled to Britain in April 1905, however, it was evident that these strategies had failed. British immigration never reached the levels he had hoped for and his anti-Dutch policies served only to antagonise and bolster an emerging Afrikaner nationalism (see Afigbo et al., 1986b: 165–167; Johnson, 2003: 72).

If the failure of this project cracked the veneer of his political faith in imperialism, Buchan's nostalgic preoccupation with the South African landscape was more deeply rooted in his personal experience of it. Working as 'Milner's "fixer"', Buchan dealt with 'difficult operations characterised by political sensitivity bordering on constitutional impropriety' (Redley, 2009: 68). This included pursuing 'on Milner's behalf a policy of taking back for use by incoming British settlers land in the former republics which had already been leased by their governments to Boer farmers' (69). Buchan was therefore responsible for implementing the most invasive aspects of Britain's imperial policy in South Africa, actively engaged in dispossession through land repossession. If his subsequent obsession with the South African landscape are explained by this experience, it was further intensified when, after 'a weighty complaint reached Milner from a local land company about the government's land policy', Buchan became the scapegoat. Accused of costing 'the government over £1,000,000' and receiving much venomous 'public criticism', Buchan decided to leave South Africa before completing the two years for which he had originally been contracted (70–71).

For Buchan, writing and landscape were deeply intertwined, as his productions of frontier geography, and particularly the South African highveld, became a space in which he could work out frontier consciousness's central paradox: 'A hundred Johannesburgs would not change the country's character. It seems not to take the impress of man', he would write (1940a: 116–117). Historically and geographically distant from South Africa, Buchan was able to portray the country as a 'Borderland' (116), a space capable of 'giving to the congested masses at home [in Britain] open country instead of blind alley' (125). Buchan's momentary metaphoric use of urban infrastructure conveys the ideological work that the frontier landscape performs for him. His conviction that the region can absorb 'a hundred Johannesburgs' without running out of 'open country' positions his literary productions of the frontier as themselves an attempt to resolve the contemporaneous crisis in capital accumulation. Buchan's imagination of South Africa as infinite rather than, as Luxemburg had argued, 'finite', fixed the contradiction faced by capital as 'the new acquisition of new markets' comes 'to an end' (2013: 223), as well as alleviating the social unrest to which increasingly proximal uneven developments gave rise. It is this paradox that gives shape to the geographical trajectories of Buchan's plots, a set of spatial dynamics that are most clearly illuminated by focusing on the infrastructural routes that cut through his frontier landscapes.

Buchan's choice of the term 'Borderland' is infused with a retrospective politics. As Gloria Anzaldúa argues, whilst borders function 'to distinguish *us* from *them*', a 'borderland is a vague and undetermined place' that is in a 'constant state of transition'; it is a zone of restless, constant movement – '[t]ension grips the inhabitants of the borderland like a virus' (1987: 3). For Arif Dirlik, borderlands are spaces that 'are essential not as cultural metaphors but as the locations for actual production and exchange relations' (1995: 230–231), a configuration that emphasises not only the infrastructures *in* literary productions of space, but also the infrastructures *of* them. The fraught socioeconomic relations of the borderlands of the world-system can be viewed through the tumultuous ideological anxieties, fissures and limitations of Buchan's literary texts. As his romance narratives respond to South Africa's industrialisation and urbanisation, they become shaped by a restless and ongoing process of 'transition'. Throughout his novels, Buchan's characters cannot sit still: they get 'stiff with doing nothing', fearful of a 'beastly stagnation' that is resolved through the production of South African space (Buchan, 2010: 264). Buchan's 'performances of space' and 'imaginative geographies' still, like Haggard's, attempt to 'fold difference into distance, simultaneously conjuring up and holding at bay the strange, the unnatural, the monstrous' (Gregory, 2004: 249). However, by repeatedly returning to the borderlands of the world-system, Buchan's literary writings might be said to incorporate a kind of 'border thinking', one that introduces 'cracks' into the 'the imaginary of the world system' (Mignolo, 2012: 22). It is from within these cracks that, as I will now explore, an anti-imperial and notably spatial resistance can be seen to emerge.

The Infrastructure of the Frontier

Set in the Scottish highlands, *Prester John*'s opening pages are littered with references which align the eleven-year-old Davie's first adventure, both geographically and ideologically, with the frontier. Though beginning in Scotland, Davie is soon sent to South Africa, where the rest of the novel is set, to make his 'fortune'. Even in this first scene, however, Davie's 'tracking' skills and his identification of 'spoor' (Buchan, 2008: 4) reveal his acquaintance with the practice of scouting that had been propagated in relation to the imperial frontier by another widely read text. Robert Baden-Powell's *Scouting for Boys* (1908) explicitly linked Britain's rise as a global power with the ideology of the frontier: 'The History of the Empire', he wrote, 'has been made by British adventurers and explorers, the scouts of the nation, for hundreds of years past up to the present time' (2004: 13). Embodying this exploratory practice, Tam, one of Davie's friends, is 'deputed to go round the edge of the cliff from which the shore was visible, and report if the coast was clear' (Buchan, 2008: 5). As the boys cautiously approach the geographic edge of the British Isles, that turn of phrase – 'the coast is clear' – takes on a literal meaning. It transpires that it is, in fact, *not* clear. Laputa, a 'black minister', is situated on the very edge of the landmass of Britain, down on the 'Dyve Burn sands' (6). The novel's geography is inflected with frontier ideology as Davie, narrating retrospectively, asks the rhetorical question: 'What kind of errand had brought this interloper into our territory?' (6). This ideological inflection takes on a further topographical dimension, as the novel's politics are translated into the three-dimensional landscape of Britain's political and geographical boundary. The beach, where Laputa stands, is located *below* the 'cliffs', whilst the boys, *above*, have 'an excellent vantage-ground' (7). The implicit hierarchies which define this confrontational borderland, invested with the racialised terminologies of 'civilisation' and 'savagery' – throughout Buchan's narrative Laputa is described as 'the black minister', with 'the whites of eyes and the red of his gums' repeatedly emphasised (2008: 7–10) – are reflected and reiterated by the topographical levels at which the representatives of each are located.

Infrastructures begin to shape this geography as soon as Davie and his friends flee *back*, away from Laputa and the frontier topography, towards 'human habitation' (11), metonymic of 'civilisation' with its significations of safety and shelter. Thus far, the novel has produced the geographical and ideological paradigm unproblematically. However, in this transitional moment, the infrastructural network that spans the landscape generates a peculiar ambivalence: 'We did not dare take the road by the links, but made for the nearest human habitation', Davie reports; when the threat of the frontier is removed just a sentence or so later, however, they join 'the highroad and trotted back at our best pace to Kirkcaple' (11). This notable shift in Buchan's description demonstrates a contingent use of the infrastructural route, one that is dependent upon his protagonists' geographical proximity to the frontier. When deep within the core circuitries of the world-system, these infrastructures are configured as secure and can thus be utilised. The boys, who shortly before 'scrambled and leaped' away from Laputa back up the cliff, once removed from the frontier scenario can simply 'trot' back home along the highroad (10–11). Whilst navigating the tension of the frontier, the infrastructural route must remain in sight of Buchan's protagonists, operating as a spatial reference point. Importantly, however, to travel directly along or upon it induces anxiety. It leaves Buchan's characters vulnerable and exposed and must be avoided.

This contingent use of infrastructure recurs consistently throughout *Prester John*. Like Haggard's imperial protagonists, Davie keeps them in view, using them to map and chart his progress through and across the landscape. However, unlike Haggard's protagonists, he repeatedly decides that to travel *along* these routes themselves is *too* dangerous. This danger is attributed to a number of factors, such as the possibility of being subject to surveillance, or being tracked or traced, a trope that is repeated throughout *The Thirty-Nine Steps*, as this chapter will show.[1] Davie's geographical

---

1   For example, at various points Davie notes that 'I would suddenly be conscious, as I walked on the road, that I was being watched' (Buchan, 2008: 34); 'I must get off the road. [...] it was only wise to leave the track which I would be assumed to have taken' (127–128). Nathan Waddell's psychoanalytic reading of the paranoia exhibited by Buchan's protagonists constructs an 'architectonics' that resembles the dynamics

location throughout *Prester John*, so often in sight of, but never actually deep within, the infrastructural networks that constitute Britain's world-empire in South Africa, enacts the ideological function of the frontier. Davie needs to have access to the 'symbolic objects' of imperial infrastructure at all times. But he also always needs to be able to move beyond them, to be one of the 'scouts of the nation', to use Baden-Powell's terminology (2005: 13), expanding these networks to facilitate capital's accumulative processes. This spatial dichotomy – a constant desire to move outwards that pulls against a conflictual need to return, or look back, to that which is expanded beyond – generates a tension that underpins the contradictions of Davie's frontier consciousness and shapes the form and plot of Buchan's literary writings.

Importantly, this tension is not static, but rather oscillates as the narrative progresses, throwing Davie back and forth as his attitude shifts in relation to his geographical location. During his initial travel away from Britain to South Africa, Davie suffers acutely from 'the loneliness of an exile' (2008: 15); when he reaches his 'final landing in Africa' he has 'lost every remnant of homesickness' (23); but then, located in his frontier trading station, and suspicious of some sort of anti-imperial activity in the region, he longs 'miserably for the places where white men were thronged together in dorps and cities' (60), tying his emotional response not only to a racial and cultural familiarity but *also* to an infrastructural one. Later in the novel, after escaping Laputa's imprisonment, in which he has been trapped for over two chapters, with the exclamation, '[a]t last I was free', rather than retreating to the safety of the British imperial military lines he does 'the craziest thing of all. [...] I started running back [along] the road we had come' (125–126). The plot oscillates geographically, a movement that both dictates, and is in turn dictated by, Davie's frontier consciousness. He perpetually shifts back and forth between an ideological commitment to the frontier, and an overwhelming desire to be relocated *back* within the safety of imperial infrastructural networks. Davie himself acknowledges this inconsistency, commenting shortly before

---

of the frontier excavated here: 'The paranoiac, burdened with feeling of smallness or insignificance, "projects" these feelings onto his environment to create an external persecuting agency that only he can detect and defeat' (2009: 126–129).

the narrative's climactic scene that 'I was now as eager to get back into danger as I had been to get into safety' (167). Oscillating between the starkly contrasting core and peripheral zones of the frontier's borderland, the novel reveals that the two socioeconomic and cultural arenas come into being through their relationship with one another. After all, Davie identifies his frontier destination, Blaauwildenesstefontein, through the spatial referent of the 'railroad' located on the 'map', from which it is 'not above ninety miles'; this locates the frontier in relation to an infrastructural demarcation, whilst also placing it, as Mr Wardlaw, Davie's companion, explains, 'in the heart of native reserves', somewhere that 'sounds like a place for adventure' (16–17).

For *Prester John*, core and periphery are constituted through both economic and cultural activity, as the novel's ideological fabric weaves these two contrasting motors of imperial expansion together into 'a field of mutually if also unevenly determining forces' (Williams, 2005: 20). Unlike *King Solomon's Mines*, *Prester John* makes no effort to conceal the socioeconomic determinants that justified infrastructural development. Mr Wardlaw's comments on Blaaudewildebeestefontein are revealing: 'It sounds like a place for adventure, Mr Crawfurd. You'll exploit the pockets of the black men and I'll see what I can do with their minds' (2008: 17). Wardlaw makes the division between ideological and economic dimensions of imperial expansion: the transmission of a 'civilising' imperial culture and the exploitation of new markets and labour forces. But the text of *Prester John* encompasses them both as a whole, consolidating them into one imperial project as a mutually substantive enterprise. Davie's job is, his uncle tells him, at the very beginning of Chapter 2 (indicatively entitled, 'Furth! Fortune!'), 'to be assistant storekeeper' for 'one of the biggest trading and shipping concerns in the world'; 'It lies with you [Davie] to open up new trade among the natives' (13–15). Davie arrives at the frontier as a representative of, and outermost link to, a global infrastructural network shaped by the dynamics of the capitalist world-system. On his arrival, he immediately sets about enmeshing local populations and socioeconomic systems into a global network of core and peripheral modes of production: there are new markets that he is keen to tap into (the 'countryside was crawling with natives') and numerous products 'which I foresaw', Davie notes, 'could be worked up into a profitable export' (30).

Davie's metonymy for global capital is reinforced by Laputa himself, the rebellious black priest who brings the frontier into being and, as already noted, is so often located at its boundary. Laputa repeatedly identifies Davie by the economic role he is performing: 'It is the storekeeper', says Laputa, even when it becomes apparent that Davie is, in fact, an intruder attempting to spy on Laputa's rebellious schemes (110). Interestingly, the novel's climactic scene hinges on the passing of an economic transaction between them, the relational axis of periphery and core manifesting even at this level of characterisation. The scene of this transaction is especially illuminating:

> 'Now see here, Mr Laputa,' I said. 'I am going to talk business. Before you started this rising, you were a civilised man with a good education. [...] I am going to make you a fair and square business proposition. [...] I offer to trade with you. Give me my life, and I will take you to the place and put the jewels in your hand. Otherwise you may kill me, but you will never see the collar of John again.'
>
> I still think that was a pretty bold speech for a man to make in a predicament like mine. But it had its effect. Laputa ceased to be the barbarian king, and talked like a civilised man. (152)

Here the narrative enmeshes economic and ideological motors of empire together, revealing their symbiotic relationship, or what Boehmer describes as their 'mutually justifying force' (2005: 37), as each facilitates the other. As he enters into Davie's business deal, Laputa's 'barbarian' attributes are quelled and he becomes 'a civilised man', just as Davie himself becomes quite literally a metonym for global capital: his own life is commodified, taking on a valuation that he is then able to trade. Emphasising this allegory, as soon as the transaction is complete and Laputa receives 'the jewels', he 'once more' becomes 'the savage transported in the presence of his fetich [*sic*]' (162). For the narrative duration of the contract, the novel momentarily resolves the tension between core and peripheral zones and the violent oscillations between them come to a standstill. Once it is broken, however, the relational economy fails and its oscillatory motion resumes: the frontier must be reproduced and conquered all over again. In this way,

Laputa seals his own fate: if Buchan's narrative is to realise its ideological resolution – the transformation of a rebellious black population into a labour force for the global capitalist economy (see MacDonald, 1994: 212) – Laputa, the only black African in the whole novel who continues to resist the hierarchical ordering of the world-system, must be sealed far beyond its infrastructural networks: 'Far from human quest he sleeps his last sleep' (Buchan, 2008: 190).

The Symbolic Cartographies of *Prester John*

The landscape of *Prester John* is far more than simply a setting in which this action takes place. It performs ideological work that is best excavated by focusing on the infrastructures that give spatial structure to the text. Reading the novel's mix of real and fictional locations as a set of spatial clues, T. J. Couzens has plotted out *Prester John*'s geography onto, and against, a historical map of South Africa. The novel's action takes place, broadly speaking, within a semicircular segment of mountain range; or as Couzens describes it, a 'whole rough U turned on its side' that 'marks the division between the highveld to the west and the bushveld (or lowveld) to the east' (1981: 2–3).[2] Buchan himself described this South African topography in his autobiography, many years later:

2   It is worth commenting that if the novel mentions recognisable geographical reference points to make its location roughly identifiable, it refutes any historical specificity, rehearsing the 'removal of all references to time' characteristic of colonialism's 'verbal economy' (Mbembe, 2001: 177). As Craig Smith demonstrates, the novel constructs 'a no-time, an imaginary moment compounding invented and actual times' that cannot be linked to a specific year in South African history – 'the story is "set" in 1870, in 1878, in 1899, in 1906, and in 1909–1910', all years with their own significant and distinctive historical events, but that exist coterminously within the time frame of the novel (1995: 181).

The country is like an inverted pie-dish, a high tableland sloping steeply into the
ocean on the south and east, less steeply to the Zambesi in the north. [...] The pie-dish
contains every variety of landscape. [...] there are a thousand hidden nooks which
recall to every traveller his own home, for it is the most versatile of lands. Yet there
is a certain subtle unity in the landscape, something indefinable which we know to
be South African. (1940a: 117)

These excerpts from Buchan's extensive description of the 'inverted pie-dish'
evidence his intimate knowledge of the *topography* of the Transvaal, and
the novel's map, included as a frontispiece to its early editions, similarly
emphasises this U-shaped landscape.

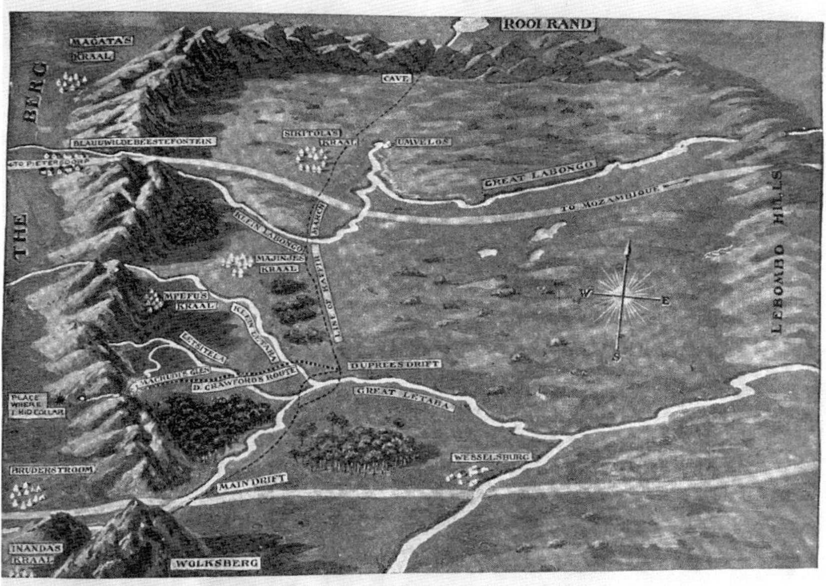

Figure 3.1: The frontispiece map included in the first editions of *Prester John*,
published in 1910 and 1912.

Prester John's map is not a conventional two-dimensional depiction
such as Haggard's, but is rather drawn from a sideways slant that visualises
the landscape's physical depth and exhibits, at least ostensibly, an increased

verisimilitude.[3] Curiously, the map that appeared as the frontispiece to the first two editions of *Prester John*, published in 1910 and 1912, is professionally drawn and marked with clear, printed labels that announce both geographical locations and scenes from the novel ('Blauuwildebeestefontein', 'Dupree's Drift', 'D. Crawford's Route [*sic*]'). These first editions also include a 'note' that reads: 'The reader is recommended to consult the map opposite the title-page for the details of the various journeys of Mr. David Crawfurd' (1910: iv; 1912: iv). By contrast, the map accompanying the 1918 and 1920 editions, whilst depicting exactly the same landscape and its corresponding labels, is roughly drawn and the accompanying text is written in a sloping longhand – indicatively, the note that directs the reader's attention to it has also been removed. It is tempting to read this counter-intuitive deterioration in the professed cartographic accuracy of the map as an aesthetic expression of Britain's waning cultural and economic – and thus representational – hegemony in the region. However, it seems more likely that this is simply due to the fact that, because of the Great War in Europe or other financial problems faced by Buchan's publishers, Thomas Nelson and Sons, the later map was a more economically viable option, cheaper to produce and reprint. We might even choose to link up these two hypotheses, reading the financial strain felt by the publishers and detectable in the map's evolving aesthetic as a direct result of Britain's deteriorating economic strength. Whatever the case, it is worth noting that the map has completely disappeared from all contemporary editions of what remains an under-read and unprofitable novel in the late twentieth and twenty-first centuries.

3   Buchan is preoccupied with the production of three-dimensional, *topographically accurate* maps, throughout his writings, so much so that the construction of topographical maps are even narrated meta-textually. For example, in a slightly later novel, *Greenmantle* (1916), Buchan's South African character Peter Pienar constructs a three-dimensional mould of the borderland he is about to traverse: 'Peter's way of doing things was all his own. He scraped earth and plaster out of a corner and sat down to make a little model of the landscape on the table, following the contours of the map. [...] He puzzled over it for a long time, and conned the map till he must have got it by heart' (2010: 264).

Figure 3.2: The frontispiece map included in two later editions of *Prester John*,
published in 1918 and 1920.

Regardless of the quality of their production, the frontispieces included
in *Prester John*'s early editions read more like paintings or 'images' than they

do maps. Huggan distinguishes maps from 'landscapes' that are more like 'cultural images', and which function in literary texts most often as part of a process of 'symbolic identification' (1994: 40). This is iterated by *Prester John*'s frontispiece – operating here as a 'cultural image' or 'landscape' rather than a conventional map – and is reiterated throughout the text as the landscape performs its ideological function. As has already been noted, the novel's opening depiction of the topography of the Scottish coastline performs ideological work, and similar agendas are embedded into the novel's production of South African space. The narrative itself invites this reading:

> It was a very bad map, for there had been no surveying east of the Berg, and most of the names were mere guesses. But I found the word 'Rooirand' marking an eastern continuation of the northern wall, and probably set down from some hunter's report. I had better explain here the chief features of the country, for they bulk largely in my story. (Buchan, 2008: 40)

Davie then goes on to give a rough sketch of the geography depicted in the novel's frontispiece. But there is a peculiar self-reflexivity in his narrative here, as the 'mere guesses' become translated into fictional locations and the 'chief features' of the landscape take on a topographical depth within it. Of course, they 'bulk largely' in terms of their physical presence and as part of the verisimilitude of the novel's representation of the landscape. Additionally, they are a prominent feature in the plot, providing an important background for the novel's action – the Rooirand, mentioned here for the first time by Davie, is the cave from which he will have to escape in the novel's climactic scene, as he literally grapples with its physical contours (191–200). But there is another reading of the novel's landscape invited by the text: this topography can be understood as actually performing, at this infrastructural level, the broader ideological resolutions and agendas that the narrative is more obviously driving towards.

At the beginning of the novel the 'grand country up there' – the high-veld that lies inland and to the west, away from the coastline – is described only as 'a grand opportunity for the [white] man who can take it'; 'there are few white men near', warns Mr Colles, Davie's employer (21). Just two chapters later, however, this geography has shifted, with the 'unknown', unchartered country now being located to the east, along the coastline. As Davie himself observes, the frontier, at this stage in the narrative, now lies 'east of the Berg' (40). But it is in the following chapter that this slow transposition of racial hierarchies onto topographical levels is completed and the ramifications of this shift begin to determine the novel's plot. Mr Wardlaw's fear of 'underrating the capacity of the native' is rooted in the geographical location of the novel's black population:

> they lived round the rim of the high-veld plateau, and if they combined could cut off the white man from the sea. I [Davie] pointed out to him that it would only be a matter of time before we opened the road again. 'Ay', he [Mr Wardlaw] said, 'but think of what would happen before then. Think of the lonely farms and the little dorps wiped out of the map. It would be a second and bloodier Indian Mutiny.' (52)

Almost a half-century after the historical event, persistent anxieties induced by the 'Indian Mutiny', already discussed in this book's first chapter, re-emerge. This fear of violent resistance is partly rooted in being too far from, or beyond, the networks of the infrastructures of transport and communication that had more fully enmeshed the Indian subcontinent into Britain's imperial and economic networks in the years following 1857. This is suggested by Davie's metaphoric use of the word 'road', as he draws on the symbolic cartographies enabled by infrastructural objects to locate himself, geographically and conceptually, on the frontier.

Interestingly, however, the population distribution that underlies this cartography is now an inversion of the traditional colonising narrative. 'White civilisation' is now located towards the interior, on the elevated plains of the highveld, afraid of being colonised by the unruly native population that is located on 'the long, unwatched coast' to the east (52). From this point in the novel, these compass orientations and topographical affiliations are reinforced: Davie repeatedly refers to 'our kindred in the West', 'the white road from the west' (with its reference both to *Undine*'s description of Kimberley's diamond road and Haggard's King Solomon's Road), and by Chapter Fourteen he comments, as he traverses the landscape: 'The Berg must be my goal. Once on the plateau I would be inside the white man's lines. Down here in the plains I was in the country of my enemies' (128). The lowveld is configured as the locale of black resistance, the highveld becoming, by about the novel's midway point, the 'white man's land'. This geopolitical configuration means that Mr Wardlaw's fears are in fact valid. The resistant black population has the 'white man's land' cornered in this geographical area, and 'if they combined [they] could cut off the white man from the sea' (52). This results in the production of three frontiers, all of which defend Buchan's beloved highveld: the rotated U-shape of the mountain ridge functions as a segregationist barricade, with the black resistance originating from, and inhabiting, the lowveld that lies between the mountains and the coastline.

With these geographical specificities established, it now transpires that the white population are defending the *interior* of Africa against an invasion from the *exterior*, or from the outside. Geographically, the project of colonisation, in which the coloniser arrives at the African coast and moves inland, is turned on its head in an ideologically significant inversion of historical reality. Davie's own arrival in South Africa enacts this process at the beginning of the novel, during which he circles the entire coastline of the Cape Colony, visiting all the key ports – Cape Town, Port Elizabeth, East London and beyond to Durban – as though patrolling it. He only disembarks when he has travelled right round the southern end of the continent, heading back up and into Portuguese South East Africa, at Lorenço Marques. The process of white colonisation moving inland was historically recent, only taking place to any significant infrastructural degree in the preceding quarter-century or so, since the commencement of the 'Scramble for Africa' and the Berlin conference of 1884 (Griffiths, 1995: 34). Nevertheless, it reflects the immediate history of South Africa's economic geography. Whilst prior to the discovery of diamonds and gold the region's economic activity had been located primarily on the 'coastal areas of the Cape and Natal', the result of the growing mining industries and the 'expanding network of trade, finance, communication and transport' that followed, 'quickly tilted the region's economic core [...] into the interior' (Lester et al., 2000: 97). Indeed, as discussed at length in the previous chapter, '[t]his shift in economic geography was manifested most obviously in the extension of a railway network centred on the mineral rinds' (97). Buchan's fictional geography positions black resistance as the invading, colonising threat, whilst simultaneously indigenising 'white civilisation' in the land it has occupied. This shift in the ideology of its topography reinforces the economic and infrastructural growth that were facilitating the uneven development of the world-system in the region, drastically altering South Africa's physical geography.

J. Hillis Miller's etymology of the term 'topography' illuminates the politics of this process. A combination of the Greek words 'topos' and 'graphein', or 'place' and 'to write' respectively, topography originally meant 'the writing of a place', or the 'creation of a metaphorical equivalent in words of a landscape' (Miller, 1995: 3). The word gradually evolved to mean the representation of a landscape 'according to the conventional signs of some system of mapping' before, in a final metamorphosis, 'the name of the map was carried over to name what was mapped' (4). The etymology of the word topography therefore traces the mechanics by which a landscape might be inflected with, if not actually produced by, ideology. A landscape can become invested with features apparently inherent to it but that are, in fact, superimposed through the ideologically refracted description of that landscape in words. 'The power of the conventions of mapping and of the projection of place names on the place are so great', argues Miller, 'that we see the landscape as though it were already a map, complete with place names and the names of geographical features' (4). *Prester John* both participates in, and narrates, this process. It reiterates Buchan's belief that the South African highveld 'is a white man's country by nature' (1940b: 121), saturating the landscape with the racial entitlement that has since led some critics, understandably, to read the novel as a 'blueprint for the perfect apartheid colony' (Smith, 1995: 175).

Prester John shows that geography and literature are not, as Mike Chang argues, 'two different orders of knowledge (one imaginative and one factual)', but rather operate 'as a field of textual genres' or surfaces waiting to be excavated and interpreted (1998: 57–58). Plot and landscape are engaged in a mutually reinforcing relationship as the novel produces South African space, one that adheres to a specifically colonial narrative. Consider the general motions of the plot: Davie, who at the beginning of the novel has never travelled to South Africa before, arrives there somewhat arbitrarily to serve the economic needs of a cross-national trading company. By the end of the narrative he has become comfortably resident in the landscape, subduing the political and military resistance of its indigenous inhabitants, extracting its various mineral resources, and even splitting his profits between between the imperial government and private companies (he sells much of the plunder to De Beers in order to avoid upsetting 'the delicate equipoise of diamond values' on the global market (Buchan, 2008: 211)). Davie allegorically enacts, in a short narrative space, two larger processes. Firstly, the plot configures the process of *settler* colonialism that Buchan believed 'must be increasingly used if both the Mother Country and the outlying Empire [were] to remain in social and economic health' (1940b: 127–128). But the trajectory of the plot, with Davie as its central linchpin, maps the processes of accumulation as critiqued by Hobson, Lenin and Luxemburg, and discussed in this book's introduction. Throughout, Davie remains on the edges of – indeed, oscillates away from and back towards – the infrastructural networks of empire that, the text makes clear, are connected to the exploitative core of the world-system. At the novel's conclusion, however, Davie conquers his fear of the frontier and is able to reside there without feeling 'cut off' from his own racial and cultural networks.[4] In turn, the resistant black population is pacified and converted into a labour force that produces a range of products for export into the world-economy.[5] 'Blaudewildebeestefontein' has, by the end of the novel, been transformed into a pacified peripheral zone. The novel itself maps a correlation between the expansive ideology of the frontier and capitalism's innate appetite for accumulation that drives it unevenly across the face of the globe.

There is, however, a political anxiety here, one that introduces a fissure, or 'crack', to use Mignolo's term (2012: 22), into the novel's ideologically shaped geography of South Africa. Buchan's passionate belief in the importance of emigration from the metropole to settler colonies across the Empire is compromised by a rift between his ideology and Britain's

4   In the novel's climactic scene in Chapter 20, when Davie makes his final return to the borderland of the frontier, the narrative now repeatedly stresses his confidence, his lack of homesickness, his 'at homeness' – his ideological restlessness that has, until this point in the narrative, condemned him to oscillate back and forth, towards and away from the frontier, is now resolved. As he comments: 'My nerves had suddenly become things of stolid, untempered iron' (182); 'now I had conquered all terror and seen the other side of fear' (184); 'I did not really fear anything' (185); 'I had no fear' (186); 'I had quite forgotten the meaning of the fear of death' (188).

5   'There you will find every kind of technical workshop, and the finest experimental farms, where the blacks are taught modern agriculture. [...] They have created a huge export trade in tobacco and fruit; the cotton promises well; and there is talk of a new fibre which will do wonders. Also along the river bottoms the India-rubber business is prospering' (Buchan, 2008: 213).

historical relations with South Africa. Written by a self-professed and politically active imperial federationist,[6] fears of the disintegration of a centralised British Empire are also implicit in the text of *Prester John*. Even as it encourages emigration and settler colonialism, the novel is also already in a process of lamentation. It anticipates the loss of the cross-national network it is simultaneously seeking to forge. As it attempts to imagine a federalised, British-ruled South Africa, it also predicts the process by which settler colonies would come to negotiate their own national independence and subsequent withdrawal from British hegemony. The historical context of *Prester John*'s production, through 1909 before its publication in 1910 (see Blanchard, 1981: 21–22), illuminates these anxieties. Despite the British victory in the Anglo-Boer War and the efforts of Milner's 'kindergarten', the project to establish a new, culturally consolidated British colony in the region had collapsed, a failure that Buchan himself experienced firsthand. The Union of South Africa in 1910 was made on terms not only 'acceptable to', but in fact 'largely suggested by the Boer Generals' who had lost the war just a few years earlier (Griffiths, 1995: 59). Britain was entering a phase of political withdrawal from Southern Africa and Buchan's novels of this period, as the following reading of *The Thirty-Nine Steps* will demonstrate, navigate the coordinates of this declining imperial hegemony.

Encoding Narrative: Landscape and Ideology in *The Thirty-Nine Steps*

The title of John Buchan's first 'Richard Hannay' novel, *The Thirty-Nine Steps*, which appeared serially in *The All Story Weekly* and *Blackwood's Magazine* during the summer of 1915, encapsulates the multidimensional

---

6   Juanita Kruse writes: 'After he returned to Britain, he used his pen to educate the public about South Africa and to spread his imperial ideal. [...] Buchan's argument for a South African federation preserving the unique features of the various states [...] foreshadowed his later justification of close imperial cooperation if not imperial federation. [...] The basic idea of preserving national integrity within larger units remained an essential feature of Buchan's imperialism throughout his life' (1989: 46–47).

interrelationship between writing, landscape and ideology that, as we have already seen, preoccupies Buchan's fiction. The titular 'Thirty-Nine Steps' is a textual code both *in* and *for* the novel: it functions as a 'clue' to some deeper meaning that, because concealed from view for much of the novel, propels the plot forward. However, as Moretti has observed of the related detective genre, 'the structure provided by clues' also creates a 'world' that, at least eventually, is 'fully understandable' and in which 'rationalisation can be reconciled with adventure' (2008: 141). The titular 'clue' and the incremental revelation of its meaning quite literally unlocks the novel's ideological efforts to 'reconcile' the contradictions of the frontier.

At first, for Hannay this clue remains undecipherable: 'one queer phrase [...] occurred half a dozen times inside brackets: "(Thirty-nine steps)" was the phrase' – 'I could make nothing of that' (Buchan, 2010: 37). This phrase, or code, holds a paradox in stasis by simultaneously signifying the presence of a deeper meaning, whilst refusing to relinquish the details of that which it conceals. The title, itself a code, thus *en*codes the contradiction of frontier consciousness into the novel – the known and the unknown, the mapped and the unmapped – that drives Hannay's movements and the plot forward through space and time. Significantly, then, the phrase is not *de*coded until the novel's closing pages when, of course, its narrative momentum abruptly ends. When it is at last deciphered, it transpires that it represents a geographical location: as Hannay realises, it is a '[p]lace where there are several sets of stairs; one that matters distinguished by having thirty-nine steps' (2010: 84). This location is also situated on Britain's geographical frontier – not the Scottish coastline of *Prester John*'s opening scene, but an even more historically and geopolitically important border given the onset of the First World War: 'somewhere on the East Coast between Cromer and Dover' (84). Buchan's fiction returns once again to a self-conscious interrogation of narrative's capacity to describe the topographies of physical space, those 'steps' suggesting not simply the flat representation of a two-dimensional map, but an area with multiple jagged and protruding edges.

The relationship between frontier consciousness and geography, as it is encoded into textual narrative, is epitomised in 'Scudder's little black pocketbook' (27). This text within the text both contains, and is contained within, the plot through which it moves. Hannay quickly realises, as he ponders the pocketbook's apparently random and nonsensical script ('jottings, chiefly figures'), that 'there was a cypher in all this' (27). Importantly, he reaches this conclusion as he travels *away* from metropolitan London, along an arterial infrastructural route (a railroad) that carves its way up through Britain into a new borderland that is, yet again, invested with the redemptive ideology of the frontier: 'I asked myself why, when I was still a free man, I had stayed in London and not got the good of this heavenly country' (27). This symbiotic relationship between geographical movement and textual decoding is rooted, by the novel's narrative, within the quite literal common *ground* of South Africa; a terrain not only geographical this time, but also historical. Hannay's conviction that the notebook contains a cypher is based on his previous experience of the South African frontier. As he recalls:

> I did a bit at it myself once as intelligence-officer at Delagoa Bay during the Boer War. I have a head for things like chess and puzzles, and I used to reckon myself pretty good at finding out cyphers. This one looked like the numerical kind where sets of figures correspond to the letters of the alphabet [...] any fairly shrewd man can find the clue to that sort after an hour or two's work. (27–28)

However, despite this skill for decoding – a thematic trope of the frontier novel that also runs through *Prester John*[7] – Hannay is not yet *in* the geographical zone of the frontier. He tries 'for hours' to decipher the code, but it is only after he leaves the infrastructural route and embarks, by foot, across the borderland of the Scottish highlands that he begins to elucidate meaning from the notebook. This landscape is repeatedly compared to South Africa, as the narrative superimposes one frontier onto another. In this 'honest-smelling hill country', each of the 'hills' shows 'as clear as a cut amethyst' (28) – as in Schreiner's *African Farm*, this crisp topographical carving might allude, albeit implicitly, to the thriving South African diamond industry. The view reminds Hannay of a specific feature of the

---

7   For example, Arcoll sends an encoded message of support to Davie, '*The Blesbok are changing ground*', that is able, because of its encoded*ness*, to 'pierce the wall' separating Davie from the British military lines (Buchan, 2008: 62–65); Mr Wardlaw, too, writes a message 'in Latin, which was not a bad cipher' (117).

colonial landscape, one that was, as I have repeatedly contended, an important borderland for Buchan: 'I felt just as I used to feel when I was starting for a big trek on a frosty morning *on the high veld*' (28, my emphasis).

Hannay's movements, from this narrative point and in both temporal and geographical terms, resemble Davie's contradictory traversal of the frontier. Hannay, like Davie, never strays too far from the infrastructural networks that run through the Scottish landscape and that have brought him from, and will return him to, the metropolitan centre. He repeatedly locates himself in relation to them, drawing on their cartographical impress as a reference point with which to make sense of an otherwise empty landscape. There 'was nothing in the landscape', he observes, before noting the 'sun glint[ing] on the metals of the [railway] line' (32). However, like Davie, Hannay often considers these infrastructural routes, in and of *themselves*, to be too dangerous to travel *on* or *along*; to do so renders him vulnerable to surveillance and pursuit. Hannay therefore oscillates between core and peripheral infrastructural zones. On one occasion he attains a balanced geographical proximity – not too far from the infrastructural routes, but not too close to them either – and significantly comments that it is the 'most peaceful sight in the world'; temporally secure, he enjoys a 'vantage-ground' from which he is able to 'scan the whole moor right away to the railway line' (32). However, this peace, and the static dynamic that momentarily underlies these passages, cannot be sustained by the relentless and restless movement of frontier consciousness. A moment later Hannay finds himself on 'a white ribbon of road' exposed to 'espionage from the air' (an 'aeroplane [that] was looking for me' flies overhead), and he quickly concludes that he 'must find a different kind of sanctuary' (32).

As the dynamic movement of the frontier intensifies, Hannay's ability to decipher the titular code increases correspondingly. The narrative overlays the practice of textual interpretation onto the novel's geography and Hannay's ever-shifting movement through it. Through an 'elaborate system of experiments' that the narrative never details, Hannay is able to find 'the key word', and within 'half an hour' he is 'reading with a whitish face and fingers that drummed on the table' (35). As for the map in the opening pages of *King Solomon's Mines*, the plot of *The Thirty-Nine Steps* is apparently encoded, in its entirety, into Scudder's notebook.

> The whole story was in the notes – with gaps, you understand, which he would have filled up from his memory. [...] The bare bones of the tale were all that was in the book – these, and one queer phrase which occurred half a dozen times inside brackets. '(Thirty-nine steps)' was the phrase; and at its last time of use it ran – '(Thirty-nine steps, I counted them – high tide 10.17pm)'. (37)

Hannay enacts a process of interpretation, or decoding, in which he fleshes out the narrative's skeletal infrastructure from his previous South African experience. Meta-textually, however, Hannay might himself be enacting the process in which ideology is inscribed into a frontier landscape *by*, or *through*, textual narrative. The passage that describes Hannay's interpretive efforts is *itself* littered with 'gaps': dashes, pauses and hesitations all draw attention, as Macherey would argue, to 'the disorder of ideology', a set of conflicts that 'cannot be isolated from the movement at the economic level' (1986: 93, 155). Hannay appears to draw attention to what Gérard Genette would call 'the frontiers of narrative', as the text attempts, yet fails, to conceal 'from us what specifically, in the very being of narrative, constitutes a problem and a difficulty, by effacing, as it were, the frontiers of its operation, the conditions of its existence' (1982: 127). After all, Buchan was personally no longer able to access the South African frontier, a frustration compounded by the gradual erosion of Britain's cultural and political hegemony in the region. For these reasons, a new peripheral space had to be produced that assuaged both Buchan's frontier consciousness and also, I argue, the uneven motions of capital accumulation. Drawing on core infrastructural routes as key reference points, Hannay repeatedly combines these with South Africa's geo-historical features in order to produce the Scottish highlands as a new frontier. The more the highlands are reconfigured as a borderland, the greater Hannay's capacity to decode and make sense of the pocket-book's narrative becomes. For Hannay, making sense of narrative and landscape are symbiotic and interwoven processes that develop, coterminously and unevenly, with the oscillating ideological movement of his frontier consciousness. The novel self-consciously highlights this process by taking the textual code, *The Thirty-Nine Steps*, as its title, as it engages in a broader ideological project that shapes all of Buchan's post-1910 novels: the production and transposition of the South African landscape into, and onto – indeed, drawing it up from within – the British Isles.

'Double Flight': The Oscillations of the Frontier

Susan Jones points out that, geographically, the novel 'takes off from the point at which the imperial romance closes' (2004: 418). Rather than beginning, as does *Prester John*, with its protagonist's movement away from the metropolitan centre to the imperial margins, Hannay is recently *returned from* South Africa when the novel commences. Back from Bulawayo, then Rhodesia, where he has been working as a mining engineer, Hannay has 'got my pile – not one of the big ones, but good enough for me' (Buchan, 2010: 13). That Hannay's modest 'pile', unlike Davie's plunder in *Prester John*, is not 'one of the big ones', is indicative of a contradiction that *The Thirty-Nine Steps* struggles so relentlessly to resolve. Contrasting with Haggard's *King Solomon's Mines*, the novel is counter-intuitively concerned to de-romanticise the South African landscape. In so doing, it repositions the ideological topography of the frontier *within Britain* through a *re*-romanticisation of the metropole. London becomes, after Hannay's thirty-seven years in South Africa, 'a sort of *Arabian Nights*' (13), and racial stereotypes seep into this inverted vision ('all capering women and monkey-faced men' (14)). This is achieved through the repeated invocation of a South African frontier context as a descriptive reference point, before the frontier's key features are then intensified. After Hannay discovers the murdered Scudder, he comments: 'I had seen men die violently before; indeed, I had killed a few myself in the Matabele War; but this cold blooded indoor business was different' (22). The violence of the Empire's urban heartland is positioned in relation to, and then described as more intense than, that of the South African frontier. This descriptive ricocheting, from one geographical context (London, or Britain) to another (the South African frontier), then back to Britain (though this time configured as a frontier), corresponds to the world-system's unevenly developing infrastructure: Buchan attempts to generate new borderlands within the very country that, according to his socioeconomic and political agenda, needs to be rejuvenated.

Figure 3.3: The frontispiece to William Booth's *In Darkest England and the Way Out* (1890).

For Buchan, as Schwarz has also argued, 'the purpose of colonial literature [...] was to allow the new nation of South Africa to be imagined *in the metropole*' (Schwarz, 2011: 262; see also Buchan, 1903). As Buchan himself commented, it was little use 'telling people they are citizens of a great Empire on which the sun never sets if they are living in slums where the sun never rises' (Kruse, 1989: 84). For Buchan, the frontier spaces of colonies such as South Africa (and later Canada) offered social and economic opportunities for Britons 'to get out of those slums and find a wider horizon if only they would emigrate' (84). William Booth had already drawn on and geographically transposed colonialism's racial, civilisational and missionary language in his study, *In Darkest England and the Way Out* (1890) into the metropole to ask: 'As there is a darkest Africa is there not also a darkest England?' (1890: 11). The image inserted as a frontispiece to Booth's commentary encapsulates the spatial layout of frontier ideology, metaphorically envisioning 'the city colony' as a tumultuous sea of 'slavery', 'prostitution', 'strikes', 'public houses' and 'gin', urban vices which are then assuaged by a brightly lit British countryside on its periphery and, beyond that, 'the colony across the sea' (ii).

The need for the sociospatial pressure valve that the frontier facilitated, ideologically, socially and economically, was felt with particular acuteness in London, the metropolitan heart of the British Empire, which was cut through with proximal yet unevenly developed core and peripheral zones. By 1909, C. F. G. Masterson commented in *The Condition of England* on the social tensions and oppositional class divisions that 'modern industrial life' had created in Britain's cities: 'the life of those who enjoy, on the one hand, in Pleasure Cities, in all branches of eager and sometimes morbid amusement; and the life of the new race which will be evolved out of these strenuous gnomes who labour in the heart of the city congestions' (1960: 84). In order to resolve, or 'fix', these spatial contradictions, the narrative of *The Thirty-Nine Steps* attempts to *remove* these problematic dynamics from its production of urban space, writing the South African landscape *into* the parts of Britain's topography that might be capable of performing the ideological work of the frontier. Like the frontispiece to Booth's *In Darkest England*, the novel's geographical and narrative trajectory establish the frontier as an antidote to the imperial capital's socioeconomic problems.

Nevertheless, fundamental to the novel's geographical movement is not simply the shift from urban London to the rural terrain of the Scottish highlands, configured by the text as a new (but still South African) frontier. At about the novel's midway point, Hannay begins to forge allegiances with the British law and, by extension, the nation-state, and the narrative's progression and geographical orientation begins to change direction. Just as Hannay is forced to flee London in a quest for, and as a result of, the novel's adventure narrative, the geography and plot of the second half of the text is determined by his need to return *from* the frontier *back* into the metropolitan centre of the British Empire. On his return, the tensions that originally drove Hannay out of the urban landscape have been resolved, albeit temporarily. In this way, the first six chapters of *The Thirty-Nine Steps* are driven by what Nathan Waddell calls a '"double-flight" narrative' (2009: 42): Hannay attempts to escape not only the spies that have murdered Scudder, but also the British 'law' which, he assumes, will mistakenly accuse him of that same murder. It is this double persecution that drives Hannay's northward adventure. Hannay is propelled by the ideological tension between anti-British terrorists and the British imperial state beyond the zone of its conflict. He plots this movement cartographically, before again drawing on his South African experience:

> I got out an atlas and looked at a big map of the British Isles. My notion was to get off to some wild district, where my veldcraft would be of some use to me, for I would be like a trapped rat in a city. (Buchan, 2010: 24)

The intensity of the conflicting ideologies bearing down on Hannay are, at this point in the narrative, transposed metaphorically onto the infrastructural density of the cityscape. His only 'notion was to get off to some wild district', a region where proximal infrastructural inequality and the social tensions they generate are removed, whilst his 'veldcraft' once again emphasises the centrality of South Africa to this geographical configuration.

However, the narration of Hannay's geographical movement is 'double-flight' in another sense as well. Just as Davie Crawfurd's adventure to the frontier in *Prester John* results in his eventual return to Britain, from around Chapter 7 of *The Thirty-Nine Steps* Hannay begins his own geographic return to the centre of the Empire, the location in and from which the narrative commenced. In addition, the plot has, by this point in the narrative, established that the terrorists are coincidentally (perhaps conveniently) located on the very edge of the borderland into which Hannay has fled. The novel narrates the resolution of its opening ideological tensions through a tactical, and distinctly geographical, repositioning of its conflictual boundaries, one enacted through the symbolic orientation of the novel's infrastructural demarcations. Lodged between these ideological forces at the beginning of the novel, Hannay feels like a 'trapped rat', a subjective response that is reflected in the lack of physical space within the urban environment. However, the journey to, and traversal across and through, the Scottish frontier, relocates the terrorist threat *outside* of that metropolitan heartland, repositioning the two ideological forces at play throughout the novel into a conveniently manageable – inside-outside, centre-periphery – geographical paradigm. The novel's frontiers are gradually 'demarcated as fixed lines', as 'marginal forms of political life, where allegiance to the central authority was graduated or variable, increasingly give way to more uniform and rigorous methods of control' – the novel produces a 'new territorial power' that, to use Mitchell's words, 'also makes possible the making of the nation' (2002: 12).

This narrative gear change significantly alters the geographical trajectory of Hannay's movements. In the opening chapters, Hannay has never had a specific *destination*, as such. Rather, he has been in a process of constant geographical flux, always moving along, between and across infrastructural routes without ever settling or assuming a position of stability. However, in Chapter 7, Hannay begins 'to feel quite kindly towards the British police', and his alignment with the ideological perspective of the state is coterminous with his beginning to travel *back* to London (65): for the first time Hannay has a specific location – Sir Walter's residency – to give his journeying direction. He immediately heads back southwards in a criss-crossing motion along British infrastructural lines that take in much of the country. The ease with which he travels along these routes, in direct comparison to the fraught anxieties of his earlier journey northward, again reveal the novel's geography to be complicit with the narrative's broader ideological resolutions. As Waddell argues, Hannay's overarching movement is 'revealed as both a literal movement through the British mainland and a mending of his previously tarnished faith in Britain's ideological institutions, one that revitalises both his own psyche and, in a symbolic sense, the political standing of the homeland itself' (2009: 43). The 'double-flight' of Buchan's narrative is therefore also a geographical one: Hannay flees the metropole towards the North, discovers the external threat present on the Scottish frontier and then heads back to the metropole again. He enacts the restless oscillation that defines frontier consciousness – after all, he has already been to, and *come back from*, South Africa, before then enacting a similar expansive and centripetal movement within Britain. Whereas in the novel's opening pages London inspired in Hannay feelings of alienation and boredom, on his return this preceding ideological conflict has been resolved by the binary orientation that the frontier allows: he now assumes a fully British national identity as he aligns himself, politically, with the state. 'You can imagine what a load this took off my mind', Hannay comments, using an indicative possessive pronoun to redefine his relationship to Britain: 'I felt a free man once more, for I was now up against my country's enemies only, and not my country's law' (Buchan, 2010: 72–73). This solidarity with the British government is reflected in his now residential comfort in London's cityscape.

But despite the ideological resolution identified by Waddell and performed by Hannay's journey up and down Britain, the text continues to be plagued by the restlessness of its protagonist's frontier consciousness. As the narrative reaches this resolution, it is severed by a break of three stars, '***', after which Hannay suddenly comments that 'I felt curiously at a loose end' (76). Though his newfound freedom allows him to move, unmolested, through London's urban spaces, he continues to oscillate between his previously realised resolution and an intensifying 'restlessness'. Importantly, it is as he walks from the wealthy urban areas through to London's more impoverished, peripheral neighbourhoods that his desire to re-enter the adventure narrative intensifies:

> At first it was very pleasant to be a free man, able to go where I wanted without fearing anything. I had only been a month under the ban of the law, and it was quite good enough for me. I went to the Savoy and ordered very carefully a very good luncheon, and then smoked the best cigar the house could provide. [...] After that I took a taxi and drove miles away up into North London. I walked back through fields and lines of villas and terraces and then slums and mean streets, and it took me pretty nearly two hours. All the while my restlessness was growing worse. I felt that great things, tremendous things, were happening or about to happen and I, who was the cog-wheel of the whole business, was out of it. (76)

Hannay's discomfort, manifesting itself in a desire to return *once again* to the frontier, occurs in response to London's impoverished urban areas. He walks through the relational zone between the core and peripheral arenas (configured in terms of economic class), descending from the wealth of the Savoy into the poverty of the city's 'slums and mean streets'. The novel meanders along Charles Booth's 'great nineteenth-century map', published as an appendix to his *Life and Labour of the People in London* (1889), which, as the segment reproduced below demonstrates, showed 'how poverty replaces wealth at every turn of the street' (Moretti, 1989: 77–78). This proximal geography of inequality and its corresponding social tensions are experienced by Hannay as he walks through the city, intensifying his need to seek out the redemptive function of the frontier. In this paragraph's final sentence, as Hannay turns back to the adventure narrative which only a few moments earlier he has been so relieved to be rid of, the infrastructural metaphor of the 'cog-wheel' is evoked to signify his imminent re-entry into that same adventure.[8] The paradoxical and perpetual movement of Buchan's frontier fiction emerges once again, disrupting the resolution for which the narrative is, nevertheless, always searching.

---

8   This metaphoric 'cog-wheel', which conflates infrastructure with imperial security, is experienced too by Kipling's titular protagonist in *Kim* (1901), as Kim similarly learns to patrol Britain's imperial frontier in India (Kipling, 2002: 234; Said, 1993: 139–143).

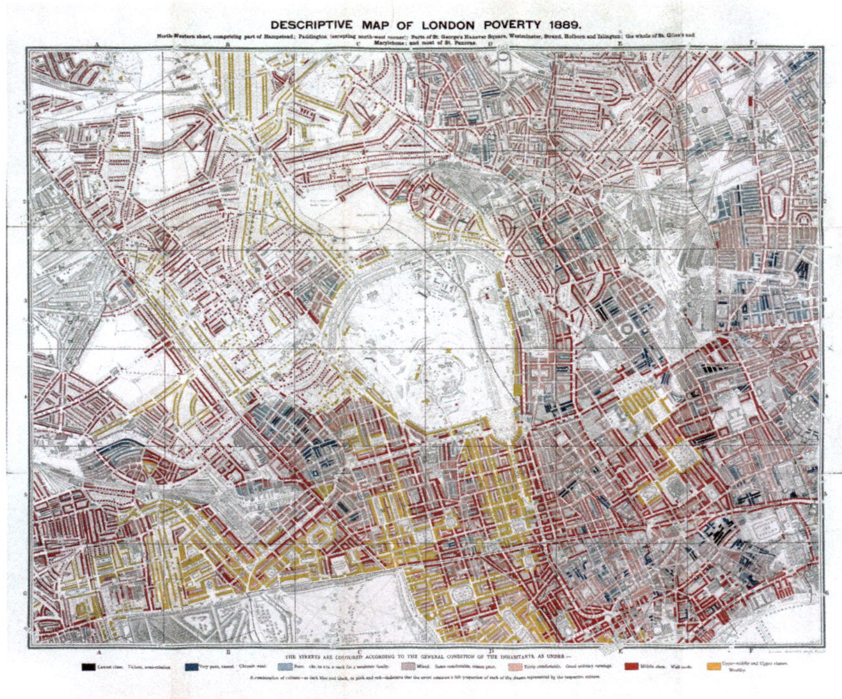

Figure 3.4: The north-western section of Charles Booth's 'Descriptive Map of London Poverty', reproduced in his *Life and Labour of the People in London* (1889).

The Thirty-Nine Steps reveals a final ideological contradiction embodied in the character of Hannay himself, one that manifests in a moment of narrative obscuration that calls the novel's representational capacities into question. David Trotter highlights the complexities of the novel's concluding scene, in which Hannay, as 'a frontiersman' – a figure 'forever excluded from the political system, and the cosy bourgeois world it protects' – comes into conflict with bourgeois society (1990: 52). In this scene, the spies, or terrorists, disguise themselves as members of the bourgeoisie, a move that at first causes Hannay to question his own instincts. 'Perhaps he is imagining it all', Trotter writes: 'The frontiersman's instincts, always at odds with those of bourgeois society, are interrogated mercilessly and then, at the last moment vindicated. A tiny gesture betrays the spies' (52). By assuming a bourgeois identity that, the novel makes clear, is content to reside at 'home' (they are, after all, 'quietly absorbed into the landscape', and repeatedly associated with domestic residences (Buchan, 2010: 91)), the spies almost elude Hannay's keen observations. He has no spatial and experiential referents with which to make sense of them; his frontier consciousness, epitomised by the veldcraft that has saved him on so many occasions throughout the novel, is here rendered impotent.

> A man of my sort, who has travelled about the world in rough places, gets on perfectly well with two classes, what you may call the upper and the lower. [...] But what fellows like me don't understand is the great, comfortable, satisfied middle-class world, the folk that live in villas and suburbs. (91)

The contradiction underlying this final scene can be configured at an infrastructural level – that is, at the level at which ideology responds to an explicitly imperial set of socioeconomic determinants. Hannay, as frontiersman, is *himself* performing an essential ideological function. Throughout the narrative, his perpetual and restless geographical movement allegorically tracks the necessity for the expansion and constant (if uneven) accumulation of capital through its ideological corollary: frontier consciousness. These movements are required to sustain, both economically and ideologically, the 'satisfied middle-class world' of the bourgeoisie, even as bourgeois values challenge frontier ideology; as Moretti observes, the 'great mechanism of adventure was being eroded by bourgeois civilisation' (2013: 16). Caught in this contradiction, Hannay realises, with horror, that he performs an ideological function for a class *whose ideology* he despises, a crisis that manifests at the level of narrative visualisation.

In this scene, the text's ability to represent that which lies before it is self-consciously interrogated. As Hannay looks at the spies around him, he realises that though there 'was nothing in their appearance to prevent them being the three that had hunted me in Scotland', there was also 'nothing to identify them' (94). Hannay 'simply can't explain why [...] I, who have a good memory and reasonable powers of observation, could find no satisfaction' (94). The narrative's capacity to describe is, in this moment, undermined. However, after drawing attention to the limits of its representational capacity, it then proceeds, *inexplicably*, to move beyond them. After another narrative break, indicated once again by three stars ('***'), Hannay immediately comments that 'something awoke in me' (95). The narrative now shifts, without justification, from a point of visual obscuration to one of clarity: 'The three faces seemed to change before my eyes and reveal their secrets. [...] The plump man's features seemed to dissolve, and form again, as I looked at them' (95). The text draws attention to its own manufactured*ness* as a representational medium by failing to explain, at a syntactical level, the shift in Hannay's powers of observation and recognition. It is for this reason that, as Alan Riach notes, this final scene has always been left out of film adaptations of *The Thirty-Nine Steps*: a visual medium cannot convey the process that Hannay, as a first person narrator, here describes (2009: 172).

This narrative opacity betrays the novel's political and economic infrastructure, as it attempts to resolve this fundamental contradiction in Hannay's frontier consciousness. Hannay, who openly rejects domesticated bourgeoisie culture, must come to terms with the realisation that he performs an ideological function *for* that same bourgeois class. Stumbling upon this fundamental paradox, the narrative then seeks to resolve it. In order to do so, the text literally *forces* the bourgeois characters that surround Hannay *out* of their domesticated, unadventurous, middle-class identities, transforming them into the complete opposite: the exterior threat that has shaped the dichotomous axis of the frontier in the first place. As Deak Nabers describes, in this scene the spies are as much 'produced' as they are 'recognised' (2001: n.pag.). After this ideological exertion, which undermine's the text's representational capacities, the narrative is unable to sustain the resolution that it has worked so hard to produce. The ending of *The Thirty-Nine Steps* is 'astonishingly abrupt' (Riach, 2009: 174), drawing to a close just a couple of pages after this scene.

Shaped by the restless oscillations of frontier consciousness, the geographical trajectories of Buchan's novels reveal 'cracks' that correspond to the uneven contradictions of capital accumulation at this historical moment. In so doing, they demonstrate the 'entangled' nature of colonial literature's mapping project and 'underline the deep "spatiality" of [the] spinning together of domination and resistance' (Sharp et al., 2005: 1).

This spatiality is not simply 'metaphorical', but rather implicates 'the countless material spaces, places and networks' – the infrastructures – that sustained, 'practically as well as imaginatively and symbolically', the British world-empire, the world-system and the ongoing resistance that challenged and shaped them both (1). However, this anti-imperial resistance mostly remains implicit throughout Buchan's literary writings, with the obvious exception of Laputa's uprising in *Prester John*. In the this book's final chapter, which turns to the work of E. M. Forster, Edmund Candler and Edward Thompson, and so back to India and its unevenly developed urban and rural zones, it becomes possible to see how late colonial literature negotiates and attempts to counter more overt expressions of anti-imperial resistance. Acknowledging the ongoing and increasingly coherent nationalist campaigns of early twentieth-century India, these literary texts are more explicitly engaged with and confronted by challenges to Britain's imperial hegemony. Like Buchan's, their productions of space take on a distinctly topographical dimension, one that is also shaped by their ideological efforts to suppress and contain the resistance they encounter. However, by reading these efforts infrastructurally, along the lines I have developed so far, the chapter will show that a form of spatial resistance still remains embedded within their various narrative structures and unevenly developed literary geographies.

CHAPTER 4

Mapping Nationalism: Allegories of Uneven Development

Introduction: Geographies of Division, Unity and Uneven Development

The short opening chapter of E. M. Forster's *A Passage to India* (1924) describes the fictional city of Chandrapore, marked by spatial segregations and unevenly developed urban infrastructure (Forster, 2005: 5–7).[1] Pankaj Mishra suggests this fictional location is based on Bankipore, where Forster had spent just three weeks in January 1913 (344), and which is located in Western Bengal. The British had partitioned the province in 1905 along communal lines, attempting to segregate Hindu centres of fomenting anti-imperial resistance from the Muslim majority in the East. In so doing, they hoped to secure Muslim loyalty – as Richard Cronin observes, the partition of Bengal was 'a classic example of "divide and rule"' politics (1977: 1). However, the partition instead ignited an atmosphere of 'anti-government agitation', culminating in the boycott of British manufactures, or *swadeshi* movement, and evolving into an increasingly unified anticolonial nationalist movement, or the 'movement for *Swaraj*' (178). Gandhi himself observed

---

1   'Amongst the many resonances of [Forster's] title is a reference to cartography, and consequently to the colonial topos of a voyage into unknown territory', Parry points out (1998: 183); another is, via Walt Whitman's poem, 'Passage to India', the great infrastructural feat of the age: the Suez Canal. In his poem, Whitman imagines a 'New' world bound together by cross-national infrastructural networks: 'by its might railway spann'd,/The seas inlaid with eloquent gentle wires [...] oceans to be cross'd, the distant brought near,/The lands to be welded together' (2004: 274–275).

that the partition had catalysed anticolonial political action, a regional resistance that soon spread across the nation: 'The Partition has caused an awakening', he wrote, and 'discontent and unrest have spread throughout the land' (2008: 133). This resistance was so widespread that on 25 August 1911, shortly before Forster himself travelled through the province, Lord Hardinge, then Viceroy, sent a dispatch not only announcing the reunification of Bengal, but also promising an increase in local self-governance (Cronin, 1977: 221–222).[2] Lord Curzon, whose reflections on frontiers were discussed in the previous chapter, predicted on the eve of the partition in 1904 that if the Raj was 'to yield to their clamour now, we shall not be able to dismember or reduce Bengal again, and you will be cementing and solidifying, on the eastern flanks of India, a force already formidable and certain to be a source of increasing trouble in future' (1987: 88). He was to be proved right.

The history of the Bengal partition gives conceptual shape to the infrastructural geographies of much anglophone colonial literature set in India in subsequent years, in particular the work of E. M. Forster (1879–1970), Edmund Candler (1874–1926) and Edward Thompson (1886–1946). Whilst the critically overlooked literature of Candler and Thompson is my main concern here, I begin with a brief reading of *A Passage to India*, as it critically opens up the issue of 'nationalism' which is the focus of this final chapter. Forster's novel negotiates an ideology that circulated through numerous polemic and historical as well as literary texts in order to justify the continuation of British rule. Many colonial writers and historians, from Alfred Lyall in 1907 – an historian cited by Candler in the epigraph to his first novel, *Siri Ram – Revolutionist* (1912) (2005: 401) – to Bruce Tiebout McCully in 1940, understood imperial rule 'as a unifying agency'

2   Though the Morley-Minto Reforms of 1909, 'a response to the intense agitation triggered by the Bengal partition, vastly extended the range of Indian participation in the governance of their country', they also embedded 'in Indian life the idea that its society consisted of groups set apart from each other', contributing to 'the flowering of a new communal rhetoric, and, ultimately, [to] the Pakistan movement' (Metcalf, 1995: 223–225).

(1940: 211–213).[3] British rule 'depended upon the ability to grasp India as a unit', argues Faisal Devji, whilst simultaneously 'understanding' and enforcing 'the fault-lines that ran across its vast expanse' (2013: 50). For colonial writers, the removal of the infrastructural framework of British governance would result in an outbreak of communalist violence and the disintegration of India as a political entity.

Conversely, notions of an inherent Indian unity informed much early nationalist writing, used by both Jawaharlal Nehru and Gandhi as a justification for independence. As Nehru writes in *The Discovery of India*:

> The unity of India was no longer merely an intellectual conception for me: it was an emotional experience which overpowered me. That essential unity had been so powerful that no political division, no disaster or catastrophe, had been able to overcome it. (Nehru, 2010: 52)[4]

Perry Anderson identifies the 'couplet' of 'diversity-unity' as an important trope 'in the official and intellectual imaginary of India' (2013: 9), and it is the slightly reconfigured notion of 'unity in diversity' – an India bound together 'into a single political community' – that underpins Sunil Khilnani's famous coinage, 'the idea of India' (1997: 5–6). As Makarand Paranjape argues, India 'as we know it today' had 'to be imagined into existence through the struggle between' colonial and national 'traditions and imaginations' (2013: 6). This chapter explores how competing geographies of division and unity, constructed through and around uneven infrastructural development in the subcontinent, underpinned colonial literature and its productions of Indian space at this historic-political moment. The novels

3   Other texts propagating this notion include William Samuel Lilly's *India and Its Problems* (London: Sands & Co, 1902) and Edwyn Bevan's *Indian Nationalism, An Independent Estimate* (London: Macmillan and Co., Limited, 1913), amongst many others.

4   As Gandhi wrote in an edition of *Young India*, published in May 1921, addressing issues of communal tension more directly: 'unity is strength [and] is in no case so clearly illustrated as in the problem of Hindu–Muslim unity. Divided we must fall. Any third power may easily enslave India so long as we Hindus and Mussalmans are ready to cut each other's throats' (2008: 191).

addressed here are explicitly concerned with the rise of Indian nationalism and the precarious legitimacy of the Raj, producing conflicting 'imaginative geographies', to use Gregory's term (2004: 12), as India's unification and division is mapped unevenly through their narratives.

A Passage to India's opening description is shaped by uneven development, albeit on a local rather than national scale. It depicts the more localised geographies of segregation demarcated by the infrastructures underpinning and facilitating the daily life of Anglo-Indians. Forster's cartographic description surveys the landscape from above, enacting and implementing the 'landscanning European eye' of the 'colonial gaze' (Pratt, 2003: 60). It reproduces the project of zoning that defined the Raj's racialised segmentation of India's colonial urban environments through '[c]ompound walls, checkpoints, imposing monuments, and intimidating boulevards' (Johnson, 2011: 5), anticipating Fanon's description of the divided colonial city (2001: 29–30). Chandrapore's 'Native town' is comprised of 'mean' streets and 'ineffective' temples, whilst the 'few fine houses' that do 'exist' are 'hidden away in gardens or down alleys whose filth deters all but the invited guest' (2005: 5). The narrative emphasises the transience of local Indian infrastructure, blurring the boundaries between man-made constructions and the surrounding natural environment. In so doing, Forster reproduces 'the binary Nature/Society' that 'is directly implicated in the colossal violence, inequality, and oppression of the modern world' (Moore, 2015: 2), and that is here measured through infrastructures as physical and symbolic objects. 'The very wood' from which the houses are built 'seem made of mud':

> So abased, so monotonous is everything that meets the eye, that when the Ganges comes down it might be expected to wash the excrescence back into the soil. Houses do fall, people are drowned and left rotting, but the general outline of the town persists, swelling here, shrinking there, like some low but indestructible form of life. (5)

Forster presents an impermanent geography, the Ganges eroding the urban environment whilst 'the general outline' remains intact, ebbing and flowing with the waters that threaten its contours. This blurring is sharply contrasted with the distinct infrastructural coordinates and rigid civil lines of the Eurasian communities, which 'stand on high ground by the railway station' away from the river's threatening waters (5). Then, shifting further upwards (Forster's topography is, like Buchan's, shaped by racial ideologies), the survey ends with 'the English people who inhabit the rise' and their concrete infrastructural environment:

> It is sensibly planned, with a red-brick Club on its brow, and further back a grocer's and a cemetery, and the bungalows are disposed along roads that intersect at right angles. It has nothing hideous in it, and only the view is beautiful; it shares nothing with the city except the overarching sky. (6)

This 'physical segregation of its ethnic, social and cultural component groups' offer the blueprints of the '*colonial city*' (King, 1976: 14). H. E. Meller documents that by 1901, the number of Indians living in British India's colonial cities amounted to three-quarters of the entire Anglo-Indian community at that time (1979: 333–335). These numbers grew throughout the first half of the twentieth century as industrial workforces inflated and urban spaces expanded to accommodate them. Cities such as Calcutta became 'practically divided into two worlds' (Bose, 1981: 3), and Kipling contrasted Calcutta's 'luxuries [...] of Sewers and Paving' with its 'great wilderness of packed houses' (2010: 59). Indeed, his short story, 'The Bridge Builders', reproduces a similar 'Nature/Society' dualism, the flowing Ganges threatening the 'Kashi Bridge – plate by plate, girder by girder, span by span', imperial infrastructure that is 'raw and ugly as original sin, but pukka – permanent – to endure' beyond 'all memory of the builder' (1990: 32–34). However, Forster's literary mapping builds on Kipling's thematic trope to do more than simply *document* these uneven rates of infrastructural development. It shows how the city's different zones are inflected with ideological agendas that, in turn, have shaped those spaces. Forster's narrative attempts to *naturalise* the indigenous architecture by emphasising its fluid quality through their metaphoric comparison with the river Ganges. But the text also shows, through the recursive self-reflexivity of this opening sequence, how this naturalisation is in fact an ideological production; read infrastructurally, Forster's urban landscape reveal colonial capitalism to be part of a *world-ecology* that is 'not the ecology of the world, but a patterned history of power, capital, and nature, dialectically joined' (Moore, 2015: 8).

Furthermore, Forster's novel links India's uneven development under British rule to the rise of nationalist resistance, albeit at the level of what Jameson would call 'national allegory' (1986: 65–88). Reapplying Jameson's concept to the subcontinent at this historical moment of its uneven assimilation into the world-system, colonial literature here becomes concerned to emphasise the infiltration of a public or political sphere into the private spheres of many of its characters' inner lives: 'their private stories are always allegories of public situations' (Szeman, 2001: 807). As Szeman reinterprets Jameson's controversial hypothesis, these texts therefore 'necessarily and directly' speak 'to and of the overdetermined situation of the struggles for national independence and cultural autonomy in the context of imperialism' (808).[5] Dr Aziz, Forster's central character, functions as an allegorical victim of the injustice of the Raj's legislative structure, a maltreatment that drives him to adopt a nationalist stance. As Alex Tickell argues, Aziz and Fielding metonymically signify 'the lost possibility of any lasting friendship between coloniser and colonised, which is registered in the novel's concluding scene' (2012: 194): '"Why can't we be friends now?" [...] "No, not yet"' (Forster, 2005: 306). Both Fielding and Aziz are unable to divide their personal lives from the broader political ideologies and sociocultural locations that they have increasingly come to signify, allegorically, throughout the text. The divide between coloniser and colonised quite literally ruptures and ruins their personal relationship, their private identities becoming representative of larger geopolitical issues.

However, this allegorical work is imbued with a deeper set of divisions that produces an 'imagined community', to use Anderson's term (2006: 5–7), divided along sectarian lines. Though Forster's experience of

5   Acknowledging Aijaz Ahmad's critique of Jameson's 'essentially descriptive' theory in the previous chapter (Ahmad, 1987: 6), by applying this concept to *colonial* literature, its 'monstrous machinery of descriptions' can be turned back upon itself. Rather than asserting generalisations about 'Third-World Literature', this reapplication instead facilitates an excavation of the political and ideological tensions embedded within these colonial texts.

India was conditioned by the partition of Bengal, the imagined cartography underpinning this final dialogue between Fielding and Aziz – who is, importantly, not Hindu but Muslim – recognises communal tensions that would lead, albeit unpredictably at the moment of Forster's writing, to another partition, that of India and Pakistan at independence in 1947 (Pandey and Samad, 2007: 18; Devji, 2013: 100).[6] Indeed, the novel self-reflexively draws attention to the way in which the Raj's 'divide and rule' ideology shapes colonial productions of Indian space.

> 'Who do you want instead of the English? The Japanese?' jeered Fielding, drawing rein.
> 'No, the Afghans. My own ancestors.'
> 'Oh, your Hindu friends will like that, won't they?'
> 'It will be arranged – a conference of oriental statesmen.'
> 'It will indeed be arranged.'
> 'Old story of "We will rob every man and rape every woman from Peshawar to Calcutta", I suppose, which you get some nobody to repeat and then quote every week in the *Pioneer* in order to frighten us into retaining you! We know!' (305–306)

In this exchange, which closes the novel, Fielding justifies British rule in the ideological terms of its role as a unifying power by gesturing towards imminent communalist tensions. But the prediction of the violence that would

6   'Colonial India was seen by its British rulers as a Hindu country', with the various other religious communities such as 'Muslims, the Sikhs, the Christians' and others, all seen rather as 'so many minorities' (Pandey and Samad, 2007: 31). The damaging infiltration of this colonial system of 'classification' and the 'advantage or disadvantage' to which a member of a majority (Hindu) or minority group would be consigned informed the political claims made on 'the eve of Partition and Independence' (31). Forster's choice to write a Muslim character as his allegorical representative of India might be read as subversive of colonialism's divisive methods of categorisation, bringing these various communal and ideological 'fault lines' to the surface. This is reflected in the novel's three sections – 'Mosque', 'Caves' and 'Temple' – which divides Hindu and Muslim communities by inserting what, as this chapter will later show, is a significantly symbolic topographical feature between their respective places of worship.

ensue were the British to leave comes not from Fielding, but rather Aziz, who satirically quotes an imagined newspaper headline. Aziz's recitation of this 'old story' suggests that it is, by the early twentieth century, a weary line of justificatory argument for Britain's continued rule. Aziz alludes to the way in which this ideology circulates through and is amplified by the British press in India through an allusion to the *Pioneer* – an 'all-India newspaper' to which Kipling himself made regular contributions (Forster, 2005: 372). The representation of India as a nation of divided cultural and religious communities is revealed to be an ideological strategy designed to justify the continuation of British rule.

At this allegorical level, Forster's novel alludes to its geopolitical and socioeconomic infrastructures, thereby undercutting the Raj's ideological arguments with the realpolitik of imperial strategy. Forster completed *A Passage to India* shortly after the First World War during a time when the technologies and, subsequently, the economies of global and imperial warfare were changing. As Rashid Khalidi observes, Winston Churchill had decided, in the first decade of the twentieth century, to construct 'a new generation of dreadnought battleships in the midst of a deadly Anglo-German naval race' (2004: 84). These ships, mounted with 'heavy, newly developed, larger fifteen-inch guns' were 'oil-powered' and, along with other technological and infrastructural developments, 'made Britain profoundly dependent on oil, a commodity that, unlike coal, had to be imported' (84–85). Mesopotamia and Persia, two areas with significant oil fields, were more accessible to Britain from its strategic foothold in India, making the subcontinent a geopolitically crucial access point. Nerendra Sarila's study of the complex geopolitical moment between the end of the Second World War in 1945 and Indian and Pakistani independence in 1947 has shown how the Raj's apparently 'selective concern for the Muslims of India' was 'not so much to protect them as to use a portion of them to realise Britain's strategic goals' (2007: 206). This is not to suggest that Forster's text is somehow consciously invoking or attempting to critique these much larger geopolitical movements, but his production of a divided colonial space still alludes to the infrastructural coordinates of the British world-empire as these were being played out on a global terrain.

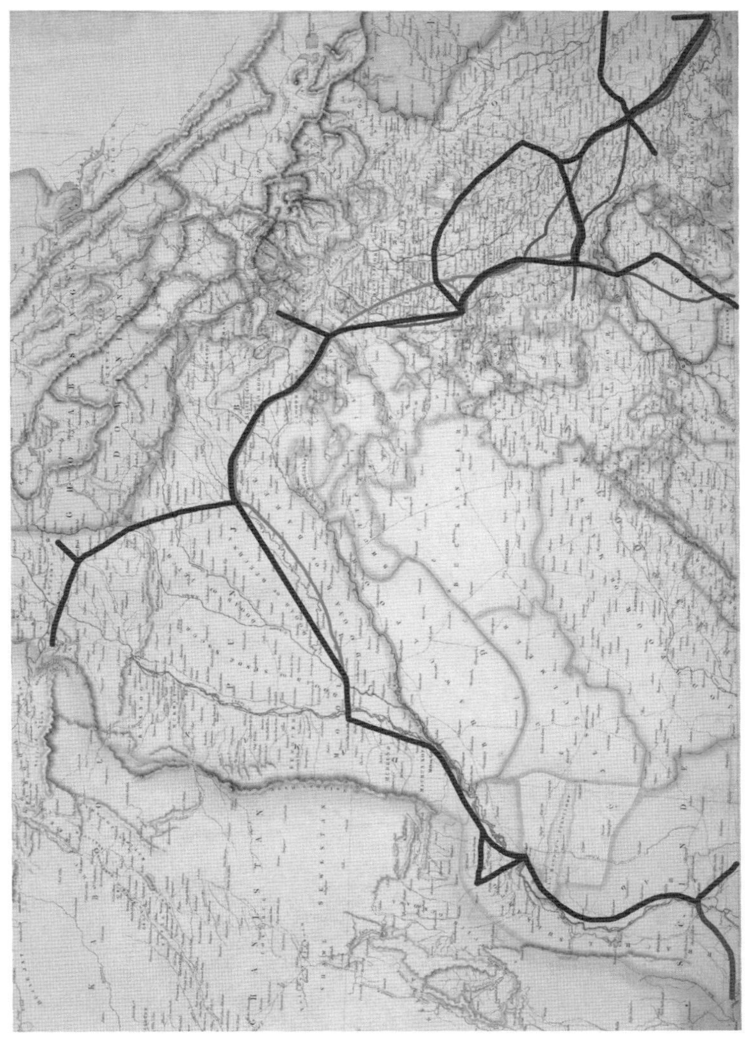

Figure 4.1: The north-western segment of a map of India produced by the geographer John Walker in 1863, showing planned arterial trunk lines and other infrastructural developments along the subcontinent's North-West frontier with Afghanistan and grouping together at Delhi. WO 78/5504, National Archives at Kew.

Whilst the British had adopted a policy of 'divide and rule in India after the bloody revolt or the Great Mutiny of 1857', continues Sarila, this had been 'a policy to control Indians, not to divide India'; this 'latter question' didn't come into play until 'the British started to plan their retreat from India' (409). Tapping into these concerns, the late colonial literature analysed in this final chapter is marked by a significant shift in imperial ideology, one that no longer attempts to justify the retention of imperial power, but rather begins to accept and imagine a post-imperial India. The ideological frameworks analysed here simultaneously struggle to redefine imperialism's infrastructural legacy, whilst also to contain anti-imperial resistance in other more strategically subtle ways. The writings of Forster, Candler and Thompson are all concerned with the rise of Indian nationalism and are infused with an acceptance of the disintegration of Britain's formal empire. In response, they frequently imagine the rise of an informal one, routed through the imperial infrastructures that the Raj would leave behind. As Mitchell points out, colonialism's 'production of maps' – and, we should add, the literary as well as the cartographic – often prefigured 'the work of twentieth-century economics, defining a contained geographical space to be organised later as a national economy' (2002: 9). As the map produced by the colonial geographer John Walker and reproduced here demonstrates, imperial infrastructural development congregated along the Raj's imperial frontiers and around its major cities, geographical lines that would come to demarcate roughly the borders and political centres of the postcolonial Indian nation. When read alongside cartographic projects such as these, it should be unsurprising that literary productions of Indian space can be seen on occasion to register the geopolitical determinants that would eventually constitute Britain's political and economic interest in the division of Pakistan from India.

Such a retrospective mapping of nationalism and these complex geographic dynamics might fall foul to what Cooper calls 'doing history backward' – something particularly common, as briefly noted in Chapter 1 of this book, to 'the study of nationalism in colonial societies': 'because we know that the politics of the 1940s and 1950s did indeed end up producing nation-states, we tend to weave all forms of opposition to what colonialism

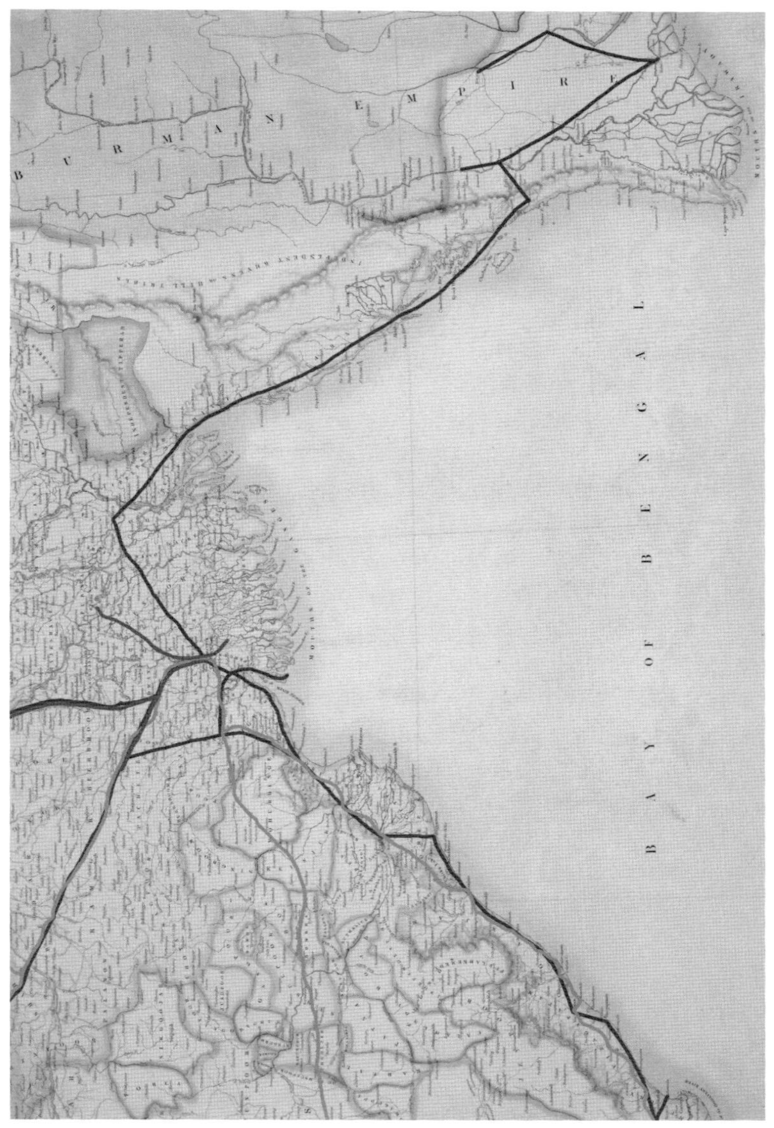

Figure 4.2: The north-eastern segment of a map of India produced by the geographer John Walker in 1863, showing planned arterial trunk lines and other infrastructural developments around the Bay of Bengal and Calcutta. WO 78/5504, National Archives at Kew.

did into a narrative of growing nationalist sentiment and nationalist organi-sation' (2005: 18). It is certainly not my intention to argue, say, that colonial literature is responding *only* to anti-imperial resistance couched in national-ist terms, that it somehow prophetically foresaw the geographic division of Pakistan from India decades before the event, or that it anticipates twenty-first-century British–India relations in any meaningful sense. It is rather to draw out the spatial complexities of imperialism's imaginative geography of the region, *particularly* as it developed in response to increasingly coherent nationalist – as well as other – resistance campaigns. After all, as Cooper continues, both 'colonial regimes and oppositions to them reshaped the conceptual frameworks in which both operated' (25). Furthermore, it is my contention that many of these dynamics, both hegemonic and resist-ant, continue to be recognisable in the 'contrapuntal geographies' of 'the colonial present' (Gregory, 2004: 12). The colonial literature studied in this final chapter conflates, often in a confused and slippery manner, imperial-ism's divisive categories of religious and cultural identification, the spatially segregationist infrastructures and rigid racial zoning of India's urban spaces, and the divided geographies of an unevenly developing India in which its rural spaces are idealised as a romanticised frontier (often, as discussed in Chapter 1, in need of imperialism's humanitarian aid). In so doing, whilst bracketed primarily under the term 'nationalism', this final chapter brings together the themes of the preceding three to emphasise the ways in which the four over-arching imperial ideologies I have identified all intersect. They here interlink and collide with one another in productive and destructive ways, never lucidly identifiable but all messily attached to, or 'entangled' with (Mbembe, 2001: 14), imperial infrastructural development.

From Forster to Candler and Thompson: Biographical Symmetries

In chronological terms, Forster's novel sits symmetrically between the years of Candler's and Thompson's literary productions. Candler published *Siri Ram – Revolutionist: A Transcript from Life, 1907–1910* in 1912, followed by its sequel, *Abdication*, in 1922. Thompson's first novel, *An Indian Day*, appeared in 1927 and his second, *A Farewell to India*, also a sequel to his first, in 1931. Indeed, Thompson's *An Indian Day*, alongside his historical work, *The Other Side of the Medal* (1925), was thought by many contemporaneous reviewers and critics to be a 'counterblast' to *Passage to India* (Lago, 2001: 210–211, 223–225). Acknowledging the 'inevitable' tendency to compare the two novels, Mary Lago argues that though 'Thompson knew his India better', it was Forster that 'wrote the better novel' (225). Curiously, Forster himself drew a direct, correlative relationship between his ability to write about India and his geographical distance from it. He reflected that though he began writing *Passage* 'before my 1921 visit', once his descriptions 'were confronted with the country they purported to describe, they seemed to wilt and go dead and I could do nothing with them. [...] The gap between India remembered and India experienced was too wide. When I got back to England the gap narrowed, and I was able to resume' (1963: 153).

Unlike Forster, Candler and Thompson invested much of their working lives in India, involved in the Raj's administration in governmental and educational capacities. They therefore developed a more intimate knowledge of its political landscape. However, as opposed to Schreiner or Plomer, for example, Candler's and Thompson's location *in* the colonial environment does not result in a formal and political radicalism, but rather a distinct conservatism.[7] Whilst Candler and Thompson were exposed to the day-to-day administration of the Raj, its hypocrisies and inefficiencies and local resistance to it, Forster was never so directly aligned with the G. O. I. nor the Anglo-Indian community, and this political and geographical distance enables Forster's undoubtedly more subversive fictional representation. For Parry, 'the indirections of its aversion to empire separate Forster's book from the self-justifying contemporaneous "problem" novels which set out to account for Indian discontent while reinstalling the British ideal of disinterested service' (1998: 178). Though Candler and Thompson come from contrasting political backgrounds, their literary voices share an explicit conservatism that comes through in the polemic tangents scattered through their novels. As a contemporaneous and comparative reference

---

7   Candler writes in his autobiography: 'I was born an unreflecting young Conservative, ready to bow my back to "the white man's burden"' (1924: 64).

point, Forster's novel thus functions as a useful intertext with which to unlock the latent politics and ideological fractures of both Candler's and Thompson's work.

If Thompson's intimate experience of the 'day-to-day political manoeuvring at the provincial level' permeates his fiction, this in fact detracts from the literary value of his novels (Lago, 2001: 225). Though both men authored polemic and historical texts as well as travel writings, Benita Parry – the only critic to have paid them extended critical attention as literary figures – has observed that there is 'often no essential difference' in the style used across these different genres. Candler's 'opinions voiced and sensations recorded in his travel books and autobiography also appear in his fiction' (1972: 132), whilst Thompson's novels detail 'debates on conflicting viewpoints among Anglo-Indians and between British and Indian' (201). The growing nationalist movement through the 1910s and 1920s forced both authors to acknowledge the increasing imminence of British withdrawal from India, and their novels negotiate these realities. Rather than struggling with anti-imperial politics at an infrastructural level, nationalism and anti-imperial resistance are placed centre-stage as their narratives' primary subject of interrogation. This plays out in open discussions of ideological differences, contested economic statistics and propagandist claims; that they are bogged down by overt politicisation is perhaps one reason for their critical neglect. Nevertheless, an infrastructural methodology that reads beyond and beneath the novels' explicit politics reveals deeper, more complex ideological struggles and tensions.

With the exception of *Siri Ram*, the novels all acknowledge the inevitability of independence. Though both Candler's and Thompson's second novels are definitely 'sequels' to their first, neither exhibits a straightforward continuity. Replicating environments, characters and themes, there is little over-arching narrative progression. That both authors fail to create strong narrative linkages across their first two novels, whilst nevertheless recycling characters and themes, is an intriguing symmetry that suggests a formal and generic tendency symptomatic of the political and economic climate in which they were written. Attempting to come to terms with ideological anxieties thrown up by Britain's withdrawal from India, both sequels return to arguments that the first novels had attempted to navigate and resolve, indicative of a reluctance to relinquish British power in India. Indeed, Gandhi once described Thompson as 'India's prisoner' (Lago, 2001: 1). The Mahatma had read Thompson's second novel, *A Farewell to India*, which concludes with an allegorical enactment of its titular declaration. Nevertheless, for the remainder of his lifetime – Thompson died on the eve of Indian independence in 1946 – he continued to return to the subcontinent and to be embroiled in its politics. Candler's sequel makes a similar titular declaration – *Abdication* – about the relinquishment of imperial rule in India. As Candler's semi-autobiographical character, Skene, comments in its final pages: 'we've abdicated and we can't have it both ways. Our conscience perhaps is not so robust as it was. Let us then hasten the wheels of Swaraj' (1993: 270). Yet, despite these explicit declarations of imperial withdrawal, a focus on the depiction of infrastructure in these texts reveals a set of ideological strategies that work to imagine Britain's continued political and economic power in the region, as well as a spatial resistance to them.

Alongside the notable similarities I have outlined, there are also some key differences between Candler and Thompson. Candler used his residency in India as a launch-pad for a string of excursions beyond the 'frontier' into 'Burma and Indo-China', which he extensively documented in his travel-writings (Candler, 1900: 60). This travel literature repeatedly rehearses the tropes of the imperial romance and exhibits a preoccupation with frontiers. Candler includes frontispiece maps that depict vast, empty spaces marked only with his (notably linear) route through them, and like Buchan's frontier characters, he is afflicted with 'the malady' of 'go-fever', 'driven to wander by the same uncontrollable impulse' that has 'impelled [him] to abandon the comforts and luxuries of civilisation' (15–16), romanticising 'places fascinating for their beauty and remoteness' (1912: x). By contrast, his literary writings repeatedly fail to move geographically or thematically beyond the politics of anticolonial nationalism. As Tickell notes, Candler is both 'an enthusiastic proponent of the "romance" of colonial adventure' and 'informed in his approach to Indian nationalist politics' (2012: 158). This conflict produces an ideological tension most clearly expressed, this chapter contends, in his literary geographies, which are in turn shaped by imperial infrastructure. The production of frontier Indian landscape that relieves the socioeconomic pressures of capital accumulation strains against the ongoing pressure to acknowledge emerging nationalist politics. The result is a literary production of a divided colonial landscape that associates certain ideological contradictions with different geographical zones in an attempt to contain them. This can, I will argue, be read as a formal expression of uneven developments not only of infrastructure, *but also* of the varying levels of nationalist consciousness as they mobilised spatially across the subcontinent.

Whilst Candler remained an apologist of Empire throughout his life, Thompson's thought followed a more radical trajectory. As Parry writes, he was 'on the left, one of the small minority who opposed' imperial policies, 'attacked Anglo-Indian attitudes' and 'attempted to explain Indian grievances to an indifferent British public' (1972: 165). As noted in Chapter 1, Thompson was already writing correctives to colonial histories of the 'Mutiny' in 1925, and he studied, translated, exchanged letters with, and became an advocate of Bengali poet and novelist, Rabindranath Tagore (see Gupta, 2003). Interestingly, Thompson was also the father of the twentieth-century historian and Marxist thinker, E. P. Thompson (1924–1993), whose work has in turn had important implications for the *Subaltern Studies* group. Thompson junior separated the concepts of 'class struggle' and 'class consciousness' so that the latter could be understood not as a necessary condition for the former but, in fact, the reverse. The result was that, as Chandavarkar explains, '[s]ince class consciousness was the product, not the prediction, of historical experience, class struggle preceded its emergence and, indeed, facilitated its development' (1997: 181–182). This loosening of class struggle from its historical bindings to a very specific stage in capitalist development meant that the analytical category could be used to describe subaltern resistance in British India: 'class struggle and the cultural and historical experience which it encompassed could [now] be studied more extensively in societies where capitalism had manifested itself weakly and unevenly' (181–182). The father's work, like Candler's, produces literary geographies that are cut through with uneven levels of infrastructural development that can be analysed, albeit indirectly, through the theoretical interventions of his son.

Despite this radical legacy and his own active criticism of British imperialism in India, Thompson's literature still offers an ideological apology for the Empire. Though he 'openly presaged the inevitable end to British authority', he 'did not escape the colonialist ideological bloc' (Boehmer, 2005: 145), remaining an advocate throughout his life of 'the British aspiration to revitalise and improve India' (Parry, 1972: 180). In 1930, Thompson wrote an extensive study of British infrastructural development in the subcontinent, *The Reconstruction of India*, which permeates his novels through ideologies of humanitarian development, or 'palliative imperialism' (Mukherjee, 2013: 17–18). Like Flora Annie Steel's short stories, Thompson's first two novels attempt to resolve the 'troubled dialectic between violation and protection, between governance and atrocity' (Pierce and Rao, 2006: 3). However, because Thompson's texts acknowledge India's imminent independence and British withdrawal, the tension is all the more problematic. The conflict between the ideological investment in infrastructure as a symbolic, civilising and humanitarian force, and that same infrastructure's facilitation of socioeconomic exploitation, uneven development and impoverishment, is further complicated by another ideological tension. Thompson expresses a patronising concern for the infrastructural development and relief works of *post*-imperial India, whilst also exhibiting a pervasive nostalgia for a romanticised, undeveloped, pre-industrial India. Like Candler, Thompson attempts to resolve these ideological tensions through a strategic literary production of an unevenly developed Indian geography.

Geographies of division shape all the landscapes in which these novels are set. After all, Forster's, Candler's and Thompson's early biographical experiences of India were forged in the politically turbulent region of Bengal, a sociopolitical environment that rocked with nationalist fervour in the aftermath of the period of partition.[8] But these mappings of differentiated geographies and uneven infrastructural developments extend beyond the political boundary enforced, then dissolved, by the Raj between 1905 and 1911. Both Candler's and Thompson's narratives engage thoroughly

8   Thompson was an educational missionary who worked as a teacher of English Literature in Bankura Wesleyan college on the western border of Bengal from 1910 (Lago, 2001: 2), whilst Candler worked as a tutor to a young Bengali rajah, followed by an appointment as principal of a Bengali college from 1905 to 1906 (Parry, 1972: 133).

with various nationalist ideologies, sometimes acknowledging them as legitimate movements whilst often working, on other narrative levels, to isolate and contain them, thereby reinstating British hegemony. Beneath the overt politics of their narratives are deeper ideological tensions at work, as the texts respond to the increased infrastructural development running unevenly through the subcontinent as well as various forms of anti-imperial and nationalist resistance. This final *infrastructural reading* of their colonial literature allows for an excavation of the ways in which imperial ideology used its physical, infrastructural developments and cartographic mappings to negotiate the increasingly prescient issue of nationalism, a set of negotiations that look forward to imperialism's ongoing socioeconomic ramifications that have informed this book's methodological practice throughout.

Before proceeding, it is necessary to clarify what is meant by 'Indian nationalism', described by Khilnani as 'a somewhat misleading shorthand phrase to describe a remarkable era of intellectual and cultural ferment and experimentation' (1997: 153). Peter Heehs helpfully breaks this activity down into four main 'factors' that drove India's successful campaign for independence from the British, and which loosely correspond to the definitions of resistance outlined in this book's introduction. They include 'pressure exerted by public bodies, notably the Indian National Congress'; 'non-violent resistance campaigns'; 'violent resistance'; and 'global and political economic changes' (2010: 153). Heehs notes that the first and second are well-remembered, celebrated and studied, whilst there is often an 'inadequate account of the third' and the fourth is 'all but' ignored (153). Here, the sporadic occurrence of *violent* resistance in both Candler's and Thompson's fiction is analysed in order to supplement the 'inadequate account' of Heeh's third category. That Candler, Thompson and Forster were located in or travelled through Bengal meant they were all geo-historically proximate to the emergence of violent terrorism as a vehicle for anti-imperial resistance (154). In addition, and as I have argued, infrastructural development was repeatedly shaped by, and contributed to, the uneven development of the world-system, and so an *infrastructural reading* necessarily acknowledges, if not foregrounds, the impact of Heeh's fourth, and thus far mostly ignored, category. As a result, the chapter stresses that whilst the imagined independent nation circulating through these colonial texts may necessitate Britain's relinquishment of its formal empire in India, these geographical imaginaries by no means predict an accompanying economic departure from the subcontinent. Nor do they concede to Nehru's unified vision, instead predicting and producing spatially the kinds of communalist divisions that would lead to the violence of Partition. India is woven into the infrastructure of the world-system and the end of the colonial project, these literary narratives predict, does not necessarily mean an end to the violence upon which that project was predicated – this violence has insinuated 'itself into the economy, domestic life, language, consciousness' (Mbembe, 2001: 174–175), and fundamentally, physical infrastructure.

The Uneven Topographies of Nationalist Ideology

The symbolic topographical feature of the cave, or caves, recurs throughout all of these novels. It is found first in Candler's *Siri Ram* (1912), reappears in Forster's *Passage* (1924), and emerges once again in Thompson's *An Indian Day* (1927). Forster's novel introduces the 'Marabar Caves' in its opening sentence, distinguishing them as topographical anomalies within the colonial terrain: 'Only in the south, where a group of fists and fingers are thrust up through the soil, is the endless expanse interrupted. These fists and fingers are the Marabar Hills, containing the extraordinary caves' (7). Indicatively, 'Part II' of the novel's three subsections is entitled 'Caves', positioning them structurally at its centre, and they perform symbolic work throughout. Mbembe's description of 'the colony' as 'a series of hollows', which in the first place manifests through the hollowness of *'physical space'* (2001: 179), perhaps explains why, as for Forster, caves too become an important symbolic trope for Candler and Thompson. As was discussed in the introduction's discussion of *spatial* resistance, it is frequently the landscapes' 'vastnesses' that, when represented in colonial literature, 'make the coloniser nervous' (179). Whilst the cave is a 'hollow' topographical feature that, like infrastructural demarcations, usefully interrupts and shapes geographical vastness for these colonial writers, it functions more than simply as a spatial reference point. This literature's production of the rural Indian landscape is more deeply shaped by anxieties around national resistance as it manifests spatially in these colonial texts, and the cave functions as a symbolic topography with which to contain it. In this strategy, Candler and Thompson follow a common colonial ideological practice: in colonial writing, 'reactive violence is a perennial theme in discussion of the countryside' because this 'resistance' opposes colonialism's 'forms of reason or logic', and therefore 'usually appears to belong to nature' (Mitchell, 2002: 14). In this way, the cave's hollowness allows Candler and Thompson, as Mbembe continues, to 'impose silences, prescribe, censure, and intimidate' (2001: 179) – even if, as I will show, this project often fails.

Both Candler's and Thompson's representation of caves can be seen as an effort to culturally 'fix' the threat posed by nationalist resistance. Both authors situate their caves in a specifically peripheral zone, beyond the core infrastructural networks of the world-system and the rigidly segregated infrastructural layouts of India's urban spaces. The activities of resistant nationalists are then restricted, spatially, to these caves. This geographical and political alignment reveals the colonial ideology embedded within the literary production of these 'unevenly developed regions (e.g. city and country)', contrasting spaces that are nevertheless imagined within the same territorial and 'national-cultural system'; as Esty argues, the nation functions to 'contain and naturalise the problem of uneven development by appeal to a common culture, language, and destiny' (2012: 26). However, the literary geographies of these colonial literary texts produce these peripheral zones (the caves) not only to contain 'the problem of uneven development', though this they do; they also attempt to delimit, isolate and undermine, spatially, different forms of nationalist resistance.

Published some twelve years before Forster's *Passage*, Candler's *Siri Ram* is the first to take a cave as its central symbolic focus: split into five 'Parts', the third is entitled 'Part III: The Cave' (2005: 395). When read comparatively, both Candler's and Forster's symbolic emphasis on the cave is intertextually and philosophically linked to Plato's 'Allegory of the Cave', raising issues of false consciousness that are mobilised by Candler to undermine the Indian nationalism his novel confronts. Debrah Raschke convincingly shows how Forster interweaves Platonic allusions into his descriptive prose before, she argues, 'then subverting them' (1997: 11). *Passage*'s materialist rejection of an idealist realm, Raschke argues, challenges the 'traditional conceptions of romance' that are built around the 'epistemological and sexual order in which pure masculine reason dominates' (11).[9] By invoking then rejecting the romance, Forster follows Schreiner by constructing a self-reflexive meta-narrative that questions its own representational capabilities. In so doing, Forster highlights the capacity for *mis*interpretation inherent in colonial productions of space, as the caves constantly evade verifiable categorisation (see, for example, Forster, 2005: 144–145). By levering open a gap between materialist and idealist philosophies, Forster's caves become a 'symptom of what the novel is unable to comprehend' (Parry, 1998: 185). Within the context of Forster's opening geographical survey, the caves elude the 'landscanning eye' of the 'colonial gaze' (Pratt, 2003: 60). *Passage* does not simply produce an Indian topography that accords with imperial ideology. Rather, it shows the way in which the production of space is always shaped by those ideologies, and in so doing, undermines them: as Aziz himself realises, Adela's 'pose of "seeing India" [...] was only a form of ruling India; no sympathy lay behind it' (Forster, 2005: 291–292). If *Passage* remains mostly silent on 'all traces of base interest – India as a source of raw materials, cheap labour, markets and investment opportunities, and India as a linchpin of Britain's wider imperial ambitions', the novel's detailed geographies nevertheless, as Parry argues, 'speak a defiant *material* presence which is both a scandal to the invaders' epistemological categories, and a threat to their boast of possessing India' (1998: 181).

9   This motif, which labels the landscape 'archetypally, as feminine', is also etched into the map in the opening pages of Haggard's *King Solomon's Mines* (2008: 21; see also Stott, 1989: 77–79). Maria Davidis has shown how 'Adela's desire for romance – her wish to explore the landscape – harkens back to male explorer figures of the past, who traditionally penetrate a fecund feminine landscape in order to bring forth its fruits for the British empire. At this point in imperial history, Adela is a reminder that the time of great imperial questing is over'; her surname, 'Quested', which 'suggests the form that romance always takes, that of the quest', is alluded to, though indicatively in its past tense form (1999–2000: 260, 266).

Approaching Candler's cave through the prism of Forster's highlights the ideological work that *Siri Ram*'s landscape performs. Candler's cave first functions to contain, delimit and control anti-imperial nationalist ideology. The depiction of the cave in *Siri Ram* is, like *Passage*'s, interwoven with Platonic allusion, but this is used to categorise nationalism as itself an explicitly *ideological* movement, thereby emphasising the *falsity* of nationalist consciousness. Whilst extended polemic debates about Indian nationalism dominate other sections of the novel, *Siri Ram*'s literary production of space attempts to resolve these challenges to imperial hegemony through this topographical feature. The physical space of *Siri Ram*'s 'Cave' becomes a shelter for Candler's nationalist insurgent, Narasimha Swami, an allegorical figure who functions as the mouthpiece for an anti-imperial, nationalist sentiment; he is a 'dangerous agitator' with 'an extraordinary influence over the youth of India' (2005: 404–405). As Stephen Morton notes, the novel itself draws 'historical comparisons' between the Swami and contemporaneous 'revolutionary publicists' such as Aurobindo Ghose (2010: 212), whose 'revolutionary politics ultimately landed him in jail' (Nandy, 1983: 92). The Swami's allegorical function is reinstated throughout this central section, whilst the cave too is invested with a distinct symbolism:

> He would sit for hours, his eyes fixed on two pebbles at his feet, restraining his breath until the material world slipped away from him and his spirit floated in ether [...] Power and influence came out of these trances. The Swami owed much of his magnetism to them and the extraordinary hold he had upon the affections and imagination of his countrymen. [...] he became a kind of superman in his own country. Images of him carved in wood and stone and cast in metal were sold in the idol shops of Kashi, where he had a great name for piety and transcendental power. (471)

This passage reverses Forster's critique, which undermines the representational capacities of colonial literature through its invocation of the 'material world below' (Raschke, 1997: 11). Instead, *Siri Ram*'s intertextual invocation of Platonic philosophy detaches the Swami's nationalism from the material geographies of a prospective Indian nation, thereby decoupling nationalism from its territorial underpinnings and isolating it as a form of false consciousness. As David Hawke argues, 'modern theories of false consciousness claim that it is produced by an imbalance in the tripartite relationship between the subject (which is the realm of ideas), the object (the world of substantial, material things), and the media of representation which negotiates between these two poles' (1996: 14). By upsetting this relationship, the cave in *Siri Ram* is invested with a process in which 'one set of ideas' seek 'to label another as false', a 'tactic' that 'can be traced to the very beginning of Western philosophy', and more specifically, to 'Plato's *Republic*' (15). *Siri Ram*'s intertextual allusion to Plato's 'Allegory of the Cave' is striking: the Swami is located in 'a cavernous cell down under the ground', at 'the far end of the cave' (Plato, 2008: 240); the 'artefacts' of 'human statuettes, and animal models carved in stone and wood and all kinds of materials' that cast shadows on the cave wall, and that the prisoners of the cave take to be material reality (240), are in *Siri Ram* circulated beyond the cave via the idolatry images of the Swami himself, 'carved in wood and stone and cast in metal' (2005: 471); finally, the Swami's nationalism is 'narrowed', or 'crystallised', through his 'flame-like energy', referencing the 'firelight burning' in Plato's cave (472). Candler's narrative attempts to delegitimise the Swami's nationalist leadership by reducing it to an idolatry reminiscent of the 'false consciousness' of Plato's 'prisoners'.

However, the realities of nationalist resistance are not so easily contained. As Rachael Corkill observes, between the years 1907 and 1910, noted in the novel's subtitle (*A Transcript from Life, 1907–1910*), 'the names of Bal Gangadgar Tilak and Aurobindo Ghose, as mouthpieces of Indian nationalism, were on the lips of anyone who professed to know anything about India' (Candler, 2005: 398). To draw on Neil Smith's terminology, the text of *Siri Ram* does not deny that nationalist ideology is 'a set of ideas rooted in practical experience'; given its historical context, it has to confess this. Rather, it seeks to emphasise that this 'given social class' – in this case a class of revolutionary nationalists – 'sees reality from its own perspective, and therefore only in part' (2008: 28). Acknowledging anti-imperial nationalism, Candler's novel then immediately sets out to reconcile it with a pro-imperial ideology. The resulting juxtaposition means that in the moment the text seeks to isolate and control nationalist thought by emphasising its ideological partiality, it must simultaneously admit the partiality of its own perspective. These unevenly competing ideologies are then mapped onto the novel's unevenly developed landscape as it is mapped through infrastructural demarcations. Though Candler's cave does not offer the level of self-critical purchase of Forster's caves, it does raise questions about the narrative's capacity both to represent and produce spaces. Drawing on Jameson's terminology from his essay 'Beyond the Cave' (itself an obvious Platonic reference), Candler's narrative is dogged by the fact that whilst 'realism is the most complex epistemological instrument yet devised for recording the truth of social reality', it must also subtly recognise, 'at one and the same time, that it is a lie in the very form itself, the prototype of aesthetic false consciousness' (1975: 8–9). By raising issues of false consciousness in order to delegitimise Indian nationalism, the text unintentionally highlights the limitations of its own ideological project as inscribed into its genre and form.

Edward Thompson's first novel, *An Indian Day*, similarly has a cave nestled at a central point in its narrative trajectory. Indeed, Parry reads Thompson's descriptions of the caves as 'derivative, drawing heavily on Forster's remarkable account of the Marabar Hills and Caves', whilst nevertheless noting a crucial distinction between them (1972: 187). Whereas for Forster 'these are multi-symbolic', Thompson's hills and caves, Parry argues, 'have a more circumscribed function, announcing the unrelenting presence of an India immensely old, remote from the British and the modern world, and contemptuous of its works' (187). The temporalities Parry ascribes to Thompson's production of Indian geography are, she notes, ideologically complicit with colonial notions of modernity that, as we have seen, manifested most obviously in infrastructural development. This passage from *An Indian Day*, which surveys the subcontinent's rural space from the perspective of an infrastructural route, is revealing:

> This was a hill outcropped from the thickest of the wilderness on the Orissa borders, and humped itself to a height of a thousand feet above the surrounding plain. [...] It was a characteristic enough hill, one of many thousands, of every height from twenty feet up to several thousand, that are scattered over India. You may see them from the train, as you go through Central India or the jungles of Chota Nagpur or Orissa. [...] The geologist finds no fossils in them. The temples of post-Aryan India seem alien, an annoying excrescence of yesterday. (Thompson, 1940: 149)

Thompson's narrative is evocative of contemporaneous travel guides, addressing the reader directly through the use of the second person pronoun, 'you',[10] and thereby implying a perspectival gaze that is geographically located on the infrastructural route – 'from the train' – cutting through the rural Indian landscape. Both hills and caves are significantly located in 'the *thickest of the wilderness* on the Orissa *borders*' (my emphasis), highlighting the peripheral location of these topographical features. The narrative positions them beyond the networks of imperial infrastructure whilst also weaving it into the core–periphery dynamics of its literary geography. Contrasting temporalities are then ascribed to this spatial production as the scientifically informed 'geologist' is juxtaposed with rural India's 'annoying excrescence of yesterday'.[11] Adopting Nandy's understanding of tradition and modernity as socially, geographically and historically contingent concepts exposes the ideological underpinnings of the contrasting temporalities with which Thompson's novel here inflects its productions of Indian space. For Nandy, the '*tradition of modernity*' is what 'the scientific and technological world-views have been trying to fob off on the rest of the world with the help of the doctrine of progress', whereas in fact '*the choice is not between traditional and modern technologies; it is between different traditions of technology*' (1978: 382). We are returned once more to WReC's emphasis on the Jamesonian singularity of modernity, as ideology and geography are symbiotically conflated through Thompson's production of Indian space (2015: 12–13).

Following *Siri Ram, An Indian Day* then continues to produce the topographical feature of the cave as both a symbolic and actual locale from which nationalist resistance emerges. It narrates this process allegorically

10   See, for example, John Murray's *The Imperial Guide to India, Including Kashmir, Burma and Ceylon. With Illustrations, Maps and Plans* (London: Alabaster, Passmore and Sons, Printers, 1904).

11   As David Arnold demonstrates through his reading of the 1909 *Imperial Gazetteer*, geology was a discipline complicit with colonialism's 'positivist logic'; its mappings of 'the physical foundations of India' and 'a survey of its human inhabitants' worked ideologically to locate the 'colonial administration' at the 'highest stage of this evolutionary saga' (2000: 131).

through the actions of Nixon, a colonial administrator, as he seeks to explain Indian unrest in the region.

> Meanwhile proof accumulated that discontent was fishing in the troubled waters of famine. The community was thrilling with excitement, winds of some mysterious terror were making men's minds a shaking grove. [...] Nixon, scanning his reports and seeking for some focus to all this wide-winging rumour, some place to search for a definite foe to strike at, settled on Trisunia. (Thompson, 1940: 149)

Trisunia, it transpires, is the name of the 'hill' described in Thompson's geographical survey. However, Nixon's decision association of this topography with anti-imperial unrest appears entirely arbitrary. Nixon actually enacts the narrative's own attempt to isolate, segregate and contain threats to its ideological perimeters within and through the spatial layout of the landscape that it depicts – and, as for Candler, the 'hollow' caves are the location best suited for this project.

The passage's opening sentence gestures towards contemporaneous debates around the relationship between British imperialism in India and the famines that had plagued the subcontinent throughout its formal rule,[12] and which can be distilled succinctly into two contrasting perspectives: whilst 'for the rulers' famine relief was configured as 'the *raison d'être* of colonialism and imperialism', 'for the ruled, famine was a direct product of the conquest of their lands by the germs, guns and the profit motives of European powers' (Mukherjee, 2013: 30–31); or as Moore would argue, it 'is not a crisis of capitalism *and* nature but of modernity-*in*-nature' (2015: 6). These debates circulate not only within the Raj's '*textualities* of governance (parliamentary papers, administrative reports, medical texts, historical and anthropological studies)', but also, as Mukherjee has shown, in 'literary narratives' of the period (31), and Thompson's novel is preoccupied with this contradiction. Whilst, like Steel's fiction, it propagates the notion of famine relief as a justification for imperial rule throughout much of the narrative,

12   Mike Davis outlines the four 'global subsistence crises' under the Raj during the latter half of the nineteenth and early twentieth centuries and includes a table that monitors the shocking 'Estimated Famine Mortality' across this period (2010: 6–7), events also documented by Navtej Singh (1996).

at this point the text alludes to the way in which nationalist movements sought to mobilise resistance from within famine stricken communities, exploiting the ongoing suffering of famine victims to further their cause. The text attempts not only to advance the humanitarian impact of imperialism that relieves famine victims living under its protectorship, but also strives to delegitimise nationalist ideology by exposing it as a coercive form of indoctrination that exploits the suffering of those that it rallies to its cause. It critiques the nationalist movement's ideological manipulation of disasters such as famines whilst failing to see its own participation in a very similar, if oppositional, process. If this is not directly acknowledged by the text, its juxtaposition of conflicting ideological perspectives works, like Candler's, to emphasise the political agendas informing its production of space. The narrative is forced to accommodate an alternative, increasingly coherent system of sociopolitical and cultural understanding in the form of growing nationalist energies, which in turn relativises and undermines its own.

Nixon's efforts to contain nationalism within a small segment of Indian landscape is symptomatic of the geographical compartmentalisation, or 'divide and rule' tactics, that underpinned counter-nationalist efforts. After Nixon identifies Trisunia as the geographical locale of nationalist unrest, the narrative describes it in greater topographical detail and links it, symbolically, to wider notions of anti-imperial resistance. The caves are presented to the reader through an intertextual repetition of Forster's own opening description of the Marabar hills:

> If you crossed Trisunia's summit, and began the northern descent, you reached a rocky surface pitted with caves and cracks [...] One of the caves went deep into the hill. No one had ever been interested or hardy enough to explore it. [...] It was from the unknown heart of this cave that Hara Deva the Destroyer was now roaring. Terrified crowds had heard him, at the spring festival; but the rumour had died away, only to be revived as the miseries of famine grew to their height. (1940: 153)

For the novel's British characters, the 'roaring stuff' emerging from an 'unknown' geographical location suggests a nationalist stronghold. As Alden, another colonial administrator, hypothesises, 'the people who started the roaring stunt have set this yarn going also, to frighten off investigators' (154–155). He continues:

I read something some time ago, about what seditionists had been doing in the Philippines. It seems they had a cave of sorts there also; and they fixed it up with a whopping megaphone. It was a place with magnificent echoes. (156)

Though invoking the 'echo' of Forster's Marabar Caves (2005: 137), another intertext is also present in this section of Thompson's novel. The cave, embedded 'deep into the hill', is uncharted territory, with no one as yet proving 'hardy enough to explore it' (Thompson, 1940: 153). Hamar, another colonial administrator, comments, 'I'm going to raid those damn caves' (155), and eventually the three British imperial characters 'entered the cave at last, cautiously and with loaded revolvers' (158). The narrative recalls Haggard's three imperial characters who, in *King Solomon's Mines*, penetrate 'the bowels of a huge snow-clad peak' where they are 'cut off from all the echoes of the world' (2008: 178). If Forster's caves subvert of the 'traditional conceptions of romance' (Raschke, 1997: 11), Thompson's cave functions as something of an ideological intermediary. It both subverts the explicitly pro-imperial allegory of Haggard's novel whilst not quite achieving the radical work of Forster's anti-imperial one. Whilst for Haggard's characters, as discussed in Chapter 2, the prospect of increased material wealth is barely concealed by their 'quest' to rescue Sir Henry's brother, within the differing context of British India in the 1920s, the motivation is instead to seek out and repress nationalist resistance. Nevertheless, recalling Jameson's argument that 'the historical moment' limits the 'number of formal possibilities' (2002: 133–135), this re-emergence of the generic contours of the imperial romance suggests that the economically exploitative motions of the world-system are still latent within the infrastructure *of* Thompson's narrative. The textual patterns and tropes playing out across different historic-geographical zones here demonstrates how colonial literature continually registers and reproduces the socioeconomic and ideological motions of the world-system, attempting and failing to fix its contradictions at the levels of form and genre.

Curiously, even though Thompson's re-writing of the cave is, like Candler's, an ideological effort to isolate and contain nationalist resistance, when his characters actually enter the cave it turns out to be empty: 'there was an easy way out to an opening in an unpathed tract of the forest. There had been cooking and sleeping and habitation in the cave', Thompson's protagonists discover, 'beyond a peradventure; but the rest was guesswork' (158). The novel configures anti-imperial nationalism as a political movement that cannot be controlled, or mapped by, the imperial government. Though the plot details the isolation, containment and infiltration of the cave, at the moment of entry Thompson's nationalists slip beyond the colonial administration's reach, escaping through the back of the cave into 'an unpathed tract of the forest' – the resistance shifts, spatially, beyond the frameworks of colonial literature's representational strategies. The narrative does not simply confess the existence of emerging Indian nationalism, but transforms it, through its symbolic topography, into a politically mobilised spatial resistance referenced within, but also always beyond, both the text's ideological and geographical frameworks. Indeed, though written in the third person, the narrative's perspectival orientation looks 'over the shoulder' of the colonial administrators who explore the cave, at no point moving beyond their personal knowledge and experience. Unlike Forster's and Candler's omniscient narrators, Thompson does not move into the consciousness, or even experience, of those that resist, unless that action is directly observed by one of his Anglo-Indian characters.

Candler's attempts to contain anxieties around anti-imperial resistance by restricting them to the cave similarly fails, as it spills over, spatially, into other geographical regions. Before retreating to his cave, the Swami makes a 'colonial pilgrimage' to Europe, especially 'England', as well as the United States. As Anderson has shown, these pilgrimages were made by bourgeois members of the colonised population to the imperial metropole to 'receive some education or training', and were linked both to the development of cross-national 'communication and transportation' infrastructures and the 'subtle, half-concealed transformation, step by step, of the colonial-state into the national-state' (2006: 114–115). The geographical coordinates of nationalism's imagined community are central to this process: there is a distinct 'isomorphism between each nationalism's territorial stretch and that of the previous imperial administrative unit', a 'similarity' that 'is by no means fortuitous; it is clearly related to the geography of all colonial pilgrimages' (114–115). Candler's novel shows that it is the Swami's cross-border geographical movements, which are then combined with the imperial transportation and communication infrastructures *within* India, that enable him to imagine a community mapped onto a specific, bordered territory: the nation.

Nehru would make a similar observation in his essay, 'The Unity of India': the 'coming of the British to India synchronised with the development in transport, communications and modern industry, and so it was that British rule succeeded at last in establishing political unity' (1941: 13). Whilst arguing that India's 'desire for unified political control' originated prior to British rule, Nehru nevertheless concedes that it was the Raj that laid the infrastructural foundations which would enable the realisation of these national imaginings.[13] It is not coincidental, then, that the literary productions of space analysed here register British India's uneven internal infrastructural development in the same moment that they negotiate the formation of the Indian nation as a distinct geographic and political entity. Candler's titular protagonist, Siri Ram, himself makes a journey across the unevenly developed terrain of the Indian subcontinent, traversing its core and peripheral zones. The geographical trajectory mapped out by the novel moves from an urban centre to a rural – and in terms of its relation to the networked world-system, economically and culturally peripheral – zone, a 'separation' that, as Jameson argues, 'becomes a vital index of the development of capitalism' (2014: 110).

The first section of *Siri Ram* works to separate nationalism from imperialism's cultural and economic circuitries as they manifest in its infrastructural networks, a division symbolically compounded through the infrastructural density of its urban environments. It produces an uneven literary geography that attempts to isolate and contain nationalism by rooting it in a peripheral zone, far from the imperial networks that it threatens.

---

13   Though Nehru and Gandhi shared ideas of a unified Indian nation, the latter did not concede, as Nehru does here, that infrastructural systems such as the railway network had played any formative role. For most nationalists, '[i]mprovement or control, not elimination of the railways, was the goal', but Gandhi was 'one of the few who contested the very presence of the railways', inverting 'every positive presentation' of them (Kerr, 2003: 313).

However, despite this ideological work, the narrative then embeds both the cave and the Swami in the material, cross-border infrastructural networks of communication that allow the Swami to spread his nationalist doctrine. 'Siva's mansion had become the Swami's office', the narrative proceeds: the cave 'floor' becomes 'littered with his torn correspondence' and 'envelopes with the American postmark' (2005: 487). The cave literally becomes coated with a correspondence that connects it to cross-national networks of nationalist resistance. This network allows for the construction of what Anderson calls 'unbound serialities' that, as Chatterjee explains, 'afford the opportunity for individuals to imagine themselves as members of larger than face-to-face solidarities' (1999: 128). The cave now becomes 'the hub of the universe; the civilised world was conspiring with [Siri Ram's] master [the Swami] to set his country free': 'Sometimes it would be a letter from an Indian in Paris or London, or an Irish professor in an American University, or some well-meaning radical in the House of Commons' (487).

The networks giving shape to this cross-national resistance complicate and undermine the simplistic spatial division between urban and rural that the broader trajectory of Candler's novel endeavours to realise. 'The town-country division inherent in capitalism' cannot be treated 'as two separate units, one developed and the other underdeveloped' – rather, they are '"areas" of differential development [that] are joined relationally' (Hopkins and Wallerstein, 1982: 180). This is mapped onto the '[o]pposition to oppression [that] is coterminous with the existence of hierarchical systems' (Arrighi et al., 2011: 29), which occurs here not in any simplistic binary sense, but *spatially*, across *Siri Ram*'s unevenly developed literary geography. When read infrastructurally, Candler's narrative details the way in which this resistance is articulated via the 'two principal varieties of antisystemic movements', each of which have contrasting spatial configurations. The first can be configured as a 'social movement' (enmeshed within cross-national, counter-networks of resistance, as 'the internationalism' of Siri Ram's and the Swami's ideology is emphasised); and the second as a 'national movement' (territorial borders give shape to the Swami's imagined community in a spatial 'liberation from the unequal relations among different zones of the modern world-system') (30–31, 54). In the novel's central section, these two movements have 'found enough tactical congruence to work together' (31), and it is imperialism's cross-national infrastructure that facilitates resistant activity (see Boehmer, 1998a: 5–6). Infrastructure has both enabled the Swami to formulate his own coherent nationalism by connecting him to a range of international social movements, whilst in turn facilitating the 'development of the sovereign and bounded state' as the 'central feature of political modernisation' (Breuilly, 2012: 170). Imperial infrastructures are configured by Candler's text no longer as symbolic and physical manifestations of imperial hegemony but instead as facilitators of anti-imperial resistance.

The ideologies informing these productions of space are themselves uneven. That is to say, different spaces, be they core or peripheral, rural or urban, perform different ideological functions inconsistently throughout the novels' duration. Within the socioeconomic context of a swiftly though unevenly industrialising India, imperial ideology shifts or, as for Buchan, oscillates, between the relational zones of core and periphery. Whilst colonial literature's symbolic cartographies attempt to divide British India's geography simplistically in two, these rigid binaries are complicated by the networked nature of the world-system as it manifests in imperial infrastructure. Focusing on the novels' infrastructures details the more complex disaggregations of core-peripheral zones that shape their geography, revealing the impoverished periphery to be at least in part a product of imperialism's development of underdevelopment, whilst Anglo-India's carefully segregated and compartmentalised urban spaces are riddled with peripheries and anti-imperial activities, as the next section will explore.

Meteorological Metaphors and Violent Resistance

Siri Ram's efforts to contain nationalism through the cartographic binary of colonial urbanity and indigenous rurality is most explicitly transgressed in the novel's final two sections Siri Ram departs *from* the cave *back towards* the urban environment of Delhi in which the novel began. On his return, he is convinced by the underground nationalist group of which he is now a member to sacrifice himself for their cause as 'hero, martyr, patriot' (2005: 548) by assassinating a colonial official. Siri Ram justifies this act of suicidal terrorism (Tickell, 2012: 159) – he will inevitably be caught, tried and hanged by the colonial government – by identifying with the imagined community of a prospective nation: '[t]onight in every city young men will be ready', he is assured – '[h]undreds of other officials will fall at the same time', and his revolutionary act will be 'be a match to light the conflagration' (537). After his arrest, Siri Ram takes comfort in the memorialisation of his martyrdom by the nationalist community for which he has died: 'The thoughts of millions were centred on him [...] thousands of cheap prints of him would be circulated in Bengal' (548–550). Comforted by these reflections, Siri Ram reaches for 'the little wafer of poison' he has smuggled into his gaol cell, opens 'the packet almost indifferently' and commits suicide (550). His political cause consumes his individual (private) identity and he enters fully into the status of national allegory.

Meanwhile, the novel's plot works to undermine Siri Ram's imagined community by dividing, and thus delegitimising, the nationalist movement. This tactic is then displaced outwards onto the literary production of Indian geography as divided, uneven and unequal. It transpires that the wider nationalist community for which Siri Ram has sacrificed himself has, in fact, no intention of initiating a movement of mass resistance. Instead, the movement's leaders have tricked Siri Ram into committing a one-off act of terrorism as part of their ongoing campaign but that, in its isolation, will prove politically insignificant. This plot twist, which is revealed through further intertextual reference to Plato's 'Allegory of the Cave', frames the national community of which Siri Ram believes he is a member as nothing *more* than 'imagined', a product of false consciousness decoupled from any territorial reality. Meeting his fellow nationalists in a dimly lit room, Siri Ram asks, 'Why was the room dark?' He is informed that '[t]he patriots always meet now in a darkened room': if a member of the group 'is taken it is easy to deny knowledge of the others. To the police, to the magistrate, to the judge, the answer is always one: "The room was dark. I could not see"' (536). Though acknowledging the 'underground' nature of these anti-imperial activists, which conspires beyond the view of the colonial gaze, the blindness emphasised here is not the government's but rather Siri Ram's. As his interlocutor points out to him: 'And they could not see you. You could not see me. You do not know what house you are in. You were taken here blindfolded' (536).

The dark chamber in which these preparatory transactions take place is evocative of the Swami's – and Plato's – cave, reducing the other members of the nationalist group to indistinguishable 'features', 'figures' and 'strange familiar voices' (535). Unable to meet them 'face-to-face', Siri Ram is literally forced to 'imagine' the community for which he is about to die (Anderson, 2006: 6). In the scene's closing moments, the Platonic imagery recurs and the narrative mechanises Siri Ram's false consciousness with an infrastructural metaphor that recalls both Kipling's Kim and Buchan's Hannay: 'Two thin wicks flickering in an earthen saucer were lighted in the niche above his head, and he was illumined fitfully like some triple-paunched idol in a cave. [...] Siri Ram was hypnotised. Thoughts revolved like wheels in his head' (538). The text rejects the possibility that Siri Ram's suicidal act is somehow related to, or constitutive of, a wider nationalist cause, emphasising instead the ideological and propagandist conditions of his resistance.

Despite these counter-nationalist strategies, Morton reads the novel, and specifically this moment of Siri Ram's conversion, within the tradition of the *Subaltern Studies* movement in order to demonstrate the limits of Candler's ideological framework. Drawing on what Dipesh Chakrabarty would call 'a subaltern past', or a 'history that resists historicisation' (2008: 9–11), Morton argues that 'a similar resistance to historicisation is evident in the ways that the insurgent acts of Siri Ram and Narasimha Swami elude the colonial intelligence gathering of the Anglo-Indian authorities' (2010: 217). Candler's colonial characters, like the novel's omniscient narrator, are unable to comprehend that 'the Swami's ascetic form of spiritualism' might provide 'a theological and rhetorical structure for the revolutionary nationalist movement' (217). The nationalist ideology to which both the Swami and Siri Ram subscribe is therefore present within the text, whilst nevertheless remaining spatially beyond the colonial apparatus. As Morton writes, 'just as Chakrabarty's subaltern past is a supplement to the historians' past, so Siri Ram's political theology is a "supplement" to Candler's post-hoc narrative of counter-terrorism' (217–218). However, this reading overlooks the novel's conclusion, when Siri Ram is eventually betrayed by his fellow nationalists. With this final movement in the text's project of delegitimisation, Candler's narrative frames Siri Ram's revolutionary ideology as 'false' not only from the perspective of his colonial characters, but also his anticolonial ones, as they dupe a young, enthusiastic militant into meaningless self-martyrdom.

Even so, Candler's text is caught in a conflictual ideological relationship with its subject material. As Parry points out, the primary focus of Candler's novel is 'the inspiration of the political upsurge' that, historically, and especially in Bengal between 1907 and 1909, had been manifesting in acts of violent nationalist resistance (1972: 149–150). The narrative details, and therefore inevitably draws attention to, moments of resistance and dissent with one hand, whilst isolating, controlling and delegitimising those same acts of violence with the other. Candler seeks to 'explain' nationalist resistance – that, given the historical surge in acts of violence, had become a substantively dangerous threat for his contemporaneous readers – without acknowledging that some of Indian nationalism's objections to Britain's imperial rule might be justifiable. This paradoxical ideological negotiation of nationalism results in a narrative jarring, or stuttering, embodied somewhat ironically in an image of revolution and repetition that recurs throughout the novel. This manifests most obviously in the novel's meteorological backdrop, as anti-imperial resistance to colonialism's 'logic' is, at this infrastructural level, conflated once again with 'nature' (Mitchell, 2002: 14).

Set temporally within the space of one year, the seasons provide contrasting atmospheric conditions to the novel's five parts. Focusing on climate reveals that the closing chapter returns the novel, ideologically, to its opening pages. 'A rainless June had succeeded a rainless April and May', the reader is informed, and the '*Ode to the Nightingale* had come round again with the revolving year, inevitable as the season' (2005: 550). Referring here to the romantic poetry taught annually on the college syllabus, and linking this to the revolution of India's seasonal climate, the novel looks backwards, returning to its opening chapters.[14] Candler's narrative performs an ideological revolution as opposed to resolution, finishing where it started, *prior* to the formations of nationalist resistance and violent terrorism that it has attempted to navigate. The text therefore fails to make any temporal or cumulative progress forward, beyond these ideological tensions. This circulatory structural motion, echoed by both Siri Ram's revolutionary thoughts that revolve 'like wheels in his head' (538) and the mechanical movement of imperial infrastructures *in* the novel, is embedded within the title's second clause – *Revolutionist*. The novel concludes with the response of another of Candler's Indian characters – Banarsi Das – to Siri Ram's death, its final sentence highlighting both the climate and his grief:

> The air was hot and gritty. Ineffectual thunder rumbled in the distance. As they drove back to the College without a word, Banarsi Das was shaken with silent weeping. (554)

Though a peripheral character in *Siri Ram*, in Candler's sequel, *Abdication*, Banarsi Das moves centre stage and himself becomes embroiled in the anti-imperial movement. The 'rumble' of thunder here provides a backdrop of pathetic fallacy for Banarsi Das's 'shaking' emotion that, though 'in the distance', is pervasive and present. The depiction of resistance through this meteorological metaphor as a distant but 'rumbling' presence shares notable similarities with Thompson's description of the intangible 'roaring', or 'bellowing, especially at night' (1940: 154–155), that emanates from the cave, distant and unseen, but definitely present.

In its closing scene, *An Indian Day* also describes the arrival of a storm, again linking this to the revolutions of India's distinct seasonal cycle.

> The Bengali year was ending. Again the Great God massed his war-clouds, and a racing tempest scoured the exhausted air. The lightnings stabbed, the thunders burst,

---

14   There is a further politics to the presence of romantic poetry running through the novel, one that recurs also in Thompson's literary writing. As Tickell argues, the novel's recurring representation of 'an Indian inability to appreciate English literature, especially its traditions of the pastoral, and where these involve "misread" romantic poetry' both references and then in turn 'effectively erases the history of Young Bengal's highly politicised transactions with romanticism' (2012: 162).

the huge red faded bowls of *simul* blossom tumbled heavily down, the leaves rent
from the tress, the black clouds strode majestically through the sky.

The first storm caught a group in Alden's compound, assembled in the hope of
tennis. They huddled on the verandah, cursed it, and watched it. (243–244)

Thompson's 'black clouds' directly inconvenience his Anglo-Indian
community, who collect on the 'verandah', an important feature of the
colonial bungalow that, as Metcalf documents, spread throughout the
Empire (2002: 6). The 'verandah' that encircled the bungalows was a
physical and symbolic location enabling 'carefully regulated intercourse'
with the colonial environment, and was often further protected by
'a large compound' (6; see also King, 1976: 123 and Glover, 2004: 61–82).
In Forster's opening cartographic survey, the rigid infrastructures and
grand architectures of Chandrapore's Anglo-Indian community perform
their intended function, segregating it from the rest of the urban environment. They operate, by contrast with the rest of the cityscape, as 'smug
redoubts' designed to make 'clear to the Raj's subjects the intrinsic separa-
tions of Indian and European societies' (Johnson, 2011: 5). However, later
in the novel, as Forster's narrative voice discusses British efforts to make
India 'harmonious all the year round', these infrastructural embodiments,
loaded symbolically with the civilisational ideology of empire, become
precarious:

The triumphant machine of civilisation may suddenly hitch and be immobilised into
a car of stone, and at such moments the destiny of the English seems to resemble their
predecessors', who also entered the country with intent to refashion it, but were in
the end worked into its pattern and covered with its dust. (2005: 199)

In Thompson's novel, the infrastructure of 'Alden's compound' fails to
entrench the Anglo-Indian occupation of space, rather disempowering the
colonial administrators. The 'group' are 'caught', isolated and contained –
trapped even – within the bungalow's barriers of segregation and demarcation, their 'huddling' together further suggesting a fear of external threat.
An Indian Day, like *Siri Ram*, concludes by aligning its narrative with the
revolution of the meteorological year, emphasising the circularity of the
temporal space it has occupied. In this concluding metaphor, these novels
indicate the onset of future revolutionary activity, each text illuminating

the other through these points of metaphorical exchange. Though Candler and Thompson tackle nationalist resistance with the intention of resolving ideological anxieties thrown up by it, their novels' conclusions instead look forward to the inevitability of further contestations; Thompson's characters only 'cursed it, and watched it' (1940: 244). As though to emphasise this circulatory movement, both novelists do return to these issues, deploying the same characters, themes and literary geographical mechanisms in their respective sequels.

This ideological circularity is embedded in the novels' geographies. If *Siri Ram*'s narrative culminates with the peripheral cave at the novel's centre, the novel's second half narrates a movement back to the infrastructural core of imperial India – both physically, in terms of the infrastructural density of the cityscape, but also socioeconomically (the infrastructures both *in* and *of* its textual terrain). Whilst the novel attempts to remove anti-imperial resistance to, and contain it within, India's rural spaces, Siri Ram commits his final violent act of resistance deep within the infrastructural environment of urban Delhi. Merivale, the colonial officer that Siri Ram assassinates, stands in

> the dimly lit spaces at the end of the station. [...] It was an interminable platform, stretching away almost to the distant signals. It might have been built for a metropolis. [...] aimless engines seemed to be eternally shunting goods trucks in the different sidings. Merivale wondered why they made these stations so big. At the far end humanity was packed thick, and there was a babel of shrill tongues, but the desert itself seemed to close in on the platform before the last lamp. (2005: 544)

Situated on the symbolic 'platform' of imperial infrastructure, Merivale looks outwards into the underdeveloped 'desert'. This peripheral geography, beyond the Raj's infrastructural network, physically closes in on the infrastructural route, an associative imagery emphasised by the scene's contrasting levels of light and dark – the desert removes the 'last lamp' from view. The physical environment anticipates Siri Ram's transgression of physical boundaries and his act of violent resistance: the assassination of Merivale. These contrasting geographies are further linked to the imperial export economy by the sounds of the 'goods trucks' that echo throughout this scene, implicitly referencing the drain theories of Dadabhai Naoroji and Romesh Chunder Dutt discussed in Chapter 1. As Siri Ram shoots Merivale, the narrative collects around the infrastructures *in* the text, symbolic objects that had historically enabled Britain's economic exploitation of the subcontinent (see Dantwala, 1973: 14).

> The noise of a train entering the station suggested to [Merivale's] flickering senses the idea of wheels. Then the supporting arm gave way under him, and he felt a twinge like a hot needle in his back. (2005: 546)

Shocked by his own actions, Siri Ram accidentally lets off another shot:

> Another bullet hit the stone coping at his feet and ricocheted into an empty goods train. [...] For a moment these two had the drama to themselves. In the din of the shrieking engines and the clang of couplings, no one recognised the sound of the revolver shot. (546)

The stray bullet momentarily draws the narrative away from the dying Merivale to hit a 'goods train' that is, significantly, 'empty', suggesting the damaging effects of famine catalysed by the 'wild trade cycle of growth and recession' of the world-system (Hall-Matthews, 2005: 68).[15] In this climactic scene, the infrastructure that has facilitated, both historically and symbolically, imperial self-assurance, military security and economic development, here obscures the act of violence, drowning out the sound of the revolver. In the concluding paragraphs of this chapter, these infrastructural demarcations are invested not with ideologies of imperial security, but rather enact, metaphorically, Siri Ram's anti-imperial efforts. As he is

15   Hall-Matthews argues that these famine crises were intensified by India's uneven development and, in particular, the inconsistent and selective development of imperial infrastructures: 'Improved transport can have a dynamic impact on society, particularly by creating access to markets with the potential to generate either profit or food insecurity. It can also cause difficulties by integrating local markets with some wider ones in which they are not competitive, including that in transport itself, but not with others of greater potential benefit' (2005: 73). Mike Davis also links these famines to India's uneven infrastructural development and the G. O. I.'s free trade policies, describing them as 'forcing houses and accelerators of the very socio-economic focus that ensured their occurrences in the first place' (2010: 15–16).

dragged away 'between two constables', he explains his actions vocally with the warning that the 'English are not long for this country' (2005: 547). This warning is then allegorically facilitated by the infrastructures that have both symbolically and physically given shape to the scene:

> The Bombay Mail with its freight of homeward-bound passengers rattled over the railway arch as they drove under. The metallic throb as it became faint in the distance sounded to them both like the knell of everything. (547)

The locomotive depicted in the chapter's concluding paragraphs, on which Merivale himself was supposed to have been travelling, actually removes its British occupants from the subcontinent, whilst the train's 'metallic throb' anticipates the 'thunder' rumbling in the novel's closing sentence (515, 554). The threat of the nationalist movement is built into the infrastructure of the narrative through this cumulative symbolic sound. Whilst the narrative's attempt to resolve this threat results in a circulatory pattern that cannot move forward, nationalism is articulated with a sense of temporal progression that predicts the Indian nation's postcolonial futurity.

An Indian Day loads yet more symbolic weight onto this meteorological metaphor. After the three protagonist's unsuccessful penetration of the cave, described above, there is a period of 'unsatisfactory weather' – 'a spate and incredible fury of rain overwhelmed the land':

> Hamar, looking from his veranda as dawn was spreading, clear at length, saw Nixon in gum-boots wading through a river that splashed and squelched round his feet. [...] He had been cooped indoors by this infernal weather, and felt he *must* get out. He invited Hamar to join him. (1940: 159)

Again located – indeed, trapped or 'cooped' – on the verandah of his bungalow, Hamar joins Nixon to face the weather, rather than remain safe within the secure, infrastructural borders of his colonial bungalow. Driven by a restlessness reminiscent of Buchan's frontier consciousness, the two men's assertion against the 'infernal weather' leads to the discovery and suppression of a potentially violent nationalist uprising, indicatively narrated through a further intertextual rewriting of Haggard's *King Solomon's Mines*. The generic coordinates of the romance evolve and shift '*in space*', 'real historical space' (Moretti, 1998: 3), as they are re-calibrated according to Thompson's different 'ideological identifications and exclusions'

(Monsman, 2010: v). The characters push 'ahead' into the 'jungle' until they reach 'the first of the broken temples', upon which is built 'a stone chariot containing effigies of Radha and Krishna' (1940: 159). This frontispiece has

> been shifted aside; beneath it a flight of steps ran down into the earth. The water was pouring down this, and half a dozen Bengalis were toiling on it, removing boxes. At sight of the police saheb panic seized them, and they bolted. The Englishmen rushed forward [...]. (159)

After the emptiness of the cave, Thompson's 'Englishmen' here stumble upon *another* hollow space embedded *within* the topography of the landscape, one that is further linked to the 'water' that has thus far kept the imperial protagonists 'cooped' up in their bungalows. The Hindu 'effigies of Radha and Krishna' recall the historical bearing of Bengali nationalist figures such as Aurobindo Ghose or Bipin Chandra Pal, who were also a template for Candler's Swami. Nationalist, meteorological and religious imagery is overlaid in this passage, as the text anxiously juggles its various ideological strategies. Just as Haggard's imperial protagonists move from 'the vast stalactite ante-cave' into 'a gloomy apartment' that 'in some past age had been *hollowed*, by hand-labour, out of the mountain' (2008: 165; my emphasis), Thompson's characters first penetrate an empty cave before then going on to discover another underground chamber. Even the 'boxes' being removed by the nationalists bear resemblance to the 'Martini-Henry ammunition boxes' discovered by Haggard's protagonists. Crucially, however, whilst Haggard's boxes are filled with 'gold pieces', Thompson's characters instead discover a vast arsenal of weaponry, described here by Nixon:

> There must be thousands and thousands of pounds' worth of revolvers and ammunition. They've got stands of rifles, too, though not so many rifles as revolvers. There's at least a couple of hundred live bombs and hand grenades, all fully detonated, and thousands of springs and bomb parts. [...] It was the ammunition and bombs that those chaps were busy removing this morning. (1940: 161)

The primary motive for the infiltration of this frontier space is no longer the barely concealed goal of retrieving the landscape's mineral wealth, nor is it to provide a redemptive pressure valve to the social tensions of the metropole. At this slightly later historical moment (1927 rather than 1885 or 1910), Thompson's repetition of the romance's key tropes now works to resolve ideological anxieties around of an increasingly coherent and potentially violent nationalist resistance.

If Thompson's protagonists do successfully discover and suppress this anti-imperial movement, the narrative still remains, as for the other romances studied in this book, self-conscious of the limits of its own representational capacities, one that is mapped out spatially according to the unevenly developed landscape. After Nixon and Hamar discover the stock of weapons, they reflect on the insufficiency of their geographical knowledge. As Nixon points out:

> Imagine yourself a young Indian! And you know every inch of this land, and you feel you can fool these sahebs and tie them up in its jungles, and have them in a fog all the time, because they *don't* know things, don't know what the folk think or feel, don't know *anything*! You'd want to take a hand in the movement! (162)

Nixon here makes a perspectival shift reminiscent of the sort we find in Steel's short stories: he attempts to imagine the Raj's unevenly developing infrastructure from a peripheral location, or 'the holes in the net', to cite Lefebvre (1998: 132). Nixon acknowledges the presence of anti-imperial activity, as he alludes to it here, whilst also emphasising that it lies beyond the borders of colonialism's cartographic exercise. This formulation is then expressed geographically as the peripheral – in both cultural and economic terms – zone of the 'jungle' becomes the locale from which this resistance originates. As the next section will further explore, the ideological and geographical productions of Thompson's literary writing suggest that it is the conditions of uneven development, as manifested in the Raj's imperial infrastructure, that actually provoke and enable the rise of nationalist movements.

'Palliative Imperialism': Producing India's Rural Space

Whilst the tumultuous climate that shapes the backdrop to *An Indian Day* has these metaphoric functions, it is still testament to the actual floods (and droughts) that plagued Calcutta and its surrounding rural regions – where

Thompson's novel is set – during this period. It was in direct response to these dramatic fluctuations in precipitation levels and climate that the Raj had established a Famine Relief and Insurance Fund in 1878, developing 'regional famine codes that instructed the organisation of local relief' from the 1880s onwards (Davis, 2010: 141). Both Candler and Thompson are preoccupied with the famine relief facilitated by forms of infrastructural development and, like Steel, use it to propagate notions of a benevolent, or 'palliative imperialism' (Mukherjee, 2013: 18). Their engagement with humanitarian ideology differs somewhat from Steel's, however, as it is used not so much to justify directly the *continuation* of imperial rule, but rather to argue that a post-imperial Indian government would not be able to provide such relief. Though the rural geographies of these novels function as a spatial mechanism designed to contain nationalist resistance, they simultaneously operate as spaces that point to the beneficence of imperial rule. Different geographical spaces, shaped by the uneven development to which they are historically subject, are themselves invested *unevenly* with different ideologies by these literary productions of colonial space.

These uneven developments can be read through *Siri Ram*'s final scene, already discussed, when we look more closely at Merivale, the British victim of Siri Ram's terrorist attack. When Siri Ram is about to murder Merivale, the narrative, like Forster's, transforms the two characters into allegories of the broader colonial-nationalist stand-off: 'For the moment he thought only of himself and Merivale, oppressor and oppressed. The Cause had narrowed down to that' (2005: 537). Whilst 'Indian nationalism' developed a 'cult of self-sacrifice and martyrdom as anticolonial resistance', argues Tickell, the British were the first 'to construct a highly exclusive, emotive Christian sacrificial *mythos* around the heroism and redemptive suffering of colonial men and women' (2012: 19). 'Merivale's heroic part in fighting a local plague academic' thus operates as a narrative counterpoint to 'Siri Ram's terrorist career' (19), as their allegorical functions are then further literalised within the text through each character's capacities for self-sacrifice or martyrdom, both men giving up their lives for their respective causes.

The tangential narrative segment of Part II of *Siri Ram*, entitled 'The Village', documents the extension of the Raj's systems of spatial regulation into a peripheral zone so that Merivale is able to undertake relief work there. As for Buchan's 'borderlands', it is in these frontier zones, where the infrastructural core and peripheral spaces meet, that the allegorical signification of Candler's imperial character becomes most neatly consolidated and self-consciously highlighted within the text. Confronted with a rural village that has fallen victim to a plague, Merivale is allegorically depicted as an invading imperialist at the outermost edges of the Raj's infrastructural network:

> He cared not for man or law. He *was* law. He might have sealed orders in his pocket to frame new codes every day to meet each new emergency. One thing only mattered. The village had to be evacuated, the houses disinfected, segregation camps and hospital camps built. He saw the work at his feet and leapt at it. Responsibility warmed him like wine. (2005: 434)

Candler's narrative self-reflexively alludes to the ideological function that this 'disaster event' plays for the justification of imperial rule. As Merivale rises to his role as 'palliative imperialist', the narrative simultaneously reveals his disregard 'for man or law'. This apparent paradox reveals the ideological work that the humanitarian relief effort is doing for imperialism's troubled self-justificatory strategies, as Merivale's assumed responsibility becomes a heady narcotic, 'like wine'. The spatial metaphor that positions the work 'at his feet', before he 'leapt at it', compounds this atmosphere of uneasy opportunism that serves the interests of the coloniser as much as it does the colonised. The irrelevance of the specifics of the disaster is itself emphasised when, on his return to Delhi, Merivale is asked by the 'first person he saw', '"where have you been all these months? Famine, wasn't it?"/Merivale explained that it was plague./"But how romantic!"' (464). The circumstances of the disaster are also dismissed by the British characters with whom Merivale converses, significantly, *inside* the symbolical architectural space of the Anglo-Indian club:[16]

---

16   Throughout Forster's *Passage*, the Anglo-Indian club is repeatedly portrayed as a racially segregated space: 'the club moved slowly; it still declared that few Mohammedans and no Hindus would eat at an Englishman's table' (2005: 60); 'there's the native, [...] we don't admit him to our clubs' (88); and as one character remarks, 'I suppose nothing that's said inside the Club will go outside the Club?' (176).

> Thus was Merivale restored to the lap of civilisation with little comment, but much inward relish. Skene had heard something of his plague adventures from Innes, but he knew it would be difficult to make him talk. Little by little, perhaps, by leading questions, he might piece out a story. (464)

Discussed as 'romantic', 'plague adventures', nothing more than 'a story', the disaster is reduced to the ideological function that it has served for imperialism's expansive and divisive spatial movements. Whilst Merivale is 'restored to the lap of civilisation' (configured spatially as the urban Anglo-Indian community), the suffering villagers are left under the rule of 'a staff of subordinates, every house disinfected and the village ringed in with police' (440). Though the text justifies the imperial intervention in the quantitive terms of the lives it has saved – '[t]hirty-two had died in the three days before the evacuation and two only in all the days afterwards' – what results is the ideological production of a new rural geography that serves imperialism's interests. Though legitimised ideologically as an expression of 'palliative imperialism', Candler's narrative exposes what Gyan Prakash describes as British imperialism's 'coherent strategy of power and identity' built through 'the structures in which the lives of its [colonised] people are enmeshed' (1999: 3). As Prakash argues, these physical technologies and imperial infrastructures, from 'railroads, steel plants, mining, irrigation, hydroelectric projects, chemical and petroleum factories' to 'public health organizations and regulations, the bureaucracy and its developmentalist routines' (3), worked to forge 'a link between space and state, making the newly configured India part and parcel of the institution of its technological configuration' (160).

Merivale's infiltration, segmentation and compartmentalisation of the village is initiated through the violent suppression of its inhabitants' 'enduring precedent for resistance' (2005: 435). The imperial occupation of this rural space is described as a brutally physical suppression of resistance to it:

As Mrinali Sinha has shown, the club is 'a quintessentially imperial institution' that operates as 'a privileged site for mediating the contradictory logic of Eurocentrism' and creates 'a distinctive colonial public sphere' (2001: 493).

> As they ran through the gate, a youth lifted an arm to bar their way. 'We do not want you here', he said, and flung a disgusting insult at them. Chauncey [Merivale's colleague] knocked him down. The two [Chauncey and Merivale] sprang on the crowd, clearing a lane with their sticks. In a moment they had the street to themselves. (436)

Candler's two imperial agents literally, and violently, clear a route for the infrastructures that will suture the village into the G. O. I.'s state bureaucracy, symptomatic of 'time-honoured contagionist practices' that sometimes placed 'temporary cordons sanitaires around whole bazaars and other native villages' (Nightingale, 2012: 133). Physically enmeshing this peripheral space into imperialism's restrictive infrastructural networks, Merivale and Chauncey in turn produce it, altering its material geography. They identify what they understand to be pre-existing cultural divisions only to entrench and reinforce them, producing a geography of segregation that infrastructurally divides the village along ethnic, communal and caste lines.

> Chauncey [...] had laid out the health and segregation camp, giving every caste its own quarter outside pollution distance, as in their homes. The Jats were in the centre, and the Kamins, or serfs, in detached camps all around, according to their degree; and the untouchables, the sweepers, and the high-defiled cobblers, farthest from the shade and the well. (435)

Of course, the text subscribes to its own ideological agendas, framing the humanitarian intervention as a justification for its restructuring of Indian space and claiming the pre-existence of social and ethnic division prior to imperial administration. Nevertheless, the text shows how the 'engineered space of colonial India' shaped not only colonialism's geographical imagination of the subcontinent, but also nationalism's (Prakash, 1999: 160). Candler describes the colonial production of a space divided between communal groups, a socio-geographical imagining that would be inherited by the 'imagined community' of independent India with disastrously violent consequences. It reveals, through its production of rural space, that, as Pandey argues, communalism 'is a form of colonialist knowledge' (2008: 6).

Thompson's second novel, *A Farewell to India* (1931), is engaged in a similar cartographic process that tries to reproduce the basic dichotomy of urban and rural zones, whilst investing each unevenly, as did the imperial romance, with different ideological functions. Rural India becomes a 'naturalised' space of 'geological accumulations and biological configurations of unpaid work' (Moore, 2015: 175), relieving the contradictions – ideological, social and economic – thrown up by the infrastructural encroachment of a swiftly industrialising Calcutta and the subcontinent's other growing urban centres. Thompson's British character, Alden, like Buchan's frontiersmen, surveys the landscape of the text's rural setting in the novel's opening pages. He turns 'into a bypath leading to the region of wilderness and forsaken temples' that 'would have brought him to the Red Tank, that swampy relic of the old days' (Thompson, 1931: 17). At this point, the rural environment is cut through with an infrastructural line that breaks up the landscape for Alden, drawing his gaze toward the neighbouring city. Following the path to the 'Red Tank', he finds that 'first it crossed a single railway line, which connected Vishnugram with the ferry of the Samodar River, twenty-eight miles away, and the dark industrial towns beyond' (17). Vishnugram is here a site of industrial production and urbanisation, whilst the rural environment is somehow separate from the city and the capitalist relations that implicitly shape it. In an effort to reconstruct the redemptive space of the frontier, Thompson reframes rural space not as a *peripheral*, but actually *pre-capitalist* landscape – an 'external nature' of the kind that had, for centuries, 'enabled capitalists and empires to construct global webs of exploitation [...] on an unprecedented scale' (Moore, 2015: 190). For Buchan as for Thompson, the frontier is 'not just there, but had to be imagined, conceptualised, and *seen*' (190; my emphasis). Looking at the Indian countryside, Alden *sees* that 'this was India, where estates are not fenced, nor are even houses over-private, except in their women's apartment' (18). If, as Jameson argues, 'one of the determinants of capitalist culture [...] is a radical split between the private and the public' (1986: 69), Thompson *produces* rural Indian infrastructure as *pre*-capitalist, 'natural' (much like Forster's descriptions of Indian architecture), external to the world-system that is in fact the cause of the area's underdevelopment.

Read more closely, however, the novel reveals the 'process of the production of nature' in which it is engaged, as it spins a necessary fiction for the story of capital accumulation (Smith, 2008: 49). Alden's observation of the 'single railway line', an infrastructural route that links the development of the city to the underdevelopment of the rural landscape, is here coterminous with the narrative's production of that rural space as a pre-capitalist 'wilderness'. The text places its content 'in historical context', revealing its representation of rural India as pre-capitalist to be, to paraphrase Smith and Moore, a product of its own ideological production. If Thompson's textual portrayal of India reproduces 'the false ideological dualism of society and nature', a focus on its mappings of infrastructural development reveal 'the real patterns of uneven development' to be a 'product of the unity of capital' (Smith, 2008: 50). Infrastructural reading here allows us to re-attach peripheral spaces to core routes, thereby realising the processes of peripheralisation that Thompson's novel is attempting to deny.

The novel's preface amplifies its spatial productions onto the subcontinent as a whole, as Thompson positions his fictional text as a map for those parts of India beyond the 'well-trodden' path of 'the tourist':

> The reader must remember that Vishnugram is not a great city, but just an entirely typical provincial town – the capital of an area of perhaps a thousand square miles. [The reader] will not be far wrong if he imagines that the conditions and circumstances amid which he finds himself [in this novel] are essentially the same in thousands of Indian provincial cities, of which the tourist necessarily can know nothing. (1931: 5–6)

The novel's patchwork literary geography of urban and rural zones are here extrapolated across the subcontinent, resolving the ideological contradictions arising from the damaging effects of British India's accelerated, though uneven and unequal, economic development, particularly as it undermines the Raj's self-justificatory rhetoric of its humanitarian role as a governmental protectorate. Another of Thompson's British characters, Findlay, reflects that '[t]here was no need for a famine to come, declared officially as such by Government; in this land there was always famine somewhere. There was always disease and suffering' (61). This final framing of the famines afflicting India's peripheral spaces as perpetual is itself a symptom of palliative ideology: India's rural space must be produced as constantly subject to disaster, from plagues to famines, so as to justify continually humanitarian intervention.

Within palliative ideology, Mukherjee writes, the 'structural relationship between imperialism's engine – industrial and financial capitalism – and disaster are not, or *cannot* [...] be imagined' (Mukherjee, 2013: 41). However, *A Farewell to India* is written some decades after the literature with which Mukherjee is primarily concerned, and which includes Steel's fiction. In the intervening years, between the end of the nineteenth century and the early 1930s, industrial and urban development in India had been pervasive. This explosion in urban, travel and communication infrastructures, and the intensification of the social and economic relations of capital that they facilitated, is registered in Thompson's novel with notable anxiety. His response is embedded within the novel's urgent production of rural space and in fact reveals, to use Mukherjee's terminology, 'the creases in the ideological façade' of palliative imperialism (18). Focusing on its intermittent representation of imperial infrastructure allows us to see how the novel actually highlights the 'structural relationship' between imperialism's infrastructural and capitalist development and the 'natural' disasters that, contradictorally, had legitimised much of that development. As the subcontinent becomes increasingly subject to the contradictions and uneven developments of the world-system, the colonial imagination of Indian space as a rural, disaster-ridden landscape has to be actively, indeed anxiously, produced and reproduced to sustain the justificatory ideology of palliative imperialism.

Resistance in the Imperial Capital: Producing Urban Space

This production of 'natural', or 'pre-capitalist' is driven by the burgeoning cityscape of Calcutta, where the proliferation of urban infrastructures creates an atmosphere of claustrophobia reminiscent of Hannay's discomfort in imperial London. Meteorologically, this is reflected in 'the heats, which were mental no less than physical' (Thompson, 1931: 40). Waiting for 'the night train' to take 'him back to Vishnugram', Alden is reduced to spending the afternoon 'shirtless on a bed, listening to the variegated noise of

Calcutta' (40). Withdrawing to the privacy of his hotel room, he listens to 'the passing voices of the modern world':

> Alden had come to equate with the metropolis other sounds also, which as yet troubled his Vishnugram hardly at all. The rattle and clank of trams, the approach and dying away of cars [...] he remembered a time when motors were hardly known in Calcutta streets. Now at whiles, especially when night was ravaged, he could have thought the whole creation was groaning together, waiting for the manifestation of – what? Some higher mechanisation, that would lift mankind out of physical weariness and all disease, but certainly out of its quick senses of light and colour and touch and sound? (41)

The different geographical segments of India through which Alden, and the novel, moves – the rural periphery, the semi-peripheral Vishnugram, and the bustling core of Calcutta – emphasise the uneven development of the Indian landscape. Though ostensibly placed on a linear developmental trajectory, the periphery being slowly accumulated by the 'modern world', Alden actually imagines these varying scales of development spatially, synchronised into a unified process ('the whole creation [...] groaning together'): these 'patterns of uneven development' become a 'product of the unity of capital' (Smith, 2008: 50).

Realising the capitalist world-system, and the uneven and unequal development it produced, to be 'a singular phenomenon' (WReC, 2015: 12), Alden is confronted with what is, more broadly, colonial literature's deepest ideological crisis: how can imperial infrastructural development – which facilitates, Luxemburg would argue, the accumulation of capital – continue if there are no rural disaster zones into which it can move? Alden's desire for '[s]ome higher mechanisation, that would lift mankind out of physical weariness and all disease' is fundamentally flawed. If this were to be realised – if imperial infrastructural development were, in the end, successful in lifting *all* of its colonial subjects out of poverty and eradicating famine and plague *indefinitely* – palliative imperialism as ideology would disintegrate. As Barnett writes of twentieth-century humanitarian intervention, 'humanitarian governance hopes to put itself out of business'; it is 'dedicated to its own destruction' (2014: 222–223). The economic determinants of colonial capitalism *and* humanitarian ideology here intersect at a point of crisis as they each realise their own finite temporalities.

Economic and ideological motors of Thompson's production of India's rural space overlap, only to be dealt with by a moment of what, returning to Macherey, is nothing more than an 'eloquent silence' (1986: 79): 'waiting for the manifestation of – what?'

Despite this colonial literature's ideological efforts toward counter-insurgency, then, it still contains 'revolutionary trajectories', to return Harvey's phrase (2012: xvii), coined in his discussion of the twenty-first-century city as a particularly productive site for sociopolitical conflict: it is 'the site where people of all sorts and classes mingle, however reluctantly and agonistically, to produce a common if perpetually changing and transitory life' (2012: 67). This scenario is produced by intensifying proximity and inequality, consequences of intensifying uneven development. Though this chapter is concerned with a very different historic and geographic space, India at this time still witnessed astonishingly swift processes of industrialisation and urbanisation, and Candler's second novel, *Abdication*, opens with a description of the 'logically planned' infrastructure of New Delhi (Candler, 1993: 1). The city, which had been 'commissioned in 1911 to facilitate the transfer of the capital of British India from Calcutta to Delhi', took only '20 years to construct' (Legg, 2007: 1). As well as being 'more centrally located', transferring the Raj's capital to Delhi also shifted its administrative centre away from 'the increasingly revolutionary [...] Bengal' (28). Stephen Legg demonstrates that the city's construction was as much a 'showcase [of] imperial sovereignty for an increasingly aggressive national audience' as it was an infrastructural transformation of a vast tract of urban space (29). But despite this astonishing project, Delhi remained cleft into two parts, denoted by temporal prefixes – 'New' and 'Old' – still used to describe the city today which are most visibly identifiable in their respective infrastructural developments. As Legg describes, 'the neo-classical monumentalism of the imperial capital, and the sterile, geometric spaces of New Delhi' contrast sharply with the 'Old' city, which is often 'depicted as an organic space of tradition and community' lacking any 'modern sanitation and infrastructure' and becoming, in the colonial imagination at least, 'a haptic and sensory place of smells, sights and contact that bewildered and beguiled Western tourists and governors alike' (1).

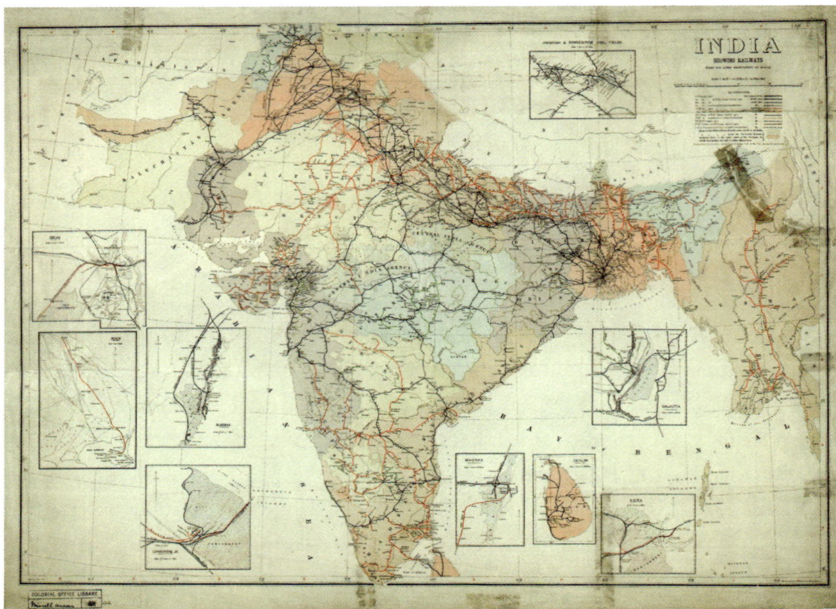

Figure 4.3: Map from the Survey of India undertaken in 1922, which details imperial infrastructural development across the subcontinent, and includes insets detailing
the infrastructural layouts of the Raj's key urban areas. Colonial Office 1047/1094,
National Archives at Kew.

These ideological associations recall the divided geographies of *Passage*'s
opening cartographic survey, demonstrative of the way in which space is
produced by literature *for* the colonial imagination. Differing spatial segments, as well as their respective inhabitants, are given temporal currencies,
positioned at alternate historical moments on a linear developmental scale
even as they continue to exist coterminously. But whilst Forster's fictional
town of Chandrapore remains starkly segregated, Candler's depiction of
Delhi interrogates and moves through these spatial divisions. Furthermore,
the narrative introduces an element of subversive self-reflexivity into its
own ability to represent the cityscape. Though designed to segregate along
hierarchical lines Delhi's co-existing populations, 'the two cities were, in

fact, governed as one and impacted upon each other in myriad ways', becoming 'intimately intwined' (Legg, 2007: 1–2). Indeed, *Abdication*'s opening sentence hints at the possibility of spatial transgression: 'Riley', Candler's British protagonist, rides 'through the Mori Gate and [leaves] Anglo-India behind him' (1993: 1). He moves through the infrastructural demarcation that separates the 'efficient, and logically planned' Anglo-Indian town of 'Thompsonpur' from the 'frank squalor of the city', spaces in turn associated with global networks of trade and capital ('the cupolaed telegraph and post offices') and economic impoverishment ('the defilement of the city') respectively (1–2).

However, Riley's subjective response to these differentiated urban spaces is contradictory: 'The frank squalor of the city pleased his eye if not his nose', whilst the rigid infrastructures and architectures of New Delhi 'depressed him' (1–2). Riley romanticises 'The City' as a space that is somehow more 'natural' than the rigid spatial segregations of Anglo-India's '"Civil Station" and cantonments' (3). The spaces are given contrasting temporalities, the newness of Anglo-India emphasised, whilst the segments of Old Delhi 'within the gate' have been, Riley observes, in existence 'since the dawn of time' (3). Positioned on a linear developmental scale, Candler's literary production of Delhi's contrasting city spaces reveals how the physical landscape is ideologically complicit, to turn to Chakrabarty, in 'Europe's acquisition of the adjective "modern" for itself' and, simultaneously, the production of the 'nightmare of "tradition" that "modernity" creates' (2008: 43–46). The text works to conceal imperialism's complicity in the underdevelopment of this part of the city by constructing it as a *pre*-capitalist, if not entirely *pre*-modern space.

Riley's status as allegorically representative of British imperialism is repeatedly emphasised: he is, notably, 'the editorial chair of the *Gazette*', a figure at the head of Anglo-Indian print production, and the narrative describes him as 'the symbol' of 'the incubus' of the Raj (6). Like Buchan's frontier characters, Riley configures the 'natural', or 'undeveloped' Old quarter as an antidote to the claustrophobic infrastructures of the Anglo-Indian city, a set of spatial movements that, as argued in the previous chapter, can be mapped onto capital's uneven accumulative processes.

> The charm of the quarter revived in him feelings which he had almost forgotten, the curiosity, the love of unfamiliar things, the itching for adventure he had felt six years earlier when he first came out to India – 'the romance of the East', still exploited by managers of theatres and novelists, though one's sensitiveness to it has been dulled by the war, which has flattened out everything or brought it too near to us [...]. (5)

Whilst producing the Old city as a redemptive frontier or borderland, Riley's affectionate observation of this peripheral space is contaminated by, as for Alden, anxieties about the loss of those spaces. Here again is the fundamental contradiction of frontier consciousness, as colonial writing has to produce and reproduce a space *beyond* infrastructural development into which it can expand. However, the self-conscious dimension of *Abdication*'s narrative here demonstrates the way in which the landscape that it represents – including those segments of the city presented as 'pre-modern' or undeveloped – are in fact *produced* by it. In so doing, it reveals that the undeveloped parts of the city are in fact part and parcel of imperialism's uneven infrastructural development, or a product of the development of underdevelopment. Whilst the 'colonial gaze' of *Passage*'s opening mapping sequence remains omniscient and all-pervasive (Pratt, 2003: 60), Candler's narrative is littered with references to perception, visibility and the ability to represent the infrastructure of the divided city. The architectural layout foregrounds the imbalance between developed and underdeveloped, or core and peripheral zones, whilst Riley's spatial movement reveals the ideological fabric overlaying them. The novel's opening lines set this recurrent theme in motion:

> Riley was aware of a *perceptible* lifting of the heart as he rode through the Mori Gate and left Anglo-India behind him. The frank squalor of the city pleased his *eye* if not his nose. Thompsonpur was efficient, and logically planned to serve the conveniences of life, but unsatisfying whether *viewed by the inward or outward eye*. (1993: 1; my emphases)

This preoccupation with *seeing* can and should be read, I want to suggest, as the spatial expression of an ideological anxiety riven by emerging Indian nationalisms.[17] Themes of visibility and knowability are written into the

---

17   Published in 1922, at the end of Gandhi's four-year-long satyagraha campaign launched in response to the Rowlatt Acts, *Abdication* deals with this strand of

infrastructural layout of the city, both facilitated and inhibited by it in equal measure. The road that connects the Anglo-Indian community to the old city is 'straight and broad; one sighted folk a mile before one met them' (1); it is constructed to facilitate visibility, as space becomes strategically geared towards the containment and suppression of insurgent activity. 'There was any amount of space in Thompsonpur', which has has 'entirely eclipsed' the 'walled city within the gate' both 'visually and materially', and '[o]ne had left it two miles behind before one reached the Mori Gate and the defilement of the city' (2–3). Infrastructural divisions, segregations and imposed distances are, the text narrates, further combined with the symbolic use of its architecture. Indeed, the pro-imperial ideology that these architectural feats instil in Riley is described as *itself* a form of infrastructure. Riley moves past

> blocks of houses, shops, and hotels. Here, too, the verandahs were roomy, the plinth high, and on the frieze above the pillars, in glazed enamelled letters, such words as Globe, Empire, British, Victoria, European, caught the eye, canalising the impressions of the Imperial-minded, which run in channels none too broad at any time. (2)

Michel Foucault indicatively used the term '*canalisation*' to 'ensure a certain allocation of people in space' and 'the coding of their reciprocal relations' (1991: 252), and Legg's book-length analysis of Delhi appropriately draws on Foucault's writings as 'a structuring analytic with which to negotiate the path from New to Old Delhi' (2007: xiv).[18] Candler's narrative here reveals the symbiotic relationship between ideology and infrastructure: New Delhi is not simply constructed as an expression of imperial ideology, a

---

Indian nationalism in particular. Thompson's second novel, *A Farewell to India*, published during another particularly intense period of Gandhian resistance – the Civil Disobedience campaign of 1930–1932 – is likewise preoccupied with Gandhian nationalism.

18 Nicholas Thomas similarly uses Foucault's concept of 'governmentality' in his assessment of the infrastructure of colonialism. He writes: 'The prison, welfare systems, town planning and political economy can all be seen as expressions of this order of governmentality, which is manifested both in colonial administration and in changes in metropolitan policies and institutions. In effect, modernity itself can be understood as a colonialist project in the special sense that both the societies internal to Western nations, and those they possessed, administered and reformed elsewhere, were understood as objects to be surveyed, regulated and sanitised' (1996: 4).

symbolic and physical manifestation of the Raj's power. That infrastructure works, in turn, to shape the thought processes of 'the Imperial-minded', the narrative listing a series of associative catchwords that are physically inscribed 'in glazed enamel letters' into the city's architecture. The ideology propagated by these architectures is itself imagined as an infrastructural edifice, its 'broad channels' locked in a dialectic with the physical space to which it responds.

Figure 4.4: Photograph of the Rajpath, or King's Way, in 2016, the arterial infrastructural route at the centre of New Delhi designed by the British architect Edward Lutyens to provide a panoramic view of the city from the Viceroy's palace.

This preoccupation with visibility and the capacity to represent persist as Riley moves into Old Delhi, the infrastructural layouts of which contrast sharply with the Anglo-Indian section of the city. He enters 'the network of alleys, too narrow to admit wheels', and by 'stretching out his arms he could almost touch the walls on either side' (4). Unlike the 'broad channels' of New Delhi, the Old city's narrow roads inhibit the imperialist's movement, as these respective infrastructures are again situated within a paradigm of contrasting temporalities: Old Delhi is filled with 'an atmosphere of ancient and undisturbed peace', invoking a pre-modern temporality that is reflected in the architectural materials out of which the buildings are constructed: 'Few of these houses had been vulgarised by modern hands. [...] the windows were corbelled, the lattices and screens fretted, the balconies supported by brackets of wood and stone' (4). 'The walls of the lower stories were all dead to the street', blocking Riley's view into the private spaces of their inhabitants. Though 'some' of 'the doors stood open', he gets only 'a glimpse of a courtyard' and immediately experiences a 'guilty sense of prying' (4). Like Thompson's character Hamar, Riley acknowledges the limits of colonial cartography, expressed here through an unevenly developed geographical terrain – for Hamar, rural, for Riley, urban.

The meteorological metaphor deployed at the end of *Siri Ram* and by Thompson throughout *An Indian Day* now recurs once more, though here the text makes the connections between the shifting climate and anti-imperial movements even more explicit: 'An atmospheric change had come over the city', observes Riley, as '[h]is sense of something impending was so strong that he even imagined a darkening of the sky' (5). The threat of an oncoming storm is no longer a meteorological backdrop to the text's plot, becoming instead part of Riley's subjective response to the imminent resistance he is about to encounter.

> Someone was shouting that the shops were already closed in every other quarter of the city. Then above the confused murmur he heard the cry of 'Mahatma Gandhi-ki-jai', and he remembered it was the *hartal*, Gandhi had been arrested. [...] All down the street behind him the dirge for the mahatma ceased, and there arose a more sinister and angry chorus, 'Hai Hai Rowlatt Bill.' It followed him through the square by Amir Khan's mosque and the relative quiet of Hari Mandi. The echo of the rhythmic beat of it sounded in his ears till he passed through the Baradari Gate and regained the complacent security of Thompsonpur. (5–7)

Within the symbolic currency of this colonial literature, the 'atmospheric' change Riley experiences is here translated from loose metaphor to direct political action through the vehicle of Gandhi, who had become by the early 1920s a metonym for 'disorder' (Cohn, 2009: 162). The 'rhythmic beat' that runs through *Siri Ram* resurfaces in *Abdication*, as what was once subtextual allusion coagulates into an organised and coherent nationalist movement present within the text. This is then inscribed back into the unevenly developed spaces of the city, as Riley retreats to 'the club [...] solid, homely, inviting, a fortress' (12), in order to escape the 'angry chorus'. Meanwhile, the Indian 'crowd' congregates in the 'open square by the mosque' (7), making use of the city's unregulated spaces to advance their protest. Though a recurrent ideological project of Candler's *Siri Ram*, *Abdication* does not even attempt to undermine the political concerns articulated by these groups. Instead, it retreats with its protagonist back into the segregated zone of the Anglo-Indian community, ignoring the resistance located spatially beyond its infrastructural barriers.

Despite the potential resistance inscribed into the spatial productions of Candler's text, this chapter has reluctantly to make, as noted at its outset, a more sceptical conclusion. If this colonial literature constructs an infrastructural framework that will be inherited by independent India, even if only on an imaginary terrain (though, as Fanon demonstrated, this is also a deeply physical one (2001: 29–31)), it remains a cultural geography riddled with social and sectarian divisions, and uneven and unequally developed urban and rural spaces. Colonial literature's imagined geographies and infrastructural circuities may have contributed to the formation of Indian nationalism, but it must be acknowledged these also exacerbated numerous violent historical processes. The notion that 'India has existed as a nation time out of mind' had been central to Nehruvian nationalism (Anderson, 2013: 96); as Nehru claimed, 'the whole history of India for thousands of years past shows her essential unity and the vitality and adaptability of her culture' (1941: 17). However, Nehru also conceded that India's deeply historical desire for 'unified political control of the whole country could not be realised' prior to British rule 'in view of the lack of means and machinery'; it was British infrastructural development, the 'railways and the other accompaniments of a modern administration', that enabled India to be both imagined and eventually consolidated as a politically unified geographical entity (18).

If Indian nationalisms were forced to imagine the new nation along the infrastructural coordinates left behind by the British, there is no reason to suppose that the various inequalities and spatial divisions (particularly communalist ones) represented and reproduced in Forster's, Thompson's and Candler's colonial literature would not gain a significant cultural as well as geographical currency in post-imperial India. Whilst the infrastructure of the Raj – its transport and communications networks, its military frameworks and state bureaucracy – may have facilitated the consolidation of a unified Indian nation, it also laid the foundations for post-imperial India's many problems: its rural and urban divisions, its communalist antagonisms and perhaps even Partition in 1947. Benedict Anderson describes this infrastructural inheritance with an illuminating metaphor: like 'the complex electrical system in any large mansion' after 'the owner has fled', 'the new owner's hand at the switch' will still flick on and activate the same infrastructural circuitry (Anderson, 2006: 160). Perry Anderson takes up his brother's infrastructural metaphor to describe Britain's departure from India in 1947: 'Having lit the fuse, Mountbatten handed over the buildings to their new owners before they blew up, in what has a good claim to be the most contemptible single act in the annals of Empire' (2013: 77).

The colonial literature discussed in this chapter constructs a new kind of imperial infrastructure that responds to the disintegration of Britain's formal empire – it looks forward to informal imperialism, but an imperialism nonetheless. For example, by highlighting communalist and other forms of social division in order to delegitimise nationalist movements, these novels look forward to Britain's geo-strategic tactics in the Partition of Pakistan and India in 1947. As Anderson argues, by inflicting 'partition on its subjects overnight' the British Empire was able to 'save its face: for Empire, now read Dominion' (2013: 77). The ideological tactics that this chapter has excavated out of colonial literature foreshadows, and eventually becomes typical of, Britain's strategic approach to decolonisation in the following decades. As Benjamin Grob-Fitzgibbon has argued, the empire sought 'to secure the colonies for the Commonwealth in an orderly transfer of power while maintaining British influence in the region and strengthening overall Western dominance in the Cold War world' (2011: 3). These literary productions of colonial space configure this shift in the imperial imagination at their infrastructural levels; they are engaged in what Gordon Martel has described, using infrastructural metaphors to described the decolonisation process, as 'a conscious design on the part of the managers to "downsize", "restructure", and "re-engineer" the imperial project' (2000: 403). They contribute to the production of a symbolic cartography that would gain wider cultural currency as Britain attempted to secure an informal cross-national infrastructure that served its post-imperial political and economic interests. The Raj's infrastructural circuitries, inherited by independent India, enabled Nehru's vision – disfigured, though it was, by the catastrophes of Partition – whilst keeping the subcontinent firmly enmeshed in the exploitative hierarchies of an unevenly developing capitalist world-system.[19]

19   The same can be said of South Africa post-1994. Patrick Bond, who traces 'how capitalist crisis coincided with the emergence of neoliberal ideas, and in turn exacerbated "uneven development"', expresses 'concern about the new government's deviation from the liberation movement mandate' as he situates 'the South African liberation struggle and the political-ideological role of the African National Congress' within the 'broader global processes also unfolding during the 1990s' (2000: 2–4).

Towards an Infrastructural Reading of the Present

Colonial literature repeatedly uses infrastructural developments as symbolic objects in its attempt to resolve contradictions emerging in and across four key strands of imperial ideology: humanitarianism, segregation, frontiers and nationalism. Infrastructure developed unevenly in different colonial situations and, funded by private investors whose speculations were secured by the imperial state, spatially fixed a moment of crisis in the world-system's accumulative processes. Correspondingly, colonial literature represented these physical embodiments of imperialism in order to achieve a cultural fix, smoothing over some of the central ideological tensions and contradictions of the period. Nevertheless, when critical attention is paid to this representation of infrastructure, these contradictions remain detectable at the level of textual form, thematic and symbolic tropes, and genre. By building on and fuelling imperial infrastructural development, colonial literature can be seen as complicit in the production of an unevenly and unequally developed landscape that has continued to scar the material and imagined geographies of now formally decolonised states, and that continue to shape the twenty-first-century's post-imperial world.

For Georges Labica, 'contemporary globalisation is nothing other than Lenin's "new imperialism", now reaching a still higher stage of development' (2007: 228). Wallerstein similarly views the recent 'protectionist thrust' of governments across the world, manifested in various forms of 'austerity' and 'repression', as symptoms of 'an ever-tighter gridlock of the system' (2013: 32). As I have be arguing, there are clearly continuities between the historical moment of high imperialism and are own that are of crucial political import. However, such broad methodological generalisations come precariously close to what Cooper calls 'the epochal fallacy' – that is, 'to see history as a succession of epochs', a practice which assumes a 'coherence that complex interactions rarely produce' (2005: 19). Analyses such as these also fall foul to a 'leapfrogging legacy', as commentators jump, for example, from the intensification of global capital mobility under the guise of 'the new imperialism' of the 1880s directly to the intensification of neoliberal policy enforcement and adoption in the 1980s under Reagan and Thatcher. Indeed, David Harvey actually names this period 'the "new" imperialism', discussing at length the transition, at the levels of state policy, media coverage and academic and other critical writings, from British to American imperialism (2005: 1–8).

Certainly, these comparisons simplify complex historical processes. They overlook 'not only the sequence of processes in the decolonisation era, but the tragedy of recent African history, people's heightened sense of possibility and the thwarting of their hopes' (Cooper, 2005: 18). Indeed, Cooper is particularly vocal in his condemnation of the use of the terms 'imperial' and 'empire' to describe the late twentieth- and early twenty-first-century geopolitical landscape, which he rightly argues has been deployed 'not only by those critical of American high-handedness in relation to its democratic pretensions, but by conservative scholars who hope to see the United States exercise the power it has' (194). These readings, Cooper argues, overlook the fact that the contemporary moment is built around an 'international system that is no longer a world of rival empires, no longer a world of bipolar conflict, but a world of extreme inequalities of wealth and power' (197), a conviction that, as I have stated from the outset, motivates the development of *infrastructural reading* as a self-consciously resistant methodological practice. Saskia Sassen, too, has convincingly demonstrated the substantial differences between these two historical moments, even if they both are marked by a notable shift in the imagination of the 'world scale': the first 'constituted through the extraterritorial projection of several major national capitalisms and geared toward building national states rather than global systems', whilst '[t]oday's global economy', launched in the 1980s, 'is constituted through an increasingly institutionalised space for operations that is both electronic and territorial, and simultaneously supra-, inter-, and subnational' (2006: 143).

Clearly, this book heeds Cooper's warning that 'we should not get carried away with the power of empires, either in the sense of a nostalgic view or of its opposite, a conception of empire as totalising power' (2005:

200). My repeated emphasis on colonial literature's representational failure is, I hope, to re-emphasise the fact that 'the story of empire is still a story of limits' (190). It is important to acknowledge that the historical specifics of imperial rule, as well as the various ideologies that both justified infrastructural development and that were dialectically reproduced by them, are no longer with us in these exact forms today. However, the resurfacing of the terms 'empire' and 'imperialism' in the writings of many contemporary critics is just as clearly a response to the recent resurgence in ideologies tainted by a rhetoric of imperialism, one that these critics are eager to resist. For example, when Deepa Kumar critiques what she decides to call 'US imperialism' (2012: 5), she does so not to reduce the analytic precision of that term. Rather, if 'the vocabulary of capitalist modernisation' propounded by British imperial ideologues was justified in part by infrastructural projects, it is to note that similar arguments have been adopted by advocates of 'the new form of imperialism initiated by the United States' (4). With this in mind, an *infrastructural reading* of the present might now be a prescient project to undertake.

Physical infrastructures, as I have argued throughout this book, fuelled imperial ideology, even if an analysis of representations of them also critically levers open the various contradictions and tensions they concealed. An ongoing 'uncritical insistence on the "progress", "advancement", "achievements", and enormous and marvellous "accomplishments"' as (one of many) justifications for the US-led invasion of Iraq in 2003 is, still in the twenty-first century, often lent authority by the construction and development of physical infrastructure projects (Rojas, 2015: xvi–xviii). Whilst performing this ideological function, infrastructure meanwhile continues to be used materially to enable the military occupation of foreign spaces: as Patrick Cockburn observed in 2007, '[e]normous concrete blocks like giant grey tombstones', erected to protect 'American checkpoints, police stations and government buildings' from 'suicide bombers', have become the 'physical symbol of the new Iraq' (2007: 116). The reapplication of coercive and divisive forms of infrastructure justified through linear (rather than uneven) developmental ideologies needs to be continuously critiqued, and its historical and cultural roots recognised and unpacked. In contemporary popular culture, infrastructure projects still generally signify an uncritical 'Western modernity', in the loosest sense – as British comedian John Oliver recently described 'infrastructure' on an episode of *Last Week Tonight*, it's 'basically anything that can be destroyed in an action movie' (2015), often at the hands of terrorists or climate disasters. Whilst it is beyond the scope of this book to bring *infrastructural reading* to bear in any thorough way on contemporary popular literary and other cultural forms, I would not be the first to read Hollywood's obsession with 'end-of-the-world scenarios', which often have the explosive destruction of infrastructure at their centre, as a kind of cultural fix. This creative destruction promises 'a revelation that all too often serves to reboot a system that has gone into crisis' (Hassler-Forest, 2012: 207–212).

Cooper concludes, fairly, that 'we need to think about empire not because it is about to be resurrected, but because it was such an important constituent of political life for so long, until so recently, and with such important effects' (2005: 158). However, in the current context of mainstream debate around empire and imperialism, it seems to me unhelpful to dismiss the groundbreaking work of historians such as Mike Davis, who has worked on imperial history throughout his academic career and who therefore has good reason to publish his writings on current US foreign policy in a collection provocatively subtitled *Essays Against Empire* (2007). Harvey justifies his own use of the term '"new" imperialism' to describe recent historical events by relating it to these mainstream debates:

> The conservative historian Niall Ferguson (whose TV series and accompanying book document, in true patriotic fashion, not only the heroic deeds of Britain's empire-builders but also the peace, prosperity, and well-being that this empire supposedly gave to the world) advises that the US must stiffen its resolve, shell out the money, and 'make the transition from informal to formal empire'. (2005: 4)

In the light of 'revisionist accounts of imperial and colonial life that have proliferated in recent years' (Gilroy, 2004a: 2–3), self-consciously foregrounding the resistant poise of my own critical practice and this book's reevaluation of colonial literature seems a necessary and productive endeavour. Rehearsing these arguments one final time, I want therefore to remind the reader once more of the resistant politics motivating this project, and express my hope that *infrastructural reading* still has a role to play in allowing us to read colonial and other archives '"against the grain"; to challenge and expand them' (Luckett, 2016: 425). By developing new 'analytical and methodological tools for debating, challenging and deconstructing inherited canons' (425), I align this project with decolonial movements such as the Rhodes Must Fall campaign, who do the important work of translating its insights into 'real action' (Prinsloo, 2015: 166).

As I have tried to show, colonial literature has contributed to the contemporary cultural conceptualisation and infrastructural manifestation of the world-system. It has helped to facilitate the ongoing 'underdevelopment' of ex-colonies by contributing to the 'extreme unevenness' of their inherited infrastructural circuitries (Amin, 1976: 201–203). 'Infrastructure does not grow *de novo*', argues Susan Leigh Star, but rather 'wrestles with the inertia of the installed base and inherits strengths and limitations from that base': '[o]ptical fibres run along old railroad lines' and cities such as Delhi remain divided into 'Old' and 'New' zones (1999: 382). The literary texts examined here have instigated and perpetuated certain infrastructural imaginings, the inheritance of which have had severe consequences for the world's postcolonial citizens. Yet they also allow us to interrogate those consequences. Dirlik observes that 'it is increasingly difficult to point to any nation or region as the centre of global capitalism', which is now constituted as 'a network of urban formations, without a clearly definable centre' (1994: 349). It is this networked world-system, comprised of infrastructural demarcations and their corresponding literary-cultural representations and ideological associations, that should continue to be the target of our critique: as Graham and Marvin write, a 'critical focus on networked infrastructure – transport, telecommunications, energy, water and streets – offers up a powerful and dynamic way of seeing contemporary cities and urban regions' (2001: 8). Dismantling the ideological investment in uneven infrastructural developments allows us to see that 'the face of modernity is not worn exclusively by the "futuristic" skyline of the Pudong District in Shanghai or the Shard and Gherkin buildings in London; just as emblematic of modernity as these are the favelas of Rocinha and Jacarezinho in Rio and the slums of Dharavi in Bombay' (WReC, 2015: 12–13).

The book has refracted its assessment of the relationship between imperial infrastructure and different kinds of spatial resistance through four paradigmatic concerns, addressed across the four chapters: humanitarianism, segregation, frontiers and nationalism, each of which continues to haunt infrastructural development in the twenty-first century. The humanitarian ideologies analysed in Chapter 1 have come increasingly 'to be used in relation to any provision of medical, shelter and food aid – even if these [are] undertaken by militaries or by state agencies following political agendas' (Weizman 2011: 51). As Barnett argues, humanitarianism has become 'a global welfare institution, and aid workers are social workers – appearing to be emancipatory when operating as mechanisms of social control': 'Global capitalism needs humanitarianism' (2014: 24), a dilemma that Flora Annie Steel was already struggling with in her short fiction at the end of the nineteenth century.

Likewise, 'the early twentieth-century mania for racial segregation', a central concern of Chapter 2, has 'left a terrible legacy for the cities of today's world – and for the larger human communities in which they are located' (Nightingale, 2012: 4). If the contemporary 'spatial politics' of 'former colonial cities' such as Johannesburg are now primarily 'about class', 'many aspects of colonial White Town/Black Town systems of race segregation continue to help carve deep social canyons that scar the vast expanses of the megacities' (402). As Chapter 2 demonstrated, literature has the capacity both to entrench and to subvert these segregationist ideologies and their physical manifestations. Whilst Haggard's literary geography implicitly advocated the separation of South Africa's white and black populations, the innovative formal strategies of Schreiner's and Plomer's fiction reveal systems of segregation to be permeable, vulnerable to transgression and subversion.

The same can be said of the themes addressed in the book's final two chapters. Aspects of frontier consciousness linger in a number of geographical locations in more violent and sinister ways than ever before. Weizman has written at length on Israel's occupation of the West Bank, where the 'dynamic morphology of the frontier resembles an incessant sea dotted with multiplying archipelagos of externally alienated and internally homogenous ethno-national enclaves' (2012: 7), and where infrastructure 'planning and architecture have become tactical tools and the means of dispossession' (5). Whilst for Buchan's Richard Hannay, 'our swords were hammered into ploughshares' (2010: 313–314), historian Arno J. Mayer has inverted this phrase – 'Plowshares into Swords' – to emphasise the increasingly violent consequences of Zionism's contemporary frontier consciousness (2008: 88). Frontier 'mythology' is, furthermore, a key factor of what Smith calls 'the new urban frontier', as gentrifiers in cities the world over exploit a 'pioneer' aesthetic to 'scrub the city clean of its working-class geography and history' (2005: 25–27). Meanwhile, Graham has shown how 'explicitly colonial models of pacification, militarisation and control, honed on the streets of the global South, are spreading to the cities of capitalist heartlands in the North' (2011: xvi-xvii), a movement between colony and metropole that the *The Thirty-Nine Steps* interrogated through the geographical oscillations of Hannay's frontier consciousness.

Finally, despite the emancipatory possibilities of the twentieth century's national-liberation movements, the new nations that emerged remained 'caught in the constraints' of the world-system (Arrighi et al., 2011: 27). Now, as Hardt and Negri have comprehensively shown, 'the concept of national sovereignty is losing its effectiveness' as the 'unity of single governments has been disarticulated and invested in a series of separate bodies (banks, international organisms of planning, and so forth, in addition to the traditional separate bodies), which all increasingly refer for legitimacy to the transnational level of power' (2001: 307). Already in the 1920s and '30s, Edmund Candler and Edward Thompson were producing literary geographies that revealed the ideologies embedded in India's infrastructural development, the cross-national nature of which would hinder later efforts toward national sovereignty. Meanwhile, whilst the nationalist liberation movements of formal decolonisation 'took shape under the headings of "emancipation" [and] "uplift"', Gilroy has since shown how 'racism, nationalism and fascism' have become 'part of a single, complex structure of modern solidarity', as 'the certainties that race provides [are] embraced as an answer' to all kinds of sociopolitical uncertainties rooted in part in the infrastructural coordinates of the world-system and its destabilisation of the nation-state (2004b: x).

Despite these various outgrowths, it is not my intention to dampen the spatial resistance excavated here with a sense of historical futility. *Infrastructural reading*, as a methodology, has enabled a specifically resistant kind of reading practice against the four thematically oppressive infrastructural and ideological formations that this book has explored. Whilst Flora Annie Steel could not relinquish her faith in the notion of imperialism as a benevolent force, her short fiction raises striking concerns about the socioeconomic effects of infrastructural development in India and exposes the hypocrisies of humanitarian ideology. If Rider Haggard propagated a segregationist ideology that would be violently realised in South Africa throughout the twentieth century, Olive Schreiner and William Plomer developed formal and textual ways of undercutting and subverting it, interrogating colonial categories of racial definition in the process. John Buchan's preoccupation with the frontier may have contributed to the formation of a range of damagingly racist tropes and stereotypes, but a closer look at his literary geographies reveal how they in fact conceive alternative, if not subversive ways of imagining the world-system's patchwork of core and peripheral zones. Lastly, though Edmund Candler and Edward Thompson sought to delegitimise the nationalist movements that threatened imperial rule and intervened in capitalism's accumulative processes, an *infrastructural reading* of their literature reveals that their efforts to isolate and contain this resistance were always doomed to fail.

Uneven infrastructural development today is most markedly seen, as Andy Merrifield has recently shown, in the world's urban spaces, where 'the progressive production of core and periphery, of centres of power and wealth as well as spaces of dispossession and marginalisation' continues unabated (2014: 10). This development manifests as 'skyscrapers as well as unpaved streets, highways as well as back roads, by-waters and marginal zones that feel the wrath of the world market' (5). Furthermore, Keller Easterling has argued that, in the twenty-first century, '[f]ar from hidden, infrastructure is now the overt point of contact and access between us all – the rules governing the space of everyday life' (2014: 11). The skylines of cities from Shenzhen and Dubai to London and Johannesburg reveal that infrastructure is no longer 'the urban substructure, but the urban structure itself' (12). But *infrastructural reading* still maintains that these infrastructural developments are intimately linked to forms of *resistance* which arise in response to, and make use of, these increasingly complex spatialities. As Merrifield continues, twenty-first-century urbanity also allows a resistance movement to 'become aware of itself, aware that other affinities exist in the world [...] in a social network connected by a certain tissuing, by a spider's webbing, by a planetary webbing' (2014: 81). *Infrastructural reading's* strategic analysis is therefore a crucial tool in the analysis of 'contemporary forms of power':

> [These] may appear to take on the shape of a multiplicity, a diffuse field of forces simultaneously aggressive and benign. It is a form of power that not only charges forward; it surrounds, immerses and embeds. Political activists must constantly invent new forms of struggle that are recognisant of this paradigm of power, but which also evade and subvert its embrace, attempt to rewire its webs in order to escape its calculation. (Weizman, 2011: 23–24)

Mindful of this 'diffuse field', this book concludes with a call for more *infrastructural readings*: the methodology needs to be redeployed in a range of different geo-historical and cultural contexts, from the period of formal decolonisation to the moment of 'the colonial present'. Whilst this book has revisited 'the colonial past in order [...] to retrieve its shapes, like the chalk outlines at a crime scene', it follows Derek Gregory by remaining conscious of 'the continuing impositions and exactions of colonialism in order to subvert them: to examine them, disavow them, and dispel them' (2004: 9). *Infrastructural reading* allows the literary critic to read, resistantly, a range of cultural productions that are both complicit with, and also subversive of, old and new modes of colonisation, oppression, dispossession and exploitation, a project that is of ever increasing urgency in the contemporary world.

Bibliography

Primary Texts

Buchan, John. 1903. *The African Colony, Studies in the Reconstruction*. London: William Blackwood and Sons.
—— 1910. *Prester John*. London: Thomas Nelson & Sons.
—— 1912. *Prester John*. London: Thomas Nelson & Sons.
—— 1918. *Prester John*. London: Thomas Nelson & Sons.
—— 1920. *Prester John*. London: Thomas Nelson & Sons.
—— 1922. *A Book of Escapes and Hurried Journeys*. London: Thomas Nelson & Sons, Ltd.
—— 1940a. *Memory Hold-The-Door*. London: Hodder and Stoughton, Ltd.
—— 1940b. *Comments and Characters*. London: Thomas Nelson & Sons, Ltd.
—— 2008. *Prester John*. Cornwall: House of Stratus.
—— 2010. *The Complete Richard Hannay Stories*. London: Wordsworth Editions, Ltd.
Candler, Edmund. 1900. *A Vagabond in Asia, with a map of the Author's Route, and Several Illustrations from Original Photographs*. London: Greening & Co., Ltd.
—— 1912. *The Mantle of the East*. London, Edinburgh, Dublin and New York: Thomas Nelson & Sons.
—— 1919. *The Long Road to Baghdad, with 19 Maps and Plans and 16 Half-tone Plates, In Two Volumes: Volume 1*. London, New York, Toronto and Melbourne: Cassell and Company, Ltd.
—— 1924. *Youth and the East, An Unconventional Biography*. Edinburgh and London: William Blackwood and Sons.
—— 1993. *Abdication*. New York: Turtle Point Press.
—— 2005. *Siri Ram – Revolutionist, A Transcript from Life 1907–1910*. In Saros Cowasjee, ed., *A Raj Collection*, pp. 393–555. New Delhi: Oxford University Press.
Conrad, Joseph. 1926. *Last Essays*, ed. Richard Curle. London: J. M. Dent & Sons.
—— 2006. *Heart of Darkness*. London: W. W. Norton & Company.
Forster, E. M. 1963. *The Hill of Devi*. London: Penguin Books.
—— 2005. *A Passage to India*. London: Penguin Classics.
Haggard, H. Rider. 1926. *The Days of My Life, An Autobiography, Volume I*. London: Longmans, Green and Co., Ltd.

——2002. *King Solomon's Mines.* Lancashire: Broadview Literary Press.

——2008. *King Solomon's Mines.* Oxford: Oxford University Press.

——2008. *She.* Oxford: Oxford University Press.

Kipling, Rudyard. 1913. *From Sea to Sea: Letters of Travel.* New York: Doubleday, Page & Company.

——1990. *The Day's Work.* London: Penguin Books.

——2002. *Kim.* London: W. W. Norton & Company.

——2006. *The Complete Verse.* London: Kyle Cathie, Ltd.

——2010. *Kipling Abroad: Traffics and Discoveries from Burma to Brazil,* ed. Andrew Lycett. London: I. B. Tauris.

Plomer, William. 1965. *Turbott Wolfe.* Toronto: Clarke, Irwin & Co., Ltd.

——1975. *The Autobiography of William Plomer.* London: Jonathan Cape, Ltd.

—— 1984a. *Selected Stories,* ed. Stephen Gray. Johannesburg: AfricaSouth Paperbacks.

——1984b. *Cecil Rhodes.* Johannesburg: AfricaSouth Paperbacks.

Schreiner, Olive. 1899. *The South African Question.* Chicago: Charles H. Sergel Company.

——1928. *Undine.* London: Harper & Brothers.

——1978. *Woman and Labour.* London: Virago Press, Ltd.

——1982. *From Man to Man.* London: Virago Press, Ltd.

——2003. *The Story of an African Farm.* Canada: Broadview Press, Ltd.

——2009. *Trooper Peter Halket of Mashonaland.* Middlesex: The Echo Library.

Schreiner, Olive, and Cronwright-Schreiner, C. S. 1896. *The Political Situation.* London: T. Fisher Unwin.

Steel, Flora Annie. 1930. *The Garden of Fidelity, Being the Autobiography of Flora Annie Steel, 1847–1929.* London: Macmillan and Co.

——1971. *Indian Scene: Collected Short Stories of Flora Annie Steel.* New York: Books for Libraries Press.

—— 2005. *On the Face of the Waters.* In Saros Cowasjee, ed., *A Raj Collection,* pp. 1–391. New Delhi: Oxford University Press.

Steel, Flora Annie, and Gardener, Grace. 2010. *The Complete Indian Housekeeper and Cook.* Oxford: Oxford University Press.

Thompson, Edward. 1930a. *The Other Side of the Medal.* London: Leonard & Virginia Woolf at The Hogarth Press.

——1930b. *The Reconstruction of India.* London: Faber & Faber, Ltd.

——1931. *A Farewell to India.* New York: E. P. Dutton & Co., Inc.

——1940. *An India Day.* London: Penguin Books, Ltd.

Woolf, Leonard. 2008. *The Village in the Jungle.* London: Eland Publishing Limited.

Secondary Texts

Abrahams, Peter. 1963. *Mine Boy*. Reading: Heineman Educational Publishers.

Afigbo, A. E., Ayandele, E. A., Gavin, R. J., Omer-Cooper, J. D., and Palmer, R. 1986a. *The Making of Modern Africa, Volume 1, The Nineteenth Century*. New York: Longman Group, Ltd.

—— 1986b. *The Making of Modern Africa, Volume 2, The Twentieth Century*. New York: Longman Group Ltd.

Ahmad, Aijaz. 1987. 'Jameson's Rhetoric of Otherness and the "National Allegory"'. *Social Text* No. 17, 3–25.

—— 2008. *In Theory: Nations, Classes, Literatures*. London and New York: Verso.

Alexander, Peter F. 1989. *William Plomer: A Biography*. Oxford: Oxford University Press.

Al-Rawi, Ahmed. 2009. 'Buchan the Orientalist: Greenmantle and Western Views of the East'. *Journal of Colonialism and Colonial History* Vol. 10, No. 2, n. pag.

Amin, Samir. 1976. *Unequal Development: An Essay on the Social Formations of Peripheral Capitalism*. Sussex: The Harvester Press, Ltd.

—— 1977. *Imperialism and Unequal Development*. Sussex: The Harvester Press, Ltd.

Amoore, Louise. 2005. *The Global Resistance Reader*. London and New York: Routledge.

Anderson, Benedict. 1998. *The Spectre of Comparisons: Nationalism, Southeast Asia, and the World*. London: Verso.

—— 2006. *Imagined Communities: Reflections on the Origin and Spread of Nationalism*. London: Verso.

Anderson, Kevin B. 2010. *Marx at the Margins: On Nationalism, Ethnicity, and Non-Western Societies*. Chicago and London: University of Chicago Press.

Anderson, Perry. 2013. *The Indian Ideology*. London and New York: Verso.

Anzaldúa, Gloria. 1987. *Borderlands: La Frontera*. San Francisco: Aunt Lute Books.

Appadurai, Arjun. 2015. 'Foreword'. In Colin McFarlane and Stephen Graham, eds, *Infrastructural Lives: Urban Infrastructure in Context*, pp. xii-xiii. London and New York: Routledge.

Archard, David. 1990. 'Paternalism Defined'. *Analysis* Vol. 50, No.1, 36–42.

Arendt, Hannah. 2004. *The Origins of Totalitarianism*. New York: Schoken Books.

Arnold, David. 1984. 'Gramsci and Peasant Subalternity in India'. *The Journal of Peasant Studies* Vol. 11, No. 4, 155–177.

—— 2000. *Science, Technology and Medicine in Colonial India*. Cambridge: Cambridge University Press.

Arrighi, Giovanni, Hopkins, Terence K., and Wallerstein, Immanuel. 2011. *Antisystemic Movements*. London and New York: Verso.

Attwell, David, and Attridge, Derek, eds. 2012. *The Cambridge History of South African Literature*. Cambridge: Cambridge University Press.

'baas, n.' *OED Online*. Oxford University Press. December 2014.

Baden-Powell, Robert. 2005. *Scouting for Boys: A Handbook for Instruction in Good Citizenship*, ed. Elleke Boehmer. Oxford: Oxford University Press.

Bal, Mieke. 1997. *Narratology: Introduction to the Theory of Narrative*. London: University of Toronto Press, Inc.

Barends, Heidi. 2015. 'Olive Schreiner's *The Story of an African Farm*: Lyndall as Transnational and Transracial Feminist'. *English Academy Review* Vol. 32, No. 2, 101–114.

Barnett, Michael. 2013. *Empire of Humanity: A History of Humanitarianism*. New York: Cornell University Press.

Barnett, Michael, and Weiss, Thomas G., eds. 2008. *Humanitarianism in Question: Politics, Power, Ethics*. Ithaca, NY and London: Cornell University Press.

Bartholomew, John George. 1909. *Imperial Gazetter of India*. Oxford: Oxford University Press.

Bartolovich, Crystal, and Lazarus, Neil, eds. 2004. *Marxism, Modernity, and Postcolonial Studies*. Cambridge: Cambridge University Press.

Beall, Jo, Crankshaw, Owen, and Parnell, Susan. 2002. *Uniting a Divided City: Governance and Social Exclusion in Johannesburg*. London: Earthscan Publications.

Beavon, Keith. 2004. *Johannesburg, The Making and Shaping of the City*. Pretoria: University of South Africa Press.

Bennett, Tony. 1982. 'Introduction'. In *Popular Culture: Past and Present*, pp. 15–19. London: The Open University Press.

——— 2003. *Formalism and Marxism*. London: Routledge.

Bennett, Tony, Martin, Graham, and Waites, Bernard, eds. 1982. *Popular Culture: Past and Present*. London: The Open University Press.

Bevan, Edwyn. 1913. *Indian Nationalism, An Independent Estimate*. London: Macmillan and Co.

Bhatia, Nandi. 1999. 'Staging the 1857 Mutiny as "The Great Rebellion": Colonial History and Post-Colonial Interventions in Utpal Dutt's *Mahavidroh*'. *Theatre Journal* Vol. 51, 167–184.

Bivona, Daniel. 1998. *British Imperial Literature, 1870–1940: Writing and the Administration of Empire*. Cambridge: Cambridge University Press.

Blanchard, Robert G. 1991. *The First Editions of John Buchan: A Collector's Bibliography*. Connecticut: Archon Books.

Bloom, Harold, ed. 1987. *Modern Critical Views: E. M. Forster*. New York: Chelsea House Publishers.

Blunt, Alison, and McEwan, Cheryl, eds. 2002. *Postcolonial Geographies*. London and New York: Continuum.

Boehmer, Elleke. 1998a. *Empire, the National and the Postcolonial, 1890–1920: Resistance in Interaction*. Oxford: Oxford University Press.

——, ed. 1998b. *Empire Writing: An Anthology of Colonial Literature, 1870–1918*. Oxford: Oxford University Press.

——2005. *Colonial & Postcolonial Literature*. Oxford: Oxford University Press, 2nd edn.

——2011. 'The Worlding of the Jingo Poem'. *The Yearbook of English Studies* Vol. 41, No. 2, 41–57.

Boehmer, Elleke, Chrisman, Laura, and Parker, Kenneth, eds. 1994. *Altered State? Writing and South Africa*. Sydney: Dangaroo Press.

Boehmer, Elleke, and Morton, Stephen, eds. 2010. *Terror and the Postcolonial*. West Sussex: Blackwell Publishing, Ltd.

Bond, Patrick. 2000. *Elite Transition: From Apartheid to Neoliberalism in South Africa*. London: Pluto Press.

Booth, Charles. 1902. *Life and Labour of the People in London*. London: Macmillan and Co., Ltd.

Booth, Howard J., and Rigby, Nigel, eds. 2000. *Modernism and Empire*. Manchester: Manchester University Press.

——2000. 'Introduction'. In *Modernism and Empire*, pp. 1–12. Manchester: Manchester University Press.

Booth, William. 1890. *In Darkest England and the Way Out*. London: The Carlyle Press.

Bosch, Tanja. 2016. 'Twitter Activism and Youth in South Africa: the Case of #RhodesMustFall'. *Information, Communication & Society*, 1–12.

Bose, Nemai Sadhan. 1981. *Racism, Struggle for Equality and Indian Nationalism*. Calcutta: Prabartak Printing and Halftone, Ltd.

Brantlinger, Patrick. 1988. *Rule of Darkness: British Literature and Imperialism, 1830–1914*. New York: Cornell University Press.

Bremner, Lindsey. 2010. *Writing the City into Being: Essays On Johannesburg, 1998–2008*. Johannesburg: Fourthwall Books.

Brenner, Neil. 2011. 'The Space of the World: Beyond State-Centrism?' In David Palumbo-Liu, Bruce Robbins and Nirvana Tanoukhi, eds. *Immanuel Wallerstein and the Problem of the World: System, Scale, Culture*, pp. 101–137. Durham and London: Duke University Press.

Breuilly, John. 2012. 'Approaches to Nationalism'. In Gopal Balakrishnan, ed., *Mapping the Nation*, pp. 146–174. London: Verso.

Brewer, Anthony. 2001. *Marxist Theories of Imperialism: A Critical Survey*. London and New York: Routledge.

Bubb, Alexander. 2013. 'The Provincial Cosmopolitan: Kipling, India and Globalisation'. *Journal of Postcolonial Writing* Vol. 49, No. 4, 391–404.

Budgen, Sebastien, Kouvelakis, Stathis, and Žižek, Slavoj. 2007. *Lenin Reloaded: Toward a Politics of Truth*. Durham and London: Duke University Press.

Burdett, Carolyn. 2001. *Olive Schreiner and the Progress of Feminism: Evolution, Gender, Empire*. New York: Palgrave.

Butlin, Robin A. 2009. *Geographies of Empire: European Empires and Colonies c.1880–1960*. Cambridge: Cambridge University Press.

Calhoun, Craig, Collins, Randall, Derluguian, Georgi, Mann, Michael, and Wallerstein, Immanuel. 2013. *Does Capitalism Have a Future?* New York: Oxford University Press.

—— 2013. 'Getting Real'. In Craig Calhoun, Randall Collins, Georgi Derluguian, Michael Mann and Immanuel Wallerstein, *Does Capitalism Have a Future?*, pp. 163–192. New York: Oxford University Press.

Callinicos, Alex. 2007. 'Leninism in the Twenty-First Century? Lenin, Weber, and the Politics of Responsibility'. In Sebastien Budgen, Stathis Kouvelakis and Slavoj Žižek, eds, *Lenin Reloaded: Toward a Politics of Truth*, pp. 18–41. Durham and London: Duke University Press.

Carruthers, Jane. 2003. 'Friedrich Jeppe: Mapping the Transvaal c.1855–1899'. *Journal of Southern African Studies* Vol. 29, No. 4, 955–976.

Carter, Paul. 1987. *The Road to Botany Bay: An Essay in Spatial History*. London: Faber and Faber, Ltd.

—— 2002. *Repressed Spaces: The Poetics of Agoraphobia*. London: Reaktion Books, Ltd.

—— 2009. *Dark Writing: Geography, Performance, Design*. Honolulu: University of Hawai'i Press.

Caygill, Howard. 2013. *On Resistance: A Philosophy of Defiance*. London: Bloomsbury.

Chakrabarty, Dipesh. 2000. *Rethinking Working-Class History: Bengal 1890–1940*. Princeton, NJ: Princeton University Press.

—— 2001. 'Clothing the political man: a reading of the use of khadi/white in Indian public life'. *Postcolonial Studies* Vol. 4, No. 1, 27–38.

—— 2008. *Provincializing Europe*. Princeton, NJ: Princeton University Press.

Chandavarkar, Rajnarayan. 1997. '"The Making of the Working Class": E. P. Thompson and Indian History'. *History Workshop Journal* No. 42, 177–196.

Chandra, Bipan. 2006. 'Economic Nationalism and the Railway Debate, circa 1880–1905'. In Roopa Srinivasan, Tiwari Manish and Silas Sandeep, eds, *Our Indian Railway: Themes in India's Railway History*, pp. 77–119. New Delhi: Foundation Books Pvt., Ltd.

Chang, Mike. 1998. *Cultural Geography*. London: Routledge.

Chatterjee, Partha. 1986. 'The Colonial State and Peasant Resistance in Bengal, 1920–1947'. *Past and Present* No. 110, 169–204.

——1999. 'Anderson's Utopia'. *Diacritics*, Vol. 29, No. 4, *Grounds of Comparison: Around the Work of Benedict Anderson*, 128–134.

——2011. *The Partha Chatterjee Omnibus*. New Delhi: Oxford University Press, 2011.

Chaudhuri, K. N., and Dewey, Clive, eds. 1979. *Economy and Society: Essays in Indian Economic and Social History*. Delhi: Oxford University Press.

Childs, Peter. 2007. *Modernism and the Post-Colonial: Literature and Empire, 1885–1930*. London: Continuum International Publishing Group.

Chrisman, Laura. 2000. *Rereading the Imperial Romance: British Imperialism and South African Resistance in Haggard, Schreiner, and Plaatje*. Oxford: Clarendon Press.

——2003. *Postcolonial Contraventions: Cultural Readings of Race, Imperialism and Transnationalism*. Manchester: Manchester University Press.

——2012. 'The Imperial Romance'. In David Attwell and Derek Attridge, eds, *The Cambridge History of South African Literature*, pp. 226–245. Cambridge: Cambridge University Press.

Clark, Nancy L., and Worger, William H. 2011. *South Africa: The Rise and Fall of Apartheid*. Edinburgh: Pearson Education, Ltd.

Clingman, Stephen. 2009. *The Grammar of Identity: Transnational Fiction and the Nature of the Boundary*. Oxford: Oxford University Press.

Cockburn, Patrick. 2007. *The Occupation: War and Resistance in Iraq*. London and New York: Verso.

Coetzee, J. M. 1980. *White Writing: On the Culture of Letters in South Africa*. London: York University Press.

Cohn, Bernard. 2009. *The Bernard Cohn Omnibus*. New Delhi: Oxford University Press.

Cooper, Frederick. 2005. *Colonialism in Question: Theory, Knowledge, History*. London: University of California Press, Ltd.

Couzens, T. J. 1981. '"The Old Africa of a Boy's Dream" – Towards Interpreting Buchan's Prester John'. *English Studies in Africa* Vol. 12, No. 1, 1–26.

Cronin, Richard Paul. 1977. *British Policy and Administration in Bengal, 1905–1912: Partition and the New Province of Eastern Bengal and Assam*. Calcutta: Firma KLM Private, Ltd.

Curzon, Lord George. 1907. *The Romanes Lectures 1907: Frontiers*. Oxford: Clarendon Press.

——1987. Letter from Lord Curzon to Lord Hamilton, Secretary of State for India, 17 February, 1904. In Vinod Kumar Saxena, ed., *The Partition of Bengal (1905–1911): Select Documents*, p. 88. Delhi: Kanishka Publishing House.

Dantwala, M. L. 1973. *Poverty in India: Then and Now, 1870–1970*. Delhi: Macmillan India.

David, Saul. 2002. *The Indian Mutiny, 1857*. London: Penguin Books, Ltd.

Davidis, Maria. 1999–2000. 'Forster's Imperial Romance: Chivalry, Motherhood, and Questing in *A Passage to India*'. *Journal of Modern Literature* Vol. 23, No. 2, 259–276.

Davies, Dominic. 2015. 'Critiquing Global Capital and Colonial (In)Justice: Structural Violence in Leonard Woolf's *The Village in the Jungle* (1913) and *Economic Imperialism* (1920)'. *The Journal of Commonwealth Literature* Vol. 50, No. 1, 45–58.

Davis, Clarence B., and Wilburn, Kenneth E., eds. 1991. *Railway Imperialism*. London: Greenwood Press.

Davis, Mike. 2007. *In Praise of Barbarians: Essays Against Empire*. Chicago: Haymarket Books.

——2010. *Late Victorian Holocausts: El Niño Famines and the Making of the Third World*. London: Verso.

Deckard, Sherae. 2016. 'Inherit the World: World-Literature, Rising Asia and the World-Ecology'. In Anna Bernard, Ziad Elmarsafy and Stuard Murray, eds, *What Postcolonial Theory Doesn't Say*, pp. 239–255. London and New York: Routledge.

Devarenne, Nicole. 2009. 'Nationalism and the Farm Novel in South Africa, 1883–2004'. *Journal of Southern African Studies* Vol. 35, No. 3, 627–642.

Devji, Faisal. 2013. *Muslim Zion: Pakistan as a Political Idea*. London: Harvard University Press.

Dewey, Clive. 1988. *Arrested Development in India: The Historical Dimension*. Riverdale: The Riverdale Company.

Dewey, Clive, and Chaudhuri, K. N., eds. 1979. *Economy and Society: Essays in Indian Economic and Social History*. Delhi: Oxford University Press.

Dirlik, Arif. 1994. 'The Postcolonial Aura: Third World Criticism in the Age of Global Capitalism'. *Critical Inquiry* Vol. 20, 328–356.

——1995. 'Confucius in the Borderlands: Global Capitalism and the Reinvention of Confuscianism'. *Boundary 2* Vol. 22, No. 3, 229–273.

——2004. 'Spectres of the Third World: global modernity and the end of the three worlds'. *Third World Quarterly* Vol. 25, No. 1, 131–148.

Duffield, Mark. 2001. 'Governing the Borderlands: Decoding the Power of Aid'. *Disasters* Vol. 24, No. 4, 308–320.

Dutt, Romesh Chunder. 1900. *Open Letters to Lord Curzon on Famines and Land Assessment in India*. London: Kegan Paul, Trench, Trübner & Co., Ltd.

——1950. *The Economic History of India in the Victorian Age*. London: Routledge & Kegan Paul, Ltd.

Dutt, Utpal. 1986. *The Great Rebellion*. Calcutta: Seagull Books.

Eagleton, Terry. 2002. *Marxism and Literary Criticism*. London: Routledge.

Easterling, Keller. 2014. *Extrastatecraft: The Power of Infrastructure Space*. London and New York: Verso.

Esty, Jed. 2007. '*The Story of an African Farm* and the Ghost of Goethe'. *Victorian Studies* Vol. 49, No. 3, 407–430.

——2012. *Unseasonable Youth: Modernism, Colonialism, and the Fiction of Development*. Oxford: Oxford University Press.

Etherington, Norman A. 1978. 'Rider Haggard, Imperialism, and the Layered Personality'. *Victorian Studies* Vol. 22, No. 1, 71–87.

Fanon, Frantz. 2001. *The Wretched of the Earth*, trans. Constance Farrington. London: Penguin Classics.

Ferro, Marc. 1997. *Colonization: A Global History*. London: Routledge.

Foster, Jeremy. 1998. 'John Buchan's "Hesperides": Landscape Rhetoric and the Aesthetics of Bodily Experience on the South African Highveld, 1901–1903'. *Cultural Geographies* Vol. 5, 323–347.

Foucault, Michel. 1991. *The Foucault Reader: An Introduction to Foucault's Thought*, ed. Paul Rabinow. London: Penguin Books.

——2001a. *Dits et Écrits I, 1954–1975*. Paris: Éditions Gallimard.

——2001b. *Dits et Écrits II, 1976–1988*. Paris: Éditions Gallimard.

Fox, Richard G. 1997. 'Passage From India'. In Richard G. Fox and Orins Starn, eds, *Between Resistance and Revolution: Cultural Politics and Social Protest*, pp. 65–82. London: Rutgers University Press.

Fox, Richard G., and Starn, Orins, eds. 1997. *Between Resistance and Revolution: Cultural Politics and Social Protest*. London: Rutgers University Press.

Frischman, Brett M. 2012. *Infrastructure: The Social Value of Shared Resources*. Oxford: Oxford University Press.

Gandhi, M. K. 2007. *An Autobiography, The Story of My Experiments With Truth*. London: Penguin Books.

——2008. *The Essential Writings*. Oxford: Oxford University Press.

Geddes, Patrick. 1947. *Patrick Geddes in India*, ed. Jacqueline Tyrwhitt. London: Lund Humphries.

Genette, Gérard. 1982. *Figures of Literary Discourse*, trans. Alan Sheridan. Oxford: Basil Blackwell Publisher.

Gilroy, Paul. 2004a. *After Empire: Melancholia or Convivial Culture?* Oxfordshire: Routledge.

——2004b. *Between Camps: Nations, Cultures and the Allure of Race*. London and New York: Routledge.

Glover, William J. 2004. '"A Feeling of Absence from Old England": The Colonial Bungalow'. *Home Cultures* Vol. 1, No. 1, 61–82.

Goodwin, Gráinne. 2013. '"An Adamless Eden": Counterpublics and Women Writers' Sociability at the fin de siècle through the Experiences of Flora Annie Steel'. *Women's History Review* Vol. 22, No. 3, 440–459.

Gott, Richard. 2012. *Britain's Empire: Resistance, Repression and Revolt*. London: Verso.

Graham, Stephen, ed. 2010. *Disrupted Cities: When Infrastructure Fails*. London: Routledge.

——2011. *Cities Under Siege: The New Military Urbanism*. London and New York: Verso.

Graham, Stephen, and Marvin, Simon. 2001. *Splintering Urbanism: Networked Infrastructures, Technological Mobilities and the Urban Condition*. London: Routledge.

Gramsci, Antonio. 1988. *The Gramsci Reader: Selected Writings, 1916–1935*, ed. David Forgacs. London: Lawrence and Wishart.

Gray, Stephen. 1986. 'William Plomer's Stories: The South African Origins of New Literature Modes'. *The Journal of Commonwealth Literature* Vol. 21, No. 53, 53–61.

Gregory, Derek. 1995. 'Imaginative Geographies'. *Progressive Human Geography* Vol. 19, No. 4, 447–485.

——2004. *The Colonial Present: Afghanistan, Palestine, Iraq*. Oxford: Blackwell Publishing, Ltd.

Griffiths, Ieuan Ll. 1995. *The African Inheritance*. London: Routledge.

Grob-Fitzgibbon, Benjamin. 2011. *Imperial Endgame: Britain's Dirty Wars and the End of Empire*. Hampshire: Palgrave Macmillan.

Guha, Ranajit, ed. 1998. *A Subaltern Studies Reader, 1986–1995*. Delhi: Oxford University Press.

Gupta, Uma Das, ed. 2003. *A Difficult Friendship: Letters of Edward Thompson and Rabindranath Tagore, 1913–1940*. Oxford: Oxford University Press.

Hall, Catherine. 2016. 'The racist ideas of slave owners are still with us today'. *The Guardian* <https://www.theguardian.com/commentisfree/2016/sep/26/racist-ideas-slavery-slave-owners-hate-crime-brexit-vote> accessed 28 September 2016.

Hall, Stuart. 1992. 'Cultural Studies and its Theoretical Legacies'. In Lawrence Grossberg, Cary Nelson and Paula A. Treichler, eds, *Cultural Studies*, pp. 277–294. New York and London: Routledge.

Hall-Matthews, David. 2005. *Peasants, Famine and the State in Colonial Western India*. Hampshire: Palgrave Macmillan.

Hanes, W. Travis III. 1991. 'Railway Politics and Imperialism in Central Africa, 1889–1953'. In Clarence B. Davis and Kenneth E. Wilburn, eds, *Railway Imperialism*, pp. 41–69. London: Greenwood Press.

Hardiman, David. 1992. *Peasant Resistance in India, 1858–1914*. Delhi: Oxford University Press.

Hardt, Michael, and Negri, Antonio. 2001. *Empire*. London: Harvard University Press.

Harlow, Barbara. 1987. *Resistance Literature*. London: Methuen, Inc.

Harnetty, Peter. 1972. *Imperialism and Free Trade: Lancashire and India in the Mid-nineteenth Century*. Manchester: Manchester University Press.

Harvey, David. 1995. *The Condition of Postmodernity*. Oxford: Blackwell Publishers.

—— 1999. *The Limits of Capital*. London: Verso.

—— 2005. *The New Imperialism*. Oxford: Oxford University Press.

—— 2006. *Spaces of Global Capitalism: Towards a Theory of Uneven Geographical Development*. London and New York: Verso.

—— 2009. *Cosmopolitanism and the Geographies of Freedom*. New York: Columbia University Press.

—— 2012. *Rebel Cities: From the Right to the City to the Urban Revolution*. London: Verso.

—— 2014. *Seventeen Contradictions and the End of Capitalism*. London: Profile Books, Ltd.

Hassler-Forest, Dan. 2012. *Capitalist Superheroes: Cape Crusaders in the Neoliberal Age*. Winchester and Washington, DC: Zero Books.

Hawkes, David. 1996. *The New Critical Idiom: Ideology*. London: Routledge.

Hawkins, Hunt. 1982. 'The Issue of Racism in *Heart of Darkness*'. *Conradian* Vol. 14, No. 3, 163–171.

Headrick, Daniel R. 1981. *The Tools of Empire: Technology and European Imperialism in the Nineteenth Century*. Oxford: Oxford University Press.

—— 1988. *Tentacles of Progress: Technology Transfer in the Age of Imperialism, 1850–1940*. Oxford: Oxford University Press.

—— 2009. *Technology: A World History*. Oxford: Oxford University Press.

Heehs, Peter. 2010. 'Revolutionary Terrorism in British Bengal'. In Elleke Boehmer and Stephen Morton, eds, *Terror and the Postcolonial*, pp. 153–176. West Sussex: Blackwell Publishing, Ltd.

Henshaw, Peter. 2003. 'John Buchan from the "Borders" to the "Berg": Nature, Empire and White South African Identity, 1901–1910'. *African Studies* Vol. 62, No. 1, 3–32.

Hobsbawm, Eric. 1959. *Primitive Rebellion*. Manchester: Manchester University Press.

—— 2007. *The Age of Empire, 1875–1914*. London: Abacus.

Hobson, J. A. 1900. *The War in South Africa: Its Causes and Effects*. London: James Nisbet and Co., Ltd.

—— 1901. *The Psychology of Jingoism*. London: Grant Richards.

—— 1988. *Imperialism: A Study*. London: Unwin Hyman, Ltd.

Hopkins, Terence K., and Wallerstein, Immanuel. 1982. *World-Systems Analysis: Theory and Methodology*. London: Sage Publications, Ltd.

Huggan, Graham. 1989. 'Decolonizing the Map: Post-Colonialism, Post-Structuralism and the Cartographic Connection'. *Ariel, A Review of International English Literature* Vol. 20 No. 4, 115–131.

——1994. *Territorial Disputes: Maps and Mapping Strategies in Contemporary Canadian and Australian Fiction*. Toronto: University of Toronto Press.

Hutchins, Francis G. 1967. *The Illusion of British Permanence: British Imperialism in India*. Princeton, NJ: Princeton University Press.

infrastructure, n. *OED*, 2nd edn, 1989 <http://ezproxy.ouls.ox.ac.uk:2277/view/Entry/95624> accessed 8 June 2012.

infrastructure. 2007. In Chris Park, ed., *A Dictionary of Environment and Conservation*. Oxford: Oxford University Press <http://www.oxfordreference.com/views/ENTRY.html?subview=Main&entry=t244.e4073> accessed 8 June 2012.

infrastructure. 2009a. In Susan Mayhew, ed., *A Dictionary of Geography*. Oxford: Oxford University Press <http://www.oxfordreference.com/views/ENTRY.html?subview=Main&entry=t15.e1667> accessed 8 June 2012.

infrastructure. 2009b. In John Black, Nigar Hashimzade and Gareth Myles, eds, *A Dictionary of Economics*. Oxford: Oxford University Press <http://www.oxfordreference.com/views/ENTRY.html?subview=Main&entry=t19.e1603> accessed 8 June 2012.

infrastructure, n. *ODO*, 2010. In Angus Stevenson, ed., *Oxford Dictionary of English*. Oxford: Oxford University Press <http://www.oxfordreference.com/views/ENTRY.html?subview=Main&entry=t140.e0410740> accessed 8 June 2012.

Jameson, Fredric. 1975. 'Beyond the Cave: Demystifying the Ideology of Modernism'. *The Bulletin of the Midwest Modern Language Association* Vol. 8, No. 1, 1–20.

——1986. 'Third-World Literature in the Era of Multinational Capitalism'. *Social Text* No. 15, 65–88.

——1990. 'Modernism and Imperialism'. In Terry Eagleton, Fredric Jameson and Edward Said, *Nationalism, Colonialism and Literature*, pp. 43–66. Minneapolis: University of Minnesota Press.

——1991. *Postmodernism, or, the Cultural Logic of Late Capitalism*. Durham: Duke University Press.

——2002. *The Political Unconscious, Narrative as a Socially Symbolic Act*. London: Routledge.

——2014. *Representing Capital: A Commentary on Volume One*. London: Verso.

Jani, Pranav. 2004. 'Karl Marx, Eurocentrism, and the 1857 Revolt in British India'. In Crystal Bartolovich and Neil Lazarus, eds, *Marxism, Modernity, and Postcolonial Studies*, pp. 81–97. Cambridge: Cambridge University Press.

Johnson, Alan. 1998. '"Sanitary Duties" and Registered Women: A Reading of *On the Face of the Waters*'. *Yale Journal of Criticism* Vol. 11, No. 2, 507–513.

——2011. *Out of Bounds: Anglo-Indian Literature and the Geography of Displacement*. Honolulu: University of Hawai'i Press.

Johnson, Robert. 2003. *British Imperialism*. New York: Palgrave Macmillan.

Jones, Susan. 2004. 'Into the Twentieth Century: Imperial Romance from Haggard to Buchan'. In Corinne Saunders, ed., *A Companion to Romance*, pp. 406–423. Oxford: Blackwell Publishing.

Karis, Thomas, and Carter, Gwendolen M., eds. 1972. *From Protest to Challenge: A Documentary History of African Politics in South Africa, 1882–1964, Volume 1: Protest and Hope, 1882–1934*. California: Hoover Institution Press.

Katz, Wendy R. 1987. *Rider Haggard and the Fiction of Empire: A Critical Study of British Imperial Fiction*. Cambridge: Cambridge University Press.

Kerr, Ian J. 1995. *Building the Railways of the Raj, 1850–1900*. Delhi: Oxford University Press.

——2003. 'Representation and Representations of the Railways of Colonial and Post-Colonial South Asia'. *Modern Asian Studies* Vol. 37, No. 2, 287–326.

Khalidi, Rashid. 2004. *Resurrecting Empire: Western Footprints and America's Perilous Path in the Middle East*. London: I. B. Tauris & Co, Ltd.

Khilnani, Sunil. 1997. *The Idea of India*. London: Hamish Hamilton, Ltd.

King, Anthony D. 1976. *Colonial Urban Development: Culture, Social Power and Environment*. London: Routledge & Kegan Paul, Ltd.

——1991. *Urbanism, Colonialism, and the World-Economy: Cultural and Spatial Foundations of the World Urban System*. London: Routledge.

——, ed. 2000. *Culture, Globalization and the World-System: Contemporary Conditions for the Representation of Identity*. Minneapolis: University of Minnesota Press.

Klein, Ira. 2000. 'Materialism, Mutiny and Modernization in British India'. *Modern Asian Studies* Vol. 34, No. 3, 545–580.

Krebs, Paula M. 1997. 'Olive Schreiner's Racialization of South Africa'. *Victorian Studies* Vol. 40, No. 3, 427–444.

Kros, Cynthia. 2015. 'Rhodes Must Fall: Archives and Counter-Archives'. *Critical Arts* Vol. 29, 150–165.

Kruger, Loren. 2013. *Imagining the Edgy City: Writing, Performing, and Building Johannesburg*. Oxford: Oxford University Press.

Kruse, Juanita. 1989. *John Buchan (1875–1940) and the Idea of Empire*. Lampeter: The Edwin Mellen Press, Ltd.

Kumar, Deepa. 2012. *Islamophobia and the Politics of Empire*. Chicago: Haymarket Books.

Labica, Georges. 2007. 'From Imperialism to Globalisation'. In Sebastien Budgen, Stathis Kouvelakis and Slavoj Žižek, *Lenin Reloaded: Toward a Politics of Truth*, pp. 222–238. Durham and London: Duke University Press.

Lago, Mary. 2001. *'India's Prisoner': A Biography of Edward John Thompson, 1886–1946*. Columbia and London: University of Missouri Press.

Larkin, Brian. 2013. 'The Politics and Poetics of Infrastructure'. *Annual Review of Anthropology* Vol. 42, 327–343.

Latham, A. J. H. 1978. *The International Economy and the Undeveloped World, 1865–1914*. London: Billing & Sons, Ltd.

Lazarus, Neil. 2011. *The Postcolonial Unconscious*. Cambridge: Cambridge University Press.

Ledger, Sally, and Luckhurst, Roger, eds. 2000. *The Fin de Siècle: A Reader in Cultural History, c.1880–1900*. Oxford: Oxford University Press.

Lefebvre, Henri. 1988. *The Production of Space*, trans. Donald Nicholson-Smith. Oxford: Blackwell Publishers, Ltd.

Legg, Stephen. 2007. *Spaces of Colonialism: Delhi's Urban Governmentalities*. Oxford: Blackwell Publishing.

Lemert, Charles, Rojas, Carlos Antionio Aguirre, and Wallerstein, Immanuel. 2016. *Uncertain Worlds: World-Systems Analysis in Changing Times*. London and New York: Routledge.

Lenin, V. I. 1934. *Imperialism, The Highest Stage of Capitalism*. London: Martin Lawrence, Ltd.

——1987. *Essential Works of Lenin: 'What Is to Be Done?' and Other Writings*, ed. Henry M. Christman. New York: Dover Publications.

Lester, Alan. 1998. *From Colonisation to Democracy: A New Historical Geography of South Africa*. London: I. B. Tauris.

Lester, Alan, Nel, Etienne, and Binns, Tony. 2000. *South Africa, Past, Present and Future: Gold at the End of the Rainbow?* Essex: Pearson Education Limited.

Lewis, Martin W., and Wigen, Kären. 1997. *The Myth of Continents: A Critique of Metageography*. London: University of California Press.

Lilly, William Samuel. 1902. *India and Its Problems*. London: Sands & Co.

Lloyd, David. 1993. *Anomalous States: Irish Writing and the Post-Colonial Moment*. Durham: Duke University Press.

Low, Gail Ching-Liang. 1996. *White Skins/Black Masks: Representation and Colonialism*. London: Routledge.

Lowry, Donald. 2016. 'The "Rhodes Must Fall" Campaign: Where Would the Destruction End?' *The Round Table* Vol. 105, No. 3, 329–331.

Luckett, Kathey. 2016. 'Curriculum Contestation in a Post-Colonial Context: A View from the South'. *Teaching in Higher Education* Vol. 21, No. 4, 415–428.

Luxemburg, Rosa. 1970. *Rosa Luxemburg Speaks*, ed. Mary-Alice Waters. London and New York: Pathfinder Press.

—— 2003. *The Accumulation of Capital*, trans. Agnes Schwarzschild. London and New York: Routledge.

Lyall, Sir Alfred. 1907. *The Rise and Expansion of the British Dominion in India*. London: John Murray.

McClintock, Anne. 1995. *Imperial Leather: Race, Gender and Sexuality in the Colonial Contest*. London: Routledge.

McCully, Bruce Tiebout. 1940. *English Education and the Origins of Indian Nationalism*. New York: Columbia University Press.

Macdonald, Kate, ed. 2009. *Reassessing John Buchan: Beyond the Thirty-Nine Steps*. London: Pickering and Chatto.

MacDonald, Robert H. 1994. *The Language of Empire: Myths and Metaphors of Popular Imperialism, 1880–1918*. Manchester: Manchester University Press.

McEwan, Cheryl. 2009. *Postcolonialism and Development*. London and New York: Routledge.

McFarlane, Colin, and Graham, Stephen, eds. 2015. *Infrastructural Lives: Urban Infrastructure in Context*. London and New York: Routledge.

Macey, David. 2012. *Frantz Fanon: A Biography*. London: Verso.

Macherey, Pierre. 1986. *A Theory of Literary Production*, trans. Geoffrey Wall. London: Routledge.

Mackenzie, Craig. 2012. 'The Metropolitan and the Local: Douglas Blackburn, Pauline Smith, William Plomer, Herman Charles Bosman'. In David Attwell and Derek Attridge, eds. *The Cambridge History of South African Literature*, pp. 360–379. Cambridge: Cambridge University Press.

Malleson, Colonel G. B. 1901. *The Indian Mutiny of 1857, with Portraits and Plans*. London: Seeley and Co. Limited.

Marks, Shula, and Rathbone, Richard, eds. 1982. *Industrialisation and Social Change in South Africa: African Class Formation, Culture, and Consciousness, 1870–1930*. London: Longman Group, Ltd.

Martel, Gordon. 2000. 'Decolonisation after Suez: Retreat or Rationalisation'. *Australian Journal of Politics and History* Vol. 46, No. 3, 403–417.

Marx, Karl. 1993. *Grundrisse, Foundations of the Critique of Political Economy*, trans. Martin Nicolaus. London: Penguin Books.

—— 1999. *Capital*, ed. David McLellan. Oxford: Oxford University Press.

—— 2006. *Karl Marx on India (1853–1862)*, ed. Iqbal Husain. New Delhi: Tulika Books.

Masselos, Jim. 2010. *Indian Nationalism: A History*. New Delhi: Sterling Publishers Private Limited.

Massey, Doreen. 1995. *Spatial Divisions of Labour: Social Structures and the Geography of Production*. New York: Routledge.

Masterman, C. F. G. 1906. *The Condition of England*, ed. J. T. Boulton. London: Methuen & Co. Ltd.

Mayer, Arno J. 2008. *Plowshares into Swords: From Zionism to Israel*. London and New York: Verso.

Mbembe, Achille. 2001. *On the Postcolony*. Berkeley: University of California Press.

—— 2008. 'Aesthetics of Superfluity'. In Sarah Nuttall and Achille Mbembe, eds, *Johannesburg: The Elusive Metropolis*, pp. 37–67. Durham and London: Duke University Press.

Meller, H. E. 1979. 'Urbanisation and the Introduction of Modern Town Planning Ideas in India, 1900–1925'. In Clive Dewey and K. N. Chaudhuri, eds, *Economy and Society: Essays in Indian Economic and Social History*, pp. 330–350. Delhi: Oxford University Press.

Meredith, Martin. 2006. *The State of Africa: A History of Fifty Years of Independence*. London: Simon and Schuster UK, Ltd.

—— 2008. *Diamonds, Gold and War: The Making of South Africa*. London: Pocket Books.

Merrifield, Andy. 2014. *The New Urban Question*. London: PlutoPress.

Metcalf, Barbara D., and Metcalf, Thomas R. 2002. *A Concise History of India*. Cambridge: Cambridge University Press.

Metcalf, Thomas R. 1995. *Ideologies of the Raj*. Cambridge: Cambridge University Press.

—— 2002. *An Imperial Vision: Indian Architecture and Britain's Raj*. New Delhi: Oxford University Press.

Mignolo, Walter D. 2011. *The Darker Side of Western Modernity: Global Futures, Decolonial Options*. Durham and London: Duke University Press.

—— 2012. *Local Histories/Global Designs: Coloniality, Subaltern Knowledges, and Border Thinking*. Princeton, NJ: Princeton University Press.

Miller, J. Hillis. 1995. *Topographies*. California: Stanford University Press.

Misra, B. B. 1990. *The Unification and Division of India*. Delhi: Oxford University Press.

Mitchell, Timothy. 1988. *Colonising Egypt*. London: Cambridge University Press.

—— 2002. *Rule of Experts: Egypt, Techno-Politics, Modernity*. Berkeley: University of California Press.

Mittelman, James H. 2000. *The Globalisation Syndrome: Transformation and Resistance*. Princeton, NJ: Princeton University Press.

Monsman, Gerald. 1991. *Olive Schreiner's Fiction: Landscape and Power*. New Jersey: Rutgers University Press.

—— 2006. *H. Rider Haggard on the Imperial Frontier: The Political and Literary Contexts of His African Romances*. Greensboro: University of North Carolina, ELT Press.

—— 2010. *Colonial Voices: The Anglo-African High Romance of Empire*. New Orleans, LA: University Press of the South.

Moore, Donald S. 1997. 'Remapping Resistance: "Ground for Struggle" and the Politics of Place'. In Steve Pile and Michael Keith, eds, *Geographies of Resistance*, pp. 87–106. London and New York: Routledge.

Moore, Jason W. 2015. *Capitalism in the Web of Life: Ecology and the Accumulation of Capital*. New York and London: Verso.

Moore-Gilbert, Bart. 2003. 'Olive Schreiner's *Story of an African Farm*: Reconciling Feminism and Anti-Imperialism?' *Women: A Cultural Review* Vol. 14, No. 1, 85–103.

Moretti, Franco. 1998. *Atlas of the European Novel, 1800–1900*. London and New York: Verso.

—— 2000. 'Conjectures on World Literature'. *New Left Review* Vol. 1, 54–68.

—— 2000. *The Way of the World: The Bildungsroman in European Culture*, trans. Albert Sbragia. London: Verso.

—— 2008. *Distant Reading*. London and New York: Verso.

—— 2013. *The Bourgeois: Between History and Literature*. London and New York: Verso.

Moroney, Sean. 1982. 'Mine Married Quarters: The Differential Stabilisation of the Witwatersrand Workforce 1900–1920'. In Shula Marks and Richard Rathbone, eds, *Industrialisation and Social Change in South Africa: African Class Formation, Culture, and Consciousness, 1870–1930*, pp. 259–269. London: Longman Group, Ltd.

Morton, Stephen. 2010. 'Terrorism, Literature, and Sedition in Colonial India'. In Elleke Boehmer and Stephen Morton, eds, *Terror and the Postcolonial*, pp. 202–225. West Sussex: Blackwell Publishing, Ltd.

Mukherjee, Upamanyu Pablo. 2013. *Natural Disasters and Victorian Empire: Famines, Fevers and the Literary Cultures of South Asia*. New York: Palgrave Macmillan.

Murphy, Patricia. 1998. 'Timely interruptions: Unsettling gender through temporality in *The Story of an African Farm*'. *Style* Vol. 32, No. 1, 80–102.

Murray, Cara. 2008. *Victorian Narrative Technologies in the Middle East*. London: Routledge.

Murray, John. 1904. *The Imperial Guide to India, Including Kashmir, Burma and Ceylon. With Illustrations, Maps and Plans*. London: Alabaster, Passmore and Sons.

Nabers, Deak. 2001. 'Spies Like Us: John Buchan and the Great War Spy Craze', *Journal of Colonialism and Colonial History* Vol. 2, No. 1, n. pag.

Nagai, Kaori, and Rooney, Caroline, eds. 2010. *Kipling and Beyond: Patriotism, Globalisation and Postcolonialism*. Basingstoke: Palgrave Macmillan.

Nandy, Ashis. 1978. 'The Traditions of Technology'. *Alternatives* Vol. 4, No. 3, 371–385.

—— 1983. *The Intimate Enemy: Loss and Recovery of Self under Colonialism*. New Delhi: Oxford University Press.

Naoroji, Dadabhai. 1901. *Poverty and Un-British Rule in India*. London: Swan Sonnenschein & Co.

Nehru, Jawaharlal. 1941. *The Unity of India, Collected Writings, 1937–1940*. Buckingham Street: Lindsay Drummond.

—— 2010. *The Discovery of India*. New Delhi: Penguin Books.

Newsinger, John. 2010. *The Blood Never Dried: A People's History of the British Empire*. London: Bookmarks Publications, Ltd.

Nightingale, Carl H. 2012. *Segregation: A Global History of Decided Cities*. London and Chicago: The University of Chicago Press.

Nuttall, Sarah. 2008. 'Literary City'. In Sarah Nuttall and Achille Mbembe, eds, *Johannesburg: The Elusive Metropolis*, pp. 195–218. Durham and London: Duke University Press.

Nuttall, Sarah, and Mbembe, Achille, eds. 2008. *Johannesburg: The Elusive Metropolis*. Durham and London: Duke University Press.

Nyman, Jopi, and Stotedbury, John A., eds. 1999. *Postcolonialism and Cultural Resistance*. Joensuu, Finland: Faculty of Humanities, University of Joensuu.

Oliver, John. 2015. 'Infrastructure: Last Week Tonight with John Oliver' <https://www.youtube.com/watch?v=Wpzvaqypav8>.

Orwell, George. 2000. *Essays*. London: Penguin Books.

Osterhammel, Jürgen, and Petersson, Niels P. 2003. *Globalization, A Short History*. Princeton, NJ: Princeton University Press.

Packenham, Thomas. 2009. *The Scramble for Africa, 1876–1912*. London: Abacus Books.

Palumbo-Liu, David, Robbins, Bruce, and Tanoukhi, Nirvana, eds. 2011. *Immanuel Wallerstein and the Problem of the World: System, Scale, Culture*. Durham and London: Duke University Press.

Pandey, Gyanendra. 2008. *The Gyanendra Pandey Omnibus*. New Delhi: Oxford University Press.

Pandey, Gyanendra, and Samad, Yunas. 2007. *Fault Lines of Nationhood*. New Delhi: Roli Books Pvt., Ltd.

Paranjape, Makarand R. 2013. *Making India: Colonialism, National Culture, and the Afterlife of Indian English Authority*. New Delhi: Springer and Amaryllis.

Parry, Benita. 1972. *Delusions and Discoveries: Studies on Indian in the British Imagination, 1880–1930*. London: The Penguin Press.

——1998. 'Materiality and Mystification in *A Passage to India*'. *NOVEL: A Forum on Fiction* Vol. 31, No. 2, Thirtieth Anniversary Issue: II, 174–194.

——2004. *Postcolonial Studies: A Materialist Critique*. New York: Routledge.

Patwardhan, Daya. 1963. *A Star of India: Flora Annie Steel, Her Works and Times*. Poona: Lokasangraha Press.

Paxton, Nancy L. 1992. 'Complicity and Resistance in the Writings of Flora Annie Steel and Annie Besant'. In Margaret Strobel and Nupur Chaudhuri, eds, *Western Women and Imperialism: Complicity and Resistance*, pp. 158–176. Bloomington and Indianapolis: Indiana University Press.

Pierce, Steven, and Rao, Anupama, eds. 2006. *Discipline and the Other Body: Correction, Corporeality, Colonialism*. London: Duke University Press.

Pile, Steve, and Keith, Michael, eds. 1997. *Geographies of Resistance*. London and New York: Routledge.

Pillay, Suntosh R. 2016. 'Silence is Violence: (Critical) Psychology in an Era of Rhodes Must Fall and Fees Must Fall'. *South African Journal of Psychology* Vol. 46, No. 2, 155–159.

Plaatje, Solomon. 1930. *Mhudi*. Oxford: Heineman Educational Publishers.

——2001. *Sol Plaatje: Selected Writings*, ed. Brian Willan. Johannesburg: Witwatersrand University Press.

Plato. 2008. *The Republic*, trans. Robin Waterfield. Oxford: Oxford University Press.

Pocock, Tom. 1993. *Rider Haggard and the Lost Empire*. London: Weidenfeld and Nicolson.

Prakash, Gyan. 1999. *Another Reason: Science and the Imagination of Modern India*. Princeton, NJ: Princeton University Press.

Pratt, Mary Louise. 2003. *Imperial Eyes: Travel Writing and Transculturation*. New York: Routledge.

Randall, Don. 2000. *Kipling's Imperial Boy: Adolescence and Cultural Hybridity*. Basingstoke: Macmillan.

——2003. 'Autumn 1857: The Making of the Indian "Mutiny"'. *Victorian Literature and Culture* Vol. 31, No. 1, 3–17.

Raschke, Debrah. 1997. 'Forster's Passage to India: Re-Envisioning Plato's Cave'. *The Comparatist* Vol. 21, 10–24.

Redley, Michael. 2009. 'John Buchan and the South African War'. In Kate Macdonald, ed., *Reassessing John Buchan: Beyond the Thirty-Nine Steps*, pp. 65–76. London: Pickering and Chatto.

Reid, Julia. 2011. '"Gladstone Bags, Shooting Boots, and Bryant & May's Matches": Empire, Commerce, and the Imperial Romance in the Graphic's Serialization of H. Rider Haggard's *She*'. *Studies in the Novel* Vol. 43, No. 2, 152–178.

Rhodes, Cecil. 1900. *Cecil Rhodes: His Political Life and Speeches, 1881–1900*. London: Chapman and Hall, Ltd.

Rhodes, Cecil. 2000. 'Speech at Drill Hall, Cape Town (18 July 1899)'. In Sally Ledger and Roger Luckhurst, eds, *The Fin de Siècle: A Reader in Cultural History, c.1880–1900*, pp. 143–144. Oxford: Oxford University Press.

Riach, Alan. 2009. 'John Buchan: Politics, Language and Suspense'. In Kate Macdonald, ed., *Reassessing John Buchan: Beyond the Thirty-Nine Steps*, pp. 171–182. London: Pickering and Chatto.

Richardson, Peter, and Van-Helten, Jean Jacques. 1982. 'Labour in the South African Gold Mining Industry, 1886–1914'. In Shula Marks and Richard Rathbone, eds, *Industrialisation and Social Change in South Africa: African Class Formation, Culture, and Consciousness, 1870–1930*, pp. 77–98. London: Longman Group, Ltd.

Roberts, Adam. 2000. *Fredric Jameson*. London: Routledge.

Robinson, William I. 2011. 'Globalisation and the Sociology of Immanuel Wallerstein: A Critical Appraisal'. *International Sociology* Vol. 26, No. 6, 723–745.

Rodney, Walter. 2012. *How Europe Underdeveloped Africa*. Oxford: Pambazuka Press.

Rojas, Carlos Antionio Aguirre. 2016. 'Introduction: Immanuel Wallerstein and the Critical "World-Systems Analysis" Perspective'. In Charles Lemert, Carlos Antionio Aguirre Rojas and Immanuel Wallerstein, *Uncertain Worlds: World-Systems Analysis in Changing Times*, pp. vii–xl. London and New York: Routledge.

Rosaldo, Renato. 1989. 'Imperialist Nostalgia'. *Representations* No. 26, *Special Issue: Memory and Counter-Memory*, 107–122.

Rothermund, Dietmar. 1970. *The Phases of Indian Nationalism and other essays*. Bombay: Nachiketa Publications Limited.

Roy, Shampa. 2010. '"A Miserable Sham": Flora Annie Steel's Short Fictions and the Question of Indian Women's Reform'. *Feminist Review* No. 94, 55–74.

Rubenstein, Michael. 2010. *Public Works: Infrastructure, Irish Modernism, and the Postcolonial*. Indiana: University of Notre Dame Press.

Rühe, Peter. 2001. *Gandhi: A Photo Biography*. London: Phaidon.

Said, Edward. 1993. *Culture and Imperialism*. London: Chatto and Windus.

———2003. *Orientalism*. London: Penguin Classics.

Sarila, Nerendra Singh. 2007. *The Shadow of the Great Game: The Untold Story of India's Partition*. London: Constable and Robinson, Ltd.

Sarkar, Sumit. 1985. *A Critique of Colonial India*. Calcutta: A. G. Printing Works.

Sassen, Saskia. 2006. *Territory, Authority, Rights: From Medieval to Global Assemblages*. Princeton, NJ: Princeton University Press.

Saunders, Corinne, ed. 2004. *A Companion to Romance*. Oxford: Blackwell Publishing.

Saxena, Vinod Kumar. 1987. *The Partition of Bengal (1905–1911): Select Documents*. Delhi: Kanishka Publishing House.

Schwarz, Bill. 2011. *The White Man's World: Memories of Empire, Volume 1*. Oxford: Oxford University Press.

Scott, James C. 1990. *Domination and the Arts of Resistance: Hidden Transcripts*. New Haven, CT: Yale University Press.

Seeley, John R. 1914. *Expansion of England: Two Courses of Lectures*. London: Macmillan and Co.

Sethi, Rumina. 2011. *The Politics of Postcolonialism: Empire, Nation and Resistance*. London: Pluto Press.

Shanmugasundaram, V. 1975. *The Drain Theory*. Madras: University of Madras, reprinted from the Indian Economic Association Conference.

Shapiro, Stephen. 2014. 'From Capitalist to Communist Abstraction: *The Pale King's* Cultural Fix'. *Textual Practice* Vol. 28, No. 7, 1249–1271.

Shapple, Deborah L. 2004. 'Artful Tales of Origination in Olive Schreiner's *The Story of an African Farm*'. *Nineteenth-Century Literature* Vol. 59, No. 1, 78–114.

Sharp, Joanne P., Routledge, Paul, Philo, Chris, and Paddison, Ronan, eds. 2005. *Entanglements of Power: Geographies of Domination/Resistance*. London and New York: Routledge.

Sharpe, Jenny. 1989. *Allegories of Empire: The Figure of Woman in the Colonial Text*. London: University of Minnesota Press.

Singh, Navtej. 1996. *Starvation and Colonialism: A Study of Famines in the Nineteenth Century British Punjab 1858–1901*. New Delhi: National Book Organisation.

Sinha, Mrinalini. 2001. 'Britishness, Clubbability, and the Colonial Public Sphere: The Genealogy of an Imperial Institution in Colonial India'. *Journal of British Studies* Vol. 40, No. 4, 489–521.

Smith, Craig. 1995. 'Every Man Must Kill the Thing He Loves: Empire, Homoerotics, and Nationalism in John Buchan's Prester John'. *NOVEL: A Forum on Fiction* Vol. 28, No. 2, 173–200.

Smith, Janet Adam. 1965. *John Buchan, A Biography*. Bristol: Western Printing Services, Ltd.

Smith, Neil. 2005. *The New Urban Frontier: Gentrification and the Revanchist City*. London: Routledge.

——2008. *Uneven Development: Nature, Capital, and the Production of Space*. Athens and London: The University of Georgia Press, 3rd edn, 2008.

Soja, Edward. 1989. *Postmodern Geographies: The Reassertion of Space in Critical Social Theory*. London and New York: Verso.

——2010. *Seeking Spatial Justice*. London and Minneapolis: University of Minnesota Press.

Srinivasan, Roopa, Tiwari, Manish, and Silas, Sandeep, eds. 2006. *Our Indian Railway: Themes in India's Railway History*. New Delhi: Foundation Books Pvt., Ltd.

Star, Susan Leigh. 1999. 'The Ethnography of Infrastructure'. *American Behavioural Scientist* Vol. 43, No. 3, 377–391.

Stoler, Ann Laura. 2002. *Carnal Knowledge and Imperial Power: Race and the Intimate in Colonial Rule*. London: University of California Press, Ltd.

——2009. *Along the Archival Grain: Thinking Through Colonial Ontologies*. Princeton, NJ: Princeton University Press.

Stott, Rebecca. 1989. 'The Dark Continent: Africa as Female Body in Haggard's Adventure Fiction'. *Feminist Review* No. 32, 69–89.

Strobel, Margaret, and Chaudhuri, Nupur, eds. 1992. *Western Women and Imperialism: Complicity and Resistance*. Bloomington and Indianapolis: Indiana University Press.

Suleri, Sara. 1992. *The Rhetoric of English India*. Chicago and London: University of Chicago Press.

Sutcliffe, Rebecca J. 1998. 'Feminizing the professional: The government reports of Flora Annie Steel'. *Technical Communication Quarterly* Vol. 7, No. 2, 153–173.

Szeman, Imre. 2001. 'Who's Afraid of National Allegory? Jameson, Literary Criticism, Globalisation'. *South Atlantic Quarterly* Vol. 100, No. 3, 803–827.

Tagg, John. 2000. 'Globalisation, Totalisation and the Discursive Field'. In Anthony King, ed., *Culture, Globalization and the World-System: Contemporary Conditions for the Representation of Identity*, pp. 155–160. Minneapolis: University of Minnesota Press.

Tally Jr, Robert T. 2013. *The New Critical Idiom: Spatiality*. New York: Routledge.

Tanoukhi, Nirvana. 2011. 'The Scale of World Literature'. In David Palumbo-Liu, Bruce Robbins and Nirvana Tanoukhi, eds, *Immanuel Wallerstein and the Problem of the World: System, Scale, Culture*, pp. 78–98. Durham and London: Duke University Press.

Tennyson, Alfred. 1998. 'The Siege of Lucknow'. In Elleke Boehmer, ed., *Empire Writing: An Anthology of Colonial Literature, 1870–1918*, pp. 59–63. Oxford: Oxford University Press.

Thomas, David Wayne. 2009. 'Liberal Legitimation and Communicative Action in British India: Reading Flora Annie Steel's *On the Face of the Waters*'. *ELH* Vol. 76, 153–187.

Thomas, Nicholas. 1996. *Colonialism's Culture: Anthropology, Travel and Government*. Oxford: Blackwell Publishers, Ltd.

Tickell, Alex. 2004. 'Negotiating the Landscape: Travel, Transaction, and the Mapping of Colonial India'. *The Yearbook of English Studies*, Vol. 34, 18–30.

——2012. *Terrorism, Insurgency and Indian-English Literature, 1830–1947*. London: Routledge.

Tidrick, Kathryn. 2013. *Gandhi, A Political and Spiritual Life*. London: Verso.

Turrell, Rob. 1982. 'Kimberley: Labour and Compounds, 1871–1888'. In Shula Marks and Richard Rathbone, eds, *Industrialisation and Social Change in South Africa: African Class Formation, Culture, and Consciousness, 1870–1930*, pp. 45–76. London: Longman Group, Ltd.

Vlies, Andrew van der. 2007. *South African Textual Cultures: White, Black, Read All Over*. Manchester: Manchester University Press.

Waddell, Nathan. 2009. *Modern John Buchan: A Critical Introduction*. Newcastle-upon-Tyne: Cambridge Scholars Publishing.

Wade, Michael. 1994. 'Trains as Tropes: The Role of the Railway in some South African Literary Texts'. In Elleke Boehmer, Laura Chrisman and Kenneth Parker, eds, *Altered State? Writing and South Africa*, pp. 75–90. Sydney: Dangaroo Press.

Wallerstein, Immanuel. 1991. *The Capitalist World-Economy*. Cambridge: Cambridge University Press.

——1992. *Geopolitics and Geoculture: Essays on the Changing World-system*. Cambridge: Cambridge University Press.

——2004. *World-Systems Analysis: An Introduction*. Durham: Duke University Press.

——2011. *Historical Capitalism*. London: Verso.

——2013. 'Structural Crisis, or Why Capitalists May No Longer Find Capitalism Rewarding'. In Craig Calhoun, Randall Collins, Georgi Derluguian, Michael Mann and Immanuel Wallerstein, *Does Capitalism Have a Future?*, pp. 9–35. New York: Oxford University Press.

Weinthal, Leo, ed. 1922. *The Story of the Cape to Cairo Railway and River Route, from 1887 to 1922. Volume One. The Record of an Imperial Project; How it Materialised to Date; and the Story of its Creators*, and *Volume Two. The Main Line as it exists to-day from the Cape to the Nile Delta*. Luton: Gibbs, Bamforth & Co.

Weizman, Eyal. 2011. *The Least of All Possible Evils: Humanitarian Violence from Arendt to Gaza*. London and New York: Verso.

——2012. *Hollow Land: Israel's Architecture of Occupation*. London: Verso.

Whitman, Walt. 2004. *The Portable Walt Whitman*, ed. Michael Warner. New York and London: Penguin Books, Ltd.

Wilburn, Kenneth E. 1991. 'Engines of Empire and Independence: Railways in Southern Africa, 1863–1916'. In Clarence B. Davis and Kenneth E. Wilburn, eds, *Railway Imperialism*, pp. 25–40. London: Greenwood Press.

Williams, Patrick. 2000. '"Simultaneous Uncontemporaneities": Theorising Modernism and Empire'. In Howard J. Booth and Nigel Rigby, eds, *Modernism and Empire*, pp. 13–38. Manchester: Manchester University Press.

——2016. 'Gaps, Silences and Absences: Palestine and Postcolonial Studies'. In Anna Bernard, Ziad Elmarsafy and Stuard Murray, eds, *What Postcolonial Theory Doesn't Say*, pp. 239–255. London and New York: Routledge.

Williams, Raymond. 1973. *The Country and the City*. London: Chatto & Windus.

——2005. *Culture and Materialism: Selected Essays*. London: Verso.

Winchester, Clarence, ed. 1937. *The Wonders of World Engineering: Epics of Conquest in Story and Picture*. London: Fleetway House.

Wisnicki, Adrian. 2007. 'Reformulating the Empire's Hero: Rhodesian Gold, Boer Veld-Craft, and the Displaced Scotsman in John Buchan's The Thirty-Nine Steps'. *Journal of Colonialism and Colonial History* Vol. 8, No. 1, n. pag.

Wittenberg, Herman. 1997. 'Imperial Space and the Discourse of the Novel'. *Journal of Literary Studies* Vol. 13, Nos. 1–2, 127–150.

Worden, Nigel. 2007. *The Making of Modern South Africa: Conquest, Apartheid, Democracy*. Oxford: Blackwell Publishing, Ltd.

WReC (Warwick Research Collective). 2015. *Combined and Uneven Development: Towards a New Theory of World Literature*. Liverpool: Liverpool University Press.

Young, Robert J. C. 2008. *Postcolonialism: An Historical Introduction*. Oxford: Blackwell Publishing, Ltd.

Žižek, Slavoj. 2008. *Violence: Six Sideways Reflections*. London: Profile Books, Ltd.

Index

RACE AND RESISTANCE ACROSS BORDERS
IN THE LONG TWENTIETH CENTURY

Series Editors:
Tessa Roynon, University of Oxford (Executive Editor)
Elleke Boehmer, University of Oxford
Victoria Collis-Buthelezi, University of the Witwatersrand
Patricia Daley, University of Oxford
Aaron Kamugisha, University of the West Indies, Cave Hill
Minkah Makalani, University of Texas, Austin
Hélène Neveu Kringelbach, University College London
Stephen Tuck, University of Oxford

This series focuses on the history and culture of activists, artists and intellectuals who worked within and against racially oppressive hierarchies in the first half of the twentieth century, and who then sought to define and achieve full equality once those formal hierarchies had been overturned. It explores the ways in which such individuals – writers, scholars, campaigners and organizers, ministers, and artists and performers of all kinds – located their resistance within a global context and forged connections with each other across national, linguistic, regional and imperial borders.

Disseminating the latest interdisciplinary scholarship on the history, literature and culture of anti-racist movements in Africa, the Caribbean, the United States, Europe, Asia and Latin America, the series foregrounds, through a cross-disciplinary approach, the transnational and intercultural nature of these resistance movements. The series embraces a range of themes, including but not limited to antislavery, intellectual and literary networks, emigration and immigration, anti-imperialism, church-based and religious movements, civil rights, citizenship and identity, Black Power, resistance strategies, women's movements, cultural transfer, white supremacy and anti-immigration, hip hop and global justice movements.

The series is affiliated with the Race and Resistance Research Programme at The Oxford Research Centre in the Humanities (TORCH), University of Oxford. Proposals are invited for sole- and joint-authored monographs as well as edited collections.

Published Volumes:

Dominic Davies, Erica Lombard and Benjamin Mountford (eds): Fighting Words: Fifteen Books that Shaped the Postcolonial World Forthcoming. ISBN 978-1-906165-55-0.

Dominic Davies: Imperial Infrastructure and Spatial Resistance in Colonial Literature, 1880–1930
2017. ISBN 978-1-906165-88-8.